Tattoos in crime and detective narratives

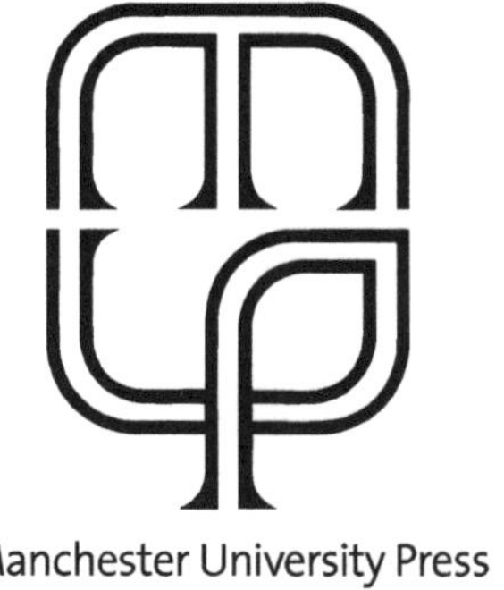

Manchester University Press

Tattoos in crime and detective narratives

Marking and remarking

Edited by Kate Watson and Katharine Cox

Manchester University Press

Published by Manchester University Press
Oxford Road, Manchester M13 9PL

www.manchesteruniversitypress.co.uk

British Library Cataloguing-in-Publication Data
A catalogue record for this book is available from the British Library

ISBN 978 1 5261 2867 6 hardback
ISBN 978 1 5261 8262 3 paperback

First published 2019
Paperback published 2025

Typeset in 10/12.5 Warnock Pro by
Servis Filmsetting Ltd, Stockport, Cheshire

Dedications
Kate would like to dedicate this collection to Sian, Sara, Pete, Rose, Terry and Zola. To Justin for first interesting her in tattoo narratives in 2005, while writing and watching his art in his studio.

Katharine would like to dedicate this collection to all tattooists for their compelling art, her sisters Helen and Mags (and their tattoos), nephew Jack and gran Sybil Olive Houlton (1923–2017).

Contents

Part 1: Psychoanalysis, patternings and the medical imagination

Part 2: Practitioners, place and contemporary identities

Part 3: Urban textualities, humans and other animals

**Part 4: Children's literature: Dark marks, scars and secret
societies**

Part 5: Film: Adaptation, memory and constructions of self

Part 6: Television: Branding, tech-noir and fan culture

Figures

Contributors

Lucy Andrew

Lucy is Lecturer in English Literature and Programme Leader of the English Degree at University Centre Shrewsbury. Her research interests are in children's literature, young adult fiction, crime fiction, comics and graphic novels, film and television, popular culture and fandom. Her first monograph, *The boy detective in early British children's literature: Patrolling the borders between boyhood and manhood*, was published by Palgrave Macmillan in 2017. She has also published articles in *Boyhood studies* and *Clues: A journal of detection* and chapters for both Palgrave's *Crime files* series and Intellect's *Crime uncovered* series. She is co-editor of *Crime fiction in the city: Capital crimes* (University of Wales Press, 2013) with Catherine Phelps. She is co-organiser of the Short Story Network with Dr Vicky Margree (University of Brighton).

Maurizio Ascari (Foreword)

Maurizio is a Senior Lecturer in English Literature at the University of Bologna (Italy). His publications include books and essays on crime fiction (*A counter-history of crime fiction*, 2007, obtained a nomination for the Edgar awards), transcultural literature (*Literature of the global age*, 2011) and inter-art exchanges (*Cinema and the imagination in Katherine Mansfield's writing*, 2014). He has also edited and translated works by Henry James, Katherine Mansfield, William Faulkner, Jack London and William Wilkie Collins.

David Beck

David completed his PhD at the University of Hull (UK). His research investigates the critical dynamic of considering Arthur Conan Doyle as either scientific or spiritual; in particular, he challenges the assumption that Doyle abandoned rational inquiry to embrace the supernatural, including spiritualism. David has recently published his article '"The dweller upon the threshold" and the infringement of the unknown in Arthur Conan Doyle's "The adventure of the Devil's foot"' in *Clues: A journal of detection* (2015) and is currently working on a monograph on Doyle.

Karin Beeler

Karin is a Professor in the English Department at the University of Northern British Columbia (Canada) where she teaches television genre and film studies courses. She has published on various aspects of telefantasy, including the role of myth in *Smallville* and *Charmed*. Selected books include *Tattoos, desire and violence: Marks of resistance in literature, film and television* (2006) and a co-edited volume, *Children's film in the digital age* (2015). Her current work continues to examine youth culture in film and television.

Kerstin Bergman

Kerstin is an expert on Nordic Noir literature, a crime fiction scholar, literary critic and a member of the Swedish Academy of Crime Fiction. She is the author of *Swedish crime fiction: The making of Nordic noir* (2014) and has also written numerous popular and scholarly articles on Swedish and international crime fiction (in English and Swedish). As an expert on crime fiction, a writer and lecturer, she runs CrimeGarden and blogs (in Swedish) about crime fiction at crimegarden.se.

Ellen Carter

Ellen is a Senior Lecturer in English Language and Translation at the University of Strasbourg, France. Her doctorate in French crime fiction was jointly awarded by the École des Hautes Études en Sciences Sociales, Paris, and the University of Auckland, New Zealand. Her crime fiction research interests centre on how cultural outsiders write, translate and read cross-cultural crime fiction. Recent publications include a chapter on translating popular fiction in *The Routledge handbook of translation and culture* (2018). Other work has been published in *(Re-)writing wrongs: French crime fiction and the palimpsest* (Cambridge scholars, 2014), *JoST: Journal of specialised translation*, *Imaginations*, and *Textus* (all 2014), and *The foreign in international crime writing: Transcultural representations* (Continuum, 2012).

Katharine Cox

Katharine is a Principal Lecturer in English at Sheffield Hallam University (UK), where she is Head of English. Katharine served on University English's Executive Committee for seven years and was Deputy Vice Chair (2016–17) and Secretary (2017–18). Recent publications include explorations of children's literature and urban space, and transgression in contemporary literature and film. Her edited collection *The transgressive Iain Banks: Essays on a writer beyond borders* (co-edited with Martyn Colebrook) was published in 2013 and included her essay 'Textual crossings: Transgressive devices in Iain Banks' fiction'. Her article on James Bond appeared in *Gender studies*: 'Becoming James Bond: Daniel Craig, rebirth, and refashioning masculinity in *Casino Royale*' (2014). Her current research focuses on the labyrinth as a lens to consider space, gender and narrative in fiction after modernism. Her essay 'Postmodern literary labyrinths: Spaces of horror reimagined' is published in *The Palgrave handbook to horror literature* (2018), edited by Laura R. Kremmel and Kevin Corstorphine.

Hywel Dix

Hywel is a Principal Academic in English and Communication at Bournemouth University. He was formerly Raymond Williams Research Fellow at the University of Glamorgan, leading to the publication of *After Raymond Williams: Cultural materialism and the break-up of Britain* (second edition, 2013). He has published extensively on the relationship between literature, culture and political change in contemporary Britain, most notably in the monograph *Postmodern fiction and the break-up of Britain* (Continuum, 2010). His wider research interests include modern and contemporary literature, postmodernism, critical cultural theory and autofiction. His monograph about literary careers entitled *The late-career novelist* was published by Bloomsbury in 2017 and an edited collection of essays, *Autofiction in English*, by Palgrave in 2018.

Peter Figler

Peter is a Lecturer in English at the University of Arizona, holding a PhD in Literature from the same institution. He specialises in twentieth- and twenty-first-century American fiction and film. His writing has appeared in the journal *Foucault studies* and *The Blackwell encyclopedia of postcolonial studies*. His scholarly interests include American Studies and state theory, and he is currently working on a book project dealing with cultural narratives and the language of everyday racism.

Ruth Hawthorn

Ruth is a Lecturer in American Literature at the University of Lincoln, having taught previously at the University of Sheffield, the University of Northern British Columbia and the University of Glasgow. Her research interests include detective fiction, the literature of LA and twentieth- and twenty-first-century elegy. She is currently completing a monograph of American detective fiction for the BAAS Paperbacks Series with Edinburgh University Press and co-editing a collection on animals in detective fiction, with John Miller, for Palgrave's *Studies in animals and literature* series.

Alexander N. Howe

Alexander is a Professor of English at the University of the District of Columbia (US) where he teaches courses on American literature, literary theory and film. His research interests focus on genre fiction, film and television and his recent publications include work on Raymond Chandler and AMC's *The walking dead*. He is the author of *It didn't mean anything: A psychoanalytic reading of American detective fiction* (McFarland, 2008) and the co-editor of *Kidding around: The child in film and media* (Continuum, 2014) and *Marcia Muller and the female private eye: Essays on the novels that started a subgenre* (McFarland, 2008). He is currently completing a manuscript on the intersections between dystopian and detective fiction.

Rebekah Humphreys

Rebekah is a Lecturer in Philosophy at the University of Wales, Trinity Saint David (UK). Her research interests include applied ethics (especially animal ethics and environmental ethics) and moral philosophy in general. Selected publications include: 'Justice and non-human beings', Part I, in *Bangladesh journal of bioethics* (7:3), 2016, pp. 1–11 (co-authored with Robin Attfield); 'Justice and non-human beings', Part II, in *Bangladesh journal of bioethics* (8:1), 2017, pp. 44–77 (co-authored with Robin Attfield); 'Dignity and its violation examined within the context of animal ethics', *Ethics and the environment* (21:2), Fall 2016, pp. 143–62; 'Biocentrism', *Encyclopedia of* global b*ioethics*, Springer, online publication 2014; hard copy published 2016; and 'The argument from existence, blood-sports, and 'Sport-slaves'', *Journal of agricultural and environmental ethics* (published by Springer), (27: 2), 2014, pp. 331–45.

Caroline Jones

Caroline is a Lecturer in Social Policy at the University of Salford (UK). She has a longstanding interest in representations of the city, fictional and otherwise, which has led to research on topics as varied as the Manchester Arena Bombing, the August 2011 UK Riots and the work of Ian Rankin. Her other main research interest is in feminism. Recent publications include 'Capital crime: Ian Rankin's Inspector Rebus and the many faces of Edinburgh' in *Crimelights: Scottish crime fiction then and now*, Wissenschaftlicher Verlag Trier, Trier, Germany (2015), and 'A matter of law and order: Reporting the Salford riots in local news webpages' *Contemporary social science* (2013) with co-author Dr Sharon Coen.

Spencer Jordan

Spencer is an Assistant Professor in Creative Writing at the University of Nottingham (UK). His novel, *Journeys in the dead season*, was published by Macmillan in 2005. In addition to his creative writing, Spencer's research includes historical and experimental writing, digital/hypertext and immersive fiction and literary geography. Recent publications include: 'Street hauntings: Digital storytelling in twenty-first century leisure cultures' (2016), 'An infinitude of possible worlds: Towards a research method for hypertext fiction' (2014) and 'The myth of Edward Colston: Bristol docks, the merchant elite and the legitimisation of authority 1860-1880' in Stephen Poole's collection: *A city built upon the water* (2013). Forthcoming publications include *Post-digital storytelling: Poetics, praxis, research* (2019), and 'Digital storytelling and performative memory: New approaches to the literary geography of the postcolonial city' (2019).

John Miller

John is a Senior Lecturer in Nineteenth-Century Literature at the University of Sheffield (UK). His research focuses on writing about animals, ecology and empire from the nineteenth century to the present, with particular emphasis on the late Victorian period. He is the author of *Empire and the animal body: Violence, identity and ecology in Victorian adventure fiction* (Anthem, 2012) and (with Louise Miller) *Walrus* (Reaktion, 2014). He is the co-editor of *Transatlantic literary ecologies* (Routledge, 2016) and *Wolves, werewolves and the gothic* (University of Wales Press, 2017).

Matt Oches

Matt completed his PhD in English Language and Literature at the University of Michigan (US). His thesis, 'The skin of modernity: Primitivism and tattooing in literature', combines Pacific and modernist studies in an examination of the role of tattooing in primitivist discourse. His project discusses the cultural exchange of tattooing and the representation of tattooed bodies in the work of James Cook, William Bligh, Herman Melville, Djuna Barnes, James Joyce and Albert Wendt.

Will Slocombe

Will is a Senior Lecturer in American Literature at the University of Liverpool (UK). He is the author of *Nihilism and the sublime postmodern* (Routledge, 2006) as well as numerous essays and articles. Recent key publications include: 'Games playing roles in the fiction of Iain (M.) Banks', in *The transgressive Iain Banks*, eds Katharine Cox and Martyn Colebrook (McFarland, 2013), 'Is metafiction an other realism? The strange case of Paul Auster and Mr Blank' in *Realism's others*, eds Geoffrey Barker and Eva Aldea (Cambridge scholars, 2010), and 'Of machine gods and technological daemons: Divine patterns in contemporary fictions of technology' in *Writing America into the twenty-first century: Essays on the American novel*, eds Elizabeth Boyle and Anne-Marie Evans (Cambridge scholars, 2010). He writes variously on education, narratives and technology, from new media to metafictions, including sf writing.

Kate Watson
Kate is a teacher of English and an independent scholar. She has been a Lecturer at Cardiff University and Cardiff Metropolitan University and has been an Honorary Research Fellow at the University of Southampton. Her research interests include crime and detective fiction, gender and women's studies, modern and contemporary literature, Victorian literature and popular culture. Her first monograph, *Women writing crime fiction, 1860–1880: Fourteen American, British and Australian authors*, was published by McFarland in 2012. She has also published articles and chapters in publications such as *Clues: A journal of detection*, *Constructing crime* (Palgrave Macmillan), *New perspectives on detective fiction* (Routledge), *Critical insights: The American thriller* (Salem Press) and Palgrave's *Crime Files* series.

Foreword

Maurizio Ascari

Given the relevance of tattoos in the varied territory of detective and crime fiction, it was high time a volume like *Tattoos in crime and detective narratives: Marking and remarking* was written. Thus it is with sincere gratitude that I thank its valiant editors – Kate Watson and Katharine Cox – and contributors for joining efforts and investigating this fascinating subject with so much energy and critical acumen. What I can offer in the space of a brief foreword is what waiters in restaurants call an 'amuse bouche', a small starter that aims to whet the appetite for more.

Tattoos are complex bodily artefacts that may include figurative and/or decorative elements (often endowed with symbolic value), also in association with writing. Harmonising with the design of the body, they fulfil an aesthetic function, but they also testify to an individual's history, personality and allegiances. The narrative potential of tattoos and related body modifications is associated with the 'life stories' of those who bear them, a coin that inevitably has two sides. In a variety of epochs and social contexts, tattoos signified ownership, as in the case of slaves and prostitutes, while fugitive slaves, criminals and deserters were also branded or otherwise marked with the aim of ensuring subsequent recognition at recapture or of preventing 'offenders' from achieving anonymity.

Given the importance branding has had throughout the centuries as an emblem of either being included in or excluded from a social group, it does not come as a surprise that it is present in literature right from the Bible. In *Genesis*, the primal murderer – Cain – is not only cursed and condemned to a life of exile, but also bears a mysterious mark, apparently to prevent others from killing him. This original outcast, an offender who cannot wash his mark of infamy clean because of divine decree, casts a long shadow over the course of the centuries.

Tattooing as a custom to mark punishment ended towards the end of the

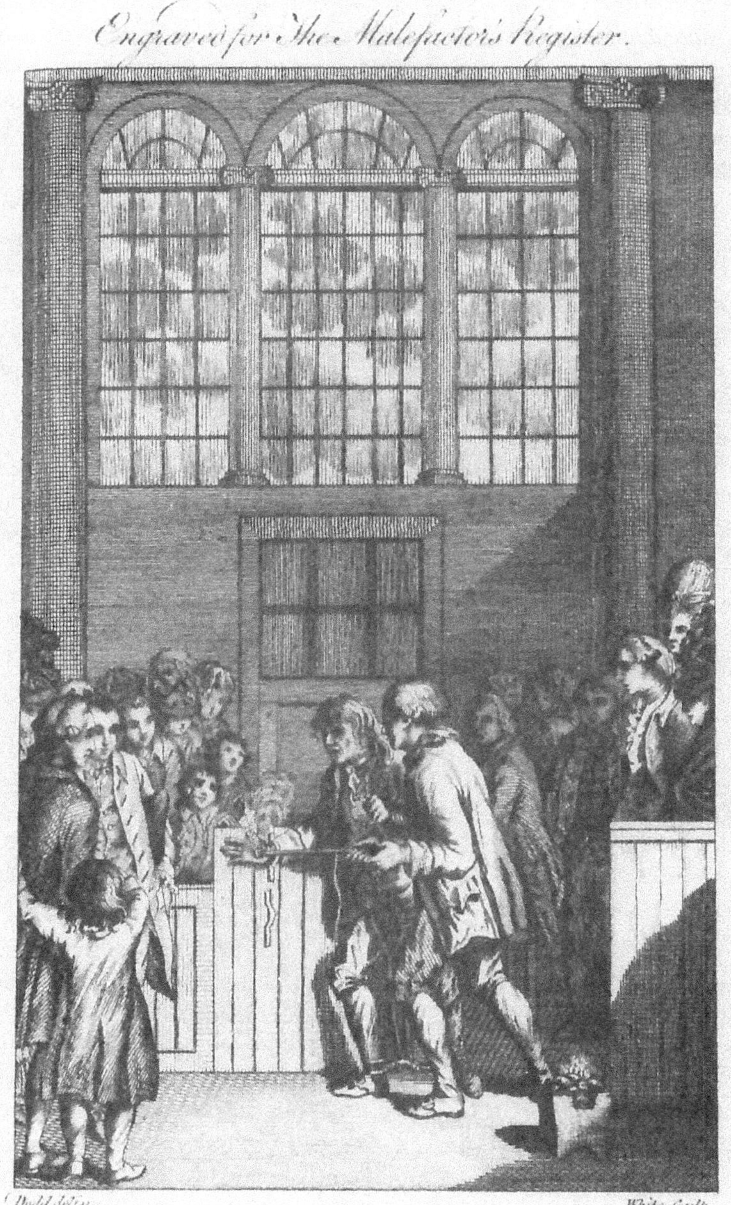

1 'Malefactor's register'.

eighteenth century, having found its way into literature thanks to works such as *The malefactors register or the Newgate and Tyburn calendars* (1779), where the anguish and spectacle of branding is clearly represented (see Figure 1). Likewise, in Alexandre Dumas's *The three musketeers* (1844), it is a *fleur de lys* mark that reveals the original guilt of the perfidious Milady de Winter. Contrasting the woman's ability to change identity, the permanence of the tattoo ultimately unmasks her, bringing her underlying nature to light.

The invention of photography and the development of forensic science definitely made branding redundant as a means of identification. In the meantime, however, a related form of body writing – criminal tattoos – had acquired new meaning in the eyes of criminal anthropologist Cesare Lombroso, whose attempt to grasp complexity by combining biological and cultural data testifies both to his intellectual daring and dangerous inclination towards self-validating theories.

Tattoos are prominent already in the first edition of *L'Uomo delinquente* (1876).[1] After describing tattoos as 'eternal traces of the ideas and passions that predominate in the man of the people' (1876: 45; my translation), Lombroso uses them to prove that deviance results from atavism (the survival of the primitive within civilisation). Statistically associating tattoos with male criminals (and a smaller minority of other social categories, from soldiers and mariners to prostitutes), Lombroso explores the tattoo's symbolic meaning, pertaining mainly to the spheres of war, love/sex, religion and profession.

Tattoos manifest allegiance to a social group and a concomitant need to prove one's courage, sexual drive and affective needs, not to mention forms of 'superstition'. Regarding tattoos as symptoms of atavism, Lombroso associates the customs of European criminals to those of extra-European 'savages' and ancient populations. Different times and spaces, different peoples and art forms are nonchalantly conflated by Lombroso, who reminds us of the importance tattoos had for ancient Britons (from the Greek *prittanoi*, tattooed) and Picts (from the Latin *picti*, painted).

Relating the disposition of tattoos to the 'professional' exposition of certain body parts (as is apparent in the case of mariners and miners), Lombroso regards this as explaining the obscene, ironic or even poetical tattoos certain prostitutes have on their private parts. To exemplify this anatomical dimension, the text features the portrait of a prisoner (see Figure 2) whose tattoos trace an affective map, displaying his vengeful nature, his love for his mother and his political allegiance, as symbolised by the emblem of the House of Savoy.

Only, this emblem is tattooed on the prisoner's penis, the glans of which shows a woman's visage. The prisoner's choice of having his genitals thus marked enables Lombroso to expand on a central aspect of his theory – the criminals' insensitivity to pain, which approaches them to savages. Everything

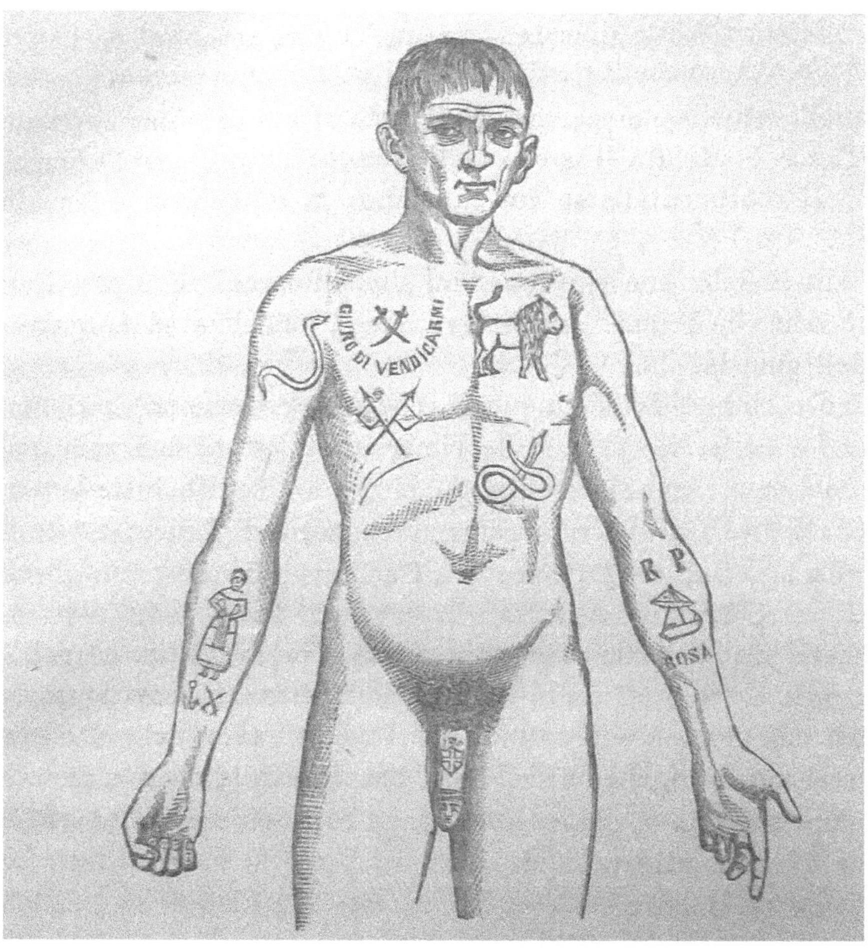

2 Cesare Lombroso's 'Prisoner with tattoos'.

is connected in this investigation of evolutionary drawbacks, which we cannot help seeing as a caricature of the positivist faith in science.

Although Lombroso's theories are thankfully no longer viable, their cultural import is undisputed since they contributed to shaping the collective imagination of the criminal at a time that was crucial to the formation of detective fiction as a literary genre. Lombroso's ideas were disseminated all over Europe and beyond. Alexandre Lacassagne's *Les tatouages: Ètude anthropologique et medico-légale* (1881) extensively discusses Lombroso's theory of atavism, partly in an attempt to revise it, while Havelock Ellis's *The criminal* (1890) includes a chapter on tattooing (see Figure 3), where the 'findings' of Italian criminal anthropologists are integrated with further data concerning Great Britain.

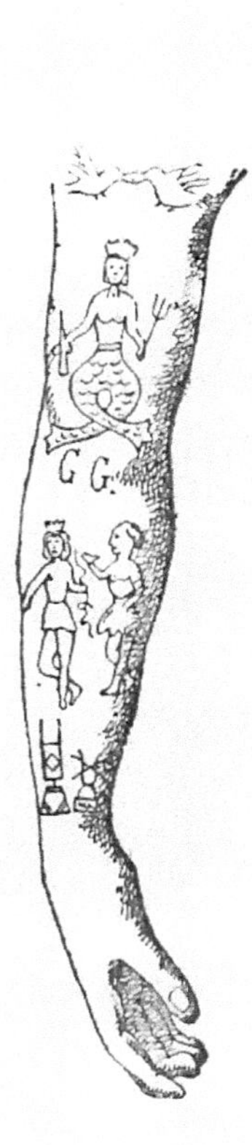

Right arm of G., French thief,
etc., expelled from France, and
wandered in Africa and Australia. (Lombroso.)

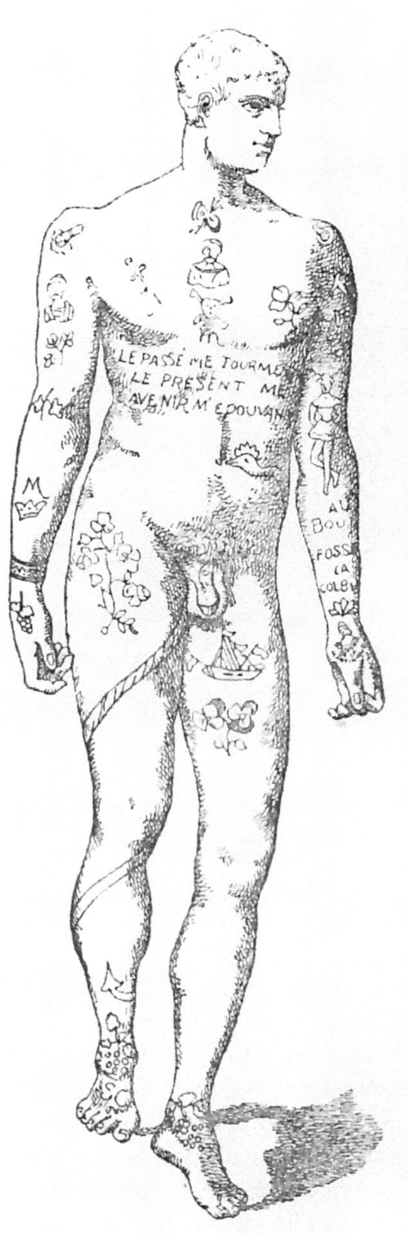

M. J., French sailor and
deserter; the nature of his
crime is unknown. (Lombroso.)

3 Cesare Lombroso's 'French sailor and deserter'.

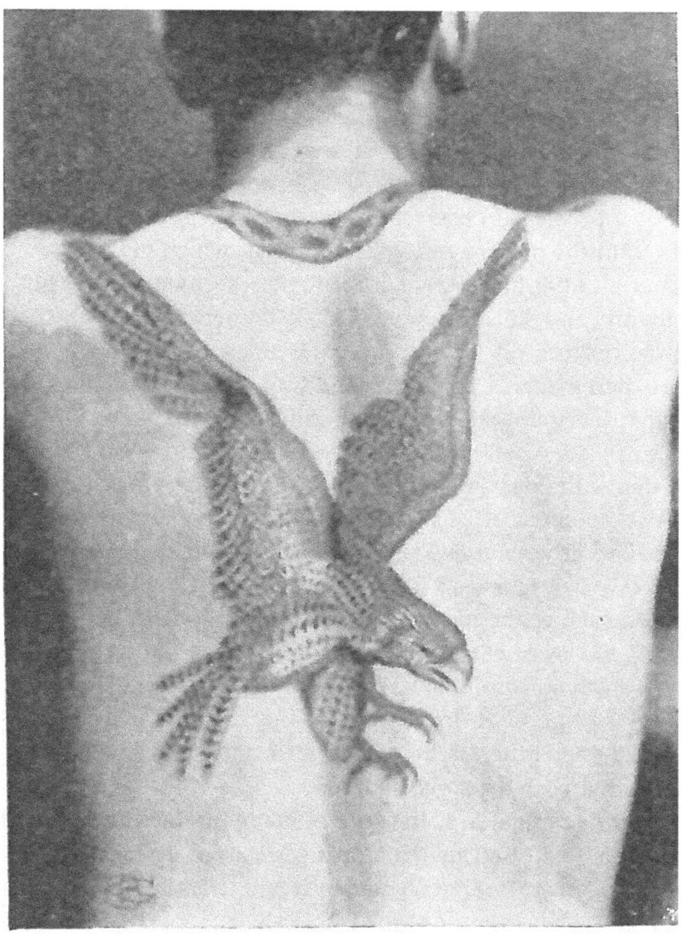

4 'Gambier Bolton's back tattooed by Sutherland Macdonald'.

Tattoos, however, were not univocally associated with crime in the context of the *fin de siècle*, as proved by an article that appeared in *The Strand magazine* in 1897. The author of 'Pictures on the human skin' – Gambier Bolton, a Fellow of the Zoological Society – presents tattoos as a form of art by means of several photographs. The article lavishes praise on Sutherland Macdonald, whose taste for painting and career in the Royal Engineers translated into the invention of the electric needle that he uses to produce 'the very finest tattooing the world has ever seen' (1897: 431). The author's enthusiasm is shown to be written on his own body in the final set of illustrations (see Figure 4).

Bolton's article testifies to what Watson and Cox label in their introduction as the first renaissance of tattooing, which was triggered by the mechanisation of the process, juxtaposing it to the second renaissance that we are currently experiencing.

Spanning the divide between criminal subcultures and pop culture, tattoos convey a flair for transgression and the primitive to which our hyper-civilised societies respond with a mixture of fear and desire. Tattoos also call our attention to the body as a signifier at the interface between the individual and society; a privileged observatory on social norms and their violation, as transpires from the present collection of essays, which offers a 'thick reading' (to paraphrase Clifford Geertz) of crime fiction, keeping in focus both text and context, literary and the anthropological phenomena.

The insightful critical investigation this team of scholars has conducted under the expert guidance of Watson and Cox enables us to reflect on the shifting relevance of criminals in fictions of crime and detection. While gothic and sensation novelists – such as Louisa May Alcott, who is paid homage in this book together with Edgar Allan Poe and Arthur Conan Doyle – freely explored the narrative potential of villains and villainesses, offenders were often confined to the background in Golden Age novels, where detection is centre stage and guilt resides with the least likely suspect. It was the twentieth-century rise of subgenres, such as the hardboiled and the psycho-thriller, that shifted the balance back, while critics responded to this metamorphosis by re-defining the genre itself, starting from Julian Symons's *Bloody murder. From the detective story to the crime novel: A history* (1972). This example was soon followed by Stephen Knight and others, who opted for the label of crime fiction as a more inclusive alternative to detective fiction.

Although the criminal is at the core of contemporary literature (and criticism), this is not to the detriment of the investigation, as the boundary between detective and offender is often blurred in recent narratives. Characters such as Leonard Shelby (*Memento* 2000) and Lisbeth Salander (*The girl with the dragon tattoo* 2005) come to mind. Both extensively discussed in this collection, their traumatic experiences translate into various forms of otherness, including an array of tattoos that testify to their multi-layered and self-conflicting personalities. These tattoos, moreover, resonate with a nearby notation concerning their talent for detection, which enables Salander 'to get *under the skin* of the person she was investigating' (2005: 33; my emphasis). We are again in the realm of complexity. These traumatised, 'vulnerable' detectives coexist within the pages of Watson and Cox's critical volume with less predictable heroes such as Harry Potter or Sam and Dean Winchester (*Supernatural*, 2005–present), whose bodily marks remind us that in order to fight the dark side one must somehow be in touch with it.

As we can see, using tattoos as a critical lens enables us to shed light on both the history of crime fiction and its present – as marked not only by the centrality of the body, but also by an investigation into the intricacies of the psyche and of social structures, of individual and collective drives, concerns and belief systems. Firmly grounded on this awareness of complexity, *Tattoos in crime and detective narratives: Marking and remarking* bravely embraces a wide array of genres, media and cultures, not to mention their unceasing hybridisation, in order to render the global dimension of crime and detective fiction. Reading this book has been an enlightening and exciting experience for me, and I can only conclude by wishing other readers the same degree of cognitive and emotional involvement.

NOTES

1 A summary of which would appear in translation as *Criminal man* in 1911.

SELECT BIBLIOGRAPHY

Gambier, Bolton (1897), 'Pictures on the human skin', *The Strand magazine*, xiii (January–June), 425–34.
Larsson, Stieg (2011), *The girl with the dragon tattoo* [*Män som hatar kvinnor*], trans. R. Keeland (London: Maclehose Press).
Lombroso, Cesare (1876), *Criminal man* [*L'Uomo delinquente*] (Milano: Hoepli).

Acknowledgements

Kate and Katharine would like to acknowledge and thank the following people and organisations that made this book possible.

Kate would like to thank:
Manchester University Press for publishing this exciting collection and to my co-editor, Katharine Cox, and our contributors for sharing the (literary) ride. Thanks to colleagues at Cardiff University and Cardiff Metropolitan University, and to Maurizio Ascari for his crime fiction expertise, kind words and feedback, as well as encouraging and jolly emails. Thank you to Rebekah Humphreys for our frequent phone conversations and ideas-bouncing sessions, and to David Lockwood for providing helpful feedback on the first iteration of our essay. Thank you to my students, who have taken an interest in my research and always ask me about my progress. Lastly, thanks to the numerous coffee houses that facilitated the inception and creation of this work.

Katharine would like to thank:
Family and friends who have put up with my distracted expression for far too long! Thank you to my co-editor, Kate Watson, and contributors in this collection who have raised thoughtful questions which have led, in turn, to a more nuanced and interesting work. Sheffield Hallam University has supported the completion of this book and encouraged me to create time for this research. Colleagues have been a great source of inspiration and comfort to me – thanks to all at Cardiff Metropolitan University (where the project began) and to all at Sheffield Hallam University. Thank you in particular to Kevin Corstorphine and Matt Steggle for their insight into new weird creatures and responses to H. P. Lovecraft. To Martin Arnold for his unrelenting interest in all areas of research and support for former colleagues. There have been numerous other

people who have helped inform this project – thank you all and my apologies for not having the space to list everyone by name. Finally to Manchester University Press: thank you for your commitment to this collection and your faith in this exciting work.

Introduction

Katharine Cox and Kate Watson

THE TATTOO SPEAKS

Focusing specifically on two periods of tattoo renaissance (1851–1914, and c. 1955 to the present),[1] this collection establishes the tattoo as a key genre convention and mimetic device that marks and remarks crime and detective narratives in complex ways. In choosing the subtitle for this book, we were mindful of Jacques Derrida's concept of 're-marking' (1992).[2] In his discussion of writing, Derrida uses the term to refer to a simultaneous act of difference and communality in writing, whereby the mark 'is a differential mark, and different from itself: different *with itself* (1992: 68; author's emphasis). The logic of this position is, as Patricia Parker notes, the uncertainty that the mark can be reduced to a 'self-contained moment of occurrence' (Parker qtd Howard and O'Connor 2008: 246). The tattoo speaks of the moment of bodily inscription but it has a life beyond this. Derrida's use of the hyphen (to re-mark) reflects the folded relationships between mark, re-mark and the deferment of ultimate meaning. We have removed the hyphen. In doing so, we unite the spoken and written word in the term 'remark' to emphasise the tattoo as narrative: and so the tattoo speaks.

This book is made up of fifteen original and scholarly chapters, which examine the tattoo and the practice of tattooing in crime and detective narratives from the mid-nineteenth century to the rebirth of the tattoo in contemporary crime and detective narratives. Tattoos and crime narratives form a twin tradition: the rise of the tattoo industry and the literary tattoo is coterminous with the birth of detective fiction in the nineteenth century and the rise of print culture and increased literacy. We argue that the tattoo is simultaneously under and over-coded (Negrin 2008); such that the act of seeing a tattoo triggers a process of detection (one that has historically been associated to criminology). Consideration of these early tattoos reveal them to be complex narrative markers which extend beyond unambiguous representations of criminology. Subsequently, the visual appeal of the tattoo is heightened through the mediums of film and television.[3] The postmodern rebirth of tattooing reflects concerns with textuality, play and deconstruction, and sees the tattoo as the ultimate representation of corporeal textuality. This recalls Western tattooing's 'very overt reproduction and recycling of prior forms [which] is [at] the very fabric of the art form' (Lodder 2015: 105). Cultural recycling is bound up with contemporary crime narratives, but these examples do more than merely replicate the uses of tattoos from earlier stories. More recently, tattooing has developed into an affirmative action. In narratives concerned with ethics, trauma and truth,[4] tattoos denote a resistance to change (Salecl in Ahmed and Stacey, 2001: loc. 959–71). This act of personal resistance and embodiment responds to postmodern and poststructuralist theories of self.

Our original contribution to knowledge is to argue beyond the tattoo as a recurrent trope in crime and detective narratives and identify its self-reflective and subversive function within the genre itself. Too often the tattoo has been analysed as an uncomplicated representation of criminality, deviance or primitivism in crime and detective narratives. Critics have ignored the complex ways tattoos offer insights into reading place, gender, animal ethics, law, violence, trauma, art, race and narrative. By responding to the sheer diversity of critical approaches that focus on the body and narrative, including, but not limited to, posthumanism, spatiality, postcolonialism, embodiment and gender studies, culminating in interdisciplinary skin studies (Ahmed and Stacey 2001), we show how the tattoo speaks. It is a complex story.

WHAT IS A TATTOO?

Tattooing permanently scars the body's largest and most visible organ: the skin. The visibly marked skin is an interpretative challenge which both reaffirms and defamiliarises our 'shared skins' (*cf* Barthes 1981). The tattoo speaks of other things, other places and other times. These revisions of place and hybridity (Angel 2012, 2017; Lodder 2015; Rogers 2015) are in dialogue with prior forms (Lodder 2015), as the private is made public and the public made private (Atkinson 2003). Unlike branding, a third-degree burn melting the epidermis and dermis layer together, or body modifications, which typically cut the skin, scoring the flesh, the practice of tattooing locates the scar within the skin's dermis. It reminds us that skin is not just surface but extends beyond the visual clue. In the practice of tattooing, layers of the skin's epidermis are repeatedly penetrated by a sharp instrument, to affect the dermis layer, and pigment applied into the wound. As part of the healing process, a scab then forms which ultimately drops off, revealing the tattoo. The gaining of a tattoo is not an instantaneous event; rather, the tattoo develops and changes over time, remaining as a scar and memory of the wound.

The significance of skin as a biological 'interface between inside and outside' is heightened by the tattoo (Stacey qtd Prosser in Ahmed and Stacey 2001, loc. 1502). This marking is a narrative act which is itself an act of remarking. As the development of skin studies has shown, our skin is already a mnemonic record, but one that is incomplete and partial. Building on Didier Anzieu's psychoanalytical considerations of skin, Sara Ahmed and Jackie Stacey (2001), Steven Connor (2001, 2004) and Jay Prosser's (2001) writings demonstrate that skin acts as an imperfect biological record, marked by trauma, age, gender, gender realignment, class, race and disease, prior to the creation of the tattoo. The tattoo overlays this imperfect mnemonic record and complicates it. The tattooing process is permanent as methods of removal, typically through either a process of effacement (Connor 2004)[5] or further scarification, remark the body.

The tattoo is a permanent act, causing both pain and pleasure, and which both conceals and reveals. Tattoos can be a means by which to identify an individual, but also connect such individuals to the collective identity of a tribe or social grouping. Just as tattoos are an imperfect individual record, they also represent collective mnemonics imperfectly. Building on Claude Lévi-Strauss's observations of Maori tattooing, tattoos speak of (and to) internal and external orders and to our contemporary existence. A social structure is communicated through the act and permanence of the tattoo to both individual and community, connecting individuals (Lévi-Strauss 1963). Lévi-Strauss sees this as a 'stamping' of image, self and tradition; however, this process might be understood to be more ambiguous. Rather than seeing the denuded skin as a limit, representing the exterior of the body and its encounter with the embodied world, the tattoo emphasises its place in a field of communicative and social exchanges.

Tattoos both reaffirm the rule of law (Connor 2001, 2004; Foucault 2006) and challenge it (Beeler 2005; Lodder 2015; Lombroso 1876; Lombroso and Ferrero 1893). Crime is inscribed on the body through forced markings, whereby slaves and criminals are identified as 'ritually polluted' (Goffman 1968: 11; qtd Prosser in Ahmed and Stacey 2001: loc. 1562). Moreover, the identification of criminal behaviours as the emergence of primitive atavistic tendencies, established by criminologists Cesare Lombroso (1835–1909) and Alexandre Lacassagne (1843–1924), informed the emergent detective genre. Drawing on Darwinian evolutionary theories and phrenology ('invented' by physician Franz Joseph Gall), Lombroso connected the tattoo with atavistic tendencies and detailed that tattooing was a symptom of degeneracy, a sign of reversion to the primitive and worthy of 'close and careful study' (2006: 58).[6]

Lacassagne's writing strikes a similar chord to Lombroso, whereby innate criminal tendencies are exposed by the criminal's primitive marking of his/ her skin which 'generally betray the profession chosen at the outset of his [*sic*] career' (in Ashton-Wolfe 1928: 281). Here tattoos are viewed as unambiguous and inalienable, reduced as Gemma Angel writes to 'only the trace, the tattoo itself' (2012: 37; see also Caplan 2000). And yet, as Angel highlights, there is a tension in Lacassagne's thinking which imbues tattoos with a loquaciousness as 'speaking scars' (qtd Angel 2012: 36).[7] The fact that these tattoos are positioned as scars that 'speak' links to the discursive nature of the tattoo and it also associates the taxonomy of the tattoo as part of scarification.

Tattoos encode the body as text on text; as the body is marked and remarked, the story changes.

TATTOOS AND SKIN STUDIES

Our consideration of tattooing is situated within the wider field of skin studies, which emerged from Sara Ahmed and Jackie Stacey's radical consideration of skin in *Thinking through skin* (2001). Here, tattooing and scarification are positioned within a focus on feminism and embodiment. Steven Connor's *The book of skin* (2004) developed Ahmed and Stacey's thinking further, in particular considering the literariness of skin. Connor's writing is informed by philosopher Michel Serres's thinking and considers the body as a site inscribed by the law (2001, 2004). Claudia Benthien's cultural history *Skin: On the cultural border between self and world* (2004) addresses skin as an organ that acts as interface and so is typified by the idea of encounter. In *Skin, culture and psychoanalysis*, Sheila L. Cavanagh, Angela Failler and Rachel Alpha Johnston Hurst use skin as a lens to consider the connection between mind and body, directly building on Didier Anzieu's concept of the 'skin ego' and in conversation with Connor's use of Serres's 'mileu' (2013; Connor 2004). In their analysis of skin, editors Caroline Rosenthal and Dick Vanderbeke note that this area is a 'largely uncharted territory' (2015: 1). Their interdisciplinary collection includes chapters examining skin in literature and film with a focus on race and trauma, with a number considering tattoos and scarification.

Sociological interest in tattooing has been active for some time and has focused on community (Davidson 2016; DeMello 2000, 2014), constructions of self (Thompson 2015), commemoration (Davidson 2016), gender (Thompson 2015) and subcultural identities (DeMello 2000). Prominent tattooed academics (Lodder, Thompson) and authors (Kathy Acker, China Miéville) have no doubt added to this interest. Ethnographic methodologies in sociology articulate contemporary tattoos as part of an individual's developing narrative (Thompson 2015), which intersect with wider cultural issues. Cultural historians DeMello (2000), Helen Rogers (2015) and anthropologist Angel (2012, 2017) have all explored the potential for tattoos to tell the stories of marginalised individuals and groups. Tattooing is also being reclaimed as an art form. Art historians, such as Lodder, have detailed the evolution of tattooing as a popularist art form which problematises areas of high–low cultural debate, distinctions between amateur and professional, which offers repetition and re-articulation of prior forms whereby tattoos both reaffirm and challenge social convention. Contemporary artistry and aesthetics of tattooing talk back to the identification of the tattooing community as being rooted in primitivism,[8] criminological and deviant practice (Angel 2013; Lodder 2011).

The systematic analysis of tattoos in literature and screen media is limited to Karin Beeler's key work *Tattoos, desire and violence: Marks of resistance in literature, film and television* (2006) and Connor's literary consideration of marked skin (2004). Beeler's detailed work examines tattoos as subversive and is an excellent companion to this collection. We develop her focus on tattooing in these different media, opening up relevant historical, sociological and philosophical ways of reading the tattoo. We identify tattooing, beyond a significant interpretative motif at the core of narratives of crime and detection, as performing a mimetic function largely overlooked and undervalued by critics. By analysing tattoo narratives, this collection paves the way for critics to understand the ways in which tattoos mark and remark the genre itself. Crime and detective narratives are revealed to be complex bodily narratives which use the motif of the tattoo to cause the reader to reflect upon the act of reading, interpretation and, at its most extreme, transform the genre itself.

We end where we began: and so the tattoo speaks.

NOTES

1 Our date ranges reflect the representations of the tattoo in crime and detective narratives which we respond to in this book. We argue that the first renaissance is a rebirth of tattooing practice represented in literature. At this time, traditional British Isles practices of pocking and pricking were being remade first through contact with other cultures and then by technological advancements. We identify a first renaissance period in literature from Melville's *Moby-Dick; Or, the whale* (see, for example, Ruggiero, 2003) to Kakfa's 'In the penal colony', examined at length by Connor (2001, 2004), Benthien (2004) and Beeler (2005) (see also Anzieu 1995; Lyotard 1993). The second period stretches from Laughton's *The Night of the Hunter* to the present. Were our date range to be led by the practice of tattooing, this would alter it to take account of specific technological advances and government legislation, so from 1891 (invention of O'Reilly's machine) and the requirement for tattooing artists to be registered in 1982 (The local government – Miscellaneous Provisions Act). A useful consideration of the professionalisation of tattooing is outlined by Ira Dye (1989).
2 Re-marking is explored in Derrida's collection of essays and interviews *Acts of literature* (1992); in particular his essay 'Mallarmé' (also known as 'The double session').
3 See, for example, representations of gender, crime, detection and tattooing in the television series *Blindspot* (NBC 2015).

4 It is not the purpose of this introduction to explore the contemporary cultural period, but there is a shift associated with ideas of metamodernism that is evident in these contemporary works, as the tattooist's ability to 'call forth' an inner truth or identity is obvious in a number of examples. This can be seen in Hal Duncan's new weird series which uses 'graving' as an external mark of bringing forth an inner self. For a detailed discussion of metamodernism, see Robin van den Akker *et al.* (eds) (2017).

5 Contemporary tattoo removal includes dermabrasion, surgery, cryotherapy and Q-switched ruby laser (Rathod *et al.* 2012).

6 Maurizio Ascari (2007) has detailed Lombroso's positioning within a (counter) history of crime fiction.

7 See also Jane Caplan (1997).

8 See primitive tattooed figures on the 1653 frontispiece from John Bulwer's *Antropometamorphoss: Man transform'd, of the artificiall changeling* (shortened title).

BIBLIOGRAPHY

Ahmed, Sarah and Jackie Stacey (eds) (2001), *Thinking through the skin* (London and New York: Routledge).

Angel, Gemma (2012), 'The tattoo collectors: Inscribing criminality in nineteenth century France', *Bildwelten des Wissens* ['Präparate' (prepared specimens)], 9.1 (Berlin: Akademie Verlag, Spring), 29–38.

— (2013), 'Atavistic marks and risky practices: The tattoo in medico-legal debate 1850–1950', in K. Siena and J. Reinarz (eds), *A medical history of skin: Scratching the surface* (London: Pickering Chatto), pp. 165–79.

— (2017), 'The modified body: The nineteenth-century tattoo as fugitive stigmata', *Victorian review: An interdisciplinary journal of Victorian studies* [*Bodily states*] 41.2, n.p.

Anzieu, Didier (2016), *The skin-ego*, intro. and trans. N. Segal (Abingdon and New York: Routledge).

Ascari, Maurizio (2007), *A counter-history of crime fiction: Supernatural, gothic, sensational* (Basingstoke and New York: Palgrave Macmillan).

Ashton-Wolfe, H. (1928), 'Tattooing and the criminal', *Illustrated London news* (11 August 1928).

Atkinson, Michael (2003), *Tattooed: The sociogenesis of a body art* (Toronto, Buffalo and London: University of Toronto Press).

Barthes, Roland (1981), *Camera lucida: Reflections on photography*, trans. R. Howard (New York: Hill and Wang).

Beeler, Karin (2005), *Tattoos, desire and violence: Marks of resistance in literature, film and television* (Jefferson and London: McFarland).

Benthien, Claudia (2004), *Skin: On the cultural border between self and world* (New York: Columbia University Press).

Bulwer, John (1653), *Antropometamorphoss: Man transform'd, of the artificiall changeling* [shortened title, 2nd edition] (London: W. Hunt). Available P.I. Nixon Medical Historical Library.

Caplan, Jane (1997), '"Speaking scars": the tattoo in popular practice and medico-legal debate in nineteenth-century Europe', *History workshop journal*, 44 (Autumn), 107–42.

— (ed.) (2000), *Written on the Body: The tattoo in European and American history* (Reaktion: London).

Cavanagh, Sheila L., Angela Failler and Rachel Alpha Johnston Hurst (eds) (2013), *Skin, culture and psychoanalysis* (Basingstoke and New York: Palgrave MacMillan)

Connor, Steven (2001), 'Mortification', in S. Ahmed, and J. Stacey (eds) (2001), pp. 36–51.

— (2004) *The book of skin* (Ithaca: Cornell University Press).

Davidson, Deborah (2016), *The tattoo project: Commemorative tattoos, visual culture, and the digital archive* (Toronto: Canadian Scholars).

DeMello, Margo (2000), *Bodies of inscription: A cultural history of the modern tattoo community* (Durham, NC and London: Duke University Press).

— (2014), *Body studies: An introduction* (Abingdon and New York: Routledge).

Derrida, Jacques (1992), *Acts of literature*, edited D. Attridge (New York and London: Routledge).

Dye, Ira (1989), 'The tattoos of early American seafarers, 1796–1818', *Proceedings of the American Philosophical Society*, 133:4 (Dec.), 520–54.

Foucault, Michel (1991), *Discipline and punish: The birth of the prison* [*Surveiller et punir: Naissance de la prison*], trans. A. Sheridan (London: Penguin Books).

— (2006), 'Utopian body', *Sensorium* (Cambridge, MA: MIT Press), 229–34.

Goffman, Erving (1968), *Stigma: Notes on the management of a spoiled identity* (Harmondsworth: Penguin).

Howard, Jean E. and Marion F. O'Connor (2008), *Shakespeare reproduced: The text in history and ideology* (Abingdon: Routledge).

Lévi-Strauss, Claude (1963), *Structural anthropology*, trans. C. Jacobson and B. Grundfest Schoepf (New York: Basic Books).

Lodder, Matt (2011), "The myth of the modern primitive", *European journal of American culture*, 30:2, 99–111.

— (2015), 'The new old style: Tradition, archetype and rhetoric in contemporary Western tattooing', in A. Lepine, M. Lodder and R. McKever (eds), *Revival: Memories, identities, utopias* (London: Courtauld Books Online), pp. 103–19.

Lombroso, Cesare (1876), *Criminal man* [*L'Uomo delinquente*] (Milano: Hoepli).

— (2006), *Criminal man* [*L'Uomo delinquente*] trans. and intro. M. Gibson and N. Hahn Rafter (Durham, NC: Duke University Press).

— and Guglielmo, Ferrero (2004), *Criminal woman, the prostitute, and the normal woman* [*La donna delinquent*, 1893], trans. and intro. M. Gibson and N. Hahn Rafter (Durham, NC: Duke University Press).

Lyotard, Jean-François (1993), 'Prescription', in R. Harvey and M. S. Roberts (eds), *Toward the postmodern* (New Jersey and London: Humanities Press).

Negrin, Llewellyn (2008), *Appearance and identity: Fashioning the body in postmodernity* (Basingstoke: Palgrave Macmillan).

Prosser, Jay (2001), 'Skin memories', in S. Ahmed and J. Stacey (eds) (2001), pp. 52–68.

Rathod, Shrinivas, Anusheel Munshi and Jaiprakash Agarwal (2012), 'Skin markings methods and guidelines: A reality in image guidance radiotherapy era' *South Asian journal of cancer*, 1:1 (Jul–Sept.), 27–29.

Rogers, Helen (2015), "'A very fair statement of his past life": Transported convicts, former lives and previous offences' (Open Library of Humanities). Available: https://olh.openlibhums.org/articles/10.16995/olh.27/ [accessed 4 December 2018].

Rosenthal, Caroline and Dick Vanderbeke (eds) (2015), *Probing the skin: Cultural representations of our contact zone* (Newcastle upon Tyne: Cambridge Scholars).

Ruggiero, Vincenzo (2003), *Crime in literature: Sociology of deviance and fiction* (London: Verso).

Thompson, Beverly Yuen (2015), *Covered in ink: Tattoos, women and the politics of the body* (New York: New York University Press).

van den Akker, Robin, Alison Gibbons and Timotheus Vermeueln (eds) (2017), *Metamodernism: Historicity, affect, and depth after postmodernism* (London and New York: Rowman and Littlefield).

PART 1

Psychoanalysis, patternings and the medical imagination

1

A knot of bodies: The tattoo as navel in Louisa May Alcott's 'V.V.: Or, plots and counterplots'

Alexander N. Howe

INTRODUCTION

The public image of Louisa May Alcott was changed forever in 1943 when Leona Rostenberg published her essay, 'Some anonymous and pseudonymous thrillers of Louisa M. Alcott', in the *Papers* of the Bibliographic Society of America. In this work, Rostenberg announced to the world that Louisa May Alcott, beloved author of *Little women* (1868), named the 'children's friend', in fact published numerous stories of intrigue anonymously (and under a variety of pseudonyms) until 1868 when she turned her energies almost exclusively to more lucrative markets. The unearthing of these thrillers began in earnest after the Second World War, but it was not until 1975 that any of the works saw print again, and the recovery was ongoing over the next two decades until Madeleine Stern published a volume of the *Collected thrillers* in 1995. The revelation of this secret publishing history is obviously tantalising for biographical criticism that would read Alcott, a celebrated nineteenth-century feminist figure, as bristling under the strictures of Victorian decorum – both within the publishing world and without.

Certainly, in Alcott's journals and correspondence there is evidence of the secret pleasure she takes in writing the thrillers, narratives that stand quite apart from the 'moral pap for the young' (Alcott qtd Cheney 2010: 296), as she described her later work. She once claimed that her 'natural ambition is for the lurid style' of 'blood and thunder tales', which might feature 'Indians, pirates, wolves, bears, & distressed damsels in a grand tableau' (qtd Smith 2000: 45). While such comments suggest the common trappings of adventure and intrigue, the 'damsels' depicted in these tales are not-so-distressed and are hardly reducible to genre fiction of the time. In this way, the thrillers are a major landmark in the history of crime fiction in North America, although Alcott's achievement on this score remains largely unacknowledged. In this chapter, I will analyse one of the perhaps better-known Alcott thrillers: 'V.V.: Or, plots and counterplots', first published in 1865 in *The flag of our Union* under the pseudonym A. M. Barnard.[1] This story of a spurned woman seeking revenge upon the aristocratic family that has wronged her is remarkable for a number of reasons, particularly for scholars of crime fiction, as we find what Nickerson has claimed is the first example of a detective in American women's writing (Nickerson 1998: 23). However, of equal interest is a tattoo on the body of the villainess, Virginie Varens, which is used to make what initially appears to be a definitive identification that ensures apprehension and punishment. Alcott muddies the waters of this common narrative trajectory significantly, a gesture that problematises any final marking – and thus knowing – of the woman. Virginie's tattoo in fact serves as the navel of the story, in the sense spoken of by Sigmund Freud, Jacques Lacan, Shoshana Felman and others – that is, a tangled knot of signification that remains impenetrable to interpretation. The navel marks that point where signification traumatically touches the body, yet in this tangle the body likewise speaks through its disruption of narrative. Alcott engages this disruption by embodying Virginie incessantly and inscrutably throughout the story, thus proleptically marking the limits of the detective's knowledge and the limits of the emergent detective genre.

GENDER AND GENRE: HYBRIDITY AND DETECTION IN THE ALCOTT THRILLERS

At the level of genre, the thrillers might be understood, initially, in terms of sensational fiction of the nineteenth century. The latter very often depicts a violent and lurid public space that reveals the idyll of the private space of the home to be a fiction. Sensational fiction is thus a sort of seamy underside of domestic fiction, although these two genres of course share the common strategy of engaging a reader's emotions rather than intellect. The intended audience of sensational writing was both men and women of the working class, and unsurprisingly working-class politics are frequently present in such tales. Importantly, in addition to introducing working-class men as protagonists, sensational fiction likewise often presents active women who are voracious and irrepressible. Alcott's thrillers certainly fit the bill on this score; however, these stories are far from formulaic potboilers. A good deal of the criticism of these stories has emanated from a biographical perspective that embraces a feminist re-interpretation of the author. This approach often limits the genre discussion to the modes of domesticity, sentimentalism and sensational literature, with little consideration of Alcott's unique voice as a crime writer (Watson 2012: 85). On the contrary, as Kate Watson argues, '[Alcott] inverted the domestic and sentimental novel and her crime-inflected stories do not efface her criminal/discursive tracks by conventionally punishing the (usually female) wrong-doer/"criminal"' (*ibid.*). The sensationalism of Alcott's thrillers blurs the distinction between public and private spaces with violence – both literal and symbolic –perpetrated by strong women characters who are, in several instances, little murderers; and as Watson suggests, justice often remains wanting.

The settings of these stories are often exotic locales derived solely from Alcott's own imagination and reading. While these distant settings are in keeping with the weekly magazines in which these stories appeared, as are Alcott's 'exotic' (or implausible) plots, this expanse is at the same time appropriate to the dominant theme of the thrillers, which is identity in crisis. It is not incidental, then, that Alcott foregrounds the act of detection in the thrillers. While detective fiction continued to be dismissed as a conservative genre in academic circles, Alcott was a savvy enough reader of Edgar Allan Poe to recognise the possibilities of critique inherent in tales of sleuthing. Much like Poe, Alcott often pairs gothic elements with detection, always with a deliberate focus on the act of reading.[2] Consequently, at the level of genre, the Alcott thrillers are hybrid texts that are as complex as they are engaging. Catherine Ross Nickerson has elaborated upon the intersection of detection and the gothic genre, particularly within early American women's detective stories (Nickerson 1998: 8). Her account interestingly examines the trope of the 'unspeakable' that the famous gothic critic Eve Sedgwick identifies, a device that is often linked to uncanny repetitions and the power of language as incantation or curse. To these ends, Sedgwick speaks of 'a kind of despair about any direct use of language' (Sedgwick 1980: 13) that is common to the gothic genre. Rather than exposing or illuminating, words only further mask and equivocate. This is precisely the presentation of language in the Alcott thrillers and 'V.V.: Or, plots and counterplots' in particular, which focuses upon the act of reading – and mis-reading. Cleverly, Alcott uses a tattoo upon the wrist of the villainess of the story to assay the limits of reference and determination from the framework of a detective narrative.

TATTOOS AND TEXTUALITY

While tattoos as identifying marks appear frequently enough in nineteenth-century literature, it is productive to briefly consider Alcott alongside her fellow dark romanticist Herman Melville. In *Moby-Dick; Or, the whale* (1851), Melville uses the tattoos of the harpooner Queequeg as identifying marks; and while these remain 'hieroglyphic' in nature, they are nonetheless discernible and representative of the sailor's experience. The tattoos are alternately referred to as a 'complete theory', a 'mystical treatise on the art of attaining truth' and a 'wondrous work in one volume' (Melville 1981: 441), and thus they offer a harmonious synthesis of the harpooner's mind, body and story – just as

Ahab's disfigurement suggests his contrasting disharmony and rage. While Ishmael assures the reader that 'what you see is what you get' with Queequeg, as his story is literally tattooed upon his forehead, clearly Melville's greater project within *Moby-Dick* is an excursion into the limits of textuality to capture experience in a perfectly transparent fashion. Here it is wise to remember that, contrary to popular belief, *Moby-Dick* actually begins with the word 'etymology'. With this gesture, Melville forcefully reminds the reader that language is the result of a process and history. Meaning is not divine or inherent in things; rather, meaning is the result of reading and interpretation. Queequeg's marks may in fact be readable, but they must be deciphered and thus interpreted; they cannot, then, function in a straightforwardly indexical fashion.[3]

However, in Alcott's story, the 'V.V.' tattoo initially presents itself as exactly such an index, and here it is perhaps helpful to move more squarely into the realm of detective fiction, albeit nearer the end of the nineteenth century, with a comparison to Arthur Conan Doyle's writing. Tattoos appear only sparingly in the Sherlock Holmes opus, although their use provides a definitive mark of identification. In *A study in scarlet* (1887), for example, a tattoo is the obvious sign missed by Watson in the midst of one of Holmes's dazzling displays of method. In this case, the mark allows the detective to identify a sergeant of the marines from across the street. In the later well-known story 'The adventure of the red-headed league' (1891), the small pink fish tattoo on Jabez Wilson's wrist allows the detective to amaze Watson and Wilson with his powers of perception. Holmes even admits to having 'made a small study of tattoo marks' and claims to have 'contributed to the literature of the subject' (Doyle 2005: 44a). Amusingly, as is often the case, Wilson is suddenly struck with the simplicity of Holmes's insight, to which Holmes responds '[o]mne ignotum pro magnifico' (2005: 44a) and then suggests that it is perhaps best to not give up his secrets. In this instance, the colour of the tattoo unmistakably indicated that Wilson had travelled to China, which in turn suggests details about his occupation. It is truly simplicity itself, as Holmes often claims, and while 'The adventure of the red-headed league' is largely comic in nature, Holmes's assessment of the simplicity of reading the tattoo perhaps ought to be taken seriously. With the tattoo, X does indeed mark the spot – something that is often quite vexing to the individual in question. The third instance of a tattoo in Holmes's stories speaks to this danger. In 'The adventure of the Gloria Scott' (1893), the individual in question, Mr Trevor, has actually gone to great lengths to obscure what he claims are the initials of a former love he had tattooed on his arm. As he says, rather poetically, '[the tattoo's meaning] is just as you say. But we won't talk of it. Of all ghosts, the ghosts of our old loves are the worst' (Doyle 2005a: 507).[4] Here again, the tattoo apparently gives away, with great ease, a past bond with another and a former self that the bearer wishes to leave behind. The fact that these initials refer to Mr Trevor's original name does not undermine this view.

The tattoo functions as a mark that binds its possessor to a given narrative; the mark upon the body does not lie. Given only three references to tattoos in the Holmes canon, one wonders if the tattoo was potentially 'too simple' a trick even for the positivist Holmes. At the very least, the great detective's application of the tattoo as identificatory mark was certainly far too literal.

Frances Mascia-Lees and Patricia Sharpe similarly analyse tattoos in literature, departing from Franz Kafka's 'In the penal colony' (1919), and posit that these marks suggest a unified body that exists outside culture. Culture writes upon the body (just as the apparatus does in Kafka's tale), inscribing it and thus limiting it to a particular social function and narrative. For men, in particular, tattoos likewise serve as a mark of a more permanent identity, something that becomes particularly appealing in a time when more traditional rites of passage fail to offer points of stable identification (Mascia-Lees and Sharpe 1992: 153–54). While this may be true for men, women on the contrary are frequently tattooed or branded to establish ownership, as is seemingly the case with Virginie Varens's tattoo, 'V.V.', where the second 'V' links her to her plundering cousin. This domination and arbitrary ownership are emphasised all the more by her subsequent pairing with Colonel Vane (though admittedly this relationship does not end in marriage). The tattoo marks Virginie as the property of either man. The men are as interchangeable as their initials, just as Virginie is interchangeable as a trophy or object of pleasure. Llewellyn Negrin has likewise analysed the potentially stabilising effects of the tattoo in response to changing notions of the self and fashion, especially for women, during the nineteenth century. When dress becomes a matter of choice and aspiration rather than a mark of an immobile identity and defined attributes, fashion is 'undercoded' and opens itself to an interchangeability of meaning (Negrin 2008: 10). Varens's play with dress and disguise, and of course the brand of ownership her tattoo is to suggest, are an apt reminder of this history and the anxiety that results from the accompanying revision of selfhood.

DOUBLENESS AND DISFIGUREMENT: SIGNS OF WOMAN'S DUPLICITY

The plot of 'V.V.: Or, plots and counterplots' is typical of the Alcott thrillers, as it is the story of a spurned woman's quest for revenge. Virginie Varens, a young Spanish *danseuse*, is bent on receiving recognition and financial support for her son from the aristocratic family of the boy's deceased father. The plot is wonderfully and unnecessarily complicated. Virginie is rescued from poverty by a predatory cousin, Victor, who expects to be repaid for his kindness with marriage. Indeed, it is Victor who kills Virginie's lover and father of her child, the titled Scotsman Allan Douglas, setting the plot into motion. After Allan's murder, Virginie spends time on the continent with her cousin, before she manages to give Victor the slip and run away to India with an affluent admirer, Colonel Vane. After the Colonel dies, Virginie returns to London posing as his widow (although the two were never married). After establishing herself as Widow Vane in London society, she then makes her way to the Douglas family estate – curiously with Victor again in tow. Her hope is to marry Earl Douglas, the family heir and cousin to her lost Allan. Unfortunately, Douglas is engaged to Diana Stuart, but the resourceful Varens quickly overcomes this obstacle.

It is only near the end of the story that the detective appears, called in based upon Douglas's suspicion that the Widow Vane is Virginie Varens. (Apparently, these suspicions are based upon information Allan communicated in letters about Virginie and public gossip about the dissolute, infamous dancer.) The detective is an old friend of Douglas's from Paris, aptly named M. Antoine Duprès. Neither an amateur nor professional detective, Duprès is a dilettante who relishes uncovering intrigue – particularly involving family conflict – within his aristocratic circles. In an introductory comment, he makes this lay status clear: 'I adore a mystery; to fathom a secret, trace a lie, discover a disguise, is my delight. I should make a fine detective' (Alcott 1995: 128). As the name M. Antoine Duprès suggests, Alcott is making a clear reference to Poe's detective Dupin, who appeared over twenty years before this story when 'The murders in the Rue Morgue' was published in *Graham's magazine* (1841). Any doubts of this homage are erased when one considers the name Duprès assumes while surreptitiously working on the case; that is, M. Dupont.

Alcott is an astute reader of Poe. Duprès exhibits not merely the basic requirements of the detective (such as keen observation, attention to detail, cunning), but likewise takes great pleasure in constructing the *text* of the mystery. In other words, like Poe's Dupin, Duprès has a literary flair and is likely himself guilty of a doggerel or two. This is all the more apparent as the story nears the climax, and the detective revels in the poetic text of his investigative summation that definitively reveals the Widow Vane to be Virginie Varens. Nearing the completion of the case, Duprès speaks of the 'grand *denouement* [that] will take place with much éclat' (Alcott 1995: 132). It is not enough that the identity of the suspicious woman should be clarified; this outing must done with a grand flourish, one that will presumably knot together the large number of remaining loose threads in the case. While the tale's finale certainly does not disappoint the reader, the sanguine aspirations of the detective are doomed to failure, as Virginie Varens manages to exact a type of revenge.

On the way to this conclusion, as is only appropriate, the detective does attempt to read the text of Varens herself one evening as he and Douglas venture into the drugged Virginie's bedroom. Adjusting the sleeping woman for better viewing, the two men first open a locket hung around her neck, which contains a picture of Allan, who looks like a brother to Douglas. On the back of this piece are inscribed the initials A. D. or Allan Douglas. Taking a key that hangs next to the locket, the two men then open Virginie's nearby jewel box. In it, they find evidence exposing Virginie as the perpetrator of a variety of recent plots, including proof that she drove Douglas's fiancée, Diana Stuart, to madness and suicide. After plundering these objects that commonly represent feminine sexuality in gothic and sensational fiction, the two men turn to the body of the woman herself for a more literal reading. Under a large bracelet that never leaves her wrist, they find the tattoo 'V.V.' underscored by a true lover's knot, confirming that the Widow Vane is in fact Virginie Varens.

Alcott's description of the tattoo is especially instructive: '[t]wo distinctly traced letters were seen, *V.V.*, and underneath a tiny true lover's knot, in the same dark lines' (Alcott 1995: 134). The emphasis upon the distinctness of the tracing indicates the force of the relationship and servitude that is referenced by the mark. Indeed, the narrator in the subsequent line calls the tattoo a brand which proves the woman's true identity and thus gives the detective Duprès a sense of satisfaction as he stands with Douglas over the helpless, immobile woman (*ibid.*:134). Mascia-Lees and Sharpe, in a discussion of the film *Tattoo* (1981), summarise this relationship well: '[tattoos] indicate not her identity but that of the man to whom she is tied; they signal sexual exclusivity, fidelity to one man, hence her identity as someone's exclusive property' (1992: 153). The tattoo thus serves to unify the duplicity of a woman and her body, reducing her to a stable identity under the sign of man. Varens accounts for her 'disfiguring' tattoo to Allan Douglas by claiming, '[Victor] set his mark upon me ... Ah, that was years ago when I cared nothing for beauty, and clung to Victor as my only friend, letting him do what he would, quite content to please him, for he was very kind, and I, poor child, was nothing but a burden' (Alcott 1995: 83). Indeed, at this point in the story, she remains engaged to Victor despite her relationship with Allan, a contingency plan that she justifies by saying she will accept Victor's proposal of marriage if 'no one else will offer me a name as he does' (*ibid.*: 83).

This play upon the inscription of gendered relations, whose greatest metaphor is the 'V.V.' upon Virginie's wrist, is ruthlessly exploited by Alcott who is constantly presenting her as reading, deciphering and equivocating signs. Lacking permanence of any kind, Varens is described as 'an apparition' and 'sylph' (*ibid.*: 82), a 'fallen angel' (*ibid.*: 85), 'fairylike' (*ibid.*: 91), a 'phantom' (*ibid.*: 111). In short, as the narrator concludes: '[e]verything about her was peculiar and piquant' (*ibid.*: 91). This notion of Virginie as nothing but disguise, a figure with no definitive identity, is suggested repeatedly throughout the story as the narrative makes characteristic references to the failure of her description, and frequently the distance of her true thoughts from the mask of her facial expressions. Here it is worth recalling the scene in which Virginie plays carnival by herself while awaiting Victor's return to her rented flat. In this scene, her dressing room is filled with seemingly endless costumes and false ornaments, and Virginie is described as 'in perfect keeping with [this display]' (*ibid*.: 121). This significant description is one of the few times in the narration that Virginie is described as being equal to an appearance, but of course the aptness of this comparison only underscores the fact that she herself is beyond description. She is nothing more than the sum of the texts she herself authors, disguises that playfully yet shrewdly capitalise upon adversaries' and readers' expectations of femininity.

Early in his investigation to prove that the Widow Vane is Varens in disguise, even the detective Duprès admits '[s]he baffles me somewhat, I confess, with her woman's art in dress' (*ibid*.: 128). The expanse and urgency of this danger is stated more plainly by Douglas in the final confrontation scene, when he accuses Varens: '[y]ou, too, disguised yourself, with an art that staggered my own senses, and perplexed Duprès, for our masculine eye could not fathom the artifices of costume, cosmetics, and consummate acting' (*ibid*.: 140). The utility of the tattoo becomes all the more apparent; without it, Virginie's identity would literally remain in play, incapable of decipherment. However, while the tattoo seems to provide a point of basic identification, the mark in the end remains as duplicitous as Varens herself. Female wiles, when expertly deployed, might avoid detection indefinitely. The adopted patronym 'Vane' is again quite telling in this regard. On the one hand it suggests Virginie's vanity, but it does first and foremost mark the vanity of the men who would presume ownership of the woman – something that Alcott endeavours to make clear throughout the story, particularly in this final confrontation scene which goes on for nearly ten melodramatic pages.

Interestingly, at the conclusion of the tale, the detective's duty of summation is transferred to Douglas alone and Duprès is not even in the same room. This curious choice maintains the detective format of denouement and exposition, but likewise preserves the drama of the thriller with Douglas's far-from-disinterested accusations. He confronts Virginie with her own narrative of deception, astutely filling in holes within the story with his own deception or deduction. Wishing to protect his family's good name by not involving the official authorities, he offers Virginie a punishment outside the law in keeping with sensation fiction's focus on women's fraught legal status: he will keep her in an 'an old gray tower, all that now remains of an ancient stronghold' kept by his family in Scotland (*ibid*.: 142). Her child will be given away to be raised by more worthy parents, leaving Virginie utterly 'cut off from the world' until her final judgement day (*ibid*.). However, before this justice can be meted out, Virginie takes her own life with poison hidden within her ostentatious pearl ring.[5] She falls dead in front of the '[h]orror-stricken' Douglas (who literally collapses). When he summons help, we are told that 'all human aid was useless, and nothing of the fair, false Virginie remained but a beautiful, pale image of repose' (*ibid*.: 143). This is the final view of the narrative gaze.

The 'capture' of Virginie may at first glance be read as just the sort of conservative ending for which detective fiction is often pilloried. The (proto-) detective exposes the villainy of the woman by reading the female body and reducing it to knowledge of the crimes and identity. The body might be safely locked away in a private tower, thus allowing women's public face – and the idea of femininity as such – to remain unsoiled and therefore pious, pure, submissive and domestic. In other words, the ideal nineteenth-century woman is protected despite this single transgression. However, this old grey tower in the end cannot contain Varens and the haunting effects of her transgressions of gender, class, romance, propriety and signification. Given this, Alcott's criticism of gender expectations is not written simply at the level of the defiant femme fatale's misdeeds; beyond the level of plot, this criticism of gender expectations and exploitation is registered in the failure of reference – through the subtext of a failed text, we might say – a practice that is so common to gothic fiction and thrillers alike. Varens thus forces the reader to consider not only double standards and demeaning treatment of women; further, she forces the reader to consider the violence of language used to identify all women, even in seemingly innocent circumstances.

Unsurprisingly, the tropes of mask and veil are fundamental to the Alcott thrillers, which are populated with numerous actresses, impersonators and manipulators. This proliferation of deception must make the reader attentive to the final description of Virginie's 'pale image of repose'. Here, Alcott brilliantly equivocates the very notion of unmasking by deflating the detective-like flourish of Douglas's narrative. As we are told plainly, there can be no peace gained from the conclusion, nor retribution for crimes committed, as we are given only the 'pale *image* of repose' (my emphasis) and not earthly or narrative repose itself. In other words, a mask remains. Virginie, or V.V., as her doubled initials suggests, escapes a final singular reference, and in this she yet excels the men of the tale and, of course, the reader.

TATTOO AS NAVEL: INTERMINABLE INTERPRETATION

This deliberate play with the meaning and permanence of signs makes a psychoanalytic reading of the tale especially fertile. To begin, a word must be said regarding the true lover's knot that is inscribed under the initials tattooed on Virginie's wrist. Over the years, this designation has been associated with a variety of ornamental knots with varying levels of decoration, particularly in artistic renderings. The actual knot itself is based upon the intertwining of two overhand knots in such a way that the resulting bows, when pulled tight, resemble a figure of eight, suggesting completed circles and likewise the mathematical symbol for infinity. Thus the two lovers' souls are entwined for all eternity. While this enmeshing is visually quite appealing and symbolically poetic, such coupling likewise suggests a potential danger in the bond to another. In medieval literature, for example, the lover's knot often references chastity and therefore the danger women always face as men's possession. In either case, what is interesting about the knot is that its strength is created simply through the looping of the simplest of knots that even a child might tie in a piece of string. The surplus of productivity and beauty that is created in this merger is not unlike that of the navel in psychoanalytic discourse, which is likewise an odd knotting, or a suture.

As has been shown, Alcott typifies this emptiness and thus defiance in the tattoo of 'V.V.', a brand upon the woman's body that does not confer the ownership it would seem to promise. That the tattoo effectively appears in the title underscores its significance, just as the subtitle, 'plots and counter-plots', suggests that Alcott's narrative, and the narrative of the tattoo itself, are far more slippery than we might first imagine. The fluidity of this mark might, then, be read through the Freudian concept of the navel. This concept is found in two brief, yet extraordinarily productive, references appearing in the early text *The interpretation of dreams* (1900). The first reference occurs in the midst of the famous interpretation of the dream of 'Irma's injection', a dream Freud himself had regarding a recalcitrant patient who was slow to accept a thera-peutic interpretation during analysis that he thought was certainly correct. As he writes:

> There is often a passage in even the most thoroughly interpreted dream which has to be left obscure; this is because we become aware during the work of inter-pretation that at that point there is a tangle of dream-thoughts which cannot be unraveled and which moreover adds nothing to our knowledge of the content of the dream. This is the dream's navel, the spot where it reaches down into the unknown. The dream-thoughts to which we are led by interpretation cannot, from the nature of things, have any definite endings; they are bound to branch out in every direction into the intricate network of our world of thought. It is at some point where this meshwork is particularly close that the dream-wish grows up, like a mushroom out of its mycelium. (Freud 1965: 564)

These dream-thoughts are, as Freud suggests shortly after this passage, 'unplumbable'; they grow up relentlessly leaving only more uncanny (and unsymbolised) life instead of a definitive point of origin (*ibid.*: 564). Freud continued to champion the efficacy of dream interpretation within analysis; however, in this passage he openly admits that his method remains powerless when confronted with the navel of the dream. As with the navel there are no 'definitive endings'.

While Freud effectively offers the concept of the navel as a dodge to his own interpretative failure, the concept becomes crucial to his subsequent reinven-tion of psychoanalysis as he abandons the archaeological metaphor of recovery (of 'lost' memories) in favour of interpretative construction in the analytic session (Verhaeghe 1999: 172–73). In Felman's well-known account of this dream, the navel marks the resistance of female sexuality to Freud's reading and the return of the body and a play of surfaces, rather than an excavation of depths. This is elaborated via a reading of the obstinate and confounding female figures within Freud's dream. These women represent, as Felman writes, 'a structured female knot which cannot be untied, a knot of female differ-entiality with respect to any given definition; a knot, in other words, which points not to the identifiability of any given feminine identity, but to the inexhaustibility, the unaccountability of female difference' (1985: 64). This tangle defies Freud's attempts at mastery. He cannot account for female identity and desire accord-ing to his conceptual framework that would mark and thus know the woman. Here it is important to recall that within the dream, Freud struggles with a bodily infection in Irma's throat.

Felman provocatively adopts this resistance inherent to the navel: '[t]o ask a question at the level of the navel is to ask a question at the level of a certain birth and of a certain scar: the question is posed out of a certain wound, a certain severance, a certain impossibility of asking' (*ibid.*: 69). What I would like to suggest is that Alcott is doing exactly that – asking a question regarding female identity in the nineteenth century at the level of the navel. In addition to the vagueness of Virginie Varens's every gesture, her body itself is incessantly spoken of as fey. In one instance, as a witness describes the events surrounding the demise of Diana Stuart, Varens (here disguised) is said to move 'as light and easy as if she hadn't no body' (Alcott 1995: 119). While such comments might at first glance seem to disembody the woman or even idealise her otherworldly beauty in a predictable fashion, it is on the contrary in these moments that Varens's body returns, standing quite apart from the more traditional markings that would make her a 'little woman' of any kind. To these ends, her tattoo is again instructive. Its literal duplicity refuses singular expression, and graphically the mark resembles the teeth of a viper, which is in fact Douglas's first description of Virginie (*ibid.*: 91). This biblical allusion to the serpent and women's alliance with evil, duplicity and knowledge is clearly not incidental. Varens's bite does indeed scar the men at the conclusion of the story, just as she herself becomes the scar of the text, taking her own life and reducing the detective and his stand-in Douglas to paroxysm.

CONCLUSION

Far from a brand or metaphorical knot binding her to a man, the 'V.V.' and true lover's knot signal both a scar and protest. The tattoo recalls Victor's attempt to possess Varens in mind and body, but its doubleness also marks Varens as the final victor as she evades Douglas's imprisonment. The surplus of the tattoo as navel is ultimately irreducible to the knowledge of the detective; it is an unsettling remainder that refuses capture and opens a space of irreducible difference. Here the tattoo becomes body art in the fullest sense, as it marks that point where language and the body collide. This interminable encounter evades all final definition and becomes, like the literal navel, a sign of creation, birth and renewal. As Fred Botting has summarised, '[t]he navel, then, is more than a figure for the eruption of the body within the network of cultural metaphors: it also irrupts within language inscribed upon the body and the unknown' (Botting 1999: 13). This disruptive energy of the navel therefore opens an 'ethical relation to otherness rather than an imperative of exclusion and mastery based upon male priority' (*ibid.*). The uncanny multiplicity knotted in the emblem 'V.V.' ceaselessly opens to something new beyond the masculine narratives of knowledge mobilised in the text. In this, Alcott's story persistently engages this 'ethical relation' and thus answers Felman's call for a feminist-inspired criticism that acts at the level of the navel.

Certainly Alcott deserves far greater recognition for the complexity of the so-called thrillers, and for 'V.V.: Or, plots and counterplots' in particular. In this tale she produces the first detective in American women's writing. This is unquestionably remarkable. However, what is all the more impressive about this story is that Alcott confronts the emergent detective genre itself with the question of the navel. In an incredibly modern and productive fashion, she mercilessly interrogates the masculine trope of investigation and its violent measure of knowledge that so frequently reduces woman to object. In so doing, she reveals the limits of its mechanism and the blind spots of the culture that embraced its model. From the perspective of detective fiction history, Alcott's name must be uttered in the same breath as Alain Robbe-Grillet, Paul Bowles, Thomas Pynchon and Sara Paretsky. These celebrated authors rigorously examine the malevolent limits of the detective narrative insofar as it is based upon a gendered knowledge that orders the world through sight, stabilisation and abstraction. In their playfulness with both language and structure, each author recreated detective fiction in innovative ways that opened the genre to difference. Alcott's story is well placed among the work of these anti-detective authors, and the fury and play of her heroine who bears the mark of prolific duplicity remain a confounding challenge. That Alcott achieved this nearly a century before these modern authors speaks all the more to the magnitude of her accomplishment.

NOTES

1 See Madeline Stern (1984) for a consideration of Louisa May Alcott's literary printing history including her use of pseudonyms. Citations from Alcott's 'V.V.: Or, plots and counterplots' are from the Stern edition (1995). See Bibliography for further details.

2 For an excellent discussion of the gothic inheritance of Poe's detective stories, see Tony Magistrale and Sidney Poger (1999).
3 See Spencer Jordan's Chapter 2 in this volume for an analysis of the tattoo, patternings and modern city, in relation to Poe's 'The tell-tale heart' and Melville's *Moby-Dick*.
4 For a detailed consideration of tattooing in the writings and personal philosophy of Arthur Conan Doyle, see David Beck's Chapter 3 in this volume. Beck argues that the trope of the tattoo is sparsely represented in the Holmes stories but is significant and complex in Doyle's medical training, spiritualist beliefs and his other historical writings.
5 The poison ring is a common trope in sensation fiction of the time, and Kathryn Simpson's fascinating work on pearls and gems as clitoral symbology is particularly resonate here in light of Varens's multiplicity. As Simpson writes, '[a]s the images of pearls and gems used as part of their clitoral symbology suggest, their [i.e., Hilda Doolittle and Virginia Woolf] writing shows an awareness that the meaning of the body, and of the female body in particular, is far from single, "natural" and fixed' (2004: 38). Even as an instrument of death, the pearl ring continues to index Varens's surplus of reference.

BIBLIOGRAPHY

Alcott, Louisa May (1995), 'V.V.: Or, plots and counterplots' [1865], in M. Stern (ed.), *Louisa May Alcott unmasked: Collected thrillers* (Boston: Northeastern University Press).
Botting, Fred (1999), *Sex, machines, and navels: Fiction, fantasy and history in the future present* (Manchester and New York: Manchester University Press).
Cheney, Ednah D. (ed.) (2010), *Louisa May Alcott: Her life, love and letters* (Carlisle, MA: Applewood Books).
Doyle, Arthur Conan (2005a), in L. Klinger (ed.), *The new annotated Sherlock Holmes: Volume 1* (New York and London: W.W. Norton and Co.).
— (2005b), *A study in scarlet* [1887], in L. Klinger (ed.), *The new annotated Sherlock Holmes: Volume 3 (novels)* (New York: W.W. Norton and Company).
— (2005c), 'The adventure of the red-headed league' [1891], in L. Klinger (ed.), *The new annotated Sherlock Holmes: Volume 2 (short stories)* (New York: W.W. Norton and Company).
— (2005d), 'The adventure of Gloria Scott' [1893], in L. Klinger (ed.), *The new annotated Sherlock Holmes: Volume 1 (short stories)* (New York: W.W. Norton and Company).
Felman, Shoshana (1985), 'Postal survival, or the question of the navel', *Yale French Studies*, 69, 49–72.
Freud, Sigmund (1965), *The interpretation of dreams* [*Die traumdeutung*, 1900], trans. J. Strachey (New York: Avon Books).
Kafka, Franz (2011) 'In the penal colony' ['*In der strafkolonie*', 1919], trans. M. Hofman (2007), *In the penal colony* (New York, London and others: Penguin).
Magistrale, Tony and Sidney Poger (1999), *Poe's children: Connections between tales of terror and detection* (Oxford: Peter Lang).
Mascia-Less, Frances and Patricia Sharpe (1992), 'The marked and the un(re)marked: Tattoo in gender and theory and narrative', in F. Mascia-Less and P. Sharpe (eds),

Tattoo, torture, mutilation, and adornment: The denaturalization of the body in culture and text (Albany: SUNY Press), pp. 145–70.

Melville, Herman (1981), *Moby-Dick; Or, the whale* [1851] (Berkley, Los Angeles and London: University of California Press).

Negrin, Llewellyn (2008), *Appearance and identity: Fashioning the body in postmodernity* (New York: Palgrave Macmillan).

Nickerson, Catherine Ross (1998), *Web of iniquity: Early detective fiction by American women* (Durham, NC: Duke University Press).

Sedgwick, Eve Kosofsky (1980), *The coherence of gothic conventions* (New York: Arno Press).

Simpson, Kathryn (2004), 'Pearl-diving: Inscriptions of desire and creativity in H.D. and Woolf', *Journal of modern literature*, 27:4 (Summer), pp. 37–58.

Smith, Gail K. (2000), 'Who was that masked woman? Gender and form in Louisa May Alcott's confidence stories', in J. Brown (ed.), *American women short story writers: A collection of critical essays* (New York: Garland), pp. 45–59.

Stern, Madeline (ed.) (1984), *The hidden Alcott* (New York: Avenel).

Verhaeghe, Paul (1999), 'Does the woman exist? From Freud's hysteric to Lacan's feminine', trans. M. du Ry (New York: Other Press).

Watson, Kate (2012), *Women writing crime fiction, 1860–1880: Fourteen American, British and Australian authors* (Jefferson and London: McFarland).

2

Making Manhattan: Urban hieroglyphics, patternings and tattoos in Edgar Allan Poe's 'The tell-tale heart' and Herman Melville's *Moby-Dick; Or, the whale*

Spencer Jordan

INTRODUCTION

From its very inception, the detective figure in crime fiction has been associated with the growth of urbanisation (Scaggs 2005; Hanson 2004). As Gillian Hanson notes, the city provided a unique setting, with its 'multi-layered historical aspects, its sense of secrecy, and its confusion of streets' (*ibid.*: 6). Yet the city was more than just an effective literary backdrop for criminal activity and subsequent detective work. Moving on from premodern crime texts such as *The Newgate calendar* (1773),[1] crime and detective writers such as Edgar Allan Poe and Arthur Conan Doyle, as well as the Mysteries of the City genre itself (Knight 2012), expressed a growing unease with modernity. With unprecedented concentrations of people crowded together, the middle classes in particular were becoming increasingly concerned with issues of urban sanitation, disease and social control during the nineteenth century. The physical space of the city itself was undergoing radical change at this time, underpinned by the growing role of cities as critical nodes in an international system of capitalist exchange (Harvey 1978). Related to this was the associated transformation of how time itself was perceived; what Anthony Giddens describes as the modern city's reordering of time and space (1996) repurposed for economic efficiency. 'Time was thus inscribed in space [...] Economic space subordinates time to itself' (Lefebvre 1991: 95). The social impact of these transformations throughout the nineteenth century are difficult to overestimate.

It was into this maelstrom of change and adaptation that the literary detective first appeared (Knight 2004, 2012). Literary detectives such as C. Auguste Dupin and Sherlock Holmes were an indirect response to the social and cultural impact of this urban modernity, as was the 'inherent individualism of the novel itself where author, hero/heroine and reader form a self-realizing triangle of security' (Knight 2012: 8). If the modern, nineteenth-century city and its people had become unknowable, then only a detective could find the 'truth', the hidden meaning that surely lay waiting to be discovered by what Poe called 'ratiocination'. As Tod Herzog notes, '[t]he detective story, like the metropolis itself, represents (and more pointedly reacts to) the most crucial experience of modernity: the alienation of the individual and the unknowability of the city and the laws that govern social interactions' (Herzog 2009: 17).

For Walter Benjamin, this sense of alienation and estrangement was a central condition of modernism, a condition for which the detective story was a key literary manifestation: '[t]he original social content of the detective story was the obliteration of the individual's traces in the big-city crowd' (Benjamin 1983: 48). G. K. Chesterton, like Benjamin, also believed that the detective story was intimately connected with urbanisation (1902). In a short essay, he described how, in the detective story, the city is rendered a place of secrets and signs, a labyrinth of hidden meaning which only the detective can properly interpret: 'there is no stone in the street and no brick in the wall that is not actually a deliberate symbol' (Chesterton 1983: 4). It is here, in the gap between chaos and order, that detective fiction was conceived. Famously, Charles Dickens wrote about joining the police on a night-time patrol across London (Dickens, 1851), an experience that no doubt influenced his creation of Inspector Bucket in *Bleak house* (1853). Inspector Bucket roamed across London, becoming the first of countless gumshoe detectives, with his 'ghostly manner of appearing' (*ibid.*: 282). The modern city existed as a paradox between planned order and rationalisation on the one hand, and the chaos and incoherence of urban sprawl on the other, a dichotomy that extended to the individualised body itself. This chapter therefore extends its analysis to both bodily tattoos and what might be called 'urban patternings', the increasing array of symbols and urban design that characterised the nineteenth-century metropolis.

This chapter undertakes a detailed analysis of Poe's short story, 'The tell-tale heart' (1843) and Herman Melville's novel, *Moby- Dick; Or, the whale* (1851).[2] While the former is a crime narrative related by a murderer with reference to police detection, the enormity of Melville's novel actually threatens to mask the elements of crime and detection that figure in the story. The crucial crime of *Moby-Dick*, of course, is the attempted murder of the eponymous beast itself, an offence made more monstrous by the whale's metaphorical relationship to notions of self and nation.

Both of these crime narratives have features of the detective novel through which the description and containment of unruly bodies is used to explore the wider socio-economic contexts of the city. Both involve patternings: the aural tattoo of the victim's heart and the imprint of the eye in 'The tell-tale heart'; and the bodily tattooing in *Moby-Dick*. Foreshadowing this chapter's discussion of the beating heart in Poe's short story, Schiffmacher states that 'tattoos function as a means of non-verbal communication' and gives the example of 'the lines on the face of the Inuit telling the tale of a murder' (Schiffmacher 2005: 12). This essence of creating rationalised patterns of meaning out of chaos remains central to nineteenth-century detective fiction. As Thomas notes, 'the literary detective transcribes the criminal body and renders it legible – in the form of fingerprints, mug shots, or various kinds of medical and legal documents' (Thomas 1999: 288). These patternings have both spatial and temporal parameters and exist not only within the city, but on the body as much as within the form and structure of the textual narrative itself. Poe's short story, for example, is bound by ideas of textual (repeated devices and images), temporal and aural patterning (sound of drums, heart beats, the pulse of a watch's minute hand, a clock sounding or the absence of these sounds). In comparison, Melville's novel is epic and digressive, and draws attention to structures or characters that offer examples of provisional mapping. In this sense, the chapter argues that the bodily tattoo should be considered part of a wider trope of patterning that is central to crime and detective fiction at this time.

Both the authors studied in this chapter were undoubtedly influenced by New York. Melville was born in Manhattan in 1819, returning to work and live there as deputy inspector of customs. As Andrew Delbanco notes: 'his sensibility, like that of all major modernist writers, had been formed by a city – specifically New York City' (Delbanco 2013: 11). Poe spent much of his life living in large urban centres, including New York for much of the 1830s and 1840s (Fisher 2010).

Like London and Paris, New York witnessed spectacular growth during the nineteenth century (Knight 2012). In 1800, its population had barely reached 60,000. Yet by 1870 Gotham could boast just under a million people (Burrows and Wallace 2000). Within a single lifespan one of the world's largest conurbations had come into being. Unlike its European rivals, however, this expansion was both planned and coordinated through the adoption of what still remains one of the city's most famous features: the grid-iron pattern of its thoroughfares, first proposed in the Commissioners' Plan of 1811 (Burrows and Wallace 2000: 419–22). As Burrows and Wallace note, the proposed grid of streets appealed to the republican predilection for 'control and balance' as well as encapsulating their 'distrust of sinuous nature' (*ibid.*: 420). Not only that, but the deliberate 'shift from naming streets to numbering them, beyond promoting efficiency, also embodied a lexicographical leveling; no longer would families of rank or fortune memorialise themselves in the cityscape' (*ibid.*: 422). The new streets and their rectilinear pattern allowed for the efficient movement of both people and commerce. The Commissioners' Plan was a key moment in the development of the market economy across the island, levelling anything in its way that did not assist in the utilitarian vision of its authors, anticipating what Haussmann was to do in Paris by forty years. As Burrows and Wallace comment, '[i]n Manhattan – a city of capital, not a capital city – considerations of efficiency and economy came first' (*ibid.*). This semi-regularised movement of individuals enforced by the grid-iron street pattern engendered a physical tattooing across the city that directly challenged existing societal structures.

Associated with this spatial rationalisation was the increasing standardisation of time. Like cityspace, time became systemised through 'technological devices (clocks, telegraph instruments), the infrastructure (telegraph lines) … necessary for the coordination of varying local times' (West-Pavlov 2013: 128). Such aural tattooing, the beating of the telegraphic pulse and the tick of the precision timepiece, became central to the development of 'absolute time [which] was from the outset intimately linked to the emergent capitalist system' (*ibid.*: 122). It was here, in this maelstrom of change and adaptation, that the modern detective was born.

EDGAR ALLAN POE'S 'THE TELL-TALE HEART' (1843)

Although Poe wrote a number of detective stories featuring the detective Chevalier Auguste Dupin, criminal detection of some kind remains a feature of many of his other short stories too (Thomas 1999: 43). 'The tell-tale heart' was first published in *The pioneer* in January 1843. Like 'The man of the crowd' (1840), it is written in the first person perspective by an unnamed narrator. The location remains unspecified but is suggestive of the claustrophobic interiority of a squalid boarding house, the type Poe was familiar with during his often peripatetic living arrangements. The narrator appears to be a misanthropic introvert, a person outside of societal norms who is suffering from a certain condition which causes 'over-acuteness of the senses' (Poe 1998: 195). In 'The tell-tale heart' the perfect crime is foiled by the murderer himself, overseen by the all seeing eye of the state. A neighbour hears a scream and lodges a complaint at one of the new police offices set up across the city; three men arrive whom the narrator assumes are police. They would not have been wearing any uniform in this period in history to denote their official status. The narrator takes them at their word, but they find nothing. As detectives, they fail. Only the murderer knows the truth. The police only find the body when the narrator spectacularly confesses after becoming unable to bear the sound of the beating heart of his victim from under the floorboards: 'I admit the deed!—tear up the planks! here, here!—It is the beating of his hideous heart!' (*ibid.*: 197). In the modern city, with its developing network of regulation and control, it is the murderer who finally reveals the truth.

There are two bodily elements of the story that relate directly to the idea of tattooing, crime and detection: the heart and the eye. Poe represents the heart as an aural tattoo while the eye is a visual imprint; both are examples of patternings. The 'hideous heart' that beats out 'a hellish tattoo' (*ibid.*: 195) dominates the second half of the story and powers the story's climax. While the rhythmic, insistent sound of the tattoo is a familiar gothic trope (the tapping at a window, knocking at a door), aural tattoos are nevertheless associated with the meanings of tattoos more widely. The tattoo in this context recalls the rhythmic Polynesian method of striking a tattoo, as well as the 'drum' of a military tattoo. The heart's sound is a regular aural tattoo that literally inscribes time into the story, a sound patterning that slowly overwhelms the narrator. Zimmerman has noted that '[t]he narrator hates the eye of an old man who has become revolting because of the passing of time, and he hears the symbols of time everywhere, even within the centre of our being – at the heart (our "ticker")' (Zimmerman 2005: 24). Drawing on James W. Gargano (1968), Zimmerman counts twenty-nine references to time alone within the story, concluding that 'The tell-tale heart' is 'obsessed with time and time passing' (Zimmerman 2005: 25).

Yet time is not just inscribed into the story through the beating heart. It is present in the very patterning of the prose itself. Like the modern city, detective fiction has always had a fixation on the representation of time (Scaggs 2005: 16). A key characteristic of detective fiction is the need for a detective to elucidate a precise chronology of past events by which to explain the present. Scaggs describes the use of the 'double rhythm' in detective fiction, a term Paul Skenazy defines as 'moving inexorably forward in time while creeping slowly backward to resolve the disruptions and violence evident in the present' (Skenazy 1995: 113). William Engel describes how this 'double rhythm' is effected within the structure of 'The tell-tale heart' by the use of chiasmus. The story is divided into two halves, each of nine paragraphs, the second reversing the order of phrase in the first. Chiasmus 'is a form of inverted parallelism that presents subjects in the order A, B, C and then discusses them C, B, A, sometimes using exact repetition, sometimes displaying the successive clauses by means of parallel syntax' (Engel 2012: 4). This attention to patternings and symmetry reinforces the reader's perception of the tattoo. The murderer is acutely aware of his victim's heartbeat. The beating, aural tattoo prompts the murderer to act fearing 'the sound would be heard by a neighbour' (Poe 1998: 195). By fetishising the heart and eye, and rendering them as synecdochic, the murderer depersonalises his victim which allows him to act. However, this linguistic function also causes the murderer's downfall. Having separated the person from these bodily functions, the heartbeat is no longer reliant on the living.

The representation of time is very different in the two halves of the story. In the first half the narrator appears outside of time – 'a watch's minute hand moves more quickly than did mine' – relating how he was able to gain entry into the old man's chamber by moving so 'slowly – very, very slowly' as to be imperceptible in the darkness (*ibid.*: 194). But then there is an immediate change at the beginning of the second half as the murder is about to be performed: 'there came to my ears a low, dull, quick sound, such as a watch makes when enveloped in cotton' (*ibid.*: 196). A heartbeat begins, a rhythmical pattern inscribed both into the story and the murderer's mind. It is this overt manifestation of syncopated time that underpins the switching of the narrator from murderer to detective, from the irrational to the rational, a transformation which finally leads him to the uncovering of his own crime.

Although the heart is a significant symbol in the story, it is the pale blue, vulture-like eye which remains the key motif. The symbolic patterning of the eye imprints itself on the murderer both prior to acting and after the murder. We are told it is an 'Evil Eye' (*ibid.*: 193). Normally it is closed but on the night of the murder the narrator finds it open at the halfway point of the story. The exact nature of the eye is never revealed and critical readings of its meaning vary greatly. Benjamin Fisher suggests that the eye is that of the old man (Fisher 2002: 87), an idea reflected in Harry Clarke's famous illustration of the story completed in 1919. Others suggest a more indeterminate nature, mirroring the elusive meaning of the story itself (Benfey 1993). If the eye is not real, then it exists as a symbol, an iconic image. E. A. Robinson, for example, emphasises the eye's subjective nature and the way Poe uses it only for psychological effect (Robinson 1971: 101). In terms of Poe's writing more generally, this notion fits with what Louise Kaplan calls Poe's 'fundamental antagonism to representational reality' (1993: 46–47). There is a similar interplay between the real and the imaginary in Poe's short story 'Gold bug' (1843) whereby, as Martin Scofield notes, the sign 'itself seems to hover between categories of natural and supernatural, literal and metaphoric, and between signifier and signified' (Scofield 2006: 39). The Evil Eye in 'The tell-tale heart' operates in the same way. Here, the eye is clearly more than a biological eye but rather a false eye, a symbol whose real power comes in what it represents. The eye is on the body but not necessarily of it, a secret that needs decoding, one of Laura Marcus's 'urban hieroglyphics' (2003: 248). As James Martel argues, one of the features of Poe's work is his focus on this question of representation: '[a]s with Benjamin too, for Poe representation is all that we have by which to organize our lives and our world' (Martel 2011: 150). For Poe, the real danger was that we took such representations to be 'true', 'natural' and/or 'divine' rather than 'delusions' (*ibid.*: 117). The eye in 'The tell-tale heart' is part of what Benjamin called phantasmagoria, a delusion, 'a *Blendwerk*, a deceptive image designed to dazzle' that nevertheless is charged with meaning (Tiedemann 2002: 938). Knight has shown that even with Dupin, there existed a conscious interplay between the rational and the irrational: 'moving from and through the scientific to the special authority of the visionary' (Knight 1980: 43). Zimmerman takes this further, noting, '[l]ike Melville's Ahab, Poe's madman in "The tell-tale heart"' particularly employs reason not only to carry out irrational acts but also to justify them' (Zimmerman 2005: 34). This tension between the rational and the irrational, between order and chaos, is one that lies at the heart of the modern city. It is no surprise to find it a major theme of contemporaneous detective fiction.

The image of the eye has a long history within human culture. The Eye of Providence (or the all-seeing eye of God) is a symbol showing an eye often surrounded by rays of light, exactly as depicted by Poe, when the narrator casts a single ray of light from the lantern onto the 'vulture eye' (Poe 1998: 193). The Eye of Providence had been incorporated into the design of the Great Seal of the United States in 1782. By the beginning of the nineteenth century, the Eye had also become a key icon within Freemasonry, representing the all-seeing Eye of God. These meanings would not have been lost on those reading 'The tell-tale heart' when it was first printed. Yet one can also read the eye as a reference to detection, as Caroline Jones and Katharine Cox's Chapter 10 in this volume demonstrates. The famous Allan Pinkerton Detective Agency, first established in 1850 in Chicago (Mackay 2007: 70), adopted the insignia of the 'wide awake human eye … with the slogan "We Never Sleep"' (*ibid.*: 71). It was this emblem that gave rise to the term 'Private Eye' as slang for a private detective. Inspector Bucket's most important feature in *Bleak House* is his stare – 'steady-looking, sharp-eyed' – as though he held supernatural powers of seeing (Dickens 1994: 282).

As a detective story, 'The tell-tale heart' presents us with a literary panopticon concentrated in a boarding house in Gotham. Michel Foucault used Jeremy Bentham's panopticon as a symbol of what he called the rise of the 'disciplinary society' during the first half of the nineteenth century (Foucault 1991: 216; Knight 2012: 8). Cities were increasingly places with 'thousands of eyes posted everywhere [...] a long hierarchized network' (Foucault 1991: 214). Crucially, at the centre of this network of regulation and control was the human body itself; what Foucault terms 'political technology of the body' to refer to this complex interplay of regulatory and bodily systems (*ibid.*: 26). Poe's police officers intervene as they are alerted to a potential breach of the peace – a shriek overheard by a neighbour. Information lodged at the police office results in their dispatch to the premises.

The eye, then, represents this growing network of surveillance and detection that was slowly permeating the city. As James Hutchisson states, '[t]he "vulture eye" suggests some observing consciousness, seeking to illuminate, to show what the narrator tries to keep dark and hidden' (Hutchisson 2005: 143). And yet, it is not the seen actions of the murderer that lead to his apprehension. Rather, it is the sound of a shriek and the incessant aural tattoo of the heart which cause the murderer to confess to his crimes. With increasing regulation on the streets, and with a network of secret informers and amateur detectives peering and listening into citizens' private lives, 'The tell-tale heart' draws on contemporaneous anxieties whereby new and expanding cities, explored by nineteenth-century crime and detective fiction, became the nexus of these 'mechanisms of subjection' (Foucault 1991: 26).

Although Henri Lefebvre does not expressly discuss tattoos, the relationship of the body to the outside world remains a critical part of his argument. Lefebvre understood the materiality of the body to be derived completely from space. The body was a 'spatial body', its material character founded on the productive rationale of that society (Lefebvre 1991: 194–203). For Lefebvre, cityspace was predicated on the complex interplay of what he termed 'spatial codes'. These codes were themselves based on the productive base of the state. However, a spatial code was 'not simply a means of reading or interpreting space: rather it is a means of living in that space, of understanding it, and of producing it' (*ibid.*: 48). Spatial codes could include both verbal and nonverbal signs.

As we have seen, Poe's Evil Eye hovers indeterminately between bodily inscription and supernatural vision. Its true nature remains unknown and, for the purposes of the story, irrelevant. For the narrator, the eye is indeed inscribed upon the body; his body. What is argued here is the meaning of that inscription is legitimated by the wider socio-economic milieu of the city. The Commissioners' attempt to control the urban form of New York, with its emphasis on market rationalisation and economy, extended to the body of each citizen. Implicit in the Commissioners' vision was both a political and a market economy in which the bodily functions of the citizen were paramount. Just as the grid served the commercial and transport requirements of each citizen, a growing, hidden, network of sewers and water pipes serviced their biological needs, while the telegraph formed an electronic communication network which linked businesses together as well as the proliferating centres of social control, such as police offices. In this sense, the grid existed both horizontally and vertically, regulating all forms of economic and social life, providing an explicit network of rationalised flow and connectivity. If the body can be understood as a node within this network of systems, then the skin is the interface between the external system of the city and the internal systems of the body, 'the scrim on which we project our greatest fantasies and deepest fears about our bodies' (Mifflin 2013: 4). It is the skin, and through that the clothes upon the skin, that provides direct interaction with the outside world.

The eye and the heart are central patternings – one physical, one aural – within the story. Each can be understood as spatial codes in the sense that they offer 'a means of reading or interpreting space' as well as 'understanding it, and of producing it' at a key moment of socio-economic development (Lefebvre 1991: 47–48). The use of spatial codes more generally across detective fiction has yet to be properly studied, yet it can be seen that a confluence between a genre explicitly interrogating social constructions of place and time and the theoretical paradigms established by Lefebvre offers much potential.

The eye and the heart within the story are at one level suggestive of the fundamental degree to which capitalist means of control had permeated society.

Both space and time within the modern city had become slaves to economic imperatives, fundamentally changing how those concepts were experienced by each city dweller. As has been discussed, crime and detective fiction, at least in part, was a means of exploring these anxieties. Yet crucially Poe is intent on showing both the extent but also the limits of this transformation. As Martel reminds us, 'Poe, perhaps more than any other writer of his time, was able to expose these changes as merely "representation" with no inherent meaning, or objectivised reality, beneath it' (Martel 2011). It is here that we find the transgressive nature of these patternings within crime and detective fiction, their existence as nothing more than delusions within the phantasmagoria, 'the whole capitalist productive process' (Tiedemann 2002: 938).

The tattoo, then, remains a central motif in the 'The tell-tale heart'. The story is riven with physical, aural and subjective patterning, an encoding that finds its way into the very structure of the text itself. The narrator becomes his own jailor, reading and misreading the proliferation of signs and symbols around him as the detectives, those two figures of modernity, look on in silence.

HERMAN MELVILLE'S *MOBY-DICK; OR, THE WHALE* (1851)

Melville's *Moby-Dick* was published eight years after Poe's 'The tell-tale heart'. On one level, the novel is a quest, a metaphysical search for truth and meaning, in which the crew of the *Pequod* follow a series of clues to the potential resolution of the plot. In this sense, *Moby-Dick* can also be considered a particular form of detective fiction, what Patricia Merivale and Susan Elizabeth Sweeney call a *metaphysical* detective story which asks questions 'about mysteries of being and knowing which transcend the mere machinations of the mystery plot' (Merivale and Sweeney 1999: 2). Merivale and Sweeney also include Poe in this category, developing a tentative genealogy of detective fiction that runs through to the postmodern authors such as Thomas Pynchon and Paul Auster. As Eric Bulson notes, 'unlike the narrative resolution of a detective story that allows for the careful reconstruction of the villain's steps, *Moby-Dick* is organised around the complete absence of that knowledge' (Bulson 2007: 48). This makes *Moby-Dick* an 'anti-detective genre' (Scaggs 2005) with its focus, as Knight explains, on questioning 'certainties about the self, the mind and the ambient world' (Knight 2004: 205).

Melville was born in New York's harbourside and took his first ocean voyage at the age of 20 (Augst 2010: 59). Like Melville, Ishmael too lives in New York. As Thomas Augst notes, 'wherever he came from, and wherever he will go, Ishmael is a New Yorker' (*ibid.*). The words could apply equally to Melville. Although the great majority of *Moby-Dick* is spent at sea, the beginning of the novel has three land-based locations, following Ishmael's progress northwards along the Eastern seaboard: Manhattan, New Bedford and finally Nantucket, where he boards the *Pequod*. Yet New York remains a central presence within the novel, the *Pequod* invisibly tied to Manhattan through the global trade links that spanned the world. As Ishmael tells us, 'people in Nantucket invest their money in whaling vessels, the same way that you do yours in approved state stocks bringing good interest' (Melville 1992: 82). In this beginning section of the novel, Ishmael is described in ways that we would now recognise as a *flâneur*, circumambulating 'the city of a dreamy Sabbath afternoon' (*ibid.*: 3), brought back to the sea when his dark moods, 'drizzly November in my soul' (*ibid.*), overwhelm him. Ishmael sees men like himself, 'silent sentinels all around the town [...] fixed in ocean reveries' (*ibid.*: 4). From the very first page a contrast is established between the ordered life of the city and the 'wild and distant seas' (*ibid.*: 8), echoing the tension between order and chaos already explored in this chapter. The oceans are depicted as beyond the civilising constraints of society, a place where a man can be truly free. Yet even in this opening chapter, the true nature of Ishmael's voyage is described as a metaphysical mystery, a physical and spiritual enigma that may be resolved during the course of the novel. The 'silent sentinels' pointing out to sea are just the first of many signs and symbols that guide Ishmael in his investigations that will ultimately lead to the white whale. This becomes more overt when Ishmael meets Queequeg, the son of a South Sea chieftain. Queequeg's body is covered with strange and indecipherable tattoos:

> This tattooing had been the work of a departed prophet and seer of his island, who, by those hieroglyphic marks, had written out on his body a complete theory of the heavens and the earth, and a mystical treatise on the art of attaining truth; so that Queequeg in his own proper person was a riddle to unfold; a wondrous work in one volume; but whose mysteries not even himself could read, though his own live heart beat against them; and these mysteries were therefore destined in the end to moulder away with the living parchment whereon they were inscribed, and so be unsolved to the last. (*ibid.*: 524)

The mystical markings of Queequeg are in contrast to the tattoos on Ishmael himself. Ishmael has had the precise dimensions of a whale's skeleton imprinted onto his right arm, 'there was no other secure way of preserving such valuable statistics' (*ibid.*: 491–92). Ishmael's tattooed sequence of numbers provides a deliberate counterpoint to the spiritual markings of the South Sea chieftain, 'part of the special category of signs in *Moby-Dick* that compellingly manifest the presence of great power and worth' (Sanborn 2011: 106–07). As we have already seen, this conflict between rationalism and irrationalism was a central feature of Poe's work; yet it also remains a key aspect of *Moby-Dick*. As David Dowling notes, '[y]earning for structure in the face of jarring ambiguity pervades the novel' noting 'the novel's tendency to place readers in a bind between precision [...] and formlessness' (Dowling 2010: 60).

In chapter four, the tattooing on Queequeg's arm, 'an interminable Cretan labyrinth of a figure', becomes interwoven with the patterning of the counterpane under which both Queequeg and Ishmael are sleeping (Melville 1992: 28). It is as though the answer to Ishmael's metaphysical investigations into humankind are there in front of him, only he can make nothing of the signs and symbols that surround him. This sense of hidden codes and signs encrypted into the very fabric of existence is a key one within *Moby-Dick*. Ishmael can be understood as a detective in the sense that he spends much of the novel trying to decipher symbols and meanings that are presented to him. The hidden prophecy of sacred texts such as the Bible is transmuted into Ishmael's unconscious interpretation of what he sees and hears. The central narrator of *Moby-Dick* occupies a distinct epistemological position, in which the world is represented as a text. Biblical writing plays a significant part here, but also the hieroglyphics and signs encoded into the world through which the *Pequod* and its crew of 'mongrel renegades, and castaways' passes (*ibid.*: 203). Ishmael is their reader, but is ultimately unable to grasp their true meaning and in the process becomes one of many postmodern detectives for whom the resolution of the story remains enigmatic.

For Paul Auster, Melville's novel was central both to New York but also the detective novel. In Auster's *The locked room* (1986), for example, the third volume in his collection *The New York trilogy* (1987), the narrator explains that his name is Herman Melville. In *The New York trilogy* it is always the writer who becomes the detective; the world is constructed through texts which are themselves founded on other fictions. The search for truth and understanding is in that sense doomed to failure. This takes us back to Poe's unpicking of representation itself, and the ultimate lack of objective meaning. As Coughlan notes, '[i]n his city of glass, Quinn is seeking exactly this world of transparency where there is a direct correspondence between the signifier and the signified, between the word and its object' (Coughlan 2006: 844). Yet for the detective 'Paul Auster' in *City of glass* (1985) and for Ishmael in *Moby-Dick*, this connection between the world and its representation is irrevocably severed. In *Moby-Dick* Ishmael is retelling the story. Ishmael exists not only as a character within the novel but is also presented to us as the writer, the metaphysical detective, trying to make sense of those things that have already happened. Queequeg's tattoos are the most famous of the long list of indecipherable signifiers that haunt the novel, the greatest being the story itself. Rational, scientific knowledge as represented by the statistics tattooed onto Ishmael's right arm are revealed to be no more than abstractions, figurative representations of a knowledge system whose claim on objectivity is itself a hapless delusion.

Queequeg remains a subversive presence. This otherness is externalised in the wild and excessive tattooing of the body, a practice common among North American, Polynesian and Maori tribes (DeMello 2000: 1–3). Indeed, as Mifflin has shown in regards to nineteenth-century women, the tattoo is very much associated with transgression. If tattoos are signifiers within a 'spatial code', then Mifflin opens up the possibility that they can operate subversively, against dominant ideology (Mifflin, 2013). Crucially for Mifflin, then, Lefebvre's 'spatial body' is a site of contestation. In this sense, tattoos can be understood as manifestations of what Lefebvre called 'representational spaces' – spaces which embody 'complex symbolisms, sometimes coded, sometimes not, linked to the clandestine or underground side of social life' (Lefebvre 1991: 33). Representational spaces include such things as ideas, concepts and theories. As a manifestation of representational space, tattoos exist, at least in part, as a subversive 'spatial code'.

As a spatial code, Queequeg's free-flowing patterning is in direct contradiction to the grid system of streets introduced in the first chapter. In fact, Queequeg is representative of the wild and excessive 'nature' that the Commissioners had tried so hard to expunge from the island. In reality, however, there were two specific areas on the island where the Commissioners' Plan failed to penetrate: the great wreath of harbourside streets and byways that swaddled Manhattan, and Sixth Ward, the heart of the island, with Five Points at its centre. It was no coincidence that these two areas were most clearly associated with the working classes. Outside of the Commissioners' grid pattern, these areas held their own distinctive spatial form, unplanned and chaotic, in dialectical opposition to the geometric regulation of Gotham's commercial districts.

It was in these two areas of New York that tattoos were most prevalent. The most popular would undoubtedly have belonged to those engaged in the maritime trade. Although there are no extant statistics, it is clear from contemporary records that many sailors considered it a rite of passage to have some insignia or other tattooed onto their hands, arms and torso (DeMello 2000). These often included depictions of the sea and shipping, both written, such as the name of a ship, and pictorial, such as anchors and figureheads.[3] These could include representations of the fantastical, such as mermaids and sea monsters (Hardy 2014). Again, these maritime tattoos can be interpreted as a separate spatial code, manifestations of a representational place utterly removed from Manhattan island (Sanborn 2011: 106–07).

In this sense, we return to the signs and secrets of Chesterton's urban detective stories. As Marcus notes, the representation of the city as a secret code became a key feature of the postmodern novel (Marcus 2003: 248). Marcus uses the neologism 'urban hieroglyphics' to refer to what she describes as spatial and temporal patterns, 'palimpsestic layerings of past events' (*ibid.*). As writers such as Auster, Iain Sinclair and Peter Ackroyd have shown, central to the discovery and decoding of these signs is the act of walking. In *City of glass*, it is Quinn's perambulations across New York that encode hidden messages into the very fabric of the city. For Auster, the detective process is primarily a spatial practice, drawing on Benjamin's notion of the *flâneur* (Benjamin 1983:

170). As Benjamin noted, '[p]reformed in the figure of the *flâneur* is that of the detective' (2002: 442).

Just as the tattoo is the manifestation of a particular representational space, then so too is the very movement of the body. For Michel de Certeau (1984), the city itself is called into existence by this spatial practice. De Certeau uses the term 'walking rhetorics' to describe this process (*ibid.*: 100) whereby 'the act of walking is to the urban system what the speech act is to language' (*ibid.*: 97). De Certeau understands walking as 'a space of "enunciation"' (*ibid.*: 98). In this sense, the detective story is a story created by the spatial practices, the urban patterning, of the detective.

As Ishmael travels across the world, the hidden secrets of Queequeg's tattoos remain a constant presence until the very end of the novel when he survives the sinking of the ship by embracing Queequeg's tattooed coffin. Like Quinn in *City of glass*, Ishmael's story is a spatial one, a physical movement from city to sea, before returning, after being rescued by the *Rachel*, back to the city again. Unlike the narrator in 'The tell-tale heart', Ishmael's investigations are of epic proportions. Yet there are significant similarities between them.

Although spatial patterning is central in both stories, so too is their temporal structure. Both evidence the 'double rhythm' of detective fiction already discussed. In *Moby-Dick*, as in 'The tell-tale heart', there remains an ongoing dichotomy between natural, bodily time and economic time. In *Moby-Dick*, this sense of 'double rhythm' is itself complicated by the *Pequod's* own movement eastwards across different time zones. The rational world of Ahab's maps and charts, with its mathematically inscribed lines of longitude and latitude, recalling the statistics tattooed onto Ishmael's arm (Bulson 2007: 43–64), is placed in direct contrast to the free-flowing hieroglyphics of Queequeg's tattoos. Time itself is encoded within the novel as both objective and systematised but also endless and free flowing. In the end, the interception of the whale by the *Pequod* remains more down to chance than rational calculation (Bulson 2007). In fact, the ending in both stories is equally open and ambiguous. As detectives, the narrators' own spatial practice is central to each story, as are the signs and hieroglyphics of the modernist city that are themselves inscribed onto the very fabric of the story.

CONCLUSION

This chapter has argued that tattooing and patterning played a crucial role in the development of the form and structure of the detective story. The context for this role was unparalleled urban growth in the first half of the nineteenth century. Ports such as New York began to acquire a global hinterland in which merchant ships such as the *Pequod* became functional nodes within the wider capitalist system (Harvey 1978). As Knight notes, port cities came to be seen as 'needing massive new systems of regulation and supervision' (2012: 6), a regulatory regime that was invested in each city as well as commercial vessels. One of the crucial themes explored here has been the underlying tension between rationality and irrationality, regulation and nature that resulted from this period. Tattooing and patterning within detective fiction was certainly symbolic of this tension. The use of Lefebvre's concept of spatial codes allows us to place the body as a key site of such regulatory systems and, perhaps more crucially, its potential contestation. The spatial practice of the body, its regulated and systematised movement through the cityspace, its attempt at deviance and boundary crossing, instantiates the very form of the city. These acts of narrative forming and decoding, what Charles Baudelaire saw as the lyrical interplay between body and city, remain at the heart of the detective story.

The inscriptions in *Moby-Dick* and 'The tell-tale heart' are spatial codes in the sense that they are products of this wider social-economic context. Yet so too, of course, is the detective novel itself, a textual patterning which tries to rationalise what Chesterton saw as an uncharted labyrinth, the detective's role both spatial in terms of progress through the city, but also deductive in terms of trying to find the hidden meaning behind signs and secrets. The aural tattooing that runs throughout 'The tell-tale heart' – such as the 'hellish tattoo of the heart', a clock sounding – reminds us that it was not just space that came under the sway of the nineteenth-century regulatory gaze. Encoded into the very structure of detective fiction is a representation of time itself, the 'double rhythm' identified by Skenazy. In their own way, both *Moby-Dick* and 'The tale-tell heart' record the social and cultural trauma engendered by the rise of modernism in which the relation of the body to the state becomes both a contested and transgressive arena of signs. Poe's Evil Eye, hovering indeterminately between realism and delusion, and Queequeg's mystical tattoos, are perhaps the most symbolic examples of the metaphysical detective novel's critical examination of Benjamin's 'phantasmagoria' in which the relationship between the world and its representation is fundamentally questioned.

NOTES

1 *The Newgate calendar; comprising interesting memoirs of the most notorious characters who had been convicted of outrages on the laws of England since the commencement of the eighteen century; with anecdotes and last exclamations of sufferers* was a series of broadsheets reported on crime from the beginning of the eighteenth century to its time of publication in 1773. The calendar was compiled in four volumes (1824–26).
2 Henceforth *Moby-Dick*. Citations are from Poe's *Selected tales* (1998) and Penguin Classics edition of Mielville's novel (1992). See bibliography for further details.
3 Matt Oches examines maritime tattoos associated with the sailors of the *Bounty* in this collection (Chapter 12).

BIBLIOGRAPHY

Augst, Thomas (2010), 'Melville, at sea in the city', in C. R. K. Patell and B. Waterman (eds), *The Cambridge companion to the literature of New York* (Cambridge: Cambridge University Press), pp. 58–75.

Auster, Paul (1985), *City of glass* (London: Penguin).

— (1986), *The locked room* (London: Penguin).

— (1987), *The New York trilogy* (London: Penguin).

Benfey, Christopher (1993), 'Poe and the unreadable: "The black cat" and "The tell-tale heart"', in K. Silverman (ed.) (1993), pp. 27–44.

Benjamin, Walter (2002), *The arcades project [Das Passagen-Werk 1982]*, trans. H. Eiland (Cambridge, MA: Harvard University Press).

— (1983), *Charles Baudelaire: A lyric poet in the era of high capitalism* (London: Verso).

Bulson, Eric (2007), *Novels, maps, modernity: The spatial imagination, 1850–2000* (London: Routledge).

Burrows, Edwin G. and Mike Wallace (2000), *Gotham: A history of New York city to 1898* (Oxford: Oxford University Press).

Chesterton, G. K. (1983), 'A defence of detective stories' [1902], in H. Haycraft (ed.) *The art of the mystery story* (New York: Carroll and Graf).

Coughlan, David (2006), 'Paul Auster's "City of glass: The graphic novel"', *Modern Fiction Studies*, 52:4, 832–54.

de Certeau, Michel (1984), *The practice of everyday life* (Berkeley: University of California Press).

Delbanco, Andrew (2013), *Melville: His world and work* (London: Picador).

DeMello, Margo (2000), *Bodies of inscription: A cultural history of the modern tattoo community* (Durham, NC: Duke University Press).

Dickens, Charles (1994), *Bleak house* [1853] (London: Penguin).

Dowling, David (2010), *Chasing the white whale: The Moby-Dick marathon; Or, what Melville means today* (Iowa: University of Iowa Press).

Engel, William E. (2012), *Early modern poetics in Melville and Poe: Memory, melancholy, and the emblematic tradition* (Farnham: Ashgate).

Fisher, Benjamin F. (2002), 'Poe and the gothic tradition', in K. J. Hayes (ed.), *The Cambridge companion to Edgar Allan Poe* (Cambridge: Cambridge University press), pp. 72–91.

— (2010) (ed.), *Poe in his own time: A biographical chronicle of his life, drawn from recollections, interviews, and memoirs by family, friends, and associates* (Iowa: University of Iowa Press).

Foucault, Michel (1991), *Discipline and punish: The birth of the prison* (London: Penguin).

Gargano, James W. (1968), 'The theme of time in "The tell-tale heart"', *Studies in short fiction*, 4, 378–82.

Giddens, Anthony (1996), *The consequences of modernity* (Stanford: Stanford University Press).

Hanson, Gillian Mary (2004), *City and shore: The function of setting in the British mystery* (London: McFarland).

Hardy, Donald E. (2014), *Sailor Jerry Collins: American tattoo master* (San Francisco: Hardy Marks Publications).

Harvey, David (1978), 'The urban process under capitalism: A framework for analysis', *International journal of urban and regional research*, 2 (1–4), 101–31.

Herzog, Todd (2009), *Crime stories: Criminalistic fantasy and the culture of crisis in Weimar Germany* (Oxford: Berghahn Books).

Hutchisson, J. M. (2005), *Poe* (Jackson: University Press of Mississippi).

Kaplan, Louise J. (1993), 'The perverse strategy in "The Fall of the House of Usher"', in K. Silverman (ed.) (1993), pp. 46–47.

Knight, Stephen (1980), *Form and ideology in crime fiction* (London: Macmillan).

— (2004), *Crime fiction, 1800–2000: Detection, death, diversity* (Basingstoke: Palgrave Macmillan).

— (2012), *The mysteries of the cities: Urban crime fiction in the nineteenth century* (London: McFarland).

Lefebvre, Henri (1991), *The production of space* (London: Blackwell).

Mackay, James (2007), *Allan Pinkerton: The first private eye* (Edison: Castle Books).

Marcus, Laura (2003), 'Detective and literary fiction', in M. Priestman (ed.), *The Cambridge companion to crime fiction* (Cambridge: Cambridge University Press), pp. 245–67.

Martel, James (2011), *Textual conspiracies: Walter Benjamin, idolatry, and political theory* (Ann Arbor: University of Michigan Press).

Melville, Herman (1992), *Moby-Dick; Or, the whale* (London: Penguin Classics).

Merivale, Patricia and Susan Elizabeth Sweeney (eds) (1999), *Detecting texts: The metaphysical detective story from Poe to postmodernism* (Philadelphia: University of Pennsylvania Press).

Mifflin, Margot (2013), *Bodies of subversion: A secret history of women and tattoo* (New York: Powerhouse Books).

Poe, Edgar Allan (1998), *Selected tales* (Oxford: Oxford University Press).

Robinson, E. A. (1971), 'Poe's "The tell-tale heart"', in W. L. Howarth (ed.), *Twentieth century interpretations of Poe's tales* (Englewood Cliffs: Prentice-Hall), pp. 94–102.

Sanborn, Geoffrey (2011), *Whipscars and tattoos: The last of the Mohicans, Moby-Dick, and the Maori* (Oxford and New York: Oxford University Press).

Scaggs, John (2005), *Crime fiction* (London: Routledge).

Schiffmacher, Henk (2005), 'On the history and practice of tattooing', in H. Schiffmacher and B. Riemschneider (eds), *1000 tattoos* (London: Taschen), pp. 6–23.

Scofield, Martin (2006), *The Cambridge introduction to the American short story* (Cambridge: Cambridge University Press).

Silverman, Kenneth (ed.) (1993), *New essays on Poe's major tales* (Cambridge: Cambridge University Press).

Skenazy, Paul (1995), 'Behind the territory ahead', in D. Fine (ed.), *Los Angeles in fiction* (Albuquerque: University of New Mexico Press), pp. 103–25.

Thomas, Ronald. R. (1999), *Detective fiction and the rise of forensic science* (Cambridge: Cambridge University Press).

Tiedemann, R. (2002), 'Dialectics at a standstill: Approaches to the *Passagen-Werk*', in G. Smith (ed.) *On Walter Benjamin: Critical essays and recollections* (Cambridge, MA: Harvard University Press), pp. 929–45.

Watson, Kate (2016), 'Mapping the mark: Tattoos, crime fiction, and gendered cartographies', in C. Cothran and M. Cannon (eds), *New perspectives on detective fiction: Mystery, magnified* (Oxford and New York: Routledge), pp. 52–71.

West-Pavlov, Russell (2013), *Temporalities* (Abingdon: Routledge).

Williams, W. (1985), 'The metropolis and the emergence of modernism', in E. Timms and D. Kelley (eds), *Unreal city: Urban experience in modern European literature and art* (Manchester: Manchester University Press), pp. 13–24.

Zimmerman, Brett (2005), *Edgar Allan Poe: Rhetoric and style* (Montreal: McGill-Queen's University Press).

3

Medical men: Speculations of morality and spirituality in Arthur Conan Doyle's writings

David Beck

INTRODUCTION

By the time Arthur Conan Doyle wrote to Dr Joseph Bell in 1892, Sherlock Holmes's fame as the world's first consulting detective was already established. Bell was famous in his own right among the medical community for being a skilled surgeon and a professor based at Scotland's Edinburgh Royal Infirmary. A champion of the medical profession, he had taught Doyle[1] and employed him as his outpatient clerk in 1878. Through this relationship, Bell influenced the creation of Holmes, a sentiment Doyle acknowledged in the letter to his mentor: '[i]t is most certainly to you that I owe Sherlock Holmes [...] Round the centre of deduction and inference and observation which I have heard you inculcate, I have tried to build up a man who pushed the thing as far as it would go' (qtd Liebow 1982: 172). Bell's inspirational traits included imagination, deductive analysis and keen observational skills, all of which were woven into Holmes's character. Bell's observational technique was a major influence upon Holmes, and became a central feature of the detective's investigative model. Holmes can 'place' people by observing their behaviour and physicality (Doyle 1926; in Klinger 2005b: 1483).[2] The study of tattoos plays a part in this technique because, as we shall see, they provide clues about a person's character, profession, criminality and locations visited. Bell's medical observational technique and Holmes's application of it are located within criminal anthropology, the systematised study of the physical and mental characteristics of a criminal. Ronald R. Thomas argues this resulted in the propagation of 'narratives that established the authority of a class of experts that could read someone's body like a text' enabling the systematised study of a criminal body (1999: 5).

Doyle's employment and adaptation of Bell's method is also relevant to the history of forensic science. For example, fingerprinting, the determination that no two fingerprints are identical, was established as valid evidence in the British courts by the turn of the twentieth century.[3] Accordingly, Holmes identifies the uniqueness of fingerprints in a number of stories including 'The sign of four' (1890) and 'The adventure of the Norwood builder', in which Lestrade belatedly confronts Holmes with 'you are aware that no two thumb-marks are alike?' (1903: 849).[4] Furthermore, Holmes makes use of identifying footprints in *The hound of the Baskervilles* (1902); develops a test for detecting old blood samples in *A study in scarlet* (1887) and identifies the idiosyncrasies of typewriters in 'A case of identity' (1891c), among others.[5]

Holmes's investigative interest in the reading of marks, brands and tattoos is a contemporaneous criminological practice. Jane Caplan reveals that the extent of tattooing in most of nineteenth-century Europe 'was uncovered only by the efforts of contemporary criminological research' (2000: 158) that associated tattooing with 'savagery and low life' (*ibid.*: 157). In this systematised examination, undertaken in the latter part of the nineteenth century by 'police and prison administrators' as well as 'prison or army doctors' (*ibid.*), the focus remained upon defining a set of physical and psychological parameters that encompassed a criminal pathology. This also informed contemporaneous concerns regarding racial degeneration and atavism. Daniel Pick observes how '[t]attooing was understood as literally the trace of a "primitive" language on the body' revealing an 'autobiography of warped inheritance, atavism and pathology' (1996: 117). The leading Italian criminologist Cesare Lombroso equated tattooing to 'a kind of hieroglyphic writing among criminals' (1876: 794). Margo DeMello makes a similar observation to Caplan by contextualising early (seventeenth century to the nineteenth century) tattoos 'as marks of savagery'. However, she identifies the 'British sailors and others' who 'eagerly received tattoos from native practitioners' as 'middlemen through which tattoos were transformed from a mark of primitivism to a mark of adventure' (DeMello 2000: 49). As we shall see in this chapter, the symbolism of tattooing in Doyle's writings was more complicated, signifying moral, criminal and spiritual turpitude as well as the aetiology of disease transference.

Sherlock Holmes remains, as Daniel Stashower notes, 'a colossus among cultural icons' (1999: xii). While it would be possible to limit a study of tattooing in Doyle's writings to Holmes and criminology, Doyle's wider appeal as a cultural figure extends beyond his detective fiction. His fictional and non-fictional writings embraced science and medicine and culminated in his public advocacy of spiritualism in 1917. His early interest in religion and morality, apparent in *The Stark Munro letters* (1895), also engaged with the infrequent, yet consistent, trope of tattooing, branding and bodily markings evident in his earlier historical novel *Micah Clark* (1889). For Bell and Holmes, tattooing provided a means of observing a subject's history, revealing past and current careers, locations visited and private details such as a hidden criminal past. Doyle's thought on tattooing was that it provided further evidence in determining vital characteristics of an individual's past, occupation and criminal propensity. Branding and tattooing reveal Doyle's adaptation of Bell's technique of observation as a literary device, yet this encompassed a wider field than detective fiction. In Doyle's medical fiction, the transposition of illness and tattooing combine with sin and suffering to leave a bodily mark which can be read to express sexual transgression. Questions of religion occur in *Micah Clarke* in which tattooing becomes a metaphor for Solomon Sprent's superficial adoption of Christianity; this overlays a simpler, personal spirituality that exists beneath the surface. In Doyle's early religious thought, he believed Christian ritual would be simplified as humanity evolved. Doyle argued: '[t]he last reformation simplified Catholicism. The coming one will simplify Protestantism. And when the world is ripe for it another will come and simplify that' (1895: 44). This 'simplified' faith will be reduced to a universal creed that will embrace all religions instituted upon an intuitive concept of morality and spirituality. In the last chapter of Doyle's autobiography *Memories and adventures* (1924), he reflected upon how his spiritual development and his literary success represented a preparatory phase for what he termed his 'psychic quest'. He stated it was 'the thing for which every preceding phase – my gradual religious development, my books' combined with his 'modest fortune' and 'physical strength' had 'all been an unconscious preparation' (1924: 395).

Despite a wealth of critical insights into Doyle's writing,[6] little or no critical attention is given to Doyle's use of tattoos in his detective and spiritual fiction.[7] The purpose of this chapter is to remedy this oversight by drawing upon the wider context of Doyle's fictional writings. As I argued previously (2013), Doyle's wider pursuits in science and spiritualism (by no means secondary in Doyle's mind or actions) undoubtedly infringe upon his fiction in, sometimes, unexpected fashion. It is within this spirit that this analysis is presented. The chapter examines the importance of tattooing, branding and other bodily markings within Doyle's Holmes stories and his historical novel *Micah Clarke*. While *Micah Clarke* is not overtly a detective novel, Doyle wrote it while he was creating Sherlock Holmes. Many elements of Clarke's character, his loyalty, tenacity and his love of adventure, would be further integrated into the personalities of Sherlock Holmes and Dr Watson. Importantly, *Micah Clarke* explores how Doyle's religious concerns were informed by medical diagnostic and observational skills, elements that would later infuse his detective fiction.

OBSERVATION AND LOCATION: DR JOSEPH BELL AND SHERLOCK HOLMES

In his autobiography, Doyle described how the observation and analytical skills instilled in Bell's students on the hospital outpatient ward were associated with 'diagnosis, not only of disease, but of occupation and character' (1924: 25). Thomas argues that the diagnostic method of observation, applied by Bell and adapted by Doyle for Holmes, appropriated the 'modern medical model for the diagnosis of crime' (1999: 188). Here, the physician's observation of a patient's case history, with its attendant environmental and physiological constituents, are applied to criminal pathology. Holmes, directly influenced by Bell, bridges the gap between medical study of the body and the development of new forensic sciences.[8] Criminality and health are connected via the detective's observational skills, modelled on late nineteenth-century medical diagnostics. Bell informed the readers of *The Strand magazine* that in instructing the treatment of disease and accident, the student must be 'taught to observe' its pathology (How 1892: 188). Observation was to be learned as a skill in itself, initially separate from medical diagnosis. Bell stated that in order to interest a student in the value of such training it would be useful to show how a 'trained use of the observation can discover in ordinary matters' the 'previous history, nationality, and occupational aspects of a patient' (*ibid.*). Some of these histories are evident in physical symptoms, such as markings upon the skin, placed there voluntarily, or otherwise.

Bell was able to discover facts about a patient's behaviour that had been hidden from the general public. One case involved Bell identifying a former soldier as a bandsman in a Highland regiment due to the 'swagger in his walk, suggestive of the Piper' and his short stature (Liebow 1982: 176). Bell's patient denied the doctor's conclusion, claiming only to have ever been a cobbler. Not to be outdone and expecting to find evidence to corroborate his observation, Bell had the man forcibly stripped by attending dressers. Bell was vindicated when he 'detected a little blue "D" branded on his skin', a mark left on the breast of British soldiers caught deserting during the Crimean War (Liebow 1982: 176). Branding as a punishment for criminal behaviour had been abolished by 1829, although desertion from the military was an exception (Science Museum n.d.). In fact, Bell's deserter may not have been literally branded with a hot iron. In J. I. Ikin's (1857) account of military branding, he noted how the branding was actually done with 'three or four needles tied together, and the letter D is pricked out in the skin under the left arm [...] in fact it is the same as tattooing' (Ikin 1857: 25). This particular conflation of branding and tattooing confers an involuntary mark of punishment. It also served as a means to prevent deserters from re-enlisting in the armed forces. This is suggestive of a wider interpretation of branding, in that it resembled an indelible mark of punishment, as well as slavery or membership of an organisation. Bell theorised that his observational method enabled him to identify a patient's history while exposing a criminal past confirmed by the presence of a hidden tattoo. This process was ripe for adaptation into a literary device; this is demonstrated in Holmes's model of detection.

Appropriately, Bell argued that the 'tattoo marks on hand or arm will tell their own tale as to voyages', referring to the tattoos worn by sailors (How 1892: 188).[9] Tattooing was strongly associated with mariners who had picked it up from abroad and also in the British army as a token of *esprit de corps*. There is a danger in adopting a generalised perspective of a tattoo's meaning. As Caplan notes 'tattoos had a cultural as well as anatomical character' determined by factors such as class, occupation and inclination, complicating an individual's motivation for acquiring one (Caplan 2000: 164). Such varied factors and motivations in receiving or in giving a tattoo present a note of caution not to take Bell's (or Holmes's) observational technique too literally. Bell acknowledged infrequent errors, citing an occasion when he observed that a patient was an army bandsman due to a paralysis of the cheek muscles caused by prolonged blowing at wind instruments. His patient confirmed Bell's observation, but revealed his instrument was a big drum (Liebow 1982: 138–39). When a client expressed a belief that Holmes could solve any puzzle, Holmes admitted that he had been 'beaten four times – three times by men, and once by a woman' (in Klinger 2005a: 137). Doyle, conscious of the demands of writing fiction, knew that an occasional lapse was the exception that proved the rule of Holmes's brilliance. Bell was probably aware of a similar effect upon his reputation. The possibility of failure, no matter how slight, enhanced the reputation of both doctor and detective.

Nonetheless, Bell contended he was able to deduce some of the locations visited by sailors via their tattoos. For example, sailors who had crossed the Atlantic Ocean sometimes wore a tattoo of an anchor, whereas a dragon signified he had visited a port in China (*Royal Museums Greenwich* n.d.). In *A study in scarlet* (1887),[10] Holmes impresses Watson by identifying a man as a former Royal Marine. Holmes explains how he came to his conclusion in a manner influenced by Bell: '[e]ven across the street I could see a great blue anchor tattooed on the back of the fellow's hand. That smacked of the sea. He had a military carriage, however, and regulation side whiskers. There we have the marine' (in Klinger 2006: 48). As with Bell, Holmes's observation of the man's physical stature is supported by the presence of a tattoo that confirms his history as a former marine. This exemplifies Doyle's fictional application of Bell's theory that tattooing confirms his initial hypothesis.[11]

The Holmes story 'The red-headed league' (1891d) is the clearest example of how tattoos appear to reveal and confirm aspects of a subject's personal history irrefutably. In this story, Holmes styles himself as an authority on tattoos, informing Watson that he had 'made a small study of tattoo marks, and [had] even contributed to the literature of the subject' (in Klinger 2005a: 44). Holmes makes this statement shortly after observing that his client, the pawnbroker Jabez Wilson, is a Freemason who had once worked in manual labour. Bell's influence upon Doyle's writing is again apparent as Holmes based his deductions on Wilson's manner of dress, his physicality and behaviour. Holmes's expertise in tattoo markings is paramount when he notes that Wilson had visited China: '[t]he fish which you have tattooed immediately above your right wrist could only have been done in China' because the 'trick of staining the fishes' scales of a delicate pink is quite peculiar to China' (in Klinger 2005a: 44). An article in *Tit-bits*, published the same year as 'The red-headed league', offers some insight regarding the location of Wilson's tattoo, though not the significance of its design. It states: '[w]ith women the decoration is usually a bee, a butterfly, a spray of flowers or a monogram. These ornaments are worn inside the wrist, so they may be hidden by the glove, if necessary' (*Tit-bits* 1891a: n.p.). Wilson's tattoo, being situated above his right wrist, may be convenient as it would be easy to hide with long sleeves. In plotting Holmes's investigations, Doyle used the motif of an easily hidden tattoo to conceal aspects of a character's past, while intentionally complicating the process of accurately applying Bell's observational technique. In 'The adventure of the Gloria Scott' (1893b), a concealed tattoo discloses a hidden criminal past, and Holmes recalls an early example of his observational skills that are, once more, influenced by Bell's technique. While on vacation from university, a younger Holmes exhibits his 'habits of observation and inference' during his stay with his friend Victor Trevor (in Klinger 2005a: 505). After briefly observing Trevor's father, Holmes deduces that the man is in fear of attack due to modifications made to his walking stick, he was once a boxer because of his damaged ears and that he had visited New Zealand and Japan (*ibid.*). Although the latter observation is not explained, based on Bell's technique Holmes's description of the senior Mr Trevor, his 'weather-beaten face', fierce eyes and mannerisms picked up during his travels where he had seen 'much of the world' would provide ample ground for observation (*ibid.*: 503). However, of interest is Trevor's tattoo of the letters 'J. A.' located on the bend of his elbow, another unusual and easily concealed place. As with Bell's branded deserter soldier, Trevor's tattoo reveals clues about his history that he would like to keep hidden. The reader is initially given Holmes's following hypothesis: the tattoos meant that in his past Trevor had been 'intimately associated with someone whose initials were J. A., and whom [Trevor] afterwards [was] eager to entirely forget' (*ibid.*: 505). Holmes was only partially correct as the initials stand for 'James Armitage' (Trevor's real name) and not, as he claimed, the initials of an old lover. It transpires that as a young man Trevor was convicted of fraud and transported to Australia upon the ship *Gloria Scott*.[12] He had managed to escape the vessel during a mutiny, eventually returning to England under an assumed identity. Holmes concluded that J. A. was someone Trevor would rather forget because the letters were 'legible, but it was perfectly clear from their blurred appearance, and from the staining of the skin around them, that efforts had been made to obliterate them' (*ibid.*: 507). Nineteenth-century techniques of tattoo removal involved skin abrasion or the injection of chemicals through the top layer of skin.[13] It was of limited success, leaving scarring as well as loss of skin pigment. In Trevor's case, the procedure resulted in some blurring but not the removal of the ink completely. Trevor attempted to erase the past and remove evidence revealing his criminal identity, an important feature in the structure of detective fiction. In Holmes's investigations, Doyle employed bodily markings to obscure, or blur, the observation and deduction of a subject's identity in a manner that cast doubt upon the efficacy of Bell's technique.

In *The valley of fear* (1915), Doyle provided a significant example of how a person's identity can be blurred by means of a brand forced upon recruits of a secret organisation called the Scowrers.[14] Holmes's attention is drawn to the brand when one is found upon the body of a murdered man at Birlstone Manor House in Sussex, England. The victim is initially believed to be John Douglas, the owner of Birlstone. Douglas is not immediately identifiable due to the damage inflicted to his face by a gunshot wound. The main clue to the victim's identity, apart from his approximate height, clothing and a missing wedding ring, is the presence of a triangle within a circle branded upon the forearm. In *The valley of fear*, the investigating doctor confuses the brand for a tattoo, further conflating the two. The brand upon the body in *The valley of fear* is voluntary, marking its bearer as an initiate in a secret criminal fraternity. The doctor examining the mark states, 'I never saw anything like it. The man has been branded at some time, as they brand cattle' (in Klinger 2006: 668). The brand was part of an initiation that all members of the Scowrers must undertake, as a test of a candidate's endurance of pain. Unlike Bell's deserter soldier, the branding in this novel is not a marker of punishment for criminal behaviour. Instead, Doyle employs it as a marker of fraternity within a secret, criminal organisation.[15] Furthermore, as with Mr Trevor and Bell's deserter, the brand is a marker for its owner's hidden past. In this story Doyle uses the mark to obscure the identity of the owner of the brand, rather than to confirm it. The mystery of Birlstone Manor revolves around identifying the killer who appears to have successfully escaped the scene of the crime. However, it is a case of mistaken identity as the dead man is not John Douglas, but Ted Baldwin, a man sent to assassinate Douglas for betraying the Scowrers. The confusion occurs due to Baldwin's similar size, his common history and his identical brand on the arm. Douglas takes advantage of their identical brands to switch places with Baldwin, hiding in the house until the investigation ended. Taken on its own the brand was a fallible source of information, creating a note of uncertainty about Bell's observational technique.

Bell and Holmes were able to apply what Holmes called 'the scientific use of the imagination' that was capable of intuitive and sometimes speculative deductions that needed to be supported by further evidence (in Klinger 2006: 436). Significantly, as Liebow (1982: 138–39) notes, Bell's deductions were not always accurate. In Holmes's fictional cases, confusion is caused by the same brand upon two men. This highlights the difficulties inherent in deciphering bodily markings based upon Bell's observational technique. Doyle was able to complicate Bell's observational method as a literary device in his detective fiction through his employment of bodily markings. Tattooing and branding took on a wider metaphorical role implying that bodily markings were inherently difficult to interpret and misleading to detectives, doctors and Doyle's readers alike.

SPIRITUALITY AND BODILY MARKINGS

In the Holmes stories, bodily markings continued to evolve from Doyle's original adaptation of Bell's observational technique. They also encompassed Doyle's religious contemplation of spiritual and moral questions. An indication of this occurs in *The valley of fear*, in which branding adopts a spiritual aspect, serving as a marker of Christian damnation. After Brother Morris, another Scowrer, unwillingly takes part in a murder, he defines his brand as a 'badge of shame on my forearm and something worse branded on my heart' (in Klinger 2006: 786). His brand signifies spiritual damnation, as well as shame and remorse. He described how he was now 'lost forever in this world, and lost also in the next' (*ibid.*: 787). Morris felt that he was a 'good Catholic' but 'the priest would have no word with me when he heard I was a Scowrer, and I am excommunicated from my faith' (*ibid.*). This touches a point close to Doyle's personal religious beliefs. He had rejected Catholicism during his education by Jesuits at Stonyhurst School in Lancashire, England. His view on religious matters was more benevolent, adopting a faith in which atonement was not only possible but an inevitable part of the soul's progression throughout its spiritual evolution. In *The vital message* (1919), Doyle argued the afterlife involved 'a gradual rise in the scale of existence without any monstrous change which would turn us in an instant from man to angel or devil' (2012: 53). Doyle retained a strong interest in religious matters throughout his life, yet religion in the Holmes stories is overlooked in critical studies. This is in some part due to Holmes's precision as a deductive reasoning machine, to which theological distraction would appear as 'grit in a sensitive instrument, or a crack in one of [Holmes's] own high-power lenses' (in Klinger 2005a: 5). While Holmes does not engage in serious religious contemplation, his speculation upon the need for deduction in religious analysis is influenced by Bell's observational method. Holmes states, '[t]here is nothing in which deduction is so necessary as in religion [...] It can be built up as an exact science by the reasoner' (*ibid.*: 686). This was a key note of Doyle's early religious questioning, stressing the importance of an un-blinkered study and reflection upon religious dogma. Uncharacteristically, Holmes continues:

Our highest assurance of the goodness of Providence seems to me to rest in the flowers. All other things, our powers, our desires, our food, are all really necessary for our existence in the first instance. But this rose is an extra. Its smell and its colour are an embellishment of life, not a condition of it. It is only goodness which gives extras. (*ibid.*: 686–87)

Holmes is directly expressing Doyle's personal religious views. This quotation was published in 1893 around the time Doyle was writing his novel *The Stark Munro letters*. As with Holmes above, he used Stark Munro to voice his spiritual concerns, writing 'Nature is the true revelation of the Deity to man. The nearest green field is the inspired page from which you may read all that is needful' (Doyle 2004: 42). In both quotations Doyle replaced Christian revelation with a metaphorical book of nature, which, as we shall see, was closely related to deism. Human reason, in conjunction with studying the world's natural laws, would be enough to reveal the existence of a non-Christian godhead. These ideas were also influenced by pre-nineteenth-century traditions of examining the natural world including natural history and philosophy.[16] The manner of religious faith Doyle advocated, whether it was his early beliefs or his later spiritualist faith, was completely independent from an external display of an organised religion. It was entirely personal, reliant upon an individual's belief. Several years after the publication of *The valley of fear*, Doyle argued that spiritualism 'abolishes the idea of a grotesque hell and of a fantastic heaven' (in Klinger 2006: 53). There existed, Doyle argued, 'endless circles below descending into gloom and endless circles above, ascending into glory, all improving, all purposeful, all intensely alive' (Doyle 2007: 75).

In *The valley of fear*, Morris's fear of eternal damnation is reminiscent of Doyle's earlier religious concerns. This idea was also expressed in the religious tattooing he incorporated in his early historical novel, *Micah Clarke*, in which tattoos illustrate the difference between an outward display of Christianity and a simpler, deeper means of religion. The novel's protagonist, Micah Clarke, seeks adventure during the failed Monmouth Rebellion (1685). Religious fanaticism and violence figure prominently in the text. Clarke is a Protestant puritan, poised against Catholic forces of King James II (James VII of Scotland). However, the novel's main theme is that of religious tolerance, which embodied Doyle's early spiritual views. Tattooing is an unusual mode of conveying this notion and yet religion is literally embodied upon Solomon Sprent, an old sailor and friend of Clarke. Sprent had served most of his life in the navy, visiting the West Indies where he was tattooed with an extraordinary design. Clarke described him thus: '[f]rom head to foot he was covered with the most marvellous tattooings, done in blue, red and green' (Doyle 1986: 29). Certainly, Bell or Holmes would have been able to observe much in the use and type of ink, yet this was not Doyle's intended purpose in this novel. Instead it is the design of the tattoos that are of interest, beginning with 'the Creation upon his neck and winding up with the Ascension upon his left ankle. Never have I seen such a walking work of art' (*ibid.*). Sprent's character militated against such an ostentatious display of his Christianity, with the narrator stating how his 'religion appeared to have all worked into his skin, so that very little was left for inner use' (*ibid.*). Doyle's thoughts upon Christianity at this time were complex. Sprent's tattoos are a metaphor for inward and outward displays of Christian worship, a distinction between the practice of religion taught through ritual, service and prayer. It is a deeper, inner belief that worked through emotion, instinctive goodness and spirituality. In predicting the future of civilisation, Stark Munro hopes that '[t]he forms of religion will be abandoned, but the essence will be maintained (*ibid.*: 235). While reflecting upon the example of Christ's life to mankind, Doyle pondered how 'the more rigid churches' could have 'got so far away from the example of their Master [Christ]', through their 'dogmatism, insistence upon forms, their exclusiveness, their pomp and their intolerance' (2012: 74).

Sprent's tattoos provide a figurative example of an outward show of Christian iconography, which had no internal value or meaning to Sprent's personal beliefs as Catholic symbolism had no relevance to Doyle. Sprent informed Clarke that had he been drowned and 'his body cast upon some savage land, the natives might have learned the whole of the blessed gospel from a contemplation of his carcass' (Doyle 1986: 29). It falls beyond the scope of the narrative in *Micah Clarke* to ponder the nature and result of such a contemplation of the Christian iconography upon Sprent's corpse. However, within the wider context of Doyle's religious thinking at this time, a body of text, without the spirit – or 'essence' as Doyle names it above – is an empty vessel, one focused solely on an outward display of Christian iconography devoid of any deeper meaning. Certainly, Doyle argued Christianity needed reform, writing in *The new Revelation* that 'Christianity must change or must perish. That is the law of life – that things must adapt themselves or perish' (2007: 54). Sprent's inner character, exhibited through his language and behaviour, did not possess Christian sentiment. The narrator of *Micah Clarke* notes Sprent's 'system was clear of [Christianity] elsewhere', being able to swear fluently in eleven languages and twenty-three dialects, regardless of the sensitive, puritanical community in which he lived (Doyle 1986: 29–30). That the Old and New Testaments could be displayed in such detail across one man's body is an extraordinary image.[17] It is in breach of scripture, which prohibits bodily markings, including tattooing, made apparent in Leviticus which states, 'Ye shall not make any cuttings in your flesh for the dead, nor print any marks upon you: I *am* The Lord' (19:28). This injunction stems from the law of Moses, prohibiting idolatrous markings on the body. Sprent's tattooing represents a discrepancy between outward appearances and an internal fact, complicating further their appearance in

Doyle's detective fiction. In *Micah Clarke* the distinction is a spiritual internal truth instead of a hidden criminal past. We discover how Sprent 'grew more sober and more thoughtful, until in his latter days he went back to the simple beliefs of his childhood' (Doyle 1986: 30). His tattoos obscure a deeper, intuitive religious sentiment that Doyle claims is common to all people.

This is an important notion for Doyle, who had keenly felt the tension between his own early, homely belief in Catholicism under the influence of his mother Mary Doyle and the harsher strain he experienced under the Jesuits at Stonyhurst. Doyle later recalled his youthful reaction to a Jesuit Father's declaration of eternal damnation to everyone outside the Church. Doyle stated how, 'I looked upon him with horror, and to that moment I trace the first rift [with the Catholic Church] which has grown into such a chasm', which developed eventually into a new religious sentiment based upon a simpler non-denominational spirituality (Doyle 1989: 21). Similarly, Sprent's regression to childhood beliefs contrasts with an outward display of Christian iconography through his tattoos, which had no core meaning. This innate spirituality remains hidden under the surface behind an outward display exhibited as vibrant, colourful markings. This underlying context of Sprent's tattoo supports Doyle's argument that Christian views should be reorganised and centred upon a simpler, underlying faith common to all religion. There should be less emphasis upon original sin, eternal damnation and outward displays of religious dogma; a notion Doyle expressed in his first unpublished novel *The narrative of John Smith*:

> the forms of religion will be abandoned but the essence maintained, so that one universal creed will embrace the whole earth, which shall preach reverence to the great Creator and the pursuit of virtue, not from any hope of reward or fear of punishment, but from a high and noble love of the right and the hatred of the wrong. (Doyle 1883: 41)

Doyle's belief in this type of faith is further demonstrated in *The Stark Munro letters* where he outlined his thoughts about a 'great Creator', a non-Christian godhead. The character Munro describes a natural religion, in that his understanding of a supreme being was not contingent upon Christianity, nor any other religion (Doyle 2004: 42). He defined the Creator as something that could be identified in 'His works, which cannot be counterfeited or manipulated' (*ibid.*). Doyle was advocating a broad deism, whereby human reason and an understanding of the natural world would reveal the existence of a Creator of the universe. Furthermore, in Doyle's medical fiction the physical symptoms of disease resemble a religious tattoo, embodying spiritual and moral implications.

By 1890, Doyle had rejected notions of biblical sin and redemption, yet his anxiety about these concepts was still expressed through physical markings.

One striking example occurs in his short story 'A medical document' (1894) that dramatises medical cases discussed by several doctors. A surgeon is consulted by a famous beauty in London society, suffering from a 'rodent ulcer [...] eating its way upwards, coiling on in its serpiginous fashion until the end of it was flush with her collar' (in Rodin and Key 1992: 210). In describing the ulcer on the woman's skin, Doyle returns to his medical roots, evident in the surgeon's reading of her symptoms. He states she is 'one of those beautiful white-and-pink creatures who are rotten with struma. You may patch but you can't mend' (in Rodin and Key *ibid.*: 211).[18] It is, in a manner similar to the brands and tattoos discussed earlier, a marker for visible and invisible qualities that are not easily read. The markings caused by the ulcer on her skin are a further indication of Doyle's religious concerns, being reminiscent of the biblical serpent from *Genesis*, with its attendant undertone of original sin. It leaves the 'red streak of its tail' below the 'line of her bust', while simultaneously coiling around her neck and 'eating its way upwards' towards her face (*ibid.*: 210). 'Serpiginous' used in this description originates from the Latin word *serpere*, meaning to creep serpent-like upon her skin. It reflected Doyle's ongoing religious concerns, apparent in the surgeon's response to her incurable condition, 'I suppose we mustn't think ourselves wiser than Providence, but there are times when one feels that something is wrong in the scheme of things' (*ibid.*: 211). In writing this story, Doyle was careful in his allusions to the patient's potential sexually transgressive nature, relying on the iconography of original sin and the surgeon's admiration for his patient's beauty and low-cut dresses.

Epidemiologists, who study the incidence, distribution and control of disease, also focused their attention upon tattooing. The anthropologist Alfred Gell indicates, in his study of Polynesian tattoos, that they have 'a pattern of occurrence, which resembles the uneven, but at the same time predictable, incidence of an illness' (Gell 1993: 20). This association of tattooing with illness shares Doyle's anxiety about some bodily markings being indicators of the spread of infection through sexual immorality. Tattooing was spread through social contact within peer groups as well as physical contact via ink and needle. Significantly, James Bradley (2000: 143) notes examples of how disease became manifest through infected tattooist's needles, demonstrating a correlation between receiving a tattoo and the spread of disease. His study of nineteenth-century military medical records report the spread of syphilitic infection in 1888 among twelve British soldiers at Portsea barracks in Hampshire, England. Within this example we witness the 'demi-metaphor of epidemiology' with the tattoo as locus and 'quasi-dermatological illness of the tattoo spreading plague-like through a segment of a regiment' (Bradley, 2000: 143). This is followed by the 'real disease of syphilis, which asserted its ascendency by transposing its own mark upon the crudely etched tattoo patterns' (*ibid.*). The primary and secondary symptoms of syphilis include sores and rashes on the body. The skin is physically branded with a disease implicated with immoral sexual conduct. As with sufferers of syphilis, a recipient of a tattoo could become unknowingly infected by a second party. Intertwined metaphors of illness and tattooing also appear in Doyle's description of Solomon Sprent, whose religious tattoos 'had broken out upon the surface [of his skin], like the spotted fever' (Doyle 1986: 29). The physical symptoms of illness in 'A medical document' function in a similar manner. The serpiginous ulcer is a bodily marking, resembling a snake winding around the woman's upper body, threatening her face. For the surgeon it is a marker for injustice inherent within Christian providence; for the reader the serpent is a metaphor for the patient's sexual transgression.

While 'A medical document' posed questions about the nature of providence, morality also exhibited a religious edge in Doyle's Holmes story 'The illustrious client' (1925). Kitty Winter, who has fallen into prostitution, gained her revenge upon Baron Gruner, the orchestrator of her misfortunes. She marks Gruner's face, with vitriol. Winter is brought to Holmes by his underworld contact, Shinwell Johnson. Watson observes Winter's features: 'on the settee was a brand which [Johnson] had brought up in the shape of a slim, flame-like young woman with a pale, intense face, youthful, and yet so worn with sin and sorrow that one read the terrible years which had left their leprous mark upon her' (in Klinger 2006: 1461). Winter is an important figure embodying the symbolism of branding, tattooing, religion, morality and illness in Doyle's fictional writings. Dr Watson's use of the word 'brand', above, supports the 'flame-like' adjective indicating a fiery element to her character. It also implies that she has been branded figuratively by the sin and sorrow that one can read in her worn features. This appears as a metaphor for disease, similar to the bodily markings in Doyle's 'A medical document'. Winter's 'leprous mark' is a metaphor for her public shame and revulsion as a consequence of her sexual immorality.

Both Winter and the female patient in 'A medical document' face social stigma and exclusion upon the discovery of their conditions.[19] In 'The illustrious client', sexual immorality is internalised by Winter and yet it is still detectable as a symbolic bodily mark. Once more Doyle engaged with his medical background and Bell's technique of reading physical marks upon the body. This reading would not be apparent in this Holmes story without a broader knowledge of Doyle's use of tattooing, combined with a recognition of the relationship between his Holmes, medical and religious writings. An understanding of Doyle's wider fictional and non-fictional writings enriches a reading of his Holmes stories. While Holmes is regarded as the arch-materialist, Doyle's wider interest in medicine, religion, observational technique, spirituality, tattooing and bodily markings are an important influence upon this character.

CONCLUSION

Tattooing was a notable part of Bell's observational technique. Accounts made by Doyle and others credit Bell with the ability to determine an individual's past, including professions, locations visited and the presence of illness. This was a major influence upon his students – notably Doyle – who adapted Bell's technique for his Holmes stories. Holmes identifies past careers and locations by reading behaviour, bodies and significantly, for this study, his clients and suspects' marks, brands and tattoos. Furthermore, tattoos reveal other information that was deliberately hidden by a subject, such as their criminal past. Doyle, conscious of the fallibility of observation, uses branding and tattooing as literary devices to misdirect his readers in at least one of Holmes's cases. Crucially, and because of Doyle's medical heritage and religious questioning, tattooing appears in his wider range of fictional writings to reveal a strong identification between illness and symptoms that left a mark upon the body. This, in turn, took on a moral and religious character that exposed Doyle's early religious doubts. In Doyle's historical novel, *Micah Clarke*, an extraordinary series of religious tattoos demonstrate the difference between an adherence to the dogma and practices of organised religion and a deeper, simpler faith that remains hidden or latent beneath the skin's surface. This is important because during this period Doyle contemplated a form of religion that incorporated a non-Christian godhead that worked through the natural world. This is a significant context for Doyle as Holmes, the exponent of empirical and deductive reason, speculated that logic was needed in religion to effect changes in religious thought and practice.

Tattooing is a minor trope within the Holmes oeuvre, but for his creator, it was a facet of his medical, spiritual and literary life. It would be inaccurate to consider Doyle's detective fiction to be separate, in any form, from his wider medical and spiritual interests and his historical writing. Tattooing provides an important example of this because it illustrates how his wider spiritual interests impinge upon his Holmes stories and vice-versa. Furthermore, without such broader contexts, tattooing would remain a sub-note of his detective fiction, limited to interpretations of nineteenth-century discussions of atavism and their influence upon the study of criminology.

NOTES

1 Doyle's early years as a general practitioner of medicine and his burgeoning interest in spiritualism is explored by Geoffrey Stavert (1987), and his life in medicine by Alvin E. Rodin and Jack D. Key (1984, 1992), who scrutinise Sherlock Holmes within the wider context of Doyle's medical fiction and non-fiction.

2 See, for example, *A study in scarlet* (1887: 40–41) and 'A scandal in Bohemia' (1891b: 9–10).

 3 For an engaging history of the colonial roots of fingerprinting, see Chandak
   Sengoopta (2003).
 4 This chapter makes reference to a wide range of Doyle's writings. Original dates of
   publication are given when referring to the writing in the main body of the chapter,
   and are listed in the Bibliography. Direct quotations are usually taken from the
   various annotated editons of Doyle's writings by L. Klinger to aid location. See
   Bibliography for further details (eds).
 5 See James F. O'Brien (2013) for a discussion of Doyle's relevance to the history of
   forensic science.
 6 Critical analysis of Doyle's detective fiction is numerous and centred, quite rightly,
   upon the public's fascination with Doyle's creation of the world's first consulting
   detective. Of particular interest are Daniel Stashower (1999), Jon Lellenberg, Daniel
   Stashower and Charles Foley (eds) (2007) and Andrew Lycett's detailed scrutiny
   of Doyle's life (2007). John Dickson Carr's biography (1949) accesses many Doyle's
   documents that have, until recently, been unavailable to researchers. Further
   reading into the wider literary context that influenced Doyle is carefully detailed
   by Richard Lancelyn Green (1986) in his annotated compilation. While James F.
   O'Brien (2013) adopts a broader perspective contextualising Holmes within the
   scientific disciplines of mathematics, biology and physics.
 7 Tattoos are sometimes listed by critics, as Katherine Ramsland does (2009), as
   drawing attention to possible markers of identity used by Doyle's mentor Dr Joseph
   Bell and later by Sherlock Holmes.
 8 For an in-depth discussion of differences between the medical study of the body and
   the development of new forensic sciences, see Ronald R. Thomas (2000).
 9 James Bradley identifies tattooing as a 'minor trope of Victorian literature' that
   includes Sherlock Holmes stories, Henry Rider Haggard's *Mr Meeson's will* (1888)
   and Fergus Hume's *Tracked by a tattoo* (1896). Kate Watson (2016) has considered
   the representation of tattooing and its ramifications in *Mr Meeson's will*, arguing its
   importance in the genealogy of the literary tattoo.
10 Val McDermid, herself a highly successful British crime writer, neatly summarises
   the cultural development of the professional detective and the advances in science
   that Doyle foreshadowed by correctly comparing Holmes's meticulous study of
   a crime scene in *A study in scarlet* (1887) with the historical specialist in early
   crime scene investigation Edmond Locard's exchange principle. 'It is impossible
   for a criminal to act', Locard noted, 'especially considering the intensity of a crime,
   without leaving traces of his presence' (qtd McDermid 2015: 5).
11 On its own the tattoo is open to misinterpretation. Hamish Maxwell-Stewart
   and Ian Duffield note the anchor was also a symbol of hope from biblical origins, illustrating the potential for misinterpreting tattoos (in Caplan 2000, see pp.
   25–28).
12 Contemporaneous commentaries held that transported convicts had their initials
   tattooed due to fear of an 'anonymous death at sea' (Bradley 2000: 150).
13 In the 1880s, Dr Gustav Variot pioneered a technique of removing tattoos by the
   use of a stick of nitrate of silver and injecting tannin. The procedure was painful and
   resulted in scarring (Morrow and Fordyce 1889: 108–09; see, for example, Cheng
   2004).
14 Doyle modelled the Scowrers upon the Molly Maguires, a secret criminal organ-

isation made up from Irish-American miners, with a hyperbolised reputation for brutal beatings and murders.

15 This is reminiscent of the Brotherhood, a secret Italian political society, in Wilkie Collins's *The woman in white* (1860) who wreak their vengeance on Count Fosco, the flamboyant criminal mastermind. Amateur detective Walter Hartright learns that members 'are identified with the Brotherhood by a secret mark, which we all bear, which lasts while our lives last' (1974: 596). Sherlock Holmes investigated crimes involving the Red Circle, another Italian secret political society, in 'The adventure of the Red Circle' (1911).

16 For a detailed discussion of natural history and philosophy, see Steven Shapin (1996) and John Hedley Brooke (1991).

17 Leviticus provides the impetus for the deranged serial killer in Stieg Larsson's crime novel *The girl with the dragon tattoo* (2005). For the titular character of this novel, Lisbeth Salander, tattooing represents non-conformity and control over her body. She has several tattoos including one as a reminder of being raped and her response to it. Furthermore, her own act of tattooing her attacker marks her revenge and eventual control over his body – indelibly marking him as a social pariah. For further discussion of tattooing and *The girl with the dragon tattoo*, see Kerstin Bergman's Chapter 6 in this collection.

18 Doyle used the term 'struma' to refer to a 'hereditary form of chronic ill-health' (Doyle 1907: 77), though it could also apply to a goitre or tumour.

19 A diagnosis of leprosy is the impetus for Godfrey Emsworth's voluntary seclusion in the Sherlock Holmes story 'The adventure of the blanched soldier' (1926), suggesting there was still a stigma attached to the disease by the turn of the twentieth century. Holmes discovers that Emsworth has in fact been misdiagnosed and suffers from 'a well-marked case of Pseudo-leprosy or ichthyosis', a condition characterised by 'dry, scaly skin' (in Klinger 2005b: 1506).

BIBLIOGRAPHY

Beck, David (2013), '"The dweller upon the threshold" and the infringement of the unknown in Arthur Conan Doyle's "The adventure of the devil's foot"', *Clues: A journal of detection*, 33:1, 62–71.

Bradley, James (2000), 'Body commodification? Class and tattoos in Victorian fiction', in J. Caplan (ed.) (2000), pp. 136–55.

Brooke, John Hedley (1991), *Science and nature: Some historical perspectives* (Cambridge: Cambridge University Press).

Caplan, Jane (ed.) (2000), *Written on the body: The tattoo in European and American history* (London: Reaktion Books).

Carr, John Dickson (1949), *The life of Sir Arthur Conan Doyle* (New York: Harper & Brothers).

Cheng, W. (2004), 'Chemical extraction technique for tattoo removal', *British journal of dermatology*, 151:6 (April), pp. 770–71.

Collins, Wilkie (1974), *The woman in white* [1860] (Harmondsworth: Penguin).

Doyle, Arthur Conan (1883), 'The narrative of John Smith', in J. Lellenberg, D. Stashower and R. Foss (eds) (London: The British Library).

— (1887), *A study in scarlet*, in Doyle, L. Klinger (ed.) (2006).

— (1890), *The sign of four*, in Doyle, L. Klinger (ed.) (2006).
— (1891a), *Tit-bits*, in Doyle, L. Klinger (ed.) (2005a).
— (1891b), 'A scandal in Bohemia' in Doyle, L. Klinger (ed.) (2005a).
— (1891c), 'A case of identity' in Doyle, L. Klinger (ed.) (2005a).
— (1891d), 'The red-headed league' in Doyle, L. Klinger (ed.) (2005a).
— (1902), *The hound of the Baskervilles*, in Doyle, L. Klinger (ed.) (2006).
— (1903), 'The adventure of the Norwood builder' in Doyle, L. Klinger (ed.) (2005b).
— (1907), *Through the magic door* (London: Smith Elder).
— (1911), 'The adventure of the red circle', in L. Klinger (ed.) (2005b).
— (1925), 'The illustrious client', in L. S. Klinger (ed.) (2005a).
— (1926), 'The blanched soldier' in Doyle, L. Klinger (ed.) (2005b).
— (1986), *The Micah Clarke* [1889] in *Sir Arthur Conan Doyle: The historical novels*. Vol. 2 (Poole: New Orchard Editions).
— (1989), *Memories and adventures* [1924] (Oxford: Oxford University Press).
— (1992), 'A medical document' [1894], in A. E. Rodin and J. D. Key (eds) (1992), n.p.
— (2004), *The Stark Munro letters* [1895] (Fairfield: 1st World Library).
— (2007), *The new revelation* [1918] (New York: Cosimo).
— (2012), *The vital message* [1919] (n.p.: The Floating Press).
— in L. Klinger (ed.) (2005a), *The new annotated Sherlock Holmes: Volume 1 (short stories)* (New York: W.W. Norton and Company).
— in L. Klinger (ed.) (2005b), *The new annotated Sherlock Holmes: Volume 2 (short stories)* (New York: W.W. Norton and Company).
— in L. Klinger (ed.) (2006), *The new annotated Sherlock Holmes: Volume 3 (novels)* (New York: W.W. Norton and Company).
DeMello, Margo (2000), *Bodies of inscription: A cultural history of the modern tattoo community* (Durham and London: Duke University Press).
Gell, Alfred (1993), *Wrapping in images: Tattooing in Polynesia* (Oxford: Clarendon Press).
Green, Richard Lancelyn (1986), *The Sherlock Holmes letters* (Iowa: University of Iowa Press).
How, H. (1892), 'A day with Doyle', *The Strand magazine*, 4 (July–December), pp. 182–88.
Ikin, J. I. (1857), 'Medical notes on the militia: n. 4', in A. Wynter (ed.), *Journal of the British Medical Association* (London: Thomas John Honeyman).
Lellenberg, Jon, Daniel Stashower and Charles Foley (eds) (2007), *Arthur Conan Doyle: A life in letters* (London: Penguin).
Liebow, Ely M. (1982), *Dr Joe Bell: Model for Sherlock Holmes* (Bowling Green: Bowling Green University Press).
Lombroso, Cesare (1876), *Criminal man [L'uomo delinquente]* (Milano: Hoepli).
Lycett, Andrew (2007), *Conan Doyle: The man who created Sherlock Holmes* (n.p.: Weidenfeld & Nicolson).
McDermid, Val (2015), *Forensics: What bugs, burns, prints, DNA and more tell us about crime* (New York: Grove).
Morrow, Howard (1889), *Diseases of the skin: An outline of the principles and practice of dermatology* (London and New York: Cassell).
O'Brien, James F. (2013), *The scientific Sherlock Holmes: Cracking the case with science and forensics* (Oxford: Oxford University Press).

Pick, Daniel (1996), *Faces of degeneration: A European disorder, c. 1848–c. 1918* (Cambridge: Cambridge University Press).

Ramsland, Katherine (2009), 'Observe carefully, deduce shrewdly: Dr. Joseph Bell', *The forensic examiner* (Fall), 77–79.

Rodin, Alvin E. and Jack D. Key (eds) (1984), *Medical casebook of Doctor Arthur Conan Doyle* (Malabar: Krieger Publishing Company).

— (1992), *Conan Doyle's tales of medical humanism and values: Round the red lamp* (Malabar: Krieger Publishing).

Sengoopta, Chandak (2003), *Imprint of the Raj: How fingerprinting was born in colonial India* (London: Macmillan).

Shapin, Steven (1996), *The scientific revolution* (Chicago: University of Chicago Press).

Stashower, Daniel (1999), *Teller of tales: The life of Conan Doyle* (New York: Henry Holt Publishing).

Stavert, Geoffrey (1987), *A study in Southsea: The unrevealed life of Doctor Arthur Conan Doyle* (n.p.: Milestone Publications).

Thomas, Ronald R. (1999), *Detective fiction and the rise of forensic science* (Cambridge: Cambridge University Press).

Watson, Kate (2016), 'Mapping the mark: Tattoos, crime fiction, and gendered cartographies', in C. A. Cothran, and M. Cannon (eds), *New perspectives on detective fiction: Mystery magnified* (Oxford and New York: Routledge), pp. 52–71.

PART 2

Practitioners, place and contemporary identities

4

From naïve artists to integrated professionals: The portrayal of tattoos in Sarah Hall's *The electric Michelangelo* and Alan Kent's *Voodoo pilchard*

Hywel Dix

INTRODUCTION

In an important early study of crime fiction, Dennis Porter suggested that a significant split took place during the nineteenth century between novels that had both a social orientation and a political commitment, and those which were more inward looking, concerned with aesthetic style and sensibility rather than with using fiction as a form of social criticism.[1] By the end of the nineteenth century, the aesthetic crime novel had become dominant over the crime novel of social commitment, so that the new figure of the detective that emerged during that period was often a fictional embodiment of the conventionally aesthetic properties of singular style, wit and mastery of language.[2]

This split within crime writing shaped many early critical assumptions about the genre, which came to be seen as 'an essentially conservative form' (Gregoriou 2007: 47). In the 1980s, when there started to be 'a growing seriousness among academics towards historical crime fiction' (Browne and Kreiser 2000: 3), much of the critical discourse argued that crime fiction was worth studying because it revealed an 'age old' human belief in the quest for finding meaning in a turbulent world (Porter 1981: 228). Such an approach, by stressing the timelessness of the basic properties of the genre, was unwittingly unhistorical. It had the effect that crime fiction came to be seen as a useful social document because it was a populist genre read by many people, and so could 'serve as a touchstone for appraising social responses to deviant conduct and disaster' (Borowitz 2002: 30) without ever amounting to seriously challenging literature.

However, since the early studies of crime fiction, significant critical developments have taken place (see, for example, Knight 2004; Rzepka 2005; Scaggs 2005). Some of the earlier assumptions about crime fiction, the identity of its readers, its aesthetic properties and its political orientations have been

questioned so that the genre is 'not necessarily' viewed as inherently conservative any longer (Johnsen 2006: 8). This is partly because as the range of
critical analyses of crime fiction has broadened, the early emphasis on the
timelessness of human inquiry and human passion has been replaced by a more
nuanced sense of how the particular crimes portrayed in crime fiction are also
situated 'in a specific historical context' (*ibid.*: 113) which can then be critically
interrogated.

This chapter argues that the critical reaction to crime writing mirrors and is
mirrored by sociological and cultural responses to the practice of tattooing. Just
as there was early critical reluctance to consider crime fiction as 'literature', so
too there has been a general reluctance on the part of the artistic establishment
to consider tattoos as 'art'. By considering representations of tattoos in crime
fiction, many of the theoretical questions that have been raised in one domain
are shown to be also relevant in the other such that the two can be made to
speak to each other.

According to Derek Roberts, tattoos and tattooing as both aesthetic object
and social practice have undergone 'drastic redefinition in recent decades'
(Roberts 2012: 153). However, he identifies a 'noteworthy reluctance' on the
part of social scientists to investigate tattoos as a 'nondeviant, mainstream
phenomenon', as if tattoos and the social practice of tattooing were *ipso facto*
socially non-normative phenomena (*ibid.*). Although Matt Lodder has questioned the assumption that tattooing is inherently transgressive (Lodder 2011:
104), contemporary mainstream culture has yet to fully claim tattoos, which
Roberts found are still associated with 'low cultural standing' (Roberts 2012:
158). He concluded that the so-called tattoo renaissance of recent decades has
been characterised by gradual evolution in social attitude rather than whole-
sale change. This has already been identified by novelist Kathy Acker, who
found that tattooing was 'very much a sign of a certain class and certain people,
a part of society that sees itself as outcast, and shows it' (Acker in Friedman
1989: n.p.).

As a sign of the gradual change in the artistic standing of tattoos,
Helen Lewis has identified occasional forays by fine artists such as Shelley
Jackson, Ann Vito Minchin and Lucien Freud into the world of tattoos.
In an interview with Lewis, Gemma Angel expressed an interest in studying and documenting the preserved skins of nineteenth-century tattooees
because to do so is to reconstruct marginalised life histories (Angel in Lewis
2013: 33). If preserving and documenting historical tattoos offers a way
of recuperating the lives of those who wore them, and whose lives would
otherwise remain unrecorded, the same can be said of certain kinds of
crime writing. Rosemary Johnsen has said of historical crime fiction that it
is important because it often focuses on groups that were disenfranchised
historically, especially women (Johnsen 2006: 12). When historical crime

fiction re-imagines the lives of women who have been excluded from the conventional literary and historical record, it provides a symbolic way of compensating for that historical exclusion. Both a historical reading of the practice of tattooing and a fictional practice of imagining lives excluded from the literary mainstream are tantamount to cultural archaeologies, recovering a sense of the lives lived by people not included in the traditional literary, historical or artistic record.

This chapter foregrounds the political, radical and social core of detective fiction through the examination of two contemporary texts, which focus on the practice and art of tattooing: Sarah Hall's *The electric Michelangelo* (2004) and Alan Kent's *Voodoo pilchard* (2010). In both novels, the 'non-metropolitan' cultural politics of much detective fiction (Knight 1995: 28) is combined with the holiday destination, still an important aspect of tattoo culture (Roberts 2012: 155). Hall's novel spans a period roughly from the end of the First World War up until the 1960s, and is an example of historical crime writing that rewrites exclusion. It is a novel in which the adjacent cultural archaeologies of tattooing and historical crime fiction are strongly associated with each other. Hall's fictional historical tattoo artists are associated with a political underclass and hence with the kinds of life and work that have traditionally been marginalised both by serious art and by canonical literature. Though the activities of Hall's tattooists are cast as 'criminal' within the social structures of Morecambe Bay and New York in the early twentieth century, they are also presented as questioning those same social structures in a politically challenging, even radical, way. In other words, Hall's 'criminal' tattooists are also to be seen as political revolutionaries precisely by refusing the distinction between art and social commitment and by bringing the activities of one into the domain of the other.

The second novel to be discussed, Kent's *Voodoo pilchard*, is set in twenty-first-century Cornwall – the setting for all of Kent's work, just as all of Hall's novels are situated (at least in part) in the north west of England. Both *The electric Michelangelo* and *Voodoo pilchard* provide a strong sense of regional British identity, and this regional identity is important in the context of the kinds of subversive, counter-cultural activity imagined. Moreover, the relationship between regional location and cultural practice forms a fruitful convergence between crime writing and tattooing. The chapter will explore how the social practice of tattooing is portrayed as a politically subversive one in the early twentieth century; and to what extent that practice is more recently portrayed as having become incorporated into the mainstream of fashion and consumer society. It will ask whether tattoos could be considered legitimate serious art in the early twentieth century and today; and how far the recognition of tattooing as legitimate art comes at the cost of compromising the politically transgressive potential of the practice.

'THE THINGS OF ART': TATTOOS AND TRANSGRESSION IN *THE ELECTRIC MICHELANGELO*

On the surface, Eliot Riley, the Morecambe Bay tattooist who apprentices the young Cyril (Cy) Parks in the first half of Hall's *The electric Michelangelo*, conforms to the notion of tattooing dominant in the early twentieth century: that it was at best tangential to genteel society and at worst on the edge of a criminal underworld. In Hall's initial portrayal, Riley's actions seem to positively invite the animosity of the town's self-appointed guardians of public morality: '[h]e drank, offended, was loud, misunderstood' (Hall 2004: 95), '[h]e went too far, got obstinate about his courtship of living wrongly and loudly and creating effrontery' (*ibid.*). The narrative emphasis on this public perception of Riley, on *the* Eliot Riley who exists only on these terms, and on the Eliot who lives as it were exclusively on the street, implies that there is another persona, another side to the character that either through accident or design eludes the public attention cultivated by his anti-social demeanour. The word that first arouses in readers the possibility of this other Riley is the word 'art', and the text's implicit question of whether or not Riley is an artist. This question can fruitfully be considered through recourse to Howard Becker's sociological concept of the 'art world'.

Becker defines an 'art world' as the sum total of social relationships and productive forces without whose mutual and carefully orchestrated collaboration no individual work of art could be created or distributed to an audience (Becker 2008: 35). The concept of the art world helps to overhaul the longstanding, romantic notion that works of art are the unique products of the individual aesthetic geniuses who produce them, and directs attention instead to the network of social, cultural, political and economic forces in which both the individual artist and his or her work are involved. The concept has the additional advantage that it draws attention to the importance of making and contesting culturally-specific value judgements: 'Art worlds typically devote considerable attention to trying to decide what is and isn't art' (*ibid.*: 36). Nicolas Michaud observes of tattoos that they 'have not been accepted into the tradition of the art world and so by the art world's standards, tattoos aren't art' (Michaud 2012: 31). However, he goes on to suggest 'this position can be challenged' (*ibid.*). *The electric Michelangelo* can be seen as a fictional embodiment of the contest for tattoos to be recognised as belonging to an art world in Becker's sense.

In cultivating a connection between the activities of Riley (which are seen as somehow not respectable, even criminal) and his work as a tattooist (which is not seen as art), Hall portrays a crisis and challenge to the notion of cultural legitimacy. In *Art and terror*, Frank Lentricchia has argued that the task of the artist has always been to try and shock an audience out of a sense of cultural orthodoxy and therefore to bring aesthetic questions to bear on the realm of politics. He proposes a definition of art that includes 'a diverse and important group of figures, and actions, not all of them artistic figures or artistic actions in the traditional sense of the word "art"' (2003: 4). This is what we find in *The electric Michelangelo.* Riley's activities have both a social outlook and a political commitment. During the General Strike of 1926 he closes his parlour to show a basic solidarity with the workers, although this gesture means a significant loss in his own income. Moreover, in his friendship with Cy's mother, Reeda, both are portrayed as politically engaged and seeking to initiate social action. Reeda stoically cares for the sufferers of consumption who cannot afford to go anywhere else. She is also a suffragette, handing out leaflets in support of women's suffrage on Morecambe promenade. The most subversive aspect of Reeda's life is the fact that she carries out illicit abortions. Thus there is a subtle continuum of activities, from caring for the sick poor (not illegal, but portrayed as being wilfully negligent of the existing social order), to the campaign for votes for women, up to the carrying out of abortions (which was illegal in the narrative setting). In this way, Hall challenges historical constructions of criminality at the same time that she reconstructs definitions of art.

Like Reeda, Hall portrays Riley as not respected among the conservative councillors of Morecambe because he willingly associates with the working class and the town's underclass – as if this were a moral failing in itself. As with Reeda's support for the suffragettes, what precisely Riley does in support of the General Strike is not specified. This might imply involvement in activity that is legally prohibited, but which readers will recognise as egalitarian in principle and hence morally 'proper'. In the midst of all this, Hall is careful to portray the practice of tattooing as a legitimate art in its own right. Furthermore she is keen to link that recognition of cultural legitimacy to a wider legitimisation of activities that might have lacked legal sanction but which nevertheless command a certain moral mandate. There is a powerful nexus between campaigning for suffrage, carrying out illicit abortions, Riley's underground art and a challenge to the bourgeois establishment more generally, as symbolised by the strike. Riley's art, in other words, is not an art for art's sake, but art in Lentricchia's sense: it both relates to activities that are not traditionally considered as art, and has a political orientation.

The electric Michelangelo is less concerned with specific crimes than with different kinds of activity that have variously been labelled as criminal. For this reason, there are not only two main crimes in the novel, but also two distinct kinds of crime. There are crimes directed against the social order of the day, which have an important political orientation; and there are crimes committed out of self-interest or personal emotion, which lack the ideological motivation of the former kind. The 'crimes' that Riley and Reeda are involved in belong to the former category: they are directed against the social order. But when Riley is targeted by a longtime rival and his hand smashed and broken at a blacksmith's stable, this is the other kind of crime. It serves no ideological purpose.[3]

After being beaten up, Riley is injured so badly he can never work again and without the ability to work he begins a slow decline which, after almost a year, culminates in his suicide. What is notable about this crime (described in the text in judicial terms as a 'sentence') is that from a purely narratological standpoint, it has no perpetrator. The identity of the assailant is neither revealed nor within the parameters of the novel even investigated. Riley is punished for his 'guilty life' (Hall 2004: 130). *The electric Michelangelo* is a crime novel without a detective. Hall is less interested in setting up a traditional 'whodunit' than in portraying a series of social relationships embodied by Riley and Reeda, and the symbolic violence to which they are subject as a result of their opposition to the political order. The assault on Riley enables the author to satirise the snobbery, prejudice and class antagonisms present in the society. Hall attempts to re-connect the aesthetic dimension of the genre with the political grounding that Porter thought had been lost during the nineteenth century. Thus the assault on Riley is not used either to launch an investigation plot or to portray the idiosyncratic style of a super sleuth, but to interrogate the inbuilt political assumptions of the society.

When Riley dies, the novel intensifies its focus on his apprentice, Cy, who emigrates to New York to set up a tattoo parlour in Coney Island. What is notable about the second half of the novel is that by substituting civil rights for the struggle of suffragettes it reflects the first half of the novel almost exactly. This continuity is important, because as Gregoriou has shown in a study of the language of crime fiction, crime novels are often constructed at the verbal level in such a way as to cultivate an affinity between apparently disparate elements, and therefore function at the level of a 'sustained metaphor' (2007: 24). Inasmuch as this is the case in *The electric Michelangelo*, the sustained metaphor is one of political struggle. Cy's parlour on Coney Island is a place where members of different races mix freely. As a result, and like Riley's tattoo shop or Reeda's guest house, it is not deemed respectable in the arena of public opinion. When a group of soldiers visit, they see it as a 'muddy bog of disapproval' (Hall 2004: 237) but nevertheless come to get tattoos. This incident is not so much about hypocrisy as about the disparity between different notions of taste and cultural capital.

It is in this transgressive location that Cy tattoos the collection of mystical eye tattoos on Grace's body that he identifies as his greatest creation: 'my Sistine Chapel' (*ibid.*: 292). Through this allusion he identifies himself as the 'electric Michelangelo' of the title, the moniker he takes on arriving in America, and this choice of forebear is significant for two reasons. It situates his tattooing practice within an artistic field that has the consecration of several centuries to lend it legitimacy. This link between tattooing and an established artistic heritage has already been outlined by Riley at the beginning of Cy's apprenticeship (initially likening his work to engraver William Blake and sculptor Gian Lorenzo Bernini) and through his sporadic teachings. Moreover, the specific alignment to Michelangelo, whose life and work were punctuated by periods of political conflict between Florence's ruling despotic Medici family and short-lived attempts to establish a Florentine republic, appears to echo the twentieth-century struggles for democracy and civil rights that form the backdrop to the novel.

Grace's choice of eye tattoos to clothe her entire body is a personal and political act, likened to a 'manifesto' (*ibid.*: 260).[4] Grace intends to reclaim her body through actualising the gaze she experiences, so that 'what they cannot do is use me with their damn eyes. Not ever again' (*ibid.*: 272). Cy's art is to combine the geography of her body and her flesh with her personality (the bringing form of an internal quality through the work) with the 'unreal' design (*ibid.*: 263), resulting in a radical rebirth. This practice of tattooing as art is compared by both Riley and Cy to that of the midwife, whereby they act to 'birth' the art. Grace is an elusive representation of the new America, a European emigre created by war, and is reborn through Cy's art as the 'Lady of Many Eyes' (*ibid.*: 271).

When Grace suffers an acid attack at the hands of Malcolm Sedak this is as much a strike against their art and hence against their anti-establishment politics as it is against her body. There is no need for an investigation (as in a classic whodunit) since readers already know the identity of the attacker. Instead there is an emphasis on the symbolic justice meted out to Sedak. He is held in an asylum, where Cy breaks in and symbolically blinds him. Justice comes not from the police or the courts, but from Cy and Grace themselves. This is significant, because it enables the attack on Grace to be ritualistically avenged, on the one hand, while also enabling Hall to portray the attacker, Sedak, as being in some respects a victim of authoritarian violence. This in turn enables her to make a Foucauldian critique of the asylum in which patients are treated like 'sick, maladjusted dogs' (*ibid.*: 313). In this way, she uses the crime structure to direct critical attention onto the exercise of violent and inhumane power by civil and bureaucratic institutions over the lives of individual citizens.

The critique of authoritarian violence is also the reason why the symbolic justice generated in the novel comes from Cy's revenge attack, rather than from the courts. As Hall is concerned to critique the operation of institutional power, justice cannot come from conventional legal process. From her hospital bed, Grace tells Cy not to drink any alcohol before carrying out the revenge attack, which must be completed 'cold in our minds' (*ibid.*: 311). In Hall's portrayal the operation of justice is measured, calculated and proportionate – even if it is at odds with the law. But for this transgression Cy cannot escape unpunished, and he pays symbolically with the end of his relationship with

Grace. The job of the artist, the novel implies, is to challenge the way we see the world, even if this comes at a high price. Through this triangular relationship, the novel deconstructs definitions of crime and punishment and asks: what is justice? What is art?

To consider how *The electric Michelangelo* constructs an implicit answer to these questions, it is useful to return to Becker's concept of the art world. As we have seen, the concept of the art world is bound up with a critical contest over what is and what is not considered to be legitimate art. As such, it is imbricated with a broader set of cultural and social value judgements, which is why the attempts by Hall's protagonists to be seen as artists are also involved with a wider set of political challenges. In *Art worlds* Becker identifies three means by which members of a nascent art world might convince others of the legitimacy of their claim to the status of artists. First, there is the development of a critical apparatus through which discussion and promotion of the work in question can take place. This is typically a workshop and/or a journal, but in Cy's case this is ultimately the completion of Grace's tattoos as she transforms into the radical physical manifestation of his art and ability.[5] Second, the demonstration that the work of the art world is distinct from mere craft or commercial activity (the difference between the tattooers' replication through use of flash designs and the tattooists' talent as a freehander); and finally the retrospective construction of a history for the work of the new art world, capable of demonstrating that it has its roots in older, already established forms of art (Becker 2008: 339). Hall sets up the evolution of tattooing practice through Polynesian techniques. Cy begins and ends his tattooing practice with the use of a bamboo shaft and hammer, which he affects to hear under the modern electrical tattooing instruments ('that original tat-tat-tat-to sound').

These means are depicted in *The electric Michelangelo* to a greater or lesser degree. Hall's writing is steeped in the research of tattoos and tattooing practice. The sailors and travellers tattooed by Cy on his crossing of the Atlantic give him physical experience of Maori, Polynesian and Japanese art, thus extending the historical rootedness of their practice onto a global scale. Riley gives Cy lessons in the history of art intertwined with politics, teaching him about Dante Gabriel Rossetti, Gustave Courbet, Édouard Manet, and Michelangelo Merisi da Caravaggio – who had 'painted the portrait of a poor carpenter' and 'dared to say that the son of God was surrogated to this old, this broken-bodied, callus-handed worker' (Hall 2004: 116–17). To Riley, all of these are appropriate 'things of art' (*ibid.*) because they challenged earlier concepts of who had the right to speak for whom and hence combined aesthetic practice with a radical social outlook. This is also why Riley has William Blake's poem 'Tyger! Tyger! burning bright' tattooed on the sole of his foot (*ibid.*: 139). If not a fully paid-up revolutionary, Blake too was a romantic free thinker in whom the twin currents of innovative artistic practice and critical social perspective also met. All of this means that although there is not a fully developed professional apparatus for discussing Riley and Cy's work as 'art' (which was the first of Becker's criterion for establishing a new art world), there are the beginnings of a distinction between art and craft (second definition) and there is also a retrospectively mediated pre-history to lend the discipline legitimacy (third criterion).

There is a good reason why Becker's criteria for defining art are only partially fulfilled in (and by) the novel. Neither Hall nor her characters Riley and Cy are really interested in subscribing to an *a priori* conception of art. Instead they are interested in challenging and changing the existing definition of it by bringing it into the political domain. The examples of major artists from history that had formed Cy's apprenticeship to Riley were those whose social roles were politically transgressive and potentially subversive of bourgeois order. By proclaiming himself a latter-day Michelangelo, Cy thus situates his practice within a longer artistic history that helps legitimise it, on the one hand, while also asserting a commitment to a radical revolutionary politics on the other. His primary artistic interest is not with abstract categories such as truth or beauty, but rather with the capacity for artistic practice to participate in political struggles on the ground. The practice of tattooing in *The electric Michelangelo* thus suggests that art is most artful when it directly confronts existing definitions of art in order to change them. Ironically, recognition of the legitimacy of the new form of art depends in part on its capacity to demonstrate an established history. This is perhaps why at the end, when the electricity fails, Cy reverts to using older Polynesian techniques for tattooing. This action underlines that his 'new' art has an ancient history, while also maintaining his position of critical outsider with regard to the established social order.

'IMPROVED MANAGEABILITY': TATTOOS AND THE LANGUAGE OF COMMERCE IN *VOODOO PILCHARD*

The electric Michelangelo ends in the 1960s when Cy's new apprentice Nina applies to art college to enhance her professional skills. This development suggests that unlike the earlier period portrayed in the novel, there are now both a relationship between tattoos and formal artistic institutions, and the beginnings of a suitable language of critical appreciation. This could be related to the wider counter-cultural developments of the 1960s compared to the 1920s, or it might represent a gradual incorporation of naïve art into the work of an integrated professional industry. Becker (2008) coined the terms 'naïve artist' and 'integrated professional' – as well as the intermediary categories of 'folk artist' and 'maverick' – to distinguish between different kinds of social relationship artists have to the various art worlds of which they are part. A naïve artist practices without regard either to the economic conditions dominant in a given field or to the aesthetic conventions of that field, and may not even recognise the validity of such conventions. By contrast, the work of an integrated professional is highly organised, technically adept and economically proficient. It relates directly to the mainstream of art, culture and commerce but its content is unlikely to be seriously innovative or challenging either to the audience or to the social hierarchy more generally. The status of naïve artist accords with the rebellious potential of the medium in which Hall's Riley and Cy both practice: it is an art that is not so much anti-art but anti-establishment in a political sense. The incorporation of that art into a cultural mainstream causes the practice to lose some of its transgressive potential: Cy's mother in the 1920s fought for women's suffrage. Nina Shearer in the 1960s is too disillusioned to even vote and seems to have lost the capacity to believe in social change. This might be because, as Raymond Williams comments in *Marxism and literature*, the dominant ideology in a given society has an almost infinite potential to incorporate emergent, oppositional tendencies to its own form of cultural and economic hegemony (Williams 1977: 121–27).

The incorporation of initially emergent, subcultural elements into the dominant ideology of capitalism, thereby neutralising the oppositional tendencies of the subculture, is what Alan Kent portrays with regard to the practice of tattooing in his novel *Voodoo pilchard* (2010), the third in a Cornish trilogy of novels about would-be rock star Charlie Kernow. At the start of *Voodoo pilchard*, Charlie has returned from touring with his band *Purple haze* and resolved to buy a house and settle down. This ironically portrays the rock and roll lifestyle as accommodated to the mainstream of commercial culture, rather than oppositional to it (see Harris 2003). Charlie's sister Jess and her partner Micky have also returned from a period of world travel to open a combined hair salon and tattoo parlour. Moreover, an unidentified street artist has started spraying graffiti on the streets and public places of Camborne. In other words, Kent uses the portrayal of rock music, tattooing and graffiti to explore the extent to which these forms of art can be considered socially subversive and how much they have become integrated to the culture of consumerism and hence to the dominant ideology of capitalism.

The potential for the dominant ideology to incorporate emergent practices is most clearly illustrated by the novel's foreclosure of the potential for revolutionary change. *Voodoo pilchard* is a parody of a gangster novel.[6] Although Porter suggests that parody can be a way of paying tribute to a genre (Porter 1981: 2), the effect of parody in *Voodoo pilchard* seems to be that the portrayal of transgressive relationships uses itself up in generating comedy rather than being converted into social action.

The plot of *Voodoo pilchard* is about local criminal boss Markie Phillips's attempt to get revenge on Ally, the woman who once jilted him, by kidnapping her son Anthony and holding him in Godrevy Lighthouse. After a series of comical blunders, Anthony is (half) rescued by the Cornish 'nationalist'

Trescothick who had earlier been tattooed with a Celtic Cross and a motto in the Cornish language recalling the Cornish uprising against Henry VIII in the sixteenth century (Kent 2010: 145). Indeed, Trescothick explains his hopes for Cornish self-determination to the tattoo artist, Micky, while he works on the tattoo. On the face of it, this recalls the political discussions that take place in the tattoo parlours of *The electric Michelangelo*, where the practice itself, because it is counter-cultural, is related to a radical, anti-establishment political praxis first in the area of female emancipation and then in the area of African-American Civil Rights. This means that in *The electric Michelangelo*, the potential for radical political change in the 1920s and 1930s was presented as a genuine possibility. In *Voodoo pilchard*, by contrast, Trescothick is a figure of fun, 'tortured' by being forced to listen to English – as opposed to Cornish – folk music. In other words, the transgressive potential of which his tattoo could be an emblem is barely operative at all. The possibility of a political revolution has been bought off by the dominance of consumer society which has incorporated the once rebellious practice of tattooing to itself. In the twenty-first century, the novel seems to say, no more revolutionary change is possible and hence the impulse towards that change expends itself in comedy and parody because no other form of closure is imaginable.

Because this incorporation has taken place, Micky's tattoo studio above the salon is portrayed in the language of bourgeois, consumerist culture appropriate to the economic order in question. He has a waiting room where 'clients could browse through his bespoke designs' (*ibid.*: 132). He also boasts an impressive range of equipment and surgical supplies, creating an impression of safety and hygiene that is very unlike the air of subcultural threat associated with tattooing in *The electric Michelangelo*:

> He double-checked the two-roll dispensers on the wall, and opened a couple of packets of tattooist's green soap, ready to go [...] By them, all the warning signs about clients needing to be over eighteen years of age, and a pad of disclaimers. (*ibid.*: 132–33)

In this description of Micky's studio, Kent emphasises three characteristics. First, the place is symbolically distinguished from other, less reputable establishments. Second, it is described as a safe place with certifiable adherence to health and safety legislation. Third, it is described as a place of artistic creativity. It is, in short, a world away from the back-street tattoo parlour of Eliot Riley in *The electric Michelangelo*, where legality was not considered and where the concept of 'clients' in a fully functioning mainstream capitalist market was alien. On the one hand, Kent's emphasis on Micky's creativity seems to suggest that in the early twenty-first century, the status of the tattooist has become fully and thoroughly elevated to that of mainstream artist which it lacked in the early twentieth. There is a critical idiom ('bespoke designs'), a medium for discussion (his catalogues) and an institutional relationship to a supplier ('Premier') that supports the identification of Micky as one of Becker's integrated professionals. As we have seen in Hall's portrayal of Cy Parks and Eliot Riley, however, the radical potential of art to imagine a revolutionary set of new social relationships is only operative to the extent that the art in question is not widely recognised as such. Riley was cast as a criminal because his activities constituted a threat to the dominant social order that existed. Micky, by contrast, offers no such threat and hence is not portrayed as a criminal, but as an innocent bystander in the gangland of Markie Phillips.

In *The electric Michelangelo*, the association between Riley's aesthetic and political transgressions is portrayed through a metaphorical affinity between his underground tattooing, Reeda's covert abortions and political subversion symbolised by the suffragettes and the General Strike of 1926. The converse of this in *Voodoo pilchard* is Kent's portrayal of the gradual loss of the socially subversive potential of tattooing and its relationship to the mainstream of consumer society, symbolised by the relationship of the tattoo studio to Jess's hair salon. Her products are advertised in the following way:

> St Meriasek Extra-Body Daily Shampoo – Super body-builder for improved manageability.
> Thickens fine and normal hair.
> Extra-body – Effectively cleanses the hair while panthenol and thickening conditioners help increase volume and and [*sic*] improve both wet and dry combing.
> (*ibid.*: 126; original presentation)

In total, forty-nine of these 'advertising' passages pervade the text of *Voodoo pilchard*. They emanate as if from a disembodied voice, not associated with any individual character though they appear connected to the plot. The cosmetic idiom and its promise of health and cleanliness speaks the language of the economic and commercial mainstream. The imbrication of cleanliness with respectability that Kent depicts in Micky's tattoo studio is replicated in the description of Jess's salon – which is in the same building. Both are thoroughly incorporated to the language and practices of the corporate world. The respectability of Jess provides a counter-balance to the criminal activities of the gangster, Markie Phillips. However, whereas Riley and Cy's crimes in *The electric Michelangelo* are carried out in the name of a wider political and egalitarian political practice, Markie's seedy activities lack solidarity to any cause bigger than himself. The same is also true of Jess and Micky's business. In this sense, whereas the 'criminals' and bourgeoisie were poles apart in *The electric Michelangelo*, their narrative function in *Voodoo pilchard* is symbolically equal. This is not because Kent believes the crime novel to be an inherently conservative form – as in earlier critical approaches to the genre. Rather, it is because he wishes to portray the loss of a radical or revolutionary political practice as a means of affirming his commitment to what is in the process of being lost.

Kent's use of a Cornish vernacular is an important part of that affirmation, because it contrasts strikingly with the managerial discourse parodied in the novel and hence contrasts also with the language of capitalism. Because hardly anyone (not even the omniscient narrator) in *Voodoo pilchard* speaks the standard English that Kent associates with a managerial class and hence with capitalist ideology, the particular achievement of the novel is to estrange the language of the dominant social order from itself. For example, Charlie's visit to the salon/studio is narrated in the following way:

> When Charlie went over t'have a geek at wha' wuz on, the plaace looked like a bombsite. [...] Y'knaw the kind of crap they have in the windows – like as if some anti-frizz is goin' t'help out in the middle of wintry, mizzly day in the middle of Bolenowe Moor. (*ibid.*: 40–41)

The narrative voice of the novel speaks a defiantly working-class idiom very unlike the commercial language of the advertisements for Jess's beauty products. As a result, the language of the economic mainstream, rather than externalising and distancing the voice and culture of the working class, is rendered external to it. At the level of language, Kent is able to say something genuinely transgressive of the dominant ideology of capitalism, because the only character in *Voodoo pilchard* who speaks the language of the economic mainstream is the thug-turned-businessman Markie Phillips. In other words, by associating the activities of commerce with those of a criminal gangster who has no interest in transforming the social order, Kent reveals an ironic disparity between the language of economic domination and those who are dominated, thereby generating a sustained critique of capitalist ideology.

The social practice of tattooing portrayed in *Voodoo pilchard* is not counter-cultural but has become assimilated to the cultural and commercial mainstream of the art and culture of which it is emblematic. Micky and Trescothick are not portrayed as criminals because their tattooing does not threaten the dominant economic order. By contrast, Markie is portrayed as a criminal because he upholds it. When he gets a tattoo, this is not so much a symbol of his criminality as of his attempts to convince the world he is going straight. Thus, to cover a rough prison tattoo, he chooses a second tattoo, the commercial logo of Truro City Football Club, which can hardly be seen as a threat to the economic order. Michael Silk, David Andrews and Cheryl Cole point out that the cultivation of a sense of loyalty to certain local and regional sports teams expresses the complex 'relationships and nuances between global brands and local cultures' in which the 're-emergence of "local" brands' often creates only 'a veneer' of local commitment when really the sports organisation in question is owned by 'various global corporations' (Silk *et al.* 2005: 2).

Markie's tattoo is an example of this nuanced expression. On the one hand, when seen in contexts not typically associated with football it might appear non-normative and even in some ways counter-cultural. On the other hand, it is also used to cultivate loyalty to sporting organisations as corporate brands, and this compromises any notion that it might express a symbolic challenge to the dominant and political order.

That Markie's tattoo represents his participation in the mainstream of consumer culture is underlined by his commercial plans for the football team, set out in a detailed business plan that looked 'like somethun' y'might be able to sell t'the International Olympic Committee or FIFA' (Kent 2010: 228). Neither the IOC nor FIFA, which aim to export sport as a consumable commodity for a global market, could seriously be seen as socially rebellious, culturally challenging or politically daring (Cloake 2014: 124–30); rather, Markie's business plan reflects his desire to be part of a competitive economic order that includes these sporting organisations. In *Voodoo pilchard*, Markie is both a criminal and a businessman, but he is no revolutionary. It is the corporate aspect of his life rather than any potential subversion that his tattoo symbolises.

CONCLUSION: THE SHIFT OF RADICAL POTENTIAL

This chapter set out to explore the portrayal of the status of tattoos by Hall and Kent by bringing aesthetic questions to bear on changing political and historical concepts of art, crime, deviance and cultural legitimacy. Hall associates the medium of tattooing with political transgression and hence with an ironic portrayal of 'deviant' behaviours in the 1920s, where the activities of suffragettes and civil rights activists were cast as 'criminal' in an attempt to discredit the challenge they posed to the political establishment. Kent represents tattoos as having become more integrated into the economic and commercial structures of daily life in the early twenty-first century. This means that they are no longer associated with 'criminality' but also means that the participation of the medium in a radical political practice has been eviscerated. Kent thus has to look elsewhere in order to generate a fictive critique of the dominant ideology of consumer culture and generates such a critique by ironically portraying the successful businessman Markie as a 'criminal'. His novel seems to suggest that the 'crimes' of a competitive, individualistic economic order are directed against the solidarity and communal interest of the disempowered working class.

The extreme polarity that exists between the portrayal of tattooing in the two novels is perhaps exaggerated as each writer strives for symbolic, novelistic and dramatic effect. Hall makes a distinction between an artistic practice that has a sociological dimension and one that is more inward looking. That distinction in turn leads her to portray two different kinds of crime: those that are directed against the social order and which hence can be interpreted as acts of solidarity and revolution; and those that are purely self-seeking. This distinction between the sociological and the individualistic in crime writing has its roots in the aesthetic turn that took place during the nineteenth century and in fact is a long-term descendant of it.

The critical sociological literature on tattooing implies that there has been a gradual shift in the social acceptability of the practice rather than a revolutionary change. Kent associates this increasing social acceptability of the medium with a loss of its earlier revolutionary potential – hence it is used in *Voodoo pilchard* as a symbol of a compromised art form whose real radical potential has shifted elsewhere. The potential for a politically subversive art form is associated in the novel not with the integrated professionalism of tattooing but with the naïve street art of graffiti.

Thorsten Botz-Bornstein has suggested that graffiti is a more subversive practice than tattooing because it permits communication 'not only between members of a community but also within urban spaces in general' (Botz-Bornstein 2012: 59). The capacity of graffiti to cross over boundaries between different kinds of urban space has the effect that it poses a challenging philosophical question about where private property begins and ends, and where public spaces begin. Since private property is the bedrock of capitalist ideology, by communicating a challenge to the notion of private ownership in an art form that literally cuts across boundaries between private and public, graffiti therefore has the potential to be activated as a revolutionary art form in opposition to the dominant economic and political ideology. This means that if used in such a way, the practice of graffiti is not merely a form of art for art's sake, it is 'not merely tattoos drawn on walls attempting to draw attention to the materiality of the body they occupy' (*ibid.*). Rather, graffiti could be a form of communication deeply bound up with the circulation and contestation of social meanings and values and hence a form of art capable of maintaining a critical stance with regard to the social order.[7] This is how Hall portrayed tattooing in the 1920s in *The electric Michelangelo* but it is a radical potential that Kent portrays as having been compromised through the incorporation into the consumerist and bourgeois mainstream in the twenty-first century in *Voodoo pilchard*. The overall findings of this chapter are necessarily provisional and point the way toward the need for further research using the methods of literary interpretation, historical analysis and sociological inquiry. Such extended research would be necessary, for example, to establish whether or not the practice of tattooing was ever as genuinely revolutionary as Hall's portrayal of it in the 1920s in *The electric Michelangelo*; or to evaluate the accuracy of Kent's assumption in *Voodoo pilchard* that tattooing today has become integrated to the dominant forms of consumerist culture and hence to the dominant ideology of capitalist society. However, the overall tendency associates tattooing with a politically engaged counter-culture in the 1920s and for this radical emancipatory agenda to have become decoupled from the medium in the early years of the twentieth century as tattooing itself receives an increasing level of cultural consecration.

NOTES

1 Porter's examples of the 'social' crime novel are Charles Dickens's *Oliver Twist* (1837) and Victor Hugo's *Last day of a condemned man* (1829). His example of the more aestheticised variety of crime writing is Thomas De Quincey's *On murder considered as one of the fine arts* (1827) (see Porter 1981: 22).
2 This is true of Edgar Allan Poe's C. Auguste Dupin and Arthur Conan Doyle's Sherlock Holmes.
3 The colours of this beating (black, red and yellow) and the colours of the infection (green and brown) mirror the tattooists' five-colour palette. Riley's trade, so intertwined with his life, is here used as a motif of his beating and signals his descent towards death.
4 Hall weaves the motif of eyes throughout the text (it appears in the opening sentence when Cy describes ways of seeing and in the first descriptions of Riley and Grace). The stylised eye as a tattoo is examined by Spencer Jordan (Chapter 2), and Caroline Jones and Katharine Cox (Chapter 10) in this collection.
5 Grace's transformation might be read purely as that of the muse of an artist (much as Claudia's decoration by her partner Arturas), but her agency and political choice of design elevate her to fellow artist and radical.
6 In the same way, Malcolm Pryce's Aberystwyth novels are also comedic parodies of the genre. In *The unbearable lightness of being in Aberystwyth* (2009) for example, Pryce parodies that assumption that tattoos are a marker of criminal or deviant behaviour (see 2009: 54, 59, 60, 75).
7 A full interrogation of Botz-Bornstein's claim for the efficacy of graffiti as a politically transgressive form of art and communication falls outside the scope of this chapter.

BIBLIOGRAPHY

Arp, Robert (ed.) (2012), *Tattoos – philosophy for everyone: I ink, therefore I am* (Chichester: John Wiley).
Becker, Howard (ed.) (2008), *Art worlds* (London: University of California Press).
Borowitz, Albert (2002), *Blood & ink: An international guide to fact-based crime literature* (Kent: Kent State University Press).
Botz-Bornstein, Thorsten (2012), 'Female tattoos and graffiti', in R. Arp (ed.) (2012), pp. 53–64.
Browne, Ray B. and Lawrence A. Kreiser (2000), *The detective as historian: History and art in historical crime fiction* (Bowling Green: Bowling Green State University Popular Press).
Cloake, Tony (2014), *Taking our ball back: English football's cultural wars* (n.p.: CreateSpace Independent Publishing).

Friedman, Ellen G. (1989), 'A conversation with Kathy Acker', *The review of contemporary fiction*, 9.3 (Fall). Available: http://www.dalkeyarchive.com/a-conversation-with-kathy-acker-by-ellen-g-friedman/ [accessed 4 December 2018].

Gregoriou, Christiania (2007), *Deviance in contemporary crime fiction* (New York: Palgrave Macmillan).

Hall, Sarah (2004), *The electric Michelangelo* (London: Faber).

Harris, John (2003), *The last party: Britpop, Blair and the demise of English rock* (London: Fourth Estate).

Johnsen, Rosemary E. (2006), *Contemporary feminist historical crime fiction* (New York: Palgrave Macmillan).

Kent, Alan (2010), *Voodoo pilchard* (Wellington: Ryelands).

Knight, Stephen (1995), 'Regional crime squads: Location and dislocation in the British mystery', in I. A. Bell (ed.), *Peripheral visions: Images of nationhood in contemporary British fiction* (Cardiff: University of Wales Press).

— (2004), *Crime fiction since 1800: Detection, death, diversity* (Basingstoke: Palgrave Macmillan).

— (2012), *The mysteries of the cities: Urban crime fiction in the nineteenth century* (London: McFarland).

Lentricchia, Frank (2003), *Crimes of art and terror* (Chicago: University of Chicago Press).

Lewis, Helen (2013), 'Will a tattoo ever hang in the Louvre?' *New statesman*, 142: 5155 (April), 32–37.

Lodder, Matt (2011), 'The myths of modern primitivism', *European journal of American culture*, 30:2, 99–111.

Michaud, Nicholas (2012), 'Are tattoos art?', in R. Arp (ed.) (2012), pp. 29–37.

Porter, Dennis (1981), *The pursuit of crime: Art and ideology in detective fiction* (London: Yale University Press).

Pryce, Malcolm (2009), *The unbearable lightness of being in Aberystwyth* (London: Bloomsbury).

Roberts, Derek (2012), 'Secret ink: Tattoo's place in contemporary American culture', *Journal of American culture*, 35:2 (June), 153–65.

Rzepka, Charles J. (2005), *Detective fiction* (Cambridge: Polity).

Scaggs, John (2005), *Crime fiction* (London: Routledge New Critical Idiom).

Silk, Michael, David Andrews and Cheryl Cole (2005), *Sport and corporate nationalisms* (Oxford: Berg).

Williams, Raymond (1977), *Marxism and literature* (Oxford: Oxford University Press).

5

Mis-reading *moko*: Cross-cultural tattooing in Caryl Férey's New Zealand crime fiction

Ellen Carter

TRADITIONAL POLYNESIAN AND NEW ZEALAND MAORI TATTOOING

This chapter introduces traditional New Zealand Maori tattooing then shows how a cultural outsider crime writer, French author Caryl Férey, appropriates and misreads the practice of Maori facial tattooing, or *moko*, in his two novels set in New Zealand: *Haka* (1998, without English translation to 2018) and *Utu* (2004, English translation 2011a). The effect of this misrepresentation is to privilege a cultural outsider readership, which leads the author to negate the complexity, ancestry and uniqueness of Maori *moko*.

Although estimates vary, New Zealand was the last major land mass to be peopled in about 800 CE. New Zealand's orginal human inhabitants arrived by canoe from islands in East Polynesia,[1] including the Society and Marquesas Islands, which are today part of French Polynesia. They brought with them the practice and varieties of tattooing from the archipelago. Polynesian tattooing was first seen in Europe in 1769 when native Polynesian Ahu-toru was brought from Tahiti to France by Louis-Antoine de Bougainville (Hemming 2006: 79), then in 1774 when Omai was taken from Raiatea to Britain by James Cook (Guest 2000: 83).[2] Both Polynesians were presented in society circles and had their likeness captured by painters such as Sir Joshua Reynolds, whose portrait of Omai 'inscribes its object with an acultural illegibility, isolated from any coherence of origin' (*ibid.*: 84). This cross-cultural exchange also marked European languages; from the Tahitian word 'tatau' stems both the English 'tattoo' (DeMello 2000: 45) and French 'tatouer'.

Facial tattoos on New Zealand Maori, a Polynesian people, are known as *moko*. *Moko* images transferred to Europe indirectly through drawings, paintings and books, including Major-General Horatio Robley's influential work *Moko or Maori tattooing*, first published in 1896. This book contains drawings and explanations gathered in 1864–65 by the author while he was fighting for the British Crown in the New Zealand wars (Phillipps 1966). Maori facial tattoos also transferred directly to Europe through collections of *toi moko* (preserved, tattooed heads), a curative process explained by Robley, who amassed his own collection, as a Maori 'acknowledgement of the nobility of its owner' (1987: 131). *Toi moko* were exchanged for goods such as muskets until the trade was officially banned in 1831, although such heads were still to be had until 1870 (Orchiston 1967: 297). The New Zealand Government is now negotiating to have all *koiwi tangata* (ancestral remains) held by museums outside New Zealand returned to Maori care (Hole 2007: 5). Since 2004, repatriations have come from fifty institutions (Aranui 2013: 4), including the British Museum (Besterman 2007) and Quai Branly, the ethnographic museum in Paris (Mortaigne 2011).[3]

Each *moko* is unique and reflects the hereditary and/or earned rank of its wearer, with different patterns for men and for women (Te Riria and Simmons 1999: 17, 22, 65). Indeed, the single term *moko* obscures the fact that different parts of the face are reserved for information about different aspects of heritage and achievement, such as tribal identification, parental lineage and work role (*ibid.*: 23–27). Borrowing Ferdinand Saussure's terms, a *moko* is a sign, with its pattern being the 'signifier' encoding the 'signified' concept that is the wearer's lineage and status, information that only cultural insiders are capable of fully decoding. If a *moko* is a sign, then the set of rules by which a certain pattern in a given facial area connotes a specific piece of information becomes the 'code' or interpretive framework for *moko* (Chandler 1994).

In the nineteenth century, it was considered bad manners for Maori to fail to identify high-ranking individuals from their *moko* (Te Riria and Simmons 1999: 75), which perhaps indicates that this process of decoding was not always straightforward for cultural insiders. When signing with the British Crown the 1840 Treaty of Waitangi – considered as New Zealand's founding document – rather than signing their names some Maori chiefs drew their *moko* (Te Awekotuku and Nikora 2010: 56), attesting both to the singularity of its design and to the respect for what it symbolises. While the practice had been on the wane, a resurgence of interest since the 1990s has seen an increasing number of Maori choosing to wear *moko* (Nikora *et al.* 2007: 481). This resurgence is due in part to a Maori renaissance born out of renewed demands for recognition of *te reo* (Maori language) as well as redressing ancient political wrongs, but it also reflects the acceptance of tattooing in contemporary New Zealand society among both Maori and non-Maori.[4]

TATTOOS IN CARYL FÉREY'S CRIME FICTION

Caryl Férey (b. 1967) is a bestselling French crime writer known for his contemporary novels in a variety of exotic locations. These locations include South Africa in *Zulu* (2008b, English translation 2010), Argentina in *Mapuche* (2012a, English translation 2013b) and two novels set in New Zealand, a country Férey has visited twice for a total of five months. In all four novels, Férey depicts the contemporary situation of indigenous peoples in countries formerly colonised by European powers through the medium of crime fiction written for a readership constituted predominately of cultural outsiders.

In his New Zealand crime fiction, Férey uses traditional tattooing in three ways: to develop the plot, to deepen characterisation and to establish the cultural background against which his intrigue plays out. In engraving deviance on faces, Férey mines a crime fiction trope that harks back to Sherlock Holmes and other early practitioners who used visual clues to identify criminals (Kustritz 2012). This references Cesare Lombroso's nineteenth-century theories of anthropological criminology, where he linked crime with inherited – often visible – characteristics (Lombroso-Ferrero 1972). Although the presence of *moko* on a body is not genetically determined, it could be argued that a biological link pertains because wearing an authentic *moko* presupposes Maori ancestry.

However, in Férey's first New Zealand novel, *Haka* (2003), tattoos only fulfil the first of these functions in relation to plot. The tattoo plays a small but important role in permitting half-Maori policeman Jack Fitzgerald to connect the murder of a Polynesian woman to a mysterious tattooed Maori cannibal sect. Férey often introduces mixed race characters through which he can explore questions of postcolonial cultural identity. However, the meaning of the ink that adorns the sect members remains unclear; when Fitzgerald tracks down the person who inked these tattoos, the artist claims not to know the designs' import beyond signifying some 'Maori rite' (2003: 290) and the term *moko* is not used. This vagueness reflects Férey's own lack of cultural knowledge at the point he wrote *Haka*, a gap brought home to him when he won a literary prize organised by a factory in France where a worker asked him: '[i]f *Haka* were transposed to France and the word "Maori" replaced by Arab, don't you think your novel could be accused of being racist?' (Férey 2013a: 143; my translation). Significantly, it is in Férey's own French cultural milieu that this lack of understanding is made evident to him. Férey explained that his knowledge of Maori culture was weak when he wrote *Haka* because: 'the first time I went to New Zealand I met very few Maori, only bouncers in bars and night clubs and a few in bars' (personal communication, 8 November 2011). Therefore, Férey does not use Jack Fitzgerald's liminal status to explore hybrid ideas of identity and meaning; rather, it highlights the outsider status of both character and author.

Férey and his readers are likely to be aware of Polynesian tattooing because of 'tribal', 'primitive' (DeMello 2000) or 'neo-tribal' (Sanders 1989:20), tattoos on All Black rugby players or celebrities such as Robbie Williams, Ben Harper or Mike Tyson (Morrison *et al.* 2005: 723) as well as the work of designer Jean-Paul Gaultier, who traced *moko* on male models in *Vogue* magazine (Lai 2010: 25–26). Another potential source of prior exposure to Maori tattooing for French readers is Jules Verne's *Les enfants du Capitaine Grant* (1868; published in English 1911), which Férey has noted as a childhood influence (as cited in Piquet 2011). In this novel a French geographer 'Jacques Paganel, during his three days'[5] captivity among the Maories [*sic*], had been tattooed from the feet to the shoulders, and he bore on his chest a heraldic kiwi with outspread wings, which was biting at his heart' (Verne 1911: 439).[6] It might be more accurate to say that Verne's character is inscribed by *kirituhi* (a writing on the skin), as his tattooing does not follow the tribal *moko* described elsewhere in the novel. It is significant to note that while this tattooing does not extend above his shoulders, he refuses to return to France as he fears ridicule. The prevalence of such references in popular culture makes it easier for Férey to introduce French readers to the idea of full facial tattoos, a concept which may have seemed outlandish, and possibly a figment of the author's cultural outsider imagination, were the novel set outside New Zealand.

Before publishing his second New Zealand novel, *Utu* (2008a), Férey deepened his cultural knowledge through reading books by French academics (Férey 2013a: 144) including those cited in *Utu*'s bibliography (2008a: 469). He also returned to New Zealand for two months on a Stendhal scholarship awarded by the French Foreign Ministry. During this visit, he spent time at local museums as well as visiting a *marae* (a Maori meeting place) where he talked to the chief. This extra time and research results in a more developed use of tattooing in his next novel, but significant issues remain.

In *Utu*, white policeman Paul Osborne inherits *Haka*'s investigation after Fitzgerald's suicide and tracks the same sect. Simultaneously, Osborne is trying to reconnect with his childhood love, the half-Maori Hana Witkaire, whose search to reconnect with her Maori identity sees her fall into the sect's clutches. As in *Haka*, Férey uses tattoos to develop *Utu*'s plot. In tracking down three brothers inked with facial tattoos that Férey now terms *moko*, *Utu*'s Osborne photographs a man with the same *moko* then canvasses experts who lead him to the artist before identifying the tattoos using the internet, which democratises access to this insider cultural knowledge:

> After a slow, laborious search, Osborne at last came across an engraving dating from the nineteenth century, the portrait of a Maori chief sporting the same *mokos*.[7] Exactly the same. They belonged to the Hauhau movement, started by

> the fanatical self-styled prophet Te Ua Haumene, whose followers recycled the language of the Biblical Apocalypse to arouse the warlike passions of the Maoris. These *mokos*, for all their refinement, were war tattoos. (2011a: 302)

Férey's choice to replicate the tattoos of Te Ua Haumene (?–1866), real-life leader of an activist Maori Christian community (Head 2010), is strange and again suggests a lack of cultural knowledge. Haumene's Christianity is diametrically opposed to the beliefs Férey gives his Hauhau sect members in his two novels, specifically the fictional sect's revivifying of ancient beliefs and pre-Christian gods (Férey 2003: 324). There are other non-Christian, *moko*-wearing representatives of nineteenth-century Maori resistance to European settlement Férey could have chosen which would be more suitable, notably Te Rauparaha (?–1849), war leader of the Ngati Toa tribe (Oliver 2014) and author of the 'Ka mate' *haka* (war dance) performed by New Zealand's All Black rugby team before test matches.

Leaving aside the appropriateness of his model, Férey's choice poses a larger question: why did he give all members of this murderous gang the same *moko* when, as we saw, each *moko* is unique and represents the lineage of its wearer? There are several layers of possible explanations here. First, that Férey was unaware of the individual nature of each *moko*. Second, that he was aware yet chose to ascribe identical *moko* as a token of gang initiation and communal identity in order to facilitate his crime fiction plot. Third, that he was aware yet chose identical *moko* to facilitate immersion of his cultural outsider readership in this cultural depiction. I reject a fourth possibility – that Férey did so to differentiate between Maori and non-Maori characters – because in interviews, he stresses his wish to avoid Manichean divides.

Whatever his motivation, in Férey's hands, *Utu*'s 'gang' *moko* tells Osborne and cultural outsider readers that the wearer belongs to the Hauhau sect and thus is not a member of 'normal' society. This dichotomy is far stronger than that which operates in New Zealand reality, where *moko* invoke belief in a cultural and spiritual practice and the establishment, rather than rejection, of societal norms. For cultural outsider readers, *moko* significance may also be diluted by the increasing ease of removing unwanted tattoos by laser treatments, which has contributed to moving tattooing from a subculture to more mainstream acceptance.

If tattoos figure prominently in the crime fiction plots of both *Haka* and *Utu*, in the latter novel Férey also uses tattoos to establish the cultural background against which his intrigue is set. For example, he explains to readers that rather than using ink, traditional Maori tattooing uses charcoal, which is applied to the skin by implements fashioned from bone. This information answers a plot point left unresolved at the ending of *Haka*: why the sect removed a femur from each victim, bones that were then fashioned into tattooing chisels (Férey 2011a: 343).

In *Utu*, Férey also uses tattooing in a third manner: to develop character-isation. He twice describes the traditional tattooing process through Hana Witkaire's eyes. She first watches someone else being tattooed:

> his thumb and index finger parting the skin like a pincer, he dug the chisel into the other man's cheek. A black liquid took root in the flesh, overflowed from the cut, flooding the motionless face of Zinzan Bee.
>
> Concentrating on his task, the tattooist wiped off the surplus with a cotton swab and completed the curve all the way up to the corners of the eyes.
>
> Hana watched him, impressed. The line was sure and regular, the designs perfectly symmetrical. He carefully wiped the face and straightened up, pleased with his work. The *moko* was finished [...] At last, he turned back toward Zinzan Bee's tattooed face. All that still remained to be done was to sew up the lips. (*ibid.*: 292–93)

Although Férey hints via the black, not red, liquid flowing over the skin, it is only the final sentence that shocks the reader into realising this is a description of post-mortem tattooing on a preserved head, the practice of *toi moko*. Originally, *toi moko* served two functions: in peacetime they were reminders of honoured ancestors, while during intertribal wars they became trophies to be captured and displayed then exchanged during parley (Palmer and Tano 2004: 3). With the arrival of Europeans, *toi moko* became commercialised as exchange goods, particularly for muskets. To meet this sudden increase in demand, the heads of slaves received the treatment previously reserved for elders. Since the designs hurriedly inked onto these lower-ranked individuals, to meet demand from cultural outsiders incapable of reading this code, did not reflect the wearer's heritage, this broke the link between the tattoo and identity.

Férey's introduction of *toi moko* in part respects the original form of this practice since this head belongs to a venerated elder: the former sect leader killed by Fitzgerald in *Haka* (Férey 2003: 337). However, since Bee wears the same *moko* as all other sect members, the designs inked on his face reflect not his ancestry but that of Te Ua Haumene (see above). Moreover, it is only fifty pages further into *Utu* that Férey explains *toi moko* (using the term *mokomokai*) for cultural outsider readers:

> *Mokos* spiralled out from the nose, thin complicated curves that covered almost the whole of the face. The eye sockets were empty, horribly empty, and the nose cut off. The lips had also been sewed up, in accordance with the old custom [...] *Mokomokai* was an old warrior practice. Like other indigenous peoples, to possess the head of an enemy chief or preserve the head of one's own grandfather was a mark of power and respect. The head was an object of worship that enhanced one's *mana*. Thus tattoed [*sic*] and prepared—eyeballs removed, nose cut off and lips sewed up—the *mokomokai* became *tapu*, sacred, a treatment slaves did not enjoy. With the arrival of the Europeans, the trade in heads had flourished—they were much in demand, not only from sailors, but from museums in the Old

World—until the British government banned this barbarous practice. (Férey
2011a: 348–49)

In this passage, Férey acknowledges the role Europeans played in developing
this 'flourishing' trade but not that many traded heads were produced to order
by sacrificing slaves.

Between the introduction and explanation of *toi moko* in *Utu*, readers receive
the tattooing process directly as Férey interweaves Hana's thoughts about her
tribe and the separatist sect with a description of the physical process she
endures as she herself is tattooed:

> The bone pierced the skin of her lips, then traced a groove toward the right-hand
> corner of her mouth [...] The bone was tearing her skin. It hurt – it hurt a lot.
> Tears rolled down her cheeks, mingling with the black liquid that would leave an
> indelible mark on her face. The chisel cut into her flesh and moved toward her chin
> [...] Hana shuddered when she saw her face. A black line now ran along her upper
> lip. On her chin, the mark of the Tainui tribe. Tears clung to her cheeks. Tears of
> blood. (*ibid.*: 324–26)

Hana is the only character for whom Férey fully explores the cultural significance of tattooing by showing her before, during and after the act of receiving
a tattoo. He is culturally correct to highlight the effect on Hana of the tattooing
process more than its product. Alfred Gell notes a key difference between
Western and Polynesian notions of tattooing: the former prioritises the result,
whereas for Polynesian peoples, 'tattooing was not a form of graphic art, but
only an abiding trace which testified to the occurrence of socially salient
blood-letting transactions' (1993: 306). However, when Osborne – who has
pursued Hana through the entire novel, their past being related in flashbacks
– catches up with her in the final scene, moments before both are blown to
smithereens, he sees for the first time 'the black tattoos adorning her beautiful
lips' (Férey 2011a: 379) and dwells on their decorative rather than symbolic
value, despite knowing she has joined the Hauhau sect. Once more, it is unclear
whether this lack of cultural understanding is Férey's own or whether he know-
ingly ascribes it to his white policeman in order to underline the cultural gap
between Osborne and Hana, the half-Maori object of his obsession.

**BEYOND TEXTUAL TATTOOING:
FÉREY'S PARATEXTUAL *MOKO***

Although Férey writes full-time, he averages four years to produce each of his
major novels. In between, he explores similar themes in other genres, often
reusing material. For example, *Utu* has a Maori chief, named Pita Witkaire,
who also appears in a children's crime fiction book, *La derniére danse des
Maoris* (2007), and a two-volume graphic crime novel: *Maori tome 1: La voie*

humaine (2013c) and *Maori tome 2: Keri* (2014). Férey based this character on a real person: Pita Sharples, who was New Zealand's Minister for Maori Affairs from 2008 to 2014 and whom Férey met during his second visit to New Zealand (Férey 2013a: 147). While Sharples himself does not wear a permanent *moko*, for certain ceremonial events he has a temporary facial tattoo applied (Nelson 2013). In the children's book and the graphic novels, Pita Witkaire has a *moko*, but he is not tattooed in *Utu*, possibly because it would have interfered with the '*moko* equals gang' plot device.

In Férey's latest work, facial *moko* tattooing assumes an overtly political role. In the second volume of the graphic novel a *moko* is layered onto a contemporary Western symbol of anti-government and anti-establishment protest: the Guy Fawkes mask from the *V for vendetta* graphic novel (Moore and Lloyd 2005) and film adaptation (McTeigue 2006); a mask that was worn by activists during the 2011–12 Occupy movement. When drawing the videoed gang rape of the daughter of Pita Witkaire – who is standing for parliamentary election on a humanist platform advocating the rejection of capitalism – Férey's illustrator, Giuseppe Camuncoli, hides her three rapists behind the mask's smile and moustache and adds *moko* tracing (Férey 2014: 8). This mixing of symbols is culturally and political potent since a white businessman ordered the rape and orchestrated the video's diffusion in order to undermine Witkaire's chances of becoming Prime Minister.

That tattoos feature in all five incarnations of Férey's crime writing set in New Zealand suggests that he regards tattooing, particularly of the face, as a marked cultural practice that lends cultural authenticity. As well as that, he is aware of the link between detective–crime novels and tattooing, discussed in other chapters of this volume. The textual significance of tattooing is accentuated by the paratextual cover images chosen by publishers. Of the eleven editions – nine in French, one in American English and one in Italian – only the earliest book does not involve depictions of Maori tattoos. While *Haka*'s initial 1998 publication displays a white woman's bloody hand lying on sand, *Haka*'s 2003 reissue by mass-market French crime fiction publisher, *Folio policier*, has a photograph of a man's tattooed back. This moves the marketing focus from a standard crime fiction trope of a dead woman to focus on the exotic and perhaps hint at the plot significance of tattooing.

Unfortunately, the chosen photograph shows Tahitian rather than New Zealand Maori tattooing, an unintended error according to *Folio policier*'s editor, Julie Maillard (personal communication, 14 December 2011). *Utu* launched with a photograph of a carved Maori statue with *moko* (2004), followed by three editions using photographs of a male face with *moko* (2008a, 2011a, 2012b). *Saga Maorie* (2011b) (an omnibus edition of *Haka* and *Utu*) has a photograph of a carved Maori statue with *moko*. Férey's children's book has appeared under two different covers (2007, 2011c), both featuring drawings of men with *moko*. Finally, placed side by side, the two volumes of Férey's graphic novel form a single image of a man with a traditionally tattooed arm (2013) facing a woman with tattooed hand (2014). This commonality suggests that Férey's publishers share his view that tattoos are iconic symbols of New Zealand culture, at least for cultural outsider readers.

MEANING AND TATTOOS IN CARYL FÉREY'S CRIME FICTION

In her cultural history of the modern tattoo community, anthropologist Margo DeMello notes that most Western tattoo shops have a 'no facial tattoos' policy:

> Facial tattoos are traditionally the mark of a convict. Even without that explicit connection, facial tattoos are extremely stigmatizing in the nontattooed world, and most tattooists do not want to contribute to marking an individual for life as an outcast. (2000: 197n)

That this Western prejudice against facial tattoos as symbolising deviance and or criminality does not pertain in Polynesian cultures[8] offered Férey the chance to demonstrate his acquired cultural knowledge by educating French readers as to this difference. Férey does not take this opportunity. Instead he perpetuates Western stigmas through, for example, Osborne saying of one *moko*-wearing sect member that: 'with those tattoos on his face, I doubt that Tagaloa was ever planning to go back to his job as a door man' (Férey 2011a: 302–03). Moreover, Férey's choice of facial *moko* as the distinguishing feature of his cannibalistic sect simplifies his crime fiction plot because such facial tattoos cannot be disguised by clothing (and a thick layer of foundation would be out of character for murderous sect members). Indeed, it may be sensible for criminals to hide behind (temporary) *moko* because Heather Buttle and Julie East (2010: 1673) report that curvilinear patterns common to *moko* reduce people's ability to recognise faces, meaning that witnesses to a crime would find it harder to pick perpetrators out of a line-up.[9]

Thus, in *Utu*, Férey offers cultural outsider readers the illusion that he is initiating them into a privileged group capable of achieving this decoding. Férey's perhaps deliberate misrepresentation of *moko* – having all gang members sport the same design, running counter to the current individualistic trend for custom motifs and idiosyncratic placement (Negrin 2008: 101) – seems credible to outsider readers who have been exposed to just enough examples of Maori and or Polynesian tattooing to be able to distinguish it from other forms.

While researching from inside the modern (American) tattoo community, anthropologist DeMello interviewed Leo Zulueta, a Hawaiian tattoo artist of Filipino descent and 'the man most responsible for the mainstream popularity of tribal tattooing' (2000: 86). Zulueta defended his appropriation of 'tribal' designs, saying: 'I know that in some countries like New Zealand, that would be horribly disrespectful to take a tribal pattern from the Maori and try to reproduce it today [...] But here in the West [*sic*] we live in such a cultural wasteland such that people tend to gravitate toward things from the past' (qtd DeMello 2000: 88). Similarly, for DeMello, choosing a 'modern primitive' tattoo: 'implies a critique of contemporary Western society, which is seen as alienating, repressive and technocratic and that lacks ritual, myth, or symbol', whereby 'participants feel that they are aligning themselves with societies and worldviews that are more pure, authentic, and spiritually advanced than the traditional Western outlook' (2000: 175).

Therefore, from an assumption that outsider readers can distinguish Polynesian-style tattooing, it is not much of a stretch for them to believe that there must be more similarity than difference between two examples of such tattooing, and a further small step to accepting that 'similar' can become 'identical' in *Utu*.

Analysing this through Saussure's lens suggests that Férey writes Osborne as uninitiated into the *moko* code system, despite Férey intending the Osborne character to act as a guide initiating outsider readers into Maori culture (personal communication, 8 November 2011) and designating him as the Auckland police force's 'Maori specialist' (Férey 2011a: 31). During *Utu*, Osborne only learns (thanks to the internet) to recognise the signifier, the physical manifestation of *moko*, not to interpret the signified concept based on the underlying code. This could be seen as an example of contemporary culture's 'undercoded' body modification experienced by the cultural outsider whereby personal symbols become blurred, mostly 'stripped of their meanings, as they are pastiched together in unexpected combinations' (Negrin 2008: 10). For Osborne, as for Férey and his cultural outsider readers, recognition without understanding is sufficient to solve the novel's mystery; or, rather, to solve the first level of the mystery. Osborne cracks the puzzle by recognising *moko* signifiers in order to identify 'who' the wearers are. However, he fails to pierce the mystery of *who* are they, in other words the heritage and personal history that should be encoded in individual *moko*.

Moreover, in *Utu* Férey does not give readers the tools to interpret *moko* themselves because he makes only vague mention of grooves, lines and curves (2011a: 324–26, 348–49). Nonetheless if, in a written text, it would have been difficult for Férey to help readers learn to read the visual language of traditional Maori tattooing, at least he could have taught them that there is a language there to be read by initiates. But by having Osborne solve *Utu*'s puzzle through the insight that members of the same gang wear the same *moko*, Férey gives readers the illusion they can understand *moko*.

CONCLUSION

When traditional Maori tattooing appears in fiction, it is often used to comment on (post)colonial attitudes (Beeler 2006: 130). An example of fictional traditional Maori tattooing occurs in the film *Utu* (Murphy and Aberdein, 1983, unrelated to Férey's novel). Set in 1870s New Zealand, the main character receives a *moko* that 'serves as a reminder of the other Maori who perished at the hands of the colonial violence and as a reflection of his resistance to the image of the non-tattooed face that characterizes the image of the white colonizers' (*ibid.*: 149). However, in the hands of a cultural outsider crime writer the symbolism of *moko* facial tattooing can become muddied.

In analysing Férey's treatment of tattoos in his crime fiction, this chapter has identified a tension in his writing between his professed sympathy for the contemporary situation of indigenous peoples in formerly colonised countries and his writing crime fiction marketed at a cultural outsider audience. This tension is nowhere more apparent than in the prominence he accords in his New Zealand novels to tattooing in general and to *moko* in particular. The *moko*'s location on the face simplifies Osborne's crime solving in *Utu* and makes *moko* powerful yet simplistic, undercoded signifiers for cultural outsider readers.

Tattoos are signs of belonging and exclusion, but they operate differently on each side of the non/tattooed divide, and this signalling is redoubled if the tattoo proclaims cultural affiliation because it overlays an insider/outsider dichotomy. Whereas the first reaction of a cultural outsider reader confronted by a non-fictional *moko* may be to fear aggression through the designs' emphasis on facial expression (McNeill 1998: 2), an insider initiated into the pertinent code can learn about the individual since, as American comedian Jimmy Kimmel put it, wearing a *moko* is 'like Facebook on your face' (2013). Thus, the language of tattooing is a code system able to be fully interpreted only by the initiated. Being able to read personal history in designs is not limited to traditional tattooing. Individuals tattooed outside tightly codified systems, such as that of New Zealand Maori, are free to combine images from different sources. Hence only the tattooed person will be able to read and understand the full story, although others may be able to piece together parts.

Férey's co-option of New Zealand Maori tattooing to lend *Haka* and *Utu* cultural credibility is only one among several ways in which he seeks to borrow authenticity (Carter and Walker-Morrison 2012). However, his use of tattooing is both the most powerful and the most misused of these techniques. Powerful because it evokes in cultural outsiders a version of New Zealand shown in tourist brochures, during rugby matches and on the skin of global celebrities. Misused because by claiming a single design per gang Férey negates centuries of insider cultural understanding.

NOTES

1 See in particular D. G. Sutton (1994: 251) for a discussion of these visitors to, and inhabitants of, New Zealand.

2 See Harriet Guest's (2000) work on eighteenth-century tattooing, art and exoticism.

3 The Universities of Aberdeen, Birmingham and Oxford have received recent publicity regarding their *toi moko* collections. Aberdeen and Birmingham Universities have actively looked to repatriate these human remains, while Oxford University continues to exhibit some specimens as part of the Pitt Rivers Museum. For press coverage see, for example: www.bbc.co.uk/news/uk-england-birmingham-24939696. Moreover, Jeffery Deaver includes such a head in a recent crime novel; see Kate Watson and Rebekah Humphreys in this collection (Chapter 7).

4 According to market research, 19 per cent of New Zealanders over 18 have been tattooed, which is one of the highest rates in the world; the figure climbs to 47 per cent for Maori and Pacific Islanders resident in New Zealand (UMR Research 2009).

5 In reality, traditional tattooing takes much longer, with one Maori chief reporting his *moko* took two weeks to complete (Cowan 1921: 242).

6 Verne may have got this idea from Englishman John Rutherford, who worked at fairgrounds displaying a *moko* and full-body tattoo he declared to have received after being captured by Maori in 1816. His claims of enforced tattooing while a prisoner in New Zealand were debunked in 1891 when it was shown that his body tattoos were Tahitian and Fijian (Oettermann in Caplan (ed.) 2000: 198–99, 295n).

7 Both Férey and his English translator use '*mokos*' as the plural of *moko*. However, the Maori language does not inflect noun plurals, a practice that has been adopted by New Zealand English for Maori loanwords (Deverson 1991: 22). Hence, this chapter uses *moko* as both a singular and plural noun.

8 New Zealand's Human Rights Commission (2010) offers advice for *moko* wearers and has mediated in several employment-related complaints (Nikora *et al.* 2007: 480).

9 A temporary *moko* has been used elsewhere as a crime fictional disguise. In episode five of the first season of the London-set television series, *Luther* (2010–13), Bristol-born, Wellington-resident scriptwriter Neil Cross (2010) disguises a kidnapper behind a drawn-on *moko*. This *moko* was so inauthentic that one reviewer, Mark Pilkington, suggested Mike Tyson as its inspiration (Pilkington 2010).

BIBLIOGRAPHY

Aranui, Amber Kiri (2013), *Kōiwi tangata report: Te Taiwhenua o Waimarāma, Kōiwi tangata provenanced to Waimarāma* (Wellington: Te Papa Tongarewa).

Beeler, Karin (2006), *Tattoos, desire and violence: Marks of resistance in literature, film and television* (Jefferson: McFarland).

Besterman, Tristram (2007), *Report to the Board of trustees of the British museum: Request from Te Papa Tongarewa for the return of sixteen Māori kōiwi tangata to New Zealand*. Available: www.britishmuseum.org/pdf/00%2022%20Tristram%20 Besterman%20report%20dated%20April%2007.pdf [accessed 1 March 2017].

Buttle, H. and J. East (2010), 'Traditional facial tattoos disrupt face recognition', *Perception*, 39, 1672–47. Available: http://doi.org/10.1068/p6790 [accessed 1 March 2017].

Carter, Ellen (2014), 'Imagining place: An empirical study of how cultural outsiders and insiders receive fictional representations of place in Caryl Férey's *Utu*', *Imaginations*, 5:1, 67–80.

— and Deborah Walker-Morrison (2012), 'Cannibalistic Māori behead Rupert Murdoch: (Mis)representations of antipodean otherness in Caryl Férey's Māori thrillers', in J. Anderson, C. Miranda and B. Pezzotti (eds) (2012), *The foreign in international crime writing: Transcultural representations* (London: Continuum), pp. 9–21.

Chandler, Daniel (1994), 'Semiotics for beginners'. Available: http://www.aber.ac.uk/media/Documents/S4B/semiotic.html [accessed 21 June 2017].

Cowan, James (1921), 'Maori tattooing survivals. Some notes on moko', *The journal of the Polynesian society*, 30:4, 241–45.

DeMello, Margo (2000), *Bodies of inscription: A cultural history of the modern tattoo community* (Durham: Duke University Press).

Deverson, T. (1991), 'New Zealand English lexis: The Maori dimension', *English today*, 7:2, 18–25. Available: http://doi.org/10.1017/S0266078400005496 [accessed 1 March 2017].

Férey, Caryl (2003), *Haka* (Paris: Gallimard).

— (2007), *La derniére danse des Maoris: French edition* (n.p.: Syros).

— (2010), *Zulu: English edition* [2008b], trans. H. Curtis (New York: Europa).

— (2011a), *Utu*, trans. H. Curtis (New York: Europa).

— (2011b), *Saga Maorie: French edition* [an omnibus edition of *Haka* and *Utu*] (n.p.: Folio Policier).

— (2013a) *Comment devenir écrivain quand on vient de la grande plouquerie internationale* (Paris: Éditions du Seuil).

— (2013b), *Mapuche: English edition*, trans. S. Rendall (New York: Europa).

— and Giuseppe Camuncoli (2013c), *Maori tome 1: La voie humaine: French edition* (Belgium: Ankama).

— and Giuseppe Camuncoli (2014). *Maori tome 2: Keri: French edition* (Belgium: Ankama).

Gell, Alfred (1993), *Wrapping in images: Tattooing in Polynesia* (Oxford: Clarendon Press).

Guest, Harriet (2000), 'Curiously marked: Tattooing and gender difference in eighteenth-century British perceptions of the South Pacific', in J. Caplan (ed.) (2000), *Written on the body: The tattoo in European and American history* (Princeton: Princeton University Press), pp. 83–101.

Head, Lyndsay (2010), 'Te Ua Haumene – biography', *Te Ara: The encyclopedia of New Zealand* (22 December). Available: https://teara.govt.nz/en/biographies/1t79/te-ua-haumene/media [accessed 17 Decemeber 2018].

Hemming, Christine (2006), 'Nine days in Nouvelle-Cythère: The origins of French artwork in the Pacific', in G. M. Cropp (ed.), *Pacific journeys: Essays in honour of John Dunmore* (Wellington: Victoria University Press), pp. 70–81.

Hole, Brian (2007), 'Playthings for the foe: The repatriation of human remains in New Zealand', *Public Archaeology*, 6:1, 5–27. Available: http://doi.org/10.1179/175355307X202848 [accessed 1 March 2017].

Kimmel, Jimmy (2013), *Interview with Sir Ben Kingsley*. Available: www.youtube.com/watch?v=z0Vobk3wrJU

Kustritz, Anne (2012), 'Born to be bad: Indeterminate sentencing and the ideology of criminal inheritance'. Presented at the Crossroads in cultural studies 9th international conference.

Lai, J. C. (2010), 'Māori culture in the modern world: Its creation, appropriation and trade' (i-call working paper no. ISSN 1664-0144), pp. 1–47. University of Luzern. Available: www.contentupdate.net/uniluadmin/web/unilu/files/i-call_working_paper02_lai.pdf [accessed 4 December 2018].

Lombroso-Ferrero, Gina (1972), *Criminal man according to the classification of Cesare Lombroso* (Montclair: Patterson Smith).

McNeill, Daniel (1998), *The face: A natural history* (Boston: Little Brown).

McTeigue, James (dir.) (2006), *V for vendetta* (n.p.: Warner Bros Pictures).

Moore, Alan and David Lloyd (2005), *V for vendetta* (New York: Vertigo).

Morrison, Toni, Gayatri C. Spivak and Ngahuia Te Awekotuku (2005), 'Guest column: Roundtable on the future of the humanities in a fragmented world', *PMLA*, 120:3, 715–23.

Mortaigne, V. (2011), 'La force vitale des Maori submerge le Quai Branly', *Le Monde* (October 11). Available: www.lemonde.fr/culture/article/2011/10/10/la-force-vitale-des-maori-submerge-le-quai-branly_1585085_3246.html [accessed 1 March 2017].

Murphy, G. and K. Aberdein (1983), *Utu* (New Zealand: Utu Productions/New Zealand Film Commission).

Negrin, Llewellyn (2008), *Appearance and identity: Fashioning the body in postmodernity* (New York: Palgrave Macmillan).

Nelson, J. (2013), *Before they pass away* (Kempen: teNeues).

Nikora, Linda Waimarie, Mohi Rua and Ngahuia Te Awekotuku (2007), 'Renewal and resistance: Moko in contemporary New Zealand', *Journal of community and applied social psychology*, 17, 477–89.

Oliver, Steven (2014), 'Te Rauparaha', *Te Ara: The encyclopedia of New Zealand* (3 July). Available: www.teara.govt.nz/en/biographies/1t74/te-rauparaha [accessed 21 June 2017].

Orchiston, Wayne D. (1967), 'Preserved human heads of the New Zealand Maoris', *Journal of the Polynesian society*, 76: 3, 297–329.

Palmer, Christopher and Mervyn L. Tano (2004), *Mokomokai: Commercialization and desacralization* (Denver: n.p.).

Phillipps, W. J. (1966), 'Robley, Major-General Horatio Gordon', in A. H. McLintock (ed.), *An encyclopaedia of New Zealand, Volume 3* (Wellington: R.E. Owen, Government Printer), n.p. Available: https://teara.govt.nz/en/1966/robley-major-general-horatio-gordon [accessed 13 March 2019].

Pilkington, Mark (2010, 2 June), 'Luther episode 5 review'. Available: www.denofgeek.com/tv/luther/9837/luther-episode-5-review [accessed 4 December 2018].

Piquet, L. (2011), 'Interview with Caryl Férey', France 5.

Robley, Horatio Gordon (1987), *Moko; Or Maori tattooing* (Papakura: Southern Reprints).

Sanders, Clinton R. (1989), *Customizing the body: The art and culture of tattooing* (Philadelphia: Temple University Press).

Sutton, D. G. (1994), 'Conclusion: Origins', in D. G. Sutton (ed.), *The Origins of the first New Zealanders* (Auckland: Auckland University Press), pp. 243–58.

Te Awekotuku, Ngahuia, and Linda Waimarie Nikora (2010), *Mau moko: Le monde du tatouage Maori*, trans. M. Orlando (Papeete: Au Vent des Îles).

Te Riria, Ko, and David R. Simmons (1999), *Moko rangatira: Māori tattoo* (Auckland: Reed).
Verne, Jules (1868), *Les enfants du Capitaine Grant* (Paris: Éditions Hetzel).
— (1911), *In search of the castaways, or the children of Captain Grant*, trans. C. F. Horne (New York: Vincent Parke).

6

Transforming tattoos of the girl with the dragon tattoo

Kerstin Bergman

INTRODUCTION

What is known in the English-speaking world as *The Millennium trilogy*, or *The girl with the dragon tattoo* series, originated as three novels published in Swedish (2005–07), written by Stieg Larsson (1954–2004).[1] One of the series' protagonists, Lisbeth Salander, sports several tattoos, among them one depicting a dragon. This facet was not used in the original Swedish titles of the novels – nor was the phrase 'the girl with the dragon tattoo' found anywhere in the novels or in Larsson's correspondence and notes – but as the novels were translated into English, the marketing focus changed completely.[2] Not only did the female protagonist, Salander, 'the ominously tattooed mystery woman', as Kirsten Mollegaard has described her, receive all the attention but also the titles of the novels were changed to reflect this (2016). In the promotion of the Swedish books the male protagonist, Mikael Blomkvist, was considered equally important. While only the title of the second Swedish novel contained an equivalent of 'the girl who …', this was turned into a catchy formula used in all three English titles. Thereby, Salander became known as 'the girl with the dragon tattoo', something that also shifted the focus from the series' explicitly feminist original marketing, expressed in the Swedish cover and title of the first novel, to Salander as a girl (not a woman) and to her body (as marked by the tattoo).[3] This chapter will explore the use and function of tattoos throughout the four Millennium novels primarily in relation to character description and development, and to gender and identity. The original title of the first novel is *Män som hatar kvinnor*, which literally translates as 'Men who hate women'. Annelie Brännström Öhman aptly describes the title change, into *The girl with the dragon tattoo*, as 'shifting the focus to an objectified image of the woman protagonist's body – thus discounting the analysis of the relation between power, gender, and sexualised violence accentuated by the original title' (2013: 69; my translation).

Larsson's novels are among the world's best-selling books of the early twenty-first century, and they have also been adapted for the screen, first in three Scandinavian films in 2009 (number one directed by Niels Arden Oplev, numbers two and three by Daniel Alfredson), followed by an American remake of the first Scandinavian film in 2011 (directed by David Fincher).[4] Furthermore, there have been two different graphic novel adaptations made of the trilogy and, perhaps more surprising, a new (Swedish) author, David Lagercrantz, was assigned to continue Larsson's work by writing a fourth novel in the series, *The girl in the spider's web* (2016).

TATTOOS AS CHARACTER DESCRIPTION

Before the reader first encounters Salander in *The girl with the dragon tattoo*, she is described by her employer, the middle-aged Dragan Armansky, for whom she works as a researcher. He portrays her as unusual, and after outlining at length her outstanding skills as a researcher, he begins to describe her physical appearance. This is where the reader gets the novel's most extensive account of her tattoos: '[s]he had a wasp tattoo about two centimeters long on her neck, a tattooed loop around the biceps of her left arm and another around her left ankle. On those occasions when she had been wearing a tank top Armansky also saw that she had a dragon tattoo on her left shoulder blade' (Larsson 2009: 35). It is thus made clear that Salander has four reasonably visible tattoos, which to other people is perceived as something characteristic about her. The tattoos are afforded different prominence in the original Swedish and English translations. The back tattoo only multiplies in the English translation, as Mikael Blomkvist 'sneaked a look at the *tattoos* on her back' (Larsson 2009, 348; my emphasis), thus indicating that there are more tattoos than just the dragon tattoo on her back. Later on, as Blomkvist becomes more intimate with her, he can add that she has 'a Chinese symbol on her hip, and a rose on one calf' (Larsson 2009: 392). By contrast, in the Swedish original Blomkvist only peeks at Salander's tattoo, in the singular (Larsson 2005: 368). In both versions of the second novel, however, as Salander removes her wasp tattoo, it is said to be one of nine, so at least two of her tattoos are never accounted for (Larsson 2006, 2010b).

Karin Beeler notes that 'the tattoo often tells its own story which runs counter to the master-narrative presented within a text, thus allowing the bearer to perform an act of resistance or subversion' (Beeler 2006: 3). In Larsson's trilogy, Salander's tattoos thus make it clear to the reader that she is different from the context she finds herself in, and this helps to establish her as the figure of resistance throughout the narrative: she is the main voice speaking out and acting up against the structural and physical violence towards women in Swedish society. Armansky, while describing Salander's physical appearance, also notes that the image of his firm, Milton Security, 'was one of conservative stability' and that 'Salander fitted into this picture about as well as a buffalo at a boat show' (Larsson 2009: 34). Furthermore, he adds that '[s]he looked as though she had just emerged from a week-long orgy with a gang of hard rockers' (*ibid.:* 35). From the start of the series it is made very clear that Salander does not adhere to the norm in the context she is in, and her tattoos are an important part of establishing this fact.

Armansky is fond of Salander and knows that she is an extremely intelligent and capable researcher, but this part of his description of her is still representative of how many (middle-aged) men of the novel view and describe Salander. Most of these men, however, are unaware of her aptitude and judge her solely by her appearance, and it is from these men that a majority of the physical and visual descriptions of Salander in Larsson's novels originate. They tend to underestimate and misjudge her, concluding that she is young and stupid. Much of the middle-aged men's judgement is based on visual attributes like Salander's piercings and tattoos, which they dismiss as juvenile and appalling. They rarely see beyond what first catches their eyes. Even Blomkvist, who knows Salander as intelligent and skillful and who even becomes her friend and lover, concludes after their first meeting that '[s]he had heaven knows how many tattoos and two piercings on her face and maybe in other places. She was weird' (2009: 319). That Salander is described this way, through the eyes of middle-aged men in particular, could be partly ascribed to their age and to the fact that they grew up before what Arnold Rubin has called the 'tattoo renaissance', when tattoos went from being marginal and even stigmatising to becoming commonplace and accepted in the Western world, starting in the 1980s (Rubin 1988).[5] However, that is not the only explanation; there is a critique embedded here of how men often tend to dismissively judge women by their looks.

By choosing this way of presenting Salander, Larsson also demands some decent interpretative and critical skills on the part of his readers. He expects them to see beyond the screen of perceptions conveyed through the eyes of most of the men in the novel, and to instead pay attention to the presentations of Salander that are more objectively told by the narrator and by a few characters in the novel who can be regarded as representing the point of view of the implicit author. These latter descriptions of Salander reveal her as a brilliant and otherwise relatively normal young woman, who has had some really traumatic experiences, making it hard for her to trust others.[6] In one instance, however, the negatively charged description of Salander in terms of her tattoos (and piercings) is effectively and explicitly shut down. This happens during the trial at the end of the third novel, when Salander's abusive childhood doctor, psychologist Peter Teleborian, is giving testimony about her and suggests that her tattoos and other body modifications indicate a self-destructive pattern and mental illness. This is an argument that Salander's lawyer, Annika Giannini, effectively comes down hard on, making Teleborian look idiotic as well as incompetent (Larsson 2010b: 642–44).

TATTOOS AS MARKERS OF INDIVIDUALITY

Salander is very much aware of the way other people perceive her, and through-out the trilogy she often uses this to her own advantage and as a means to an end. In combination with her outfits, makeup and hair, her visible tattoos complete the image of a goth or rocker. She signals that she does not really belong in, or identify herself with, mainstream society, and prefers to be left alone. Mollegaard notes that Salander's most visible tattoos, particularly 'the wasp and the dragon tattoos, [are] emblematically inked onto Salander's body as warnings', a type of warning that also 'disturbs and antagonizes conven-tional social values about female purity and beauty' (Mollegaard 2016: 351). Judging from the way (most) others in the series view her, Salander is often successful in achieving a standoffish and cautioning response to her appearance. Nevertheless, sometimes her appearance is still interpreted as one of vulnerabil-ity and indicates that she is an easy target of abuse – as in the case of her legal guardian Nils Bjurman. This is also an interpretation of her looks that she is very much aware of, though, as she notes that '[i]n her world', the 'natural order of things' was that '[a]s a girl she was legal prey, especially if she was dressed in a worn leather jacket and had pierced eyebrows, tattoos, and zero social status' (Larsson 2009: 213). Clearly her looks, including her tattoos, are here associated with social class and (lack of) status, something that in her own eyes makes her an easy target of abuse. Mollegaard stresses how 'tattoos have a long history in Western culture of signaling an affiliation with non-mainstream, especially low-class groups' (Mollegaard 2016: 353), and Jane Caplan emphasises the tattoo 'as a marker of difference, an index of inclusion and exclusion' (Caplan 2000: xiv). In Salander's case it is more a question of perceived affiliation. She is a loner, but still her tattoos function as markers of low social status in the eyes of others; thus marking exclusion rather than inclusion and also being read in ways she does not want or intend. This somewhat negative effect is simultaneously countered, or balanced, by the way her looks tend to make people keep their distance and underestimate her. It is very clear that the meaning and status of her tattoos can be read in the Western tradition, where tattoos historically and culturally 'have been a metaphor for ambiguity' (*ibid.*: xxiii).

The one tattoo that stands out most in Salander's case is the dragon tattoo. Not only is it her largest tattoo and the one most frequently mentioned in the novels, it has also contributed to her establishment on the crime fiction scene worldwide. It is never made clear in Larsson's novels, however, what the tattoo represents. One of the tattooed women that Victoria Pitts interviewed also has a dragon tattoo, and after describing a history of sexual molestation during her childhood, the woman concludes that '[t]he dragon was really about finding my way to stand on my own two feet [...] being in the world on my own as a real person'. She further says the idea was for her to 'visualize a dragon guarding a cave as a process of overcoming fear', and that her 'way of dealing with it was to make myself one with the dragon and make the dragon become me' (Pitts 2003: 58). Perhaps Salander choosing the dragon tattoo could be similarly explained, and her dragon then be interpreted as a response to her traumatic and abusive childhood. The placement could perhaps be read as the dragon always 'has her back', and so watches out for her. Mollegaard (above) describes the dragon tattoo, just like the wasp tattoo, as a warning. Similarly, Deborah Henderson reads the tattoo in the context of Old Norse mythology where dragons are evil, and she draws parallels between the fire of dragons and Salander setting fire to her father. Henderson then interprets the placement of the dragon tattoo as an indication that Salander has put 'her evil dragon of her father' behind her (Henderson 2014: 1055–56). In his extensive work on the cultural history of the dragon, which includes analysis of *The girl with the dragon tattoo*, Martin Arnold reads the tattooed Salander as an avenging female fury, where 'no man, no matter how physically powerful he might be, is safe' (Arnold 2018: chapter 10; see also Shippey 2016). Arnold reads the tattooed dragon as a female figure that has been co-opted and subverted by patriarchy, which causes a distortion of its earlier representations (2018), and so is apposite for reclamation in Larsson's feminist project. More common among the criticism of the trilogy, however, is to connect the dragon to a series of Asian references in relation to Salander. Most interesting is perhaps Mollegaard's interpretation, as she regards Salander as a combination of two archetypes of Asian popular culture, 'the dragon lady (an untrustworthy, although not necessarily evil character) and the *waif-fu* (the tiny, pretty girl who turns out to be an amazing martial arts fighter)' (2016: 358; author's emphasis).[7] The symbolic meaning of the dragon tattoo in relation to who Salander is can thus be interpreted in many ways.

Another interesting aspect of Larsson's use of the dragon tattoo is how he lets it grow in size throughout the first two novels, something that is left out of the English translation. In Larsson's original Swedish version of *The girl with the dragon tattoo*, Armansky, as previously quoted, first notes that Salander's dragon tattoo was placed on the shoulder blade. When Blomkvist then describes the tattoo, he explains that it was 'stretched over her back, from the right shoulder blade and down to her buttocks' (Larsson, 2005: 413; my translation). In the English translation, however, this passage has been 'corrected', so Armansky's and Blomkvist's descriptions of the tattoo match, and there Blomkvist observes 'the dragon at her shoulder blade' (Larsson 2009:

392). In addition to Armansky and Blomkvist, Salander herself provides further detail of her dragon tattoo in the second novel, where she admires it in a mirror, 'the tattoo on her back – it was beautiful, a curving dragon in red, green, and black' (Larsson 2010a: 120). In the Swedish original, however, the description continues and she sees how the dragon 'started on her shoulder and its winding tail continued down over her buttock and ended on her thigh', something the English translation fails to mention (Larsson 2006: 106; my translation).[8] Larsson thus lets the tattoo continually grow throughout the narrative, from being located on the shoulder blade, to stretching down to the buttocks, and finally reaching the thigh. This could be read as a parallel to how Salander grows as a person throughout the trilogy. The English translator, however, has chosen to fix the size of tattoo according to Armansky's description of it, regarding his view as authoritative, while Lagercrantz in his addition to the series has chosen to enlarge the tattoo throughout, thus making Blomkvist's or Salander's view authoritative. Also notable is that while people around Salander tend to describe her using black as her only colour, Salander herself sees multiple colours as she describes her appearance in the above quoted passage.

TATTOOS: TELLING A STORY OF PAIN AND SURVIVAL

Karin Beeler stresses the importance of the narrative of the genesis of tattoos (2006: 2). This is clearly also something that is crucial both to Salander herself and to the narrator of Larsson's novels. Furthermore, according to Rachel Rodgers and Eric Bui, Salander's tattoos (and piercings) 'tell a story: her story' (2011: 31). After Salander is raped by Bjurman for the second time, she visits a tattoo parlor to get a new tattoo, a 'narrow band' around her ankle, and describes it to the tattoo artist as 'a reminder' (Larsson 2009: 237). To the reader, this also puts some of her previous tattoos into context, and it seems reasonable to assume that at least the bands she already has on her left ankle and left bicep have a similar origin and purpose. This is also argued by Rachel Rodgers and Eric Bui, who add that 'using a tattoo to remember or commemorate a trauma is a relatively frequent motivation for victims of trauma' (2011: 33). Pitts notes that in contemporary subcultural discourse, this is something particularly associated with 'women's assertion of control over their bodies' (Pitts 2003: 56). Furthermore, Susan Benson stresses that in Western culture today, body modifications, such as tattoos, are associated 'with possession, fixity and the stabilization of the self through and in cor-poreality' (Benson 2000: 237). Alessandra Lemma similarly describes that four out of five people with tattoos that she has interviewed talk about their tattoos 'as acts of taking control over their body, or more generally over their life' (Lemma 2010: 154). Read in such a context, Salander is reclaiming herself as she reclaims her body by making the new tattoo; her body is not the same as before the rape, but it is hers again, and she is the one to own and control it.

Moreover, there is the connection between tattoos and pain. The tattoo artist points out that '[t]he skin is very thin there [on the ankle]. It's going to hurt a lot', something that Salander sees no problem with (Larsson 2009: 237). Clearly the pain of the tattooing process is also part of the 'reminder' for her. Mollegaard further points to the fact that '[p]art of the message communicated through body modifications [such as for example tattoos] is visual testimony of stamina and the ability to endure pain, both highly-valued cultural ideas with deep roots in the West's political history of torture, martyrdom, self-flagellation, hunger strikes, and other expressions of political zealotry or religious devotion'(Mollegaard 2016: 354). With Salander, the tattooing certainly functions as a demonstration of stamina, although the religious connotations are missing and the political connotations are only implicit, connected to her as a (feminist) fighter of men and structures that abuse women throughout the series. Rodgers and Bui further interpret the pain of the process as Salander 'proving to herself that the pain inflicted upon her [by Bjurman] was not unbearable since she herself could choose to experience more pain. She is making a statement that her body is her own' (Rodgers and Bui 2011: 34).[9] In the third novel, when her doctor asks about the dragon tattoo, Salander states that she had reasons she does not want to reveal for getting it, and that the inking did hurt (Larsson 2010b: 226). In light of Salander choosing an ankle tattoo in the first novel after Bjurman's rapes, it is reasonable to assume that the dragon tattoo constitutes a similar reminder (though a more elaborate one) and that the pain of the process is also an important part of it for Salander.

Additionally, Benson emphasises the importance of the '*processes* of bodily inscription' in contemporary culture (Benson 2000: 237; my emphasis). Similarly, Lemma notes that 'body modification accrue[s] psychic significance not simply from the final, visible product, but for some people, perhaps even primarily, from the *process* of physical transformation – a process that mirrors that of birth', the painful 'birth' of a new, transformed, body (and self) (Lemma 2010: 156; author's emphasis). Mollegaard further points out that 'contemporary tattooing and piercing practices include many aspects of magic and belief, such as the totemic or protective power of a tattoo or piercing, the meaning it symbolizes for the bearer and what it signifies for others, the symbolic meaning of the place on the body where it is situated, and the ritual significance of its application to the skin' (Mollegaard 2016: 352–53). Possibly the pain of the application process in combination with the mnemonic function of the tattoo(s) are meant to protect Salander from repeated harm by reminding her not to put herself in a similar situation of vulnerability again. The placement of some of the tattoos, resembling restraints around her ankle (or possibly ankles, we do not know which ankle the new tattoo is on) and her arm, can also be interpreted as a way of reminding Salander not to let anyone control her physically against her will again. The placement of the new tattoo is a clear reference to how Bjurman tied her up during the second rape where 'she felt him putting something around her ankles, spread her legs apart and tie them so that she was lying there completely vulnerable' (Larsson 2009: 234). There are also parallels to how she was strapped down in the psychiatric ward as a child, where her doctor 'grabbed hold of one ankle, forced her knee down with his other hand, and fastened her foot with a leather strap' and then 'tied down her other foot', an experience in the past that could possibly be the origin behind one of her previous tattoos (Larsson 2010a: 6). Whether her other tattoos – the dragon, the wasp, the rose and the Chinese character – function similarly as such reminders remains undetermined. That they are signs of what Mollegaard describes as 'stamina and the ability to endure pain' is nevertheless evident (2016: 354).

TATTOOING AS DEFEATING EVIL

Salander leaves the traumatic encounters with Bjurman permanently marked by a tattoo, but she is not the only one. As part of her revenge, after raping Bjurman, and while he is still tied up, Salander tattoos him. When finished, she examines her work: '[t]he letters looked at best impressionistic. She had used red and blue ink. The message was written in capitals over five lines that covered his belly, from his nipples to just above his genitals: I AM A SADISTIC PIG, A PERVERT, AND A RAPIST' (Larsson 2009: 246). This is something completely different from the discreet reminder tattoo Salander gets herself. Bjurman's tattoo is a physical punishment, as well as a means to warn others who might encounter him. Salander's aim is to keep him away from all women in the future. Sheng-mei Ma has described Salander tattooing Bjurman as 'the reverse of Salander getting a tattoo herself'. For her, 'tattoos are writings on the body for self-identity, but her quintessential dragon design is veiled from the public, as Bjurman would undoubtedly hide his true identity and shame. Duality by design, tattoos both reveal and conceal the one wearing them' (Ma 2014: 59–60). Later, Salander ponders whether Bjurman 'would ever take his clothes off in front of a woman again, and if he did, how was he going to explain the tattoos on his stomach? And the next time he went to the doctor how would he avoid taking off his clothes?' (Larsson 2009: 520). The idea that he will have the tattoo removed does cross her mind – as after tattooing him she checks up on him occasionally to make sure he makes no such attempts (Larsson 2010a: 46). Still, there is a sense conveyed in the novel that Bjurman's tattoo is permanent, that it will make him perpetually suffer and will work as a kind of visual 'chastity belt' for the rest of his life – which it also most likely does, as when he is killed in the second novel he still has the tattoo (*ibid.*: 335). As Mollegaard points out, the tattoo is also a way to 'emasculate him without actually removing any parts of his reproductive organs' (2016: 363).

TATTOO REMOVAL: A SIGN OF CHANGE

Salander herself does remove one of her tattoos, though. In addition to being crime novels, Larsson's narrative can simultaneously be read as a coming-of-age story, where Salander grows from being almost like an isolated and surly teenager who trusts no one, to being a grown-up woman who shops at IKEA and even has friends.[10] As she notes about halfway into the trilogy, '[s]he felt that some fundamental change had taken place or was taking place in her life [...] Maybe it was the adult world which was belatedly pushing its way into her life' (Larsson 2010a: 23). Part of her transformation is also physical, as she gets breast implants, takes out most of her piercings and has the wasp tattoo on her neck removed (*ibid.*: 23–24; 120). Rodgers and Bui refer to their research on body modifications, and note that just like with Salander, 'individuals who have acquired multiple body modifications, tend to gradually remove them as they find meaning and purpose in their lives and curb risky behaviors' (Rodgers and Bui 2011: 40). This further supports a reading of Salander's narrative as a coming-of-age story. The permanence of the removal of the visible tattoo constitutes a step from Salander's – often self-imposed – outsider position, towards a more mainstream and grown-up look. Rodgers and Bui also point to Salander's 'shift away from body modifications in the form of tattoos and piercings to cosmetic surgery' (her breast implants), and interpret this as something that 'brings Salander closer to social ideals of beauty and indicates a willingness to be more part of society' and 'conveys the change in her relationship with the world and herself' (*ibid.*: 43). This changed relationship, and the end of Salander's coming-of-age story, is further summarised in her conclusion at the end of the trilogy, where she notes that: '[f]inally it was all over. The story that had begun on the day she was born had ended at the brickworks. She was free' (Larsson 2010b: 741). At that point Salander is ready to put her childhood behind her and move out into the world as a free and adult woman.

The removal of the visible tattoo also makes Salander more flexible in terms of easily being able to change her appearance, for example transforming into her alter egos of the classy Irene Nesser and Monica Sholes, without having to spend 'a long time masking the tattoo on her neck with a thick layer of skin-coloured lotion and powder over it', the way she has to at the end of the first novel (Larsson 2009: 523). Salander herself stresses how 'the wasp [tattoo] was conspicuous and it made her easy to remember and identify', and that this was why she had it removed (Larsson 2010a: 23).[11] Blending in and being less identifiable thus seem to be her main motivations behind removing the tattoo. Rogers and Bui suggest that Salander's 'willingness to use her appearance to achieve certain goals also emphasizes a lack of group affiliation expressed by her body modifications' (Rogers and Bui 2011: 35). As previously discussed, her tattoos are not there to show belonging, but rather the opposite, and this is emphasised by her lack of nostalgia in removing the tattoo. That it is specifically the wasp tattoo that is removed also carries meaning. Rogers and Bui point out that Salander's wasp tattoo 'serves as a coded message of her other identity' and to the high status she possesses in the hacker community (*ibid.*: 33, 39).[12] Her hacker name is Wasp, and the removal of the wasp tattoo can thus also be interpreted as her going even deeper under cover, as further hiding her secret identity as a hacker. Rogers and Bui suggest that the motive of the tattoo is also 'an attempt to signal to others that she can be dangerous', like a wasp (*ibid.*: 33). This is also something she hides by removing the tattoo.

TATTOOS AS A GAME OF IDENTITY

Despite having grown up and moved on throughout the trilogy, during the trial in the final novel, Salander 'dresses up' as her former outsider self. Blomkvist is clearly shocked as she first enters the court room, wearing a top that 'barely covered her many tattoos', and he continues to notice her numerous piercings, her 'uneven stubble' of a hairdo and her excessive makeup. 'Then he realized that Salander was in costume [...] here in the district court she had exaggerated her style to the point of parody. It was no accident, it was part of Giannini's strategy' (Larsson 2010b: 611–12). Rodgers and Bui suggest that this is a way to show contempt for a court system that is a representative of the same authorities that have abused her before (2011: 36). However, this is not the main function or purpose of Salander's choice of court outfit. As Katarina Gregersdotter observes, by dressing up like this Salander 'is removing all traces of the traditionally sexually attractive woman' (2013: 86). Instead she is emphasising the vulnerable and lost child who puts on a costume to look tough and hard. Still, this time Salander uses her outfit not to scare people off, but rather to show her vulnerability, to show herself to be an easy target, as 'legal prey' with no social status, as previously discussed (Larsson 2009: 213). Mollegaard explains that Salander's 'provocative self-fashioning sets her tough looks up against the history of her childhood, which, as it unfolds in the courtroom, renders her punk masquerade into a pathetic and painful cover for her broken childhood and her status as ward of the state' (2016: 355). At this point in the story, Salander has grown up and gained further insights about the world around her. She is well aware of the impression her appearance makes, and skilfully uses this to her advantage.

DAVID LAGERCRANTZ'S TAKE ON SALANDER'S TATTOOS

David Lagercrantz only mentions Salander's tattoos three times in *The girl in the spider's web*, despite continuously making a big deal about the way the character looks in general, with her hair, the way she dresses and her piercings. The first time her tattoos are mentioned in Lagercrantz's story is illustrative of how she is described in general in his novel. On this occasion the description of her is given by a young computer scientist: '[s]he was tattooed and pierced and all that crap and looked like a heavy rocker or goth or punk, plus she was thin as hell' (Lagercrantz 2016: 48). Here it is clear that the mentioning of the tattoos functions mainly as part of creating a picture of someone who looks different, and that the difference is viewed in a condescending way, similar to the way Larsson's middle-aged men view Salander. However, the tattoos are only rarely mentioned in Lagercrantz's descriptions – partly perhaps since the novel is set in November and early December, when the tattoos are covered up by clothing. The only exception is during a scene in a car where Salander gets undressed to bandage a wound. Afterwards, the driver of the car is able to tell the police it was her because he 'saw that she had a large tattoo of a dragon all the way up her back. That same tattoo was mentioned in one of the old newspaper articles' (*ibid.*: 293). The articles referred to were those written during events in Larsson's second and third book. In this instance, the tattoo is used as a firm confirmation of identity, rather than as something defining Salander as Other. However, it is also clear that in comparison with how the dragon tattoo is initially described by Armansky in Larsson's first novel, Lagercrantz has made Salander's tattoo notably larger, more in line with how Larsson later lets Blomkvist and Salander herself, respectively, describe the tattoo, as previously argued. Lagercrantz's choice of the larger tattoo makes the tattoo more defining of who Salander is, making her into 'the girl with the dragon tattoo' of the English title, instead of regarding the tattoo as just one of her many attributes. This is her main and (in this context) her only identifying mark. Lagercrantz's use of the dragon tattoo for identification is also reminiscent of how unknown dead bodies, or found body parts, in crime fiction are often eventually identified by some characteristic tattoo.

In Lagercrantz's novel, Salander's tattoos appear only in one more context, and that is when Mikael Blomkvist is nostalgically reminiscing: 'he thought about a dragon tattoo on a skinny pale back, a cold snap at Hedeby Island in the midst of a decades-old missing-person-case and a dug up grave in Gosseberga that was nearly the resting place of a woman who refused to give up' (*ibid.*: 58).[13] The first event he refers to is from Larsson's first novel when Blomkvist and Salander had a sexual relationship while spending time together in the cold cabin in Hedestad. The second event is from Larsson's second novel, when Salander almost died and Blomkvist came to her rescue. In the first case,

Salander's dragon tattoo thus takes on a sexual function, a type of function it never had in Larsson's novels.[14] The second reference, however, contributes to shaping an image of Salander as someone who is both vulnerable and needing to be taken care of – an image of her that is not common with Larsson – and a survivor, which is exactly how Larsson portrays her most of the time. As the episode of the grave took place, however, Blomkvist did not actually see Salander's tattoo – he was not even at the site of the dug-up grave – and when he later found Salander at Zalachenko's farmhouse close to the grave, she was still fully clothed (Larsson 2010a: 710).[15] Rather than referring to something Blomkvist actually experienced at the time, his memory of the tattoo and Salander's slim back thus represents more generally the combination of vulnerability and strength he sees as characteristic for Salander, two features that are also evident in her final showdown with Zalachenko and Niederman, which concludes *The girl who played with fire*.

Lagercrantz's portrayal of Salander's tattoos and their functions is thus much less complex and less extensive than Larsson's, and with Lagercrantz the reader only gets to see what functions the tattoos have for others, never for Salander herself. In Lagercrantz's narrative her tattoos have solely the dual function of distancing others from her (the computer scientist), and making them feel closer to her (Blomkvist and the man in the car).

One reason why Larsson's use of tattoos is more complex is naturally a result of him establishing the characters, primarily the character of Lisbeth Salander. When Lagercrantz takes up the torch, readers are already well acquainted with Salander and her history. Furthermore, as I have explored, as part of his feminist project Larsson uses the tattoos to describe how Salander reclaims and 'owns' her body and how this is related to how she evolves and grows throughout the trilogy, a development that is virtually complete by the end of the third novel. The rationale for Lagercrantz using Salander's tattoos in a similar way is thus effectively undermined, as his Salander is no longer struggling with growing up and finding her identity and place in the world. It is also worth noting that the function of the tattoos in novels by both authors is related to personal character development and in relation to others, rather than to any specific conventions of the crime fiction genre. In particular, Larsson puts great emphasis on exploring and evolving the crime genre, but the only way the tattoos can possibly be read as related to such a project is, in the establishment of Salander as a hardboiled hero, as a loner and outsider.[16] As previously discussed, the role of the tattoos in that process is relevant almost only in relation to how other people in Larsson's novels perceive Salander, not to who she really is. Lagercrantz uses Salander's dragon tattoo only once for identification in classic crime fiction manner, while Larsson even makes a point of Salander being impossible for the police to locate, even though she 'had tattoos all over her body' (Larsson 2010a: 434). Despite the central role of tattoos in portraying

Larsson's Salander, perhaps tattoos after the tattoo renaissance have lost some of their criminal associations and functions in crime fiction.

NOTES

1 This chapter gives the original date of publication when discussing the novels. Quotations are given from the edition used by the author. See Bibliography for further details (eds).

2 See John-Henri Holmberg (2011), especially page 35.

3 I have previously discussed the Swedish original cover of Larsson's first novel more extensively in Bergman (2013), see in particular pages 39–40.

4 The three Scandinavian films were also released as a television series called *Millennium* in six episodes in 2010 with added material that was cut when making the film versions.

5 Nevertheless, some scholars, for example John Gray and Karin Beeler, still contend 'that the tattoo continues to be associated with difference' (Beeler 2006: 4).

6 See Bergman (2012: 142). During the course of the trilogy, Mikael Blomkvist becomes increasingly more representative of the implicit author's view of Salander; initially, perhaps the best example is her former legal guardian Holger Palmgren.

7 Catherine (Kay) G. Valentine also discuss Salander's Asian-ness in relation to the figure of the Dragon Lady (2012: 94) as does Martin Arnold who terms Salander 'a psychologised dragon-woman' (2018: n.p.). For further consideration of Salander as an embodiment of female fury, see Tom Shippey's online lecture 'Lisbeth Salander: Avenging female fury'. We are grateful to Martin Arnold for this reference (eds).

8 The cover of the first Swedish edition of the second novel also shows how the dragon's head is placed high on Salander's left shoulder, close to her neck (Larsson 2006: front cover). The cover of the first novel (original edition) does not portray Salander, but she features on the cover of the third novel's original edition, and there her neck and shoulder, where the dragon's head is placed in the second cover picture, are visible, but there is no tattoo (Larsson 2007: front cover).

9 When recounting details of Bjurman's rape in the third novel, Salander describes how he commented on her having 'several tattoos and piercings', and that this made him conclude that she enjoyed pain, resulting in him pushing a needle through her nipple (Larsson 2010b: 427). This can be read as further strengthening the argument that Salander needs to make her body her own again, but also as further explaining why she, as part of her revenge on Bjurman, 'pierces' his body with the tattooing needle (see Larsson 2009: 246).

10 I have previously discussed this in Bergman (2012: 142).

11 Stieg Larsson's intention was to write ten novels in the Millennium series, and according to his partner, Eva Gabrielsson, who is the only one who knows anything about the planned continuation of the series, '[e]ach time she [Salander] has managed to extract her revenge on someone who has hurt her, physically or mentally, she will remove one of her tattoos that represents that particular hurt' (qtd John-Henri Holmberg 2011: 230). In light of what transpires in the first three novels, however, this does not make sense. Holmberg goes as far as to suggest that the wasp tattoo must have represented Bjurman's abuse of Salander, but that appears very

far-fetched as she had it beforehand, and as she gets another tattoo associated with Bjurman raping her (cf. Holmberg 2011: 231).

12 Rodgers and Bui suggest that removing the wasp tattoo is Salander's way of saying 'that her work no longer defines her' (2011: 39), but I would rather argue that the purpose is to further hide her illegal hacking activities, not to say that these are no longer important to her.

13 The English translator has done some serious editing here. Not only is this scene moved – in Lagercrantz's Swedish original it is placed directly in association with Blomkvist's conversation with the computer scientist mentioned earlier but in the English version there is another scene placed in-between – but also the translator has added the parts in the quote specifying the missing-person case and how Salander, 'a woman', was connected to the dug-up grave. That clarification is not present in Lagercrantz's original.

14 In some scholarship, for example in Mollegaard (2016: 352–53), it is claimed that Salander's tattoos do have a sexual connotation, that they in Mollegard's words 'eroticize her body' (2016: 352) in Larsson's novels. I would argue, however, that this reflects a more general view of or attitude towards tattoos, rather than anything actually present in Larsson's novels.

15 See Larsson 2010a: 710 (the dug-up grave) and 724 (Blomkvist finds and saves Salander).

16 I have discussed Larsson's use of crime fiction genres extensively in Bergman (2013).

BIBLIOGRAPHY

Arnold, Martin (2018), *Dragon-power: From ancient mythology to 'Game of thrones'* (London: Reaktion).

Beeler, Karin (2006), *Tattoos, desire and violence: Marks of resistance in literature, film and television.* (Jefferson: McFarland).

Benson, Susan (2000), 'Inscriptions of the self: Reflections on tattooing and piercing in contemporary Euro-America', in J. Caplan (ed.) (2000), pp. 234–54.

Bergman, Kerstin (2012), 'Lisbeth Salander and her Swedish crime fiction "sisters": Stieg Larsson's hero in a genre context', in D. King and C. L. Smith (eds), *Men who hate women and women who kick their asses: Stieg Larsson's millennium trilogy in feminist perspective* (Nashville: Vanderbilt University Press), pp. 135–44.

— (2013), 'From "The case of the pressed flowers" to the serial killer's torture chamber: The use and function of crime fiction subgenres in Stieg Larsson's *The girl with the dragon tattoo*', in R. Martin (ed.), *Critical insights: Crime and detective fiction* (Ipswich: Salem Press), pp. 38–54.

Caplan, Jane (2000), 'Introduction', in J. Caplan (ed.) (2000), pp. xi–xxiii.

— (ed.) (2000), *Written on the body: The tattoo in European and American history* (London: Reaktion).

Gregersdotter, Katarina (2013), 'The body, hopelessness, and nostalgia: Representations of rape and the welfare state in Swedish crime fiction', in B. Åström, K. Gregersdotter and T. Horeck (eds), *Rape in Stieg Larsson's Millennium trilogy and beyond: Contemporary Scandinavian and Anglophone crime fiction* (London: Palgrave Macmillan), pp. 81–96.

Henderson, Deborah (2014), 'Thor's mighty hammer: Christianity, justice and Norse mythology in Stieg Larsson's *Millennium Trilogy*', *The journal of popular culture*, 47:5, 1047–61.

Holmberg, John-Henri (2011), 'The novels you read are not necessarily the novels Stieg Larsson wrote', in D. Burstein, A. de Keijzer and J.-H. Holmberg (eds), *The tattooed girl: The enigma of Stieg Larsson and the secrets behind the most compelling thrillers of our time* (New York: St. Martin's Griffin), pp. 29–41.

Lagercrantz, David (2016), *The girl in the spider's web*, trans. G. Goulding (London: MacLehose Press/Quercus).

Larsson, Stieg (2005), *Män som hatar kvinnor* (Stockholm: Norstedts).

— (2006), *Flickan som lekte med elden* (Stockholm: Norstedts).

— (2007), *Luftslottet som sprängdes* (Stockholm: Norstedts).

— (2009), *The girl with the dragon tattoo*, trans. R. Keeland (London: MacLehose Press/Quercus).

— (2010a), *The girl who played with fire*, trans. R. Keeland (New York: Vintage Crime/Black Lizard).

— (2010b) *The girl who kicked the hornets' nest*, trans. R. Keeland (London: MacLehose Press/Quercus).

Lemma, Alessandra (2010), *Under the skin: A psychoanalytic study of body modification* (London and New York: Routledge).

Ma, Sheng-mei (2014), 'My aspergirl: Stieg Larsson's Millennium trilogy and visualizations', *The journal of American culture*, 37:1 (2014), 52–63.

Mollegaard, Kirsten (2016), 'Signs taken for warnings: Modification and visual pleasure in *The girl with the dragon tattoo*', *The journal of popular culture*, 49:2, 347–66.

Pitts, Victoria (2003), *In the flesh: The cultural politics of body modification* (New York: Palgrave MacMillan).

Rodgers, Rachel, and Eric Bui (2011), 'The body speaks louder than words: What is Lisbeth Salander saying?', in R. S. Rosenberg and S. O'Neill (eds), *The psychology of the girl with the dragon tattoo* (Dallas: Smart Pop/BenBella Books), pp. 29–44.

Rubin, Arnold (1988), 'Tattoo renaissance', in A. Rubin (ed.), *Marks of civilization: Artistic transformations of the human body* (Los Angeles: Museum of Cultural History/ University of California, Los Angeles), pp. 233–62.

Shippey, Tom (2016), 'Lisbeth Salander: Avenging female fury' [online lecture]. Available: www.thegreatcoursesplus.com/heroes-and-legends-the-most-influenti al-characters-of-literature [accessed 5 December 2018].

Valentine, Catherine (Kay) G. (2012), 'Tiny, tattooed, and tough as nails: Representations of Lisbeth Salander's body', in D. King and C. L. Smith (eds), *Men who hate women and women who kick their asses: Stieg Larsson's Millennium trilogy in feminist perspective* (Nashville: Vanderbilt University press), pp. 88–97.

PART 3

Urban textualities, humans and other animals

7

The killing floor and crime narratives: Marking women and nonhuman animals

Kate Watson and Rebekah Humphreys

INTRODUCTION

The English word 'tattoo' is derived from the Tahitian term 'tatau' and denotes the corporeal practice to 'puncture or mark […] on skin' (Taliaferro and Odden 2012: 4). Tattoos are just one example of body modification practices and marks made on skin. However, this type of body modification in contemporary crime fiction relates female victims to industrial treatments of nonhuman animals. This chapter specifically examines the equation of women and nonhuman animals, using the tattoo and the imprinting and branding of animals for meat to provide a critique of animal studies in and via crime fiction. We argue that there is an emergent subgenre of crime fiction – 'killing floor' crime fiction – which uses the tropes and practices of butchery. These fictions focus on the mutilation of women, the puncturing of their skins and the equation of their bodies with meat (which symbolically feeds and sustains the male killer). The increased technology and use of factories to literally rip nonhuman animals apart mirrors the way that women's bodies are dehumanised, fragmented and inscribed in these contemporary crime fictions.

In this chapter we will be concerned with the tattoo in contemporary crime fiction and marking of the body in a broad sense, including literal marking of the skin, as in the marking and 'scarification' of skin and bodies via cutting, branding, slicing and butchering. We are also concerned with how such marking and scarification can function as a representation and reflection of the perceived value of certain beings, particularly of nonhuman beings and women, and of their status in society; a value and status 'inscribed by culture and counterinscribed by individuals' (DeMello 2000: 9). Relatedly, this chapter provides an analysis of the marking, both literal and metaphorical, of nonhuman beings and women via an examination of contemporary crime narratives, including Jeffery Deaver's novel *The skin collector* (2014b) and Peter Robinson's

Abattoir blues published in 2014.[1] In doing so, it links the exploitation and objectification of the bodies of women and of nonhumans.

MARKING AND CONSUMPTION:
WOMEN AND CRIME NARRATIVES

Representations of food, cooking and consumption in crime fiction have a long history and have been documented in recent fiction and criticism.[2] Indeed, the genre of crime fiction and its sub-genres can be viewed as a recipe – or recipes – made up of particular conventions and 'ingredients'. Crime and detective narratives often reflect the dominant viewpoint of a particular culture, unmasking a society's hierarchical structures and ideologies. In particular, the language used in such narratives can sometimes be found to reflect cultural norms relating to the hierarchal status of humans and nonhumans. Interestingly, there are strong analogies between the use of nonhuman beings in modern-day practices (such as factory farming and animal experimentation) and the position of women in contemporary crime fiction who are repeatedly 'bound, gagged, strung up or tied down, raped, sliced, burned, blinded, beaten, staved, suffocated, stabbed, boiled or buried alive' (Mann 2009: n.p.).

The imagery of butchering is often used to describe acts of sexual violence against women; though usually women in such narratives (unlike nonhuman beings in reality) are not literally reduced to pieces of meat, but are only metaphorically reduced to meat.[3] As Gill Plain has noted, 'flesh becomes meat and sex mutates into butchery' in twentieth-century crime narratives (Plain 2001: 232). We say 'usually' for cannibalism is not unknown in such narratives, and is famously evinced by Thomas Harris's cannibalistic serial killer Dr Hannibal Lecter (who made his first novelistic appearance in *Red dragon* (1981)). Discussing Harris's sequel, *The silence of the lambs* (1988), Plain discusses '[t]he 'meatification' of [Clarice] Starling' (Plain 2001: 235), commenting how '[i]n the red-blooded machismo of the FBI, Starling is nothing more than "poultry" – a cheap, expendable alternative to "real" meat' (*ibid.*: 233). Time and time again, women are connected to meat, crime and sex. Understanding the metaphor of butchering depends on the reader's awareness that many animals are literally butchered (see Adams 2010: 86) – made into pieces of meat – and also depends on the ways in which they are actually treated (especially at the slaughterhouse) and the methods by which their bodies are literally fragmented.

Significantly, the animals themselves are often absent from such images of butchering, and this absence is a disturbing reflection of 'the dominant reality that renders real animals invisible and masks violence' (Adams 2010: 93). Helene Tursten's *The torso* [*Tatuerad torso*] (1999) takes steps in this direction, reading the necrosadistic murder-mutilation (of men and women) in these terms: '"[t]o murder a human being and then take apart the body piece by piece like a … roasted chicken. It's damned disgusting!'" (Tursten 2006: 16).[4] It is, though, the cooked meat/consumable object that is visible in this comparison.

This reading of women, nonhumans and consumption is extended in *The skin collector*. One of the series' figures, Amelia Sachs (who works with and is partner to NYPD detective Lincoln Rhyme), links murder and cannibalism specifically to marking and modification: '[c]utting throats, cannibalism, Sachs reflected. Talk about body modification' (Deaver 2014b: 114). The novel's front cover draws on the well-established connection between the killer as artist in crime narratives, stating that 'Death is his art'.[5]

While poison administered via food is a longstanding favourite means of murder (for example, Dorothy L. Sayers's *Strong poison* (1930)), the poison trope is reworked in a postmodern fashion in Deaver's narrative, with the principle criminal – Billy Haven – tattooing his victims using poison rather than ink. He refers to such inscriptions as 'a Billy Mod' (2014b: 10) and is subsequently named 'the poison tat artist' (*ibid.*: 29). These acts and markings – which are carried out in New York's underground tunnels, and significantly in a former slaughterhouse (see the section 'The invisible animal') – serve as cryptic clues and are part of Billy's larger plan, titled 'the Modification', where he would employ '[p]oison to destroy the poisoned city' (*ibid.*: 301, 363). Billy also refers to this destruction as '[a] plague' (*ibid.*: 351), drawing on images of disease.

There are many connections made between Deaver's 1997 novel, *The bone collector* (2014a); for example, Billy is inspired by his predecessor's *modus operandi*. *The skin collector* is also undeniably inspired by previous tattoo/crime narratives, and it self-referentially draws attention to Stieg Larsson's *The girl with the dragon tattoo* (2005) thriller throughout the novel. The interconnection of gender, the tattoo, textual branding, crime and nonhumans (pigs) is also apparent in Larsson's novel, where Lisbeth Salander tattoos 'I AM A SADISTIC PIG, A PERVERT, AND A RAPIST' (Larsson, 2008: 235; author's emphasis) on her sexual assailant. Billy's inscription of his victims (both men and women) in *The skin collector* plays on the association of the sexual element and serial killing of women. Billy's first victim, Chloe, details how 'what she'd been expecting, dreading, wasn't happening. In a way, though, this was worse because *that* – ripping her clothes off and then what would follow – would at least have been understandable. It would have fallen into a known category of horror. This was different' (Deaver 2014b: 6).

The considerations detailed above support the reading that crime and detective narratives can offer a platform from which modern-day views of women and of nonhuman animals can be explored. Further, since marking and scarification of women is frequently conveyed through the metaphor of meat and butchering in such narratives, they provide a means by which the literal and metaphorical marking of the bodies of women and of animals can be analysed.

To further draw out these associations, we will first set up the positioning of nonhuman animals in crime narratives.

NONHUMAN ANIMALS AND CRIME NARRATIVES

Animals or animal-references in crime narratives have a long genealogy. Examples include the detective figure of 'Mr Samuel Ferret' in 'The experiences of a barrister' (Warren 1856) and dog detectives.[6] As well as detecting figures, animal villains and/or animals that are complicit (willingly or unwillingly) in crime have appeared: consider Edgar Allan Poe's famous orangutan in 'The murders in the Rue Morgue' (1841), the use of an anthill (under a beaten and stripped body) in Charles De Boos' *Mark Brown's wife: A tale of the goldfields* (1871), the tarantula as torture instrument in Patricia Cornwell's *Predator* (2005) and the killings in *The bone collector*, which utilise rats and mad dogs. *The skin collector* also has a strong focus on animals.

There also are many representations of murder or mutilation of animals in crime narratives. A few examples include Errol Childress's dog in *True detective* (Series 1, 2014), the murder of animals and women in Larsson's *The girl with the dragon tattoo*, and an old case where a dog had been shot in Cornwell's *All that remains* (1992). In the latter text, Kay Scarpetta notes how '[d]uring my career I had autopsied tortured dogs, mutilated cats, a sexually assaulted mare, and a poisoned chicken left in a judge's mailbox. People were just as cruel to animals as they were to each other' (Cornwell 1993: 256).[7]

Moreover, animal representation and attendant hierarchies apply to 'the female's place in the hierarchy of animal life' (Lombroso and Ferrero 2004: 41). Cesare Lombroso and Guglielmo Ferrero in their 1893 work, *The female offender [La donna delinquente]*, draw on the Victorian human–animal divide and natural selection. They detail the physical and psychological features that classify criminals and discuss the nature of lesbianism and its causes – specifically prison – which causes the women 'prisoners [to] resemble animals' (Lombroso and Ferrero 2004: 177). Their gendered 'zoological scale' includes spiders, birds, worms, crustaceans, mammals, carnivores and primates. They state that: 'among the inferior animals, female dominance in size and strength is typical. It manifests itself strongly in the zoological world and extends even to some species of birds. But little by little as one goes up the scale, the male begins to approach the female and then to become stronger, so that among the mammals without exception the male rules over the species' (*ibid.*: 44). Deaver draws on this connection between natural selection and crime in *The skin collector*, when Rhyme muses that '[n]atural selection applies to criminal activity, as well as to newts and simians' (2014b: 428).[8] The same applies to Billy's red centipede tattoo with human eyes; when attacking Chloe – his first victim – his criminal acts, tattoo and identity become entwined: he is 'her attacker, the yellow-face insect' (*ibid.*: 8). The text describes this tattoo – and Billy's rationale – in further detail:

> The creature was about eighteen inches long. Its posterior was at the middle of his biceps and the design moved in a lazy S pattern to the back of his hand, where the insect's head rested – the head with a human face, full lips, knowing eyes, a nose, a mouth encircling fangs.
>
> Traditionally, people tattooed themselves with animals for two reasons: to assume attributes of the creature, like courage from a lion or stealth from a panther. Or to serve as an emblem to immunize them from the dangers of a particular predator.
>
> Billy didn't know much about psychology but knew that, between the two, it was the first reason that had made him pick the creature with which to decorate his arm. (*ibid.*: 208–09)

The strong animal (and gendered experimentation) connection in *The skin collector* is accentuated by the numerous referrals to H. G. Wells's *The island of Dr Moreau* (1896): this is Billy's favourite book, and a quotation from Wells's text is used as the preface to the novel. Billy explicitly compares 'the Modification' with Doctor Moreau's vivisection experiments (*ibid.*: 301).

Centipedes, while ostensibly innocuous creatures, are both predators and highly venomous. They are also usually subterranean and they move quickly; as such, they can go unnoticed and are not easy to detect. Therefore, Billy's choice of tattoo correlates to both his criminal being and actions: the ink that he uses for his tattoos is a deadly venom, intended to poison slowly. Billy (and his symbolic centipede tattoo) seeks to torture and kill those weaker than himself. Further, just as the aforementioned zoological scale might be interpreted as a hierarchal ordering of nature, perhaps similarly the narrative we tell ourselves about nonhuman animals used in modern-day practices is a narrative which relates to the hierarchical structure of our society; a structure in which humans dominate and exploit other animals, and a culture in which the exploitation of nonhuman animals has become normalised. We tend not to see our treatment of nonhuman animals as problematic because the idea that their domination is part of a natural ordering has been entrenched throughout history. Their treatment in experiments and in meat production is generally deemed to be acceptable, and in this way somehow established as defensible. As Carol Adams claims, '[b]ecause of the dominant discourse which approves of meat eating, we are forced to take the knowledge that we are consuming dead animals and accept it, ignore it, neutralize it, repress it' (2010: 241). For Adams, the dominant discourse is not only anthropocentric but patriarchal too:

> Eating animals acts as a mirror and representation of patriarchal values. Meat eating is the re-inscription of male power at every meal. The patriarchal gaze sees

not the fragmented flesh of dead animals but appetizing food. If our attitudes re-inscribe patriarchy, our actions regarding eating animals will either reify or challenge this received culture. (*ibid.*: 241)

Whether or not one agrees with Adams's feminist critique of patriarchy and her view that our eating of nonhumans represents patriarchal norms, our normalised attitudes towards such beings mirror a cultural paradigm which is certainly anthropocentric, and that cultural paradigm reinforces our attitudes. In some sense parallel to Adams's views, Dinesh Joseph Wadiwel explores links between human violence against women and against animals, arguing that, with respect to sexual violence against women (and analogous to violence towards animals), such 'violence maintains male domination against women, and simultaneously articulates a binary between "man" and "woman" as normative gender constructions' (2015: 9). Moreover, Wadiwel emphatically claims (in relation to violence inflicted upon animals in commercial practices) that 'mass orchestrated violence against animals both maintains systems of human domination and ... constructs epistemologically how we understand the "animals" as a discursive category that is opposed and subordinated to the "human"' (*ibid.*: 9). In some sense, then, many nonhumans are already 'marked' or 'inscribed' (by a human-centred culture and by individuals) as objects, as consumables, even before they come into existence. Moreover, while many crime fiction narratives readily utilise abattoir imagery with male killers who perceive women as meat, nonhuman beings themselves are not 'seen' in the narratives. It is rather the women's flesh as meat (and treated as meat, treated as poorly as animals used in modern farming), which is held in the male gaze.

MARKING AND METAPHOR

Furthermore, language performs a marking function, both for women and for nonhumans. For example, Dr Jordan in Margaret Atwood's *Alias Grace* (1996) seeks to define and brand Grace via his language and evocative thoughts: '[m]urderess, *murderess*, he whispers to himself. It has an allure, a scent almost ... He imagines himself breathing it as he draws Grace towards him, pressing his mouth against her. *Murderess*. He applies it to her throat like a brand' (Atwood 1997: 453). Here, it is the male who has the power to figuratively brand the female with his sexualised discourse and his body. Christiana Gregoriou, discussing linguistic deviance in contemporary crime fiction, has identified and examined animal metaphors in James Patterson's Alex Cross series of novels – particularly *Along came a spider* (1993) and *Cat and mouse* (1997). These are the 'KILLERS ARE SPIDERS metaphor' and the 'KILLERS ARE ANIMALS/ INSECTS TO BE FED metaphor' (Gregoriou 2007: 80; author's emphasis.). She elaborates further:

> The overall use of such conceptual metaphors in the Patterson series establishes
> the criminals as a special kind of human species, one that is driven to criminality
> because they felt it was *necessary* for them to do so. Just like animals hunting to be
> fed, criminals are 'justified' as a species that cannot help but kill in order to survive.
> At the same time, criminal behaviour is presented as 'viewed' by an audience of
> common people who seek entertainment; in this sense, criminal behaviour forms
> part of the social structure, and is *wanted* rather than not. (*ibid.*: 82)

Such metaphorical readings correlate to *The skin collector*, especially Billy's connection to animals and his prominent centipede tattoo. David Lagercrantz's sequel to Stieg Larsson's Millennium novels, *The girl in the spider's web* (2016), again (by virtue of its title) makes these connections.[9]

It is noteworthy that (similarly to how we tend to view animals) the human killers (in the aforementioned metaphors and in crime narratives generally) are sometimes characterised as purely instinctive beings; indeed, they are presented as lacking control over their murderous acts. Just as animals are not held responsible for their actions for the reason that they are thought to lack moral agency, killers (often characterised as 'mad', 'inhuman', 'deranged' or regarded as mentally ill) are deemed to lack the agency required to refrain from criminal and immoral behaviour. But nonhumans' supposed instinctiveness and lack of agency are also the very reasons we sometimes use to justify our exploitation of nonhumans and justify our un-empathic behaviour towards them,[10] rather than – as in the case of the human killers in the crime narratives – reasons for evoking a certain degree of sympathy because, in the words of Gregoriou, 'they cannot help but kill in order to survive'. However, just as it is problematic to read nonhuman animals as purely instinctive beings, lacking rationality, so too is it problematic to read humans (in this case, murderers) in this way.

Further, human killers are 'reduced' to nonhuman animals; a reduction that assumes that humans are not animals, and that animals are somehow inferior in comparison to *Homo sapiens*. This imagery is strengthened by the species of animals which are used in the metaphors (arachnids and insects are often animals by which many people are repelled). Thus, nonhuman animals again take the brunt; they become (those humans we characterise as) debased. But interestingly what both humans and animals more widely are capable of in reality is hidden in these narratives (humans as capable of morally atrocious acts, and animals as capable of more than purely instinctive ones).

THE INVISIBLE ANIMAL: MARKING NONHUMAN VIA MARKING WOMEN

While animal advocates are often concerned about our use of language in relation to how we speak about nonhuman animals, particularly those animals which are systematically and routinely exploited by humans, feminists too are often concerned about how language serves to reinforce the objectification of women in a dominant patriarchal culture. This is not surprising for, as Kemmerer notes, the oppressions of women and of nonhuman animals (as well as the oppressions of other beings) are linked 'by common ideologies, by institutional forces, and by socialisation that makes oppressions normative and invisible' (2011: 11). Objectification may be seen as a key feature that links these oppressions (*ibid.*: 6). In so far as those beings which are oppressed are viewed as objects and consumables, their exploitation is considered to be permissible. Indeed, objectification reduces that which is oppressed from a living being to something to be used at (humanity's) will.

The imagery of butchering in relation to women and sexual violence against women originates in the literal oppression of nonhuman animals (particularly, although not exclusively, of farm animals) by both men *and* women, as well as in the cruelties inflicted upon farm animals (and animals used for purposes other than meat production, including, most notably, animals who are farmed for their fur). Yet the animal is usually absent in such imagery. As Adams notes, '[a]nimals are the absent referent in the act of meat eating; they also become the absent referent in images of women butchered, fragmented, or consumable' (2010: 13). She argues that

> The absent referent is that which separates the meat eater from the animals and the animal from the end product. The function of the absent referent is to keep our 'meat' separated from any idea that she or he was once an animal ... to keep something from being seen as having been someone. Once the existence of meat is disconnected from the existence of an animal who was killed to become that 'meat', meat becomes unanchored by its original referent (the animal), becoming instead a free-floating image, used often to reflect women's status as well as animals. (*ibid.*: 13)

Yet it could be said that while animal bodies are an absent referent in meat eating, the way in which they are absent referents in images of women butchered may appear different. In the first case, we hide our knowledge of what we eat; in the second, the killer emulates the butchering of animals, but (one might claim) he does not hide anything from himself (or from the reader). However, the butchering act by the murderer may be seen to be a transformative one. Turning women into meat at the very least enables the murderer to reduce women to objects the exploitation of which is normalised (and perhaps turning women into meat may even mask the murder itself).

With respect to crime narratives, the farm animal often appears invisible in the butchering imagery that is used, yet such imagery depends on the way we treat such animals. While the bodies of farm animals are literally manipulated, modified, crushed, sliced, force-fed, starved, cut and hacked, so too are the bodies of women in some crime and detective narratives (especially where cannibalism is involved); narratives which make use of imagery of the slaughterhouse. This is evinced in *The bone collector*. Below, the perpetrator imagines with admiration the actions of Schneider (an early twentieth-century killer):

> Beneath Schneider's bed, a constable found a diary … 'Bone' – (Schneider wrote) – 'is the ultimate core of a human being … Once the façade of our intemperate ways of the flesh, the flaws of the lesser Races, and the weaker gender, are burnt or boiled away, we are – all of us – noble bone … (2014a: 254).

While this quotation makes explicit the patriarchal hierarchy discussed above, and makes obvious reference to the ways in which the female victims are killed, the imagery used may be seen to describe the ways in which the bodies of farm animals are literally marked in the production process (burnt, boiled, stripped clean of flesh; and shockingly in some cultures it is not unknown for animals used in certain practices to be buried or burnt alive). In the same narrative, when summarising the behaviour of the perpetrator and comparing it to that of Schneider, Lincoln Rhyme notes that '[t]he MOs were the same – fire, animals, water, boiling alive' (*ibid.*: 395). Even the titles of crime and detective novels use such butchering imagery: consider, for example, *Abattoir blues* by Peter Robinson and *The body farm* by Patricia Cornwell, which associates bodies and farming (1994).

Images of meat and butchery with reference to female victims are plenteous in *The bone collector*. The perpetrator appears to enjoy butchery, and even has a painting on his wall of '[a]n eerie, moon-faced butcher, holding a knife in one hand, a slab of meat in the other' (2014a: 402). Places connected with slaughterhouses also feature prominently: the perpetrator's house is located near an old tannery (*ibid.*: 385), and a stockyard is the scene for an attempted murder of one of the victims; a female victim who is significantly portrayed as a lamb led to slaughter (*ibid.*: 167). In spite of copious associations between butchering, meat and females, the animal is (in Adams's words) the 'absent referent' in all these images (which further points to its invisible exploitation).

Further, in *The skin collector* Billy's second victim – Samantha Levine – is murdered in a nineteenth-century slaughterhouse culling area underground, which makes the connections between butchery and murderer even more explicit:

> In a different century … these corridors had been used to direct cattle to two different underground abattoirs here on the West Side of Manhattan.
>
> Healthy cows were directed to one doorway, sickly to another. Both were slaughtered for meat but the tainted ones were sold locally to the poor … The more robust cattle ended up in the kitchens of the Upper East- and Westsiders and the better restaurants in town.
>
> Billy didn't know which of the exits was for healthy beef, which was for sickly … He wished he knew because he wanted to tattoo the young lady in the tainted beef

> corridor – it just seemed appropriate. But he'd decided to do this mod in the place
> where the livestock cull had been made: the octagon itself. (Deaver 2014b: 182–83)

This quotation plays on a range of hierarchies, and the victim is presented as not just meat but 'tainted' meat. At the crime scene, Amelia draws connections to the Bone Collector's use of a former slaughterhouse: '[s]he remembered that the perp seemed to be influenced by the Bone Collector; that the killer had used a former slaughterhouse as a place to stash one of his victims – and staked her down, bloody, so she would be devoured alive by rats' (*ibid.*: 191).

MASKED OBJECTIFICATION

However, this imposed narrative is not absent in all crime novels. *Abattoir blues* is one such text which, while using the imagery of butchering and meat, makes fairly explicit the treatment of animals at the slaughterhouse and also draws attention to the ways in which animals are treated as consumables, as merely part of a production process. In this text the perpetrator is a former slaughterman and butcher who uses a stun-gun as his murder weapon, and this leads the detective, Annie, to make enquiries at a local abattoir where she is sickened by what she witnesses:

> Three monorails of dead animals slowly moved down the length of the abattoir. At each stage of the way, slaughtermen performed their specialised tasks, such as slitting the throat for bleeding, spraying with boiling water to loosen the skin, then the actual skinning and disemboweling and careful removal of valuable organs … The stench was awful. Annie tried to keep her eyes averted … but it was impossible. There was something about the ugly violent death that demanded one's attention, so she looked, she watched, she saw. And heard: the discharge of the bolt guns, the buzz of the mechanical saws, and the change in pitch when they hit bone as the head was cut off and the animals split in half. It was almost unthinkable that someone had done this to Morgan Spencer. (2015: 267–68)

Here, and elsewhere in the text, the treatment of nonhuman animals is made visible. The nonhuman animal is not absent from the imagery; rather, the literal treatment of nonhuman animals is explicitly associated with the treatment of the murder victim. In this way, the connection between female victim and non-human victims is foregrounded and the absent referent made visible. Annie, a vegetarian, is aware of the fact that the treatment of animals at the slaughter-house is purposely concealed from the public's view, and she strongly rejects one attempted justification for such treatment (a justification which appeals to the claim that the animals are unaware of their fate) (*ibid.*: 265). Annie refuses to make palatable or sanitise a practice which, if made visible, would be seen to be horrific and, for Annie, even murderous. She faces the situation head on, perceiving that which is normally shied away from ('the terrified animals' and 'the horrors being committed on the killing floor' (*ibid.*: 265)); that which is usually unheard and unseen.

Usually, though, our objectification of nonhuman animals as meat products renders the living beings as absent from the process of consumption and from our thoughts. This is evident in the language we use in relation to nonhuman animals generally and to the beings we eat. While women in crime narratives are recurrently described using this objectified language, animals are referred to as objects using the pronoun 'it', suggesting that the being to whom we are referring is nothing more than a mere inanimate object. We buy 'meat' not dead animals and we eat 'lamb chops', 'beef steaks', 'pork chops', not the dead parts of once-living individual sheep, cows and pigs. The living subject, as well as his or her slaughter, blood and suffering is missing from our view, from our consciousness and thus from our considerations. As Wadiwel claims, '[t]he image that one finds on some butcher shop signs, or on the side of refrigerated trucks, featuring a smiling cartoonised cow or pig slicing at their own bodies with a knife, attests to the causal way in which everyday violence is discursively hidden from view' (2015: 57). Similarly, Kirsty Dunn (in relation to an analysis of Michel Faber's *Under the skin* (2000)) discusses how language can camouflage not only sexual violence against women, but against animals too, 'hiding in plain sight' (2017: 152) the severe sufferings inflicted upon animals used in the meat industry (*ibid.*: 158). The once-living being, at the end of the production process, becomes so fragmented in a literal sense that we fail to see the truth behind every piece of animal flesh.

Other uses of language serve to reduce women to sexualised parts or to objects to be eaten or consumed by men. Consider, for example, 'fresh meat', a term used to refer to a young prostitute, 'dead meat', a term used to refer to an older prostitute (Adams 2004: 11), 'piece of skirt', 'piece of ass', 'tasty chick' and 'eye-candy'. Note also that, for the most part, nonhuman animals are referred to, and the metaphor of meat eating is employed. Moreover, the expression 'he made me feel like a piece of meat' is not uncommon. This expression is used in *Abattoir blues* when Alex (the girlfriend of a witness) comments on the behaviour of the victim: '[y]ou know, it's just like, if you're a woman he makes you feel like a piece of meat' (2015: 54). The explicit suggestion behind this expression tends to be that women should not be treated as pieces of meat. But when this expression is used an underlying (and implausible) implication tends to be that since nonhuman animals are literally viewed as meat then treating them as such is somehow justifiable. Indeed, such a well-used expression could be seen to convey a particular societal norm; that is, that it is permissible to treat nonhuman animals as pieces of meat, as objects to be consumed, but not permissible to do the same to human beings. But such a norm ignores dominant ideologies that link the oppression of women and animals, including anthropocentric and patriarchal ideas, the latter which, for Adams, are reflected in and substantiated by the patriarchal gaze (see above).

In using exploitative and hostile language, women are reduced to those nonhuman beings who are routinely objectified, fragmented, consumed, but so too are the women themselves, as subjects of their own lives, made absent and invisible through language which reinforces the historical idea of women as sexualised objects to be viewed and consumed, and as beings which lack agency and individuality. In *The skin collector* Billy thinks about reducing Amelia to an object in this way (and an object to be marked) when he states: '[o]h, he wanted so badly to get her on her back and give her one of his special mods' (Deaver 2014b: 153).[11] As with the language we use in relation to meat eating, the reality of the subject is masked. Similarly to nonhuman animals, women are 'marked' as something other than they are. Indeed, the exploitative language used to describe women negates their subjectivity, thereby maintaining a distance between the subject which oppresses and the being or 'object' which is oppressed.

In *The skin collector*, the character of Pamela resists this language and, despite being forcibly tattooed by Billy with 'splitter' tattoos, she rejects his patriarchal plan for her, speaks back and leaves a literal mark/'mod' of her own:

> 'You were my Lovely Girl. You'd grow up to be my woman and the mother of our children.'
>   'Like I was some kind of cow, some kind of fu---'
>   Striking like a snake, he jabbed his fist into her cheek, bone to bone. She inhaled at the pain.
>   'I won't warn you again. I'm your man and I'm in charge. Understand?' (*ibid.*: 380)

Her response – armed with a box cutter – is telling: '[t]he blade connected with Billy's cheek and mouth. Not like the slush sound of a stabbing in movies. Only the silent cutting of flesh. Pam leapt over the coffee table and headed for the front door, calling, "Okay, there's a mod for you, asshole"' (*ibid.*: 391). Pamela, here, invokes this hierarchical conflation of women as object and meat. That said, Pamela refers to the cow in a way which coveys the normality of *its* exploitation, implying that while it is unacceptable to define women as baby-making machines, defining female cows in this way is the norm. The female cow here becomes the object which lacks agency, the object whose life is not its own, and in reality it is used and exploited by both men and women alike.[12]

IDENTITY AND FORCED NARRATIVES

Autonomously chosen and acquired permanent tattoos are often thought to have a meaning that goes beyond the inscription of the actual tattoo artwork.

Indeed, in so far as one considers one's identity to be constituted at least partly by bodily continuity then, for such persons, 'tattoos are not just part of their body; they are part of themselves', or at least part of their narrative identity (Fruh and Thomas 2012: 88). While the tattooed person's body and psychological characteristics change and develop over time, their tattoo is an enduring mark (at least for the duration of their lifetime); a permanent reminder or individuating symbol. Admittedly, a tattoo will change as the skin changes and ages, but unless the tattoo is literally cut from the skin, then it remains part of one's body (and remains as such even if it is removed because tattoo removal results in significant scarring and skin alteration). However, while some tattoos can be associated with a person's attempt to individuate, some people acquire tattoos in an attempt to integrate themselves into a particular social group in which having a certain mark on one's skin identifies one as part of a larger group of persons. These notions of marking/tattooing and identity are played with in *The skin collector*. It transpires that Billy draws his insect tattoo in water-soluble ink (used for tattoo outlines) in order to enable him to switch between identities: Billy, the Underground Man and Seth. Here, it is the male who has control over his marks and representation. In Deaver's novel, it is not just the criminal who is 'modded'. Tattoo artist, 'TT' says to Rhyme: '"[h]ey, looks like you're one of us, dude."[...] "You're modded." [...] He pointed to Rhyme's arm, where scars were prominent, from the surgery to restore motion to his right arm and hand' (2014b: 245). So too is the other criminal, the Watchmaker, 'modded'. Rhyme tells him: 'you've changed – modded, if you will – again, right? Since we've run the picture' (*ibid.*: 416). Compared to the marked victims, the other 'marked' male figures in this novel have greater freedom and power. Correspondingly, the marking or branding of nonhumans in some sense signifies that their lives are *not* their own; that *their* narrative is perceived as really *our* narrative; nonhumans are largely viewed as ours to be consumed.

This connects to the *forced* marking of the skin, and in particular the forced marking of the skin of nonhuman beings. The skin of nonhumans, particularly those used in the practices of farming and of animal experimentation, is often marked either with a number or by piercing an identification tag through the skin (usually through the ear). These methods of marking are used in order to identify the nonhuman animal as, for example, an animal used in a certain experiment or belonging to a particular person.[13] For many people, such marking is merely considered as something that is done for a particular purpose, with no hidden meaning. But that they are identified in such ways is not insignificant; the way in which a nonhuman is identified establishes something about what that being is, or more accurately, about what humans' view that being to be; the being is reduced to merely a number, or a piece of property, or a consumable object. Billy's tattooed marks on his female victims do signify a hidden meaning, but they also are associated with experimentation and 'belonging' to Billy's 'modification' plan. His tattoo modifications connect the women as a group. They are ordered to form a select group in his own mind; *his* women. The women are emphatically identified by Billy with meat through his butchery practices.

CONCLUSION

In contemporary crime narratives we repeatedly see the trope/s of the butchered, branded, scarred and marked woman. Further, such markings extend to tattoos and to other bodily imprints, both literal and metaphorical. Language itself plays an important factor in such social and gendered inscriptions. However, such markings (seen and unseen) relate to not only women and crime fiction, but also to the lesser-known or examined connections between crime fiction, (marked/imprinted) women and the objectification of nonhumans. As well as reflecting the dominant hierarchical power structures in society, language and crime fiction also (at least implicitly) reinforces them, and cements people's general beliefs that the oppression of nonhuman beings (and women) is not only the norm but permissible. Being aware of such connections affords new ways of viewing such relationships and prompts further examinations into analogies between the literary and literal marking of women and nonhuman animals respectively in relation to issues of oppression and objectification.

NOTES

1 This chapter gives the original date of publication when discussing the novels. Quotations are given from the edition used by the authors. See Bibliography for further details (eds).

2 For example, see Verdaguer (2001), Michelis (2010), Watson (2012), Do (2013), Rowland (2015), Franks (2013) and Baučeková (2015). In Patricia Cornwell's forensic detective novels, Kay Scarpetta often focuses on preparing, cooking and eating food (including meat). For example, when Kay is cooking Marino dinner in *All that remains* (1992), he makes an analogy between eating, cutting and death, stating '[m]aybe you ought to forget cutting up dead bodies and open a restaurant' (Cornwell 1993: 167).

3 It is important to note that some men in crime fiction have also been treated in this manner (for example, the immanent sexual and murderous attack on Stieg Larsson's journalist, Mikael Blomkvist, in *The girl with the dragon tattoo* (2005), and a man being sexually tortured with cooking utensils in Val McDermid's *The mermaids singing* (1995)). For a discussion of this latter text, see Watson (2012).

4 In this novel, Detective Inspector Irene Huss's husband is a chef, and there is a focus on both family meals and what Irene and her colleagues are eating throughout the novel. There is a particular emphasis on vegetarian dishes and lifestyle in the Huss household, which starkly contrast to both this quotation and the (male and female) murders that take place.

5 Examples include Thomas De Quincey's famous 'On murder considered as one of the fine arts' (1827), Val McDermid's *The mermaids singing* (1995), Peter Ackroyd's *Dan Leno and the limehouse golem* (1994).

6 See Watson (2011).

7 This is reiterated later with the intentional neck breaking of Socks the kitten in *The body farm* (1994) and in *From Potter's field* (1995), when Scarpetta tells Wesley that she is 'so tired of cruelty. I'm so tired of people beating horses and killing little boys and head-injured women' (Cornwell 1996: 71).

8 Humans are explicitly couched in animal terms throughout Agatha Christie's *And then there were none* (1939). When five individuals are left, the novel states '[a]nd all of them, suddenly, looked less like human beings. They were reverting to more bestial types' (Christie 2007: 225). Ultimately, Vera Claythorne says to Blore and Lombard: '[d]on't you see? We're the Zoo ... Last night we were hardly human anymore. We're the Zoo ...' (Christie 2007: 265).

9 See Kerstin Bergman's Chapter 6 in this collection for discussion of David Lagercrantz's *The girl in the spider's web* (2016), a sequel to Stieg Larsson's Millennium novels.

10 It is beyond the scope of this chapter to provide a detailed outline of the treatment of animals in the practice of factory farming, but for a descriptive and visceral overview of the treatment of factory-farmed animals, see Kemmerer (2011: 'Appendix'), Singer (1995: ch.3), and Harrison (1964). For information on the treatment of animals in experiments, see Singer (1995: ch.2).

11 'Mods' are short for 'modifications' in the novel.

12 See Kemmerer (2011: 'Appendix').

13 Here, analogies can be made with the forced branding of human prisoners in Nazi concentration camps, who were branded with a number as a method of identification. Like branded nonhuman beings, such humans were reduced to a mere commodities or disposable objects.

BIBLIOGRAPHY

Adams, Carol J. (2004), *The pornography of meat* (New York and London: Continuum).

— (2010), *The sexual politics of meat: A feminist-vegetarian critical theory* [20th anniversary edn] (New York, London, New Delhi and Sydney: Bloomsbury).

Atwood, Margaret (1997), *Alias Grace* [1996] (London: Virago Press).

Baučeková, Silvia (2015), *Dining room detectives: Analysing food in the novels of Agatha Christie* (Newcastle upon Tyne: Cambridge Scholars Publishing).

Christie, Agatha (2007), *And then there were none* [originally published as *Ten little niggers* 1939] (London: HarperCollins).

Cornwell, Patricia (1993), *All that remains* [1992] (London: Time Warner).

— (1995), *The body farm* [1994] (New York: Warner Books).

— (1996), *From Potter's field* [1995] (London: Warner Books).

Deaver, Jeffery (2014a), *The bone collector* [1997] (London: Hodder and Stoughton).

— (2014b), *The skin collector* (London: Hodder and Stoughton).

DeMello, Margo (2000), *Bodies of inscription: A cultural history of the modern tattoo community* (Durham, NC: Duke University Press).

Do, Tess (2013), 'Food and crime fiction: Two complementary approaches to the

Vietnamese past in Tran-Nhut's *Les travers du docteur'*, *Edible alterities: Perspectives from la Francophonie* (Special issue), *PORTAL journal of multidisciplinary international studies*, 10:2, 1–20.

Dunn, Kirsty (2017), '"Do you know where the light is?" Factory farming and industrial slaughter in Michel Faber's *Under the skin'*, in A. Potts (ed.), *Meat Culture* (Leiden and Boston: Brill), pp.149–62.

Faber, Michel (2000), *Under the skin* (Edinburgh: Canongate Books).

Franks, Rachel (2013), 'Developing an appetite for food in crime fiction', *TEXT: Cookbooks: Writing, reading and publishing in culinary literature in Australia*, 24, 1–9.

Fruh, Kyle, and Emily Thomas (2012), 'Tattoo you: Personal identity in ink', in R. Arp (ed.), *Tattoos: Philosophy for everyone: I ink, therefore I am* (Oxford: Wiley-Blackwell), pp. 83–95.

German, Lindsey (2003), 'Women's liberation today', *International socialism journal*, 101, n.p.

Gregoriou, Christiana (2007), *Deviance in contemporary crime fiction* (Hampshire and New York: Palgrave Macmillan).

Harrison, Ruth (1964), *Animal machines: The new factory farming industry* (London: Vincent Stuart).

Kemmerer, Lisa (2011), 'Introduction' and 'Appendix', in L. Kemmerer (ed.), *Sister species: Women, animals, and social justice*, (Urbana, Chicago and Springfield: University of Illinois Press) 1–43, 173–85.

Larsson, Stieg (2008), *The girl with the dragon tattoo* [2005], trans. R. Keeland (London: MacLehose Press).

Lombroso, Cesare and Guglielmo Ferrero (2004), *Criminal woman, the prostitute, and the normal woman*, [1893] trans. and intro. N. H. Rafter and M. Gibson (Durham, NC: Duke University Press).

Mann, Jessica (2009), 'Crimes against fiction', *Standpoint* (9 Sep). Available: www.standpointmag.co.uk/node/2045 [accessed 12 April 2013].

McHugh, Susan (2011), *Animal stories: Narrating across species lines* (Minneapolis and London: University of Minnesota Press).

Michelis, Angelica (2010), 'Food and crime: What's eating the crime novel?', *European journal of English studies*, 14:2, 143–57.

Plain, Gill (2001), *Twentieth-century crime fiction: Gender, sexuality and the body* (Edinburgh: Edinburgh University Press).

Robinson, Peter (2015), *Abattoir blues* [2014] (London: Hodder and Stoughton, 2015).

Rowland, Susan (2015), 'Cooking the books: Metafictional myth and ecocritical magic in "cozy" mysteries from Agatha Christie to contemporary cooking sleuths', in C. Cothran and M. Cannon (eds), *New perspectives on detective fiction: Mystery, magnified* (Oxford and New York: Routledge), pp. 157–72.

Singer, Peter (1995), *Animal liberation* [2nd edn] (London: Pimlico Press).

Taliaferro, Charles, and Mark Odden (2012) 'Tattoos and the tattooing arts in perspective: An overview and some preliminary questions', in R. Arp (ed.), *Tattoos: Philosophy for Everyone* (Oxford: Wiley-Blackwell), pp. 3–13.

Tursten, Helene (2006), *The torso* [*Tatuerad torso*] [1999], trans. K. E. Tucker (New York: Soho Press).

Verdaguer, Pierre (2001), 'The politics of food in post-WWII French detective fiction', in L. R. Schehr and A. S. Weiss (eds), *French food: On the table, on the page, and in French culture* (New York: Routledge), pp. 184–202.

Wadiwel, Dinesh Joseph (2015), *The war against animals* (Leiden and Boston: Brill).

Warren, Samuel (1856), 'The experiences of a barrister' series [1849–50], in *Chambers's Edinburgh journal.*

Watson, Kate (2011), 'The hounds of fortune: Dog detection in the nineteenth century', *Clues: A journal of detection*, 29:1, 16–25.

— (2012), 'Engendering violence: Textual and sexual torture in Val McDermid's *The mermaids singing*', in C. Gregoriou (ed.), *Constructing crime: Discourse and cultural representations of crime and 'deviance'* (Hampshire and New York: Palgrave, Macmillan), pp. 194–208.

8

The tattoo wakes: Sentient ink, curatorship and writing the new weird in China Miéville's *Kraken: An anatomy*

Katharine Cox

INTRODUCTION

China Miéville is an innovative writer and critic of fantasy fiction, who emerged as part of the British sf/f renaissance at the end of the 1990s. His consideration of the new weird as a politically engaged form of fantasy is a direct challenge to theories of science fiction, building on Darko Suvin's hierarchy of sf (1979, 1983) that prioritises the value and potential of science fiction over fantasy (see Chu 2010; Vint 2015).[1] Miéville's apotheosis of the new weird is achieved in his novel *Kraken: An anatomy* (2010) through both form and content (Miéville 2009).[2] In *Kraken*, by recombining the twin foundations of modern detective and weird fiction,[3] Miéville 'was deliberately writing something big and monstery' (Miéville qtd *Socialist worker* 2010: n.p.). Through marking and remarking – metaphors of ink, tattooing and detection – writing the new weird is aligned to the process of tattooing. I argue this remarking process exposes the depth of the weird beyond the narrative of the modern and new weird that Miéville theorises. While Miéville's critical readings locate the genre in modernity, the reader can, in following his character Billy Harrow's detective[4] and interpretative lead, reveal the historical depths of the weird obscured by Miéville's curatorship.

WEIRD WRITERS, WEIRD CREATURES

Miéville's writing is explicitly informed by the weird tradition, both the modern weird, which he acknowledges, and the older weird related to fate and determinism, which I argue he suppresses in his critical writing. Though the weird has been under theorised, the genre is now receiving attention from author–critics M. John Harrison (2003, reproduced in VanderMeer and VanderMeer 2008), Jeff VanderMeer (2008, in VanderMeer and VanderMeer 2008) and in particular from Miéville, whose essay 'Long live the new weird' acts as a manifesto (2003; see also 2011).[5] These authors actively reposition the genre's politics (see Miéville 2011; Luckhurst 2016),[6] and are keen to see a form that is 'capable of speaking outwards with confidence' (Harrison in VanderMeer and VanderMeer 2008: 331). There is a thriving cross-fertilisation of ideas among these authors, who acknowledge explicit influence from *Weird tales* onwards.

In Harrison's discussion thread of 2003, he asks a community of writers, readers and fans the primary question 'The new weird. Who does it?'. The ownership of the term is reinforced later in the thread whereby Henry positions the idea of the new weird as an argument 'between a bunch of writers who read each other, who sometimes influence each other, sometimes struggle against that influence' (Henry qtd Harrison 2008, in VanderMeer and VanderMeer 2008: 329). A number of key discussions and publications shape the new weird. These include Miéville's guest editorship of a special edition of *Third alternative* (2003) which includes his essay 'Long live the new weird', M. John Harrison's discussion board (2003), Ann and Jeff VanderMeer's publication *The new weird* (2008) and 'Weird Council: An international conference on the writing of China Mieville [*sic*]' (2012). Its writers are ideologically engaged in writing socialist-informed fantasy as a political response after the Seattle WTO demonstrations of 1999 (Sust *et al.*, in VanderMeer and VanderMeer 2008: 349–62; Malcolm-Clarke 2008; Miéville 2003, 2011). These writers self-consciously re-appropriate the literary legacy and mythos of (modern) weird fiction as focalised by H. P. Lovecraft's creative and critical work. The unknowingness and impenetrability of the weird is central to Miéville's critique of Lovecraft and he conflates this with uniqueness in response to modernity. Lovecraft's concern with racial degeneracy is inverted as the new weird promotes possibility in a multi-species milieu.

In *Kraken*, Miéville's godhead is a preserved giant squid, the 'default' contemporary monster (Miéville 2011; see also Corstophine 2011 and Luckhurst 2014), re-imagined through the lens of new weird fiction. This is not the fear or horror-inspired manifestation described by Lovecraft in 'Notes on writing weird fiction' (1938), but rather the ironic repositioning of a weird creature, causing a transmutation of awe.[7] As a post-Lovecraftian story the godhead is comically grotesque, the cult it inspires dysfunctional, and it serves as a reminder of the ironic return of the new weird. Despite the apparent otherness of the squid, what better creature to worship than this with its sacs of ink 'waiting for us, aeons before writing' (Miéville 2010: 402)?

As Miéville demonstrates in his critical writings, the new weird is a reframing of past traditions whereby as author he acts in part as a 'conduit' (Jordan qtd Miéville 2011). However, Miéville demonstrates a far more selective approach in his discussion and curatorship of weird writing. I use the concept of 'curatorship' as it conveys an active role of construction and management combined with the care of a custodian (*OED* n1). The term also encompasses the role of his character Harrow in identifying, preserving and naming the squid. Across his critical writing, Miéville details and limits the periods of the weird as: pre-weird (associated with Jules Verne and Victor Hugo's seafaring narratives); the locus of the weird or *haute* weird (in particular, with Lovecraft)[8] and new weird (including Neil Gaiman, Stephen King, Michael Moorcock and Miéville; see Miéville 2008, 2009, 2011). It is clear that Miéville is emotionally and ideologically invested in the political potential of new weird. He identifies a lineage of weird writing born out of 'crisis-blasted modernity' (Miéville 2011: n.p.). Contrary to Miéville's identification of new weird's monsters as the offspring of nineteenth-century literary sea-creatures, I argue the 'vaguely familiar' feeling they evoke (Malcolm-Clarke 2008: 338)[9] is born of much earlier weird heritage which re-emerges in *Kraken*.

Miéville's discussions of the weird emphatically reject the idea of weird texts prior to these 'pre-weird' texts of the nineteenth century. In doing so, he suppresses mythological examples of weirdness and earlier literary examples of archetypal monsters of the weird, typically from the deep ocean. I assert both genres can be traced to ancient texts and the default weird creature, the monstrous Kraken, found in an array of different literatures. Miéville, on the other hand, claims to find no historical precedent for the tentacular Kraken in 'Gothic or traditional precedents (in "Western" aesthetics)' (Miéville 2008: 105). It is precisely his emphasis on the newness and unknowability of the weird that causes him to close off these earlier examples.

An exploration of the etymologies of 'new' and 'weird' challenge Miéville's neat lineage of the critical form. 'Weird' is an old term with etymological variants in Old English, High German and Norse. The *Oxford English dictionary* lists the supernatural quality of weird (1b; 4a; 5d) but also notes the older and more numerous meanings associated with prophesying fate (1a; 2a, b; 3a, c; 4b; 5b, c). Prominent examples of weird individuals able to tell the future include the Norns (fates) in Norse mythology, who spin out each wo/man's thread of life, the Sybils from Roman mythology, who variously read fate from books or speak as oracle, culminating in the representation of the weird/wyrd sisters in *Macbeth*. 'New' might suggest a renewal of an existing form, recalling the obsolete and rare uses of 'new' as a verb (*OED*).[10] The coupling of 'new' with 'weird' places joint emphasis on both terms. In so doing, Miéville's reengagement with the weird evokes past tropes that predate the modern weird authors Edgar Allan Poe, Arthur Machen, Algernon Blackwood, Lovecraft and others.

Miéville's choice of a cephalopod as godhead foregrounds an earlier literary and mythological lineage. Taking the Kraken as an example, there are descriptions of squid-like monsters ranging from Norse mythology, to ancient Greece (Homer's Scylla and Charybdis, the combat of Hercules against Triton, representations from the 'Minoan' period including pottery and a preserved fresco at Knossos 2000–1000 BCE) to the biblical Leviathan and the 'polyp' of Pliny the elder's *Naturalis historia*. It is evident that records of strandings of giant squid are more frequent from 1860 onwards and the creature is represented in the literature of Victor Hugo and Jules Verne among others. The decision to refer to the squid as 'Kraken' foregrounds earlier literary and mythological influences though, as well as encourages the reader to read the beast through literature from Alfred Tennyson, John Wyndham and Hugh Cook. 'Kraken' is a term of Norwegian descent and refers to a gigantic creature, perhaps 'the largest and most surprising of all the animal creation' (Berthelson 1755 qtd *OED*); a harbinger of Apocalypse, it is often represented as sleeping in the deep (Miéville refers to this in the chapter 'Universal sleeper'). Lovecraft's Cthulhu, a tentacular alien-hybrid, draws on Tennyson's Kraken in its deep, near-eternal sleep (Corstophine 2011: n.p.). However, Miéville repeatedly downplays representations of cephalopods in pre-nineteenth-century literature as he seeks to delimit the meanings of the creature, as his character Harrow does in naming the squid as specimen (Miéville 2010: 461). Groundbreaking research into giant squid by Tsunemi Kubodera and Kyoichi Mori (2005) captured images of a fearsome predator which dramatically revised scientific and historical depictions of the squid. These active and predatory traits support the squid's literary history – a lineage Miéville is keen to mask – as a fearsome monster of the deep. Miéville's attempts to define the lineage of his monster and the parameters of the new weird, mirrored by Harrow's role as curator, ultimately undermines this project. The reader's attention is drawn to failure of taxonomy to sustain order.

ILLUSTRATED MEN: TATTOOS AND CRIME

Tattoos are foregrounded in *Kraken* through a series of illustrated men; principally, Tattoo and Grisamentum. There is symmetry between Tattoo and Grisamentum, both in terms of their criminal activities, which shaped London (Miéville 2010: 367), and their representation through sentient ink. Tattoo has been extracted from his body by Grisamentum, his essence bound to tattooing ink before being imprisoned onto the unsuspecting Paul through the process of tattooing. 'Whatever nasty miracle it was had en-dermed him had thrown away his name as well as his body. Everyone knew they used to know what he was called, including him, but no one recalled it now' (*ibid.*: 97). This creative revenge backfires. Despite being disembodied and then trapped within a 'mobile skin prison' (*ibid.*: 377), Tattoo prevails and tricks Paul into re-assembling his criminal empire.

Ironically, this physical 'prison' houses Tattoo but does not have the power to restrict his criminal activities. The proto-criminologist Cesare Lombroso (1876) identified tattooing as the visual stigmas and signifiers of criminality, representing an internal degeneration. There is no internal degeneration to be measured in Tattoo but he does confirm Lombroso's essentialist view of criminality. Tattoo is criminal incarnate, a 'criminarch'. Descriptions of Tattoo emphasise his hierarchical power and social position as 'eminence', 'boss' (Miéville 2010: 337), 'criminarch' (97), 'Svengali' (380) and 'illicit king' (97). Crucially, these descriptions stop short of describing him as divine. When explaining to Harrow about Tattoo, Dane transitions between classifying Tattoo as a thing or person but emphasises his earthliness through criminality: '"[t]hat tattoo's a god?" "*Fuck* no. It's a criminal. A fucking villain is what he is"' (*ibid.*: 78). In structuralist terms, Tattoo is both the signifier and the signified. Revealed as Tattoo, he literally is crime.

The capitalised letter indicates a name as well as an occupation. Tattoo is, as Karl Marx outlines, the 'criminal who produces crimes' (1956: n.p.). As employer, he revels in transforming his minions into their labour functions (his watchman has the head of a dog, his hired muscle have fists for heads). Tattoo is pre-eminently a boss. He is revealed as a capitalist essentialist whose labour and delegation of labour define him. Without him, his outsourced gangs continue in increasingly chaotic frenzies (Miéville 2010: 380–81). He is the tattooed representation of a head, making him both the virtual and actual head of a body politic of crime which emphasises the modified body (giant fist heads, naked body transmitters), and the body he lost.

Tricked and coerced into reforming Tattoo's criminal empire, Paul is scarred both physically, by the process of tattooing, and psychologically by the 'en-dermed' tyrant. Unhappy and unfortunate in his body, during a brief period of freedom Paul attempts to remove the t/Tattoo. Finding legitimate opportunities for tattoo removal closed to him, he attempts a painful and unorthodox removal through the use of sandpaper.[11] This process recalls the use of sandstone to remove layers of (indigenous) skin by early missionaries in Polynesia (after *Leviticus* 19:28), called Holystoning. After finally prevailing against Tattoo, Paul chooses to retain Tattoo as a tattoo. By using magic, he effectively gags the criminal by inking his mouth closed. This stops Tattoo's voice but not his eyes or his mind. It recalls the power that Tattoo exerted over Paul, restricting his movements and threatening to incapacitate him through amputation. As Paul notes, in a rephrasing of Tattoo's threats: '[i]f he gives me too much shit I might blind him' (Miéville 2010: 479). Without his voice Tattoo is truly trapped.

If Tattoo is a criminarch, Grisamentum's imaginative desire to bond with Kraken ink reveals him as a supra-criminal. Grisamentum cheats death through combining his essence (contained in the ashes following his cremation) with water, glue and rich knack to become an ink. Making ink from burnt matter recalls Pliny's descriptions of the process from mixed water and 'soot' (n.p.). Pliny also refers to the practice of extracting ink from polyps or cuttlefish as sepia. Grisamentum's mixing with different inks explores both the human-made and natural forms of ink. He is transformed: 'with the kraken's ink, ink also, the two inks, one new ink, and changed' (Miéville 2010: 459). As a scholar of London and its traditions (*ibid*.: 204), Grisamentum chooses an old ink factory in London to digest the Krakenists's library and to finally mix with the squid ink.

Far from maintaining a balance of order in the criminal underworld of London, as supposed by the police and the Krakenists, Grisamentum, temporally thwarted by his disease and transformation into an embodied ink, craves total power. Believing the squid to be a Kraken, Grisamentum's existentialist desire is to bind with the cephalopod's ink so that he can write the doctrine of his new world. To be '[t]he very writing on the wall. The logbook, the instructions by which the world worked. Commandments' (Miéville 2010: 402). Unlike Tattoo who is literal and so limited, Grisamentum's form of tattooing, by using himself as ink, reveals protean and authorial potential.

In contrast to Tattoo's rebirth which confirms his nature as criminal, transfiguration is prevented for Grisamentum until he can join with the squid's ink. After his initial reduction to ash, mixed to form a type of ink, he also bonds with ink drawn from the Kraken library to imbibe knowledge of the squid (*ibid*.: 441). Although he appears reliant on Byrne his partner to transcribe his inked instructions, he is also able to change, encharming paper to create a tiger and in his inkform writes spells on the body that kill. Grisamentum as the combined ink is revealed as briefly 'authorial' and able to remake place as he 'writes' (*ibid*.: 459). As the embodiment of *logos*, from the polysemic λόγος in ancient Greek, Grisamentum reflects the term's etymology that includes 'word' and 'ground'. As λόγος, he is the divine Word of God (*John* I: i) able to remake place through a genesis.[12] His adaptability makes him more versatile than Tattoo but ultimately more vulnerable too. Made new in his compound inkform, he is susceptible to Harrow's persuasion as bottle prophet.

NEW WEIRD DETECTIVE FICTION: PROPHETS, BELIEF AND INK

There are a series of crimes, detectives and manners of detecting presented in the novel. Examples range from the unorthodox but institutional detectives that make up the Fundamentalist and Sect-Related Crime Unit, the abstract spiritual police entities, Marge's social-networking to discover the cause of her boyfriend Leon's death, to the 'patchwork detections' undertaken by Paul to overcome Tattoo (Miéville 2010: 407). Unbound by the procedures of mundane policing, the FSRC pressurise suspects where with '[a] few cosmetic knacks [...] his skin looked quite untouched, all his bruises glamoured away' (*ibid*.: 305, see also 203) and take inspiration from fictional detectives to construct virtual officers to apply occult jurisprudence. These generalised police entities reflect stereotypes from golden age television police procedurals: *The sweeney, The professionals* along with their 'fetishised' representation in *Life on Mars* (*ibid.*: 191).

The most prominent detective in the novel, Harrow, inhabits a variety of guises, including curator, detective and prophet.[13] As detective he seeks to read past events, isolate clues to logically identify the thief who stole the squid. He is changed into a prophet through his weird encounters with sentient ink. Although Harrow is not visibly transformed in Tattoo's utilitarian workshop it does serve to make him aware of another London, one that 'he recognised no more than if it were Tripoli' (*ibid.*: 73). In *Empire of the senseless*, Kathy Acker considers the origin of the tattoo from overseas and comments that to see a tattoo outside of its seafaring milieu was to witness 'icons of power and mystery designating realms beyond normal land-dwellers' experience' (qtd Temple 2012). Tattoo does this literally. To see Tattoo is to reveal this inner London of Londonmancers, chaos Nazis and gods. Harrow's reluctance to acknowledge this other London can be read in the way in which he refers to Tattoo as 'tattoo' (Miéville 2010: 91, 98, occasional uppercase 97). In comparison, the third person narrative, Dane and the other Krakenists all capitalise the 'T' of Tattoo. It is not until Harrow believes in the alternative London and his place as a prophet within it that he refers to the Tattoo with deference (*ibid.*: consistently from p. 137 onwards).[14]

As a prophet, his role is weird. He is expected to read and narrate events before they happen by interpreting God's Word; in this instance through the practice of drinking squid ink. Harrow is widely regarded by weird Londoners as a Kraken prophet. His prophetic dreams, created by his initial submersion via squid ink, allow him to return to the watery depths where in '[a]we, not fear' he sees his squid specimen sinking downwards 'still in suspension in its tank' (*ibid.*: 80–81). His visions emphasise the squid as a bottled or tanked specimen. Billy's final dream, unbidden by the ink, sees the bottle without the squid: '[h]e felt the universe, exasperated, was giving him an insultingly clear insight, that he was simply missing' (*ibid.*: 212). Harrow as prophet recalls the reluctant Sibyl, a Roman priestess charged with speaking as an oracle. As the novel progresses, it becomes obvious that he has been chosen as a messiah by another ancient force. London is riddled with memory angels, with one charged with protecting the museum's exhibits, including the giant squid. The museum's angel takes the form of a bottle. Due to a joke about being the first child created by *in vitro* fertilisation (a test-tube baby), Harrow is mistaken for being a bottle prophet: '*you came, born not of woman but of glass*' (*ibid.*: 292; author's emphasis), Harrow's destiny is as a '*bottle* prophet' (*ibid.*: 460; author's emphasis).[15] The author draws the reader's attention towards this by using weird as an adverb. The term '[fiasco] was weirdly tenacious in his head' (*ibid.*). Language and the ability to persuade are central to the role of the prophet (though not the original Sibyl who was, at times, crucially ignored). Harrow understands this when he reminds himself that the etymology of 'fiasco' refers to an Italian bottle (n.1. *OED*). The memory angel considers him a bottle prophet because language has the ability to persuade.

Harrow's investigations into the theft of the squid narrow the potentiality of both Londons, promising instead a 'closed-down future' (Miéville 2010: 241) where 'other maybes [... are] drying up, one by one' (*ibid.*: 187). The role of language to actualise other possibilities is key here. There are different versions of meaning-making represented by Tattoo (a structuralist harking after the 'perfect' semantic moment) and Grisamentum (a poststructuralist). Harrow, meanwhile, has evolved beyond this. He combines imaginative thinking with literal understanding of metaphor. As he begins to belong in the alternant London, he gives 'equal ontological weight to both the metaphor and the thing it "really" stands for' (Vint 2015: 51). As Christopher Palmer claims, '[l]iteralism is important to the whole project of *Kraken*' (2014: 171). This is reflected in Miéville's multi-faceted approach to the idea of the tattoo, which functions in both literal and metaphorical forms.

By acting as a custodian, Harrow mediates Grisamentum and our understandings of the *Architeuthis* and reduces it from mythical 'Kraken' to specimen (and not even representative of the genus), whose ink is tainted as a result. Ultimately, Harrow names the squid coupled with written evidence: '[i]t's a specimen and it's in the books [...] We've written it up' (Miéville 2010: 461). He reveals that his 'Archie' is a specimen, created through human taxonomy and preservation.[16] His verbal persuasion is heard by the universe which causes the inks to curdle, turning against one another. In his destruction, Grisamentum is effectively covered up by the ink in the process of being 'overwritten [...] effaced by ink (*ibid.*). A fitting end for this scholar, criminal and tattooist.

The central battle represented by the sentient inks of Tattoo and Grisamentum is about the nature of writing and interpretation. Power is repeatedly presented through the written word. Harrow notes: '[t]his has always been about *writing*' (*ibid.*: 402; author's emphasis), but it is also about the reception and interpretation of writing and the persuasion that ensues. As prophet, Harrow rewrites Grisamentum's victory. He is able to impose a taxonomy (reducing the divine Kraken to *Architeuthis*, a specimen) which ultimately contains and constrains Grisamentum's power. With his categorisation of the squid, Harrow defeats Grisamentum's poststructuralist project, reinforcing boundaries and structural order, at least superficially. Here, at the end of the novel, Miéville reveals that this process of curation, is contingent upon argumentation and belief: '[it's] all a matter of persuasion' (*ibid.*: 468). In doing so, Miéville effectively offers an implicit challenge to his own curated theorisation of the new weird.

CONCLUSION

Miéville's subtitle for the novel is 'an anatomy', but it would be more accurate to call it a curation, as Miéville defines and explores the territory of the new weird, mediated through the modern weird. The novel's attention to language, rhetoric and interpretation heightens the reader's awareness of Miéville's own acts of persuasion. The use and practice of the tattoo to write the new weird is revealed as polysemic and, beyond Miéville's curatorship, it remarks and speaks of older meanings. By considering metaphors of ink, tattoo and tattooing as representative of the new weird's complex associations with body, place and meaning, this chapter challenges Miéville's theorisation of the new weird and details a historically nuanced understanding of the relationship between writing, detection and tattooing in weird fiction. Representations of sentient ink and tattoos to mark a locus of the new weird are ultimately revealed as textual and semantic remarkings which challenge Miéville's theorisation. These tropes serve to highlight a belonging which far exceeds the modern tradition. The weird as part of crisis-blasted modernity opens up to older, suppressed representations of the weird associated with the idea of the Kraken, the etymology of 'weird' and the associations of the tattoo which are active in the text.

Miéville's use of tattoos as a metaphor for writing highlights the body's potential as a site to reclaim power in literature more widely. Emphasis on modes of ink and tattooing can be extended and used as a means to explore contemporary ontological debates of self, embodiment and representation. Miéville's curatorship of the new weird and the development of the genre masks the extent to which weirdness is a feature of literature more widely. In doing so, the new weird is effectively challenged in the very novel Miéville uses to celebrate the genre but, conversely, demonstrates a broader potential. Rather than move on and identify the 'Next Weird' (J. VanderMeer in VanderMeer and VanderMeer 2008), it is time to read the markings and remarkings of weirdness within contemporary literature as a whole. By engaging with writing fantasy, place and the body, this consideration has the potential to re-evaluate the importance of weirdness and fantasy as a means of textualising, articulating and empowering contemporary representations of self.

NOTES

1 Donna Haraway goes even further and claims that these new weird creatures, the borders between human, nonhuman animal and our ecology inform and articulate our contemporary epoch, in her book *Staying with the trouble: Making kin in the Chthulucene* (2016).

2 Ann and Jeff VanderMeer (2008) suggest Miéville's *Perdido Street Station* (2000),

the first of his Bas Lag trilogy, is a fulcrum of writing the new weird. I argue that this is surpassed by *Kraken*.

3 Both genres evolved through dime novels in the years 1860–1915 (Bedore 2013) and were consolidated in the genre-based pulp fiction golden age (1920s–1930s). Despite the complementary publishing history of these genres, they are dealt with separately by critics.

4 Harrow's name is perhaps a pun on the tattooing torture machine in Franz Kafka's 'In the penal colony' (1919).

5 See Jeff VanderMeer and Martin Šust *et al.* (both in VanderMeer and VanderMeer 2008). The discussion thread is reprinted in the same volume (*ibid.*: 317–32). Ann and Jeff VanderMeer's collection *The new weird* (2008) is an innovative publication which combines analytical and creative extracts. It reproduces significant, and some multi-authored, work concerning the genre.

6 Modern weird is defined by, and associated with, H. P. Lovecraft, who espoused racist, misogynist, xenophobic views and rhetoric in his fiction and letters (see in particular Houellebecq 2008). Both Miéville and Michel Houellebecq highlight Lovecraft's treatment of race but do so with recourse to his style by identifying the powerful affect of his writing to inspire horror, awe and fear. Houellebecq recalls Lovecraft's style as a 'poetic trance' achieved through an aesthetics of hate (Houellebecq qtd Miéville n.d.). However, Miéville does address these features of Lovecraft's writing through his own creative work in the recovery of the weird.

7 The theft of the cephalopod from London's Natural History Museum mirrors the madcap hi-jinx of Disney's film *One of our dinosaurs is missing* (1975).

8 It is easy to be critical of Lovecraft and his oeuvre. His writing style is at best patchy; however, critics such as Joshi (1990) and Houellebecq (2008) have sought to establish this as part of his deliberate style.

9 See Paul Kincaid for a discussion of these types of godhead in post-1992 sf as a response to global religious conflict (2008).

10 There are a number of sf subgenres that use the term 'new'. These include new space opera, new wave fabulism and the new weird (see Kincaid 2008). Definitions of science fiction and fantasy are notoriously fraught, but newness is often key to different emergent subgenres.

11 In 'The illustrated man', which fuses of elements of the weird and detection, Ray Bradbury's tattooed protagonist recalls various means to remove his bewitched illustrations: 'sandpaper, acid, a knife' (2008: n.p.), to no avail.

12 I am grateful to Dr Harriet Earle who pointed out the ways in which Miéville is engaging with *logos* and its etymology.

13 These interpretative roles are prominently represented in Antiquity by the binary representations of proto-detective Oedipus and the blind prophet Tiresias.

14 A similar process can be traced in Dane's experience. When Harrow meets Simon (a teleporting Trekkie) he immediately recognises his constructed familiar as a Tribble (Star Trek original series, series 2 episode 15 'The trouble with tribbles' 1967). Dane's lack of general knowledge about the series causes him refer to the creature in the lower case (see Miéville 2010: 217).

15 Harrow is repeatedly associated with glass. His spectacles highlight both his kinship with the glass of the memory angel but also his lack of insight as prophet; rather like a specimen himself, he ends the novel expectant 'behind glass' (Miéville 2010: 481).

16   This categorisation of the creature in human terms recalls Jules Verne's depiction
     of the terrific cephalopod in *20,000 leagues under the sea* (1869). Despite Miéville's
     concerns that Verne's cephalopod is 'de-weirded' through human observation and
     rationalised enquiry (2011), this same consideration forms the crux of his dénoue-
     ment between Harrow and Grisamentum.

BIBLIOGRAPHY

Bedore, Pamela (2013), *Dime novels and the roots of American detective fiction* (London: Palgrave Macmillan).

Bradbury, Raymond (2008), *The illustrated man* [1952] [ebook version] (London: Harper Collins).

— (2013), 'The illustrated woman' [1961], *The machineries of joy* [ebook version] (London: Harper Collins).

Chu, Seo-Young (2010), *Do metaphors dream of literal sleep?: A science-fictional theory of representation* (Harvard: Harvard University Press).

Corstorphine, Kevin (2011), 'Day of the tentacle?' University of Stirling: The gothic imag-ination. Available: www.gothic.stir.ac.uk/guestblog/day-of-the-tentacle/ [accessed 21 June 2017].

Foucault, Michel (2006), 'The Utopian body', *Sensorium* (Cambridge, MA: MIT Press), pp. 229–34.

Haraway, Donna (2016), *Staying with the trouble: Making kin in the Chthulucene* (Durham, NC: Duke University Press).

Harrison, John M. [and others] (2003), 'The new weird. Who does it? What is it?' [discussion board], reproduced in A. and J. VanderMeer (eds) (2008), *The New Weird* (San Francisco: Tachyon), pp. 317–31.

Houellebecq, Michel (2008), *H.P. Lovecraft: Against the world, against life*, trans. D. Khazeni (London: Orion).

Joshi, S. T. (1990), *The modern weird tale* (Jefferson: McFarland).

Kincaid, Paul (2008), *What it is we do when we read science fiction* (Essex: Beccon Publications).

Kubodera, Tsunemi and Kyoichi Mori (2005), 'First-ever observations of a live giant squid in the wild', *Proceedings of the Royal Society B: Biological Sciences* 272:1581, 2583–86.

Lombroso, Cesare (1876), *Criminal man* [*L'Uomo delinquente*] (Milano: Hoepli).

Lovecraft, H. P. (1938), 'Notes on writing weird fiction', *Supramundane stories* (spring).

Luckhurst, Roger (2016), 'Weird stories: The potency of horror and fantasy', in D. Head (ed.), *The Cambridge history of the English short story* (Cambridge: Cambridge University Press), pp. 447–63.

Malcolm-Clarke, Darja (2008), 'Tracking phantoms' in A. and J. VanderMeer (eds), *The New Weird* (San Francisco: Tachyon).

Marx, Karl (1956), *Theories of surplus value: Part I* (Moscow: Foreign Languages Publishing House).

Miéville, China (n.d.), 'China Miéville on a favourite New York Story'. Available: www.youtube.com/watch?v=mSxm_nhqDyw [accessed 21 June 2017].

— (2003), 'Long live the new weird', *Third alternative*, 35 (Summer), n.p.

— (2008), 'Multilateralism as terror: International law, Haiti and imperialism', *Finnish yearbook of international law*, 19. Available: http://eprints.bbk.ac.uk/783 [accessed 21 June 2017].

— (2009), 'Long live the new weird', *Extrapolation*, 35.

— (2010), *Kraken: An anatomy* (London: Pan Macmillan).

— (2011), 'M.R. James and the quantum vampire weird; Hauntological: Versus and/ or and and/or or?' Available: www.thing.net/~rdom/ucsd/Zombies/Quantum%20 Vampire.pdf [accessed 11 September 2018].

Palmer, Christopher (2014), 'Ordinary catastrophes: Paradoxes and problems in some recent post-Apocalypse fiction', in G. Canavan and K. S. Robinson (eds), *Green planets: Ecology and science fiction* (Middletown: Wesleyan University Press), pp. 158–78.

Socialist worker (2010), 'Kraken: China Miéville interview', *Socialist worker*, 2202 (18 May) Available: http://socialistworker.co.uk/art/20857/Kraken%3A+China+Mi% C3%A9ville+interview [accessed 21 June 2017].

Sukin, Darko (1979), *Metamorphoses of science fiction: On the poetics and history of a literary genre* (New Haven and London: Yale University Press).

— (1983), *Victorian science fiction in the UK: The discourses of knowledge and of power* (Boston: G.K. Hall).

Šust, Martin, Michael Haulica, Hannes Riffel, Jukka Halme and Konrad Walewski (2008), 'European editor perspectives on the new weird', in A. and J. VanderMeer (eds) (2008), pp. 349–62.

Temple, Emily (2013), 'Literary ink: Famous authors and their tattoos' (23 June). Available: http://flavorwire.com/311333/literary-ink-famous-authors-and-their-tattoos/ [accessed 21 June 2017].

VanderMeer, Ann and Jeff VanderMeer (eds) (2008), *The New Weird* (San Francisco: Tachyon).

VanderMeer, Jeff (2008), 'The new weird: "It's alive?"' in A. and J. VanderMeer (eds) (2008), pp. ix–xviii.

Verne, Jules (1869), 'Vingt mille lieues sous les mers', *Magasin d'éducation et de récréation* [serialised], (2017), *20,000 leagues under the sea: English edition* [1872], trans. and intro. David Coward (ed.) (London: Penguin Classics).

Vint, Sherryl (2015), 'Ab-realism: Fractal language and social change' in C. Edwards and T. Venezia (eds) *China Miéville: Critical essays* (Canterbury: Gylphi).

'Weird Council: An international conference on the writing of China Mieville' [*sic*] (2012), Available: https://www.sas.ac.uk/videos-and-podcasts/culture-language-and-literature/weird-council-international-conference-writing-0 [accessed 17 December 2018].

PART 4

Children's literature:
Dark marks, scars and secret societies

9

Dark marks, curse scars and corporal punishment: Criminality and the function of bodily marks in the *Harry Potter* series

Lucy Andrew

INTRODUCTION

Although the *Harry Potter* series is traditionally positioned within the fantasy genre, it can also be read as a crime narrative with Harry as the 'ultimate detective' at its heart (Zipes 2002: 179). Charles Elster argues that 'Harry is a detective in the tradition of Philip Marlowe and Nancy Drew, and the series is more clearly in the mystery genre than the fantasy genre' (2003: 206). Certainly, Harry begins the series like Nancy Drew: an amateur investigator, uncovering secrets, solving mysteries and combating evil. As Christopher Routledge observes in his assessment of the first four books in the series, Harry and his companions' investigative process 'is one of gathering clues [...] forming theories about "whodunit"' and 'finding justice for the wrongly accused' (2001: 205). This is certainly true of the first three books, where Harry must expose the concealed 'criminal' character and exonerate those who are suspected. In *The philosopher's stone* (1997), Harry discovers that it is the ostensibly harmless Professor Quirrell rather than the openly unpleasant Professor Snape who is attempting to steal the Philosopher's Stone. In *The chamber of secrets* (1998), he identifies Tom Riddle as the heir of Slytherin who sets the basilisk on Hogwarts' students, proving the innocence of Hagrid, who has been arrested for the crime, in the process. In *The prisoner of Azkaban* (1999), Harry learns that it is Peter Pettigrew, rather than his own godfather, escaped convict Sirius Black, who betrayed Harry's parents by revealing their whereabouts to Voldemort. Here, the criminal figures disguise their identities to evade capture: Professor Quirrell wears a turban which conceals the face of his master, Voldemort, with whom he now shares a body; an imprint of Tom Riddle is concealed within an old diary which, it later transpires, is a Horcrux containing part of Voldemort's soul; and Peter Pettigrew is an Animagus who can transform into a rat and who escapes detection by remaining in his animal form as Ron Weasley's pet rat, Scabbers, for several years. In true clue-puzzle form, the resolution of the narrative occurs when Harry uncovers these concealed criminals and the threat dissipates – temporarily at least.

However, the (re)introduction of Voldemort's Dark Mark, the symbol branded upon his Death Eaters in *The goblet of fire* (2000), marks a crucial transition in the series from the clue-puzzle form, which has long been popular in children's literature, to a more mature type of crime narrative in which criminality is openly expressed and pervasive. The Dark Mark indicates the shift from a concealed, conquerable foe to a publicly recognised terrorist organisation. The series' crime narrative, and the Dark Mark in particular, is tied up with issues of terror, intimidation, control, possession, punishment and, more broadly, identity and morality. Both Voldemort's Dark Mark and Harry's lightning-bolt scar, a product of Voldemort's failed killing curse against Harry, dominate the second half of the series and are, initially at least, representative of the fight between good and evil, hero and villain, detective and criminal. This chapter will examine how bodily marks – namely brands and scars – contribute to the changing nature and complexity of the series' overarching crime narrative, examining the symbolic status and functions of these marks and considering the role that they play in reconfiguring the identities of and relationships between criminal, victim and seeker of justice as the series progresses.

The 'whodunit' element which Routledge identifies in the first four books is eradicated at the end of *The goblet of fire* when the concealed criminal Barty Crouch Junior, has, by the time he is exposed, brought about Voldemort's restoration to his former body. Coinciding with the maturation of the protagonist and the series' initial child readers and the growth of the series' adult audience (Falconer 2009: 15–16), *The goblet of fire* is more 'adult' than its predecessors, particularly in terms of the escalation of violence. It is the first book in which any serious crimes occur directly within the narrative – with the murders of Frank Bryce, Barty Crouch Senior and Cedric Diggory – and in which one of the criminal culprits, Barty Crouch Junior, is punished by the Ministry of Magic, receiving the Dementor's kiss for his crimes. From here onwards, the emphasis is not so much on 'whodunit' but on how to thwart the powerful criminal organisation – the Death Eaters and their leader, Voldemort – who are now threatening to terrorise the wizarding world once more. The resolution of the mystery and black and white morality of the early books is replaced by the irresolution of criminal threats and the moral complexity of the later texts, which incorporate 'shades of grey and the relativity of good and evil' (Klaus 2012: 32). Here, Harry's world and work are now more akin to that of Philip Marlowe than that of Nancy Drew. The series has evolved from a child-friendly mystery to a quasi-adult crime narrative and Voldemort's Dark Mark, Harry's curse scar and other bodily marks play a key role in signifying this transition.

MARKS OF DARKNESS: MARKING THE CRIMINAL

With the re-emergence of the Dark Mark and the Death Eaters in *The goblet of fire*,[1] Harry now knows who his enemies are: they are helpfully marked out for him by 'something like a vivid red tattoo – a skull, with a snake protruding from its mouth' (Rowling 2000: 560), which is visible on the left forearm. The imagery is obvious. The skull signifies death and the snake is the symbol of Voldemort's ancestor Salazar Slytherin, co-founder of Hogwarts, who in his time campaigned for the removal of Muggle-born students from the school. Voldemort and his Death Eaters take this campaign to its furthest extreme as they seek to purify wizard stock by exterminating Muggles, Muggle-borns and all who sympathise with them. In this context, Harry's lightning-bolt scar takes on a new significance. He is no longer just 'the boy who lived' (Rowling 1997: 18), the sole survivor of Voldemort's fatal attack upon the Potter family, but 'the Chosen One' (Rowling 2005: 43), the 'light' avenger, ready to strike down his 'dark' foes; specifically, the bearers of the Dark Mark and its creator.

While, technically, the Dark Mark is a brand which each Death Eater has 'burnt into him by the Dark Lord' (Rowling 2000: 606), the initial description of Wormtail's Mark in the scene in *The goblet of fire* recalls 'something like a vivid red tattoo'. Within a few sentences it is identified as a 'brand' (*ibid.*: 560), but on one level the Dark Mark can clearly be read as a gang tattoo. Karin Beeler asserts that '[i]n the minds of the general public, tattoos are often linked to violence in the context of gangs and prison culture' (2006: 96). The Death Eaters' Dark Mark – consisting of a skull and snake – fits in with '[t]he stereotypical image of the biker sporting a demonic tattoo [which] comes to mind in relation to gangs' (*ibid.*), and is perceived as such by the law-abiding citizens of the wizarding world as a symbol of violence and antisocial behaviour. From the point of view of the Death Eaters, the Dark Mark distinguishes them as a subcultural group, an elite representing Voldemort's inner circle, who recognise themselves as being genetically superior to the majority of the wider wizarding community.[2] From the perspective of this wider wizarding community, however, the Dark Mark distinguishes the deviant from the normative, the criminal from the upstanding citizen. For Hermione, the fact that Sirius Black, who has been wrongly convicted of murder and identified as a Death Eater by the Ministry, 'hasn't got the Mark' (Rowling 2003: 297) should be enough to absolve him of guilt in the Ministry's eyes. Harry takes a similar view when it comes to his schoolboy rival Draco Malfoy. Convinced that Malfoy has 'replaced his father as a Death Eater' (Rowling 2005: 125) and is working on a secret project from within Hogwarts, Harry tries to prove this to his friends by presenting them with evidence that Malfoy now bears Voldemort's Mark: 'In Madam Malkin's. She didn't touch him, but he yelled and jerked his arm away from her when she went to roll up his sleeve. It was his left arm. He's been branded with the Dark Mark' (*ibid.*). For Harry and company, the absence or presence of the Dark Mark is, for most of the series at least, a shorthand for innocence or guilt.

Just as real-life tattoos become 'a marker of difference, an index of inclusion and exclusion' and 'inscribe various kinds of group membership often in opposition to a dominant culture' (Caplan 2000: xiv), so the Dark Mark signifies membership of an exclusive and subversive group in the form of Voldemort's select criminal gang. As Severus Snape explains to the Minister for Magic: '[e]very Death Eater had the sign burnt into him by the Dark Lord. It was a means of distinguishing each other, and his means of summoning us to him. When he touched the Mark of any Death Eater, we were to Disapparate, and Apparate, instantly, at his side' (Rowling 2000: 616). The power of the Dark Mark, therefore, is not just symbolic. It has magical properties, which enable it to be used for practical purposes. It becomes a 'private means of communication' (Rowling 2007: 481) between Voldemort and his followers. Just as Voldemort can summon the Death Eaters, so they can summon him when necessary – a privilege which is not granted to all supporters of the Dark Lord. For example, when werewolf Fenrir Greyback and his Snatcher companions capture Harry, Ron and Hermione in *The deathly hallows* (2007), he is forced to bring them to the Death Eaters at Malfoy Manor rather than summon Voldemort himself, since 'only Voldemort's inner circle were branded with the Dark Mark: Greyback had not been granted this highest honour' (Rowling 2007: 368).

The power of the Dark Mark goes beyond its use as a direct line of communication to Voldemort. It also enables its bearer to threaten and intimidate in order to achieve their aims in the name of the Dark Lord. When the Dark Mark first (re)appears in *The goblet of fire*, not on the arm of a Death Eater, but 'etched against the black sky like a new constellation' (Rowling 2000: 115–16) at the Quidditch World Cup, Harry and Ron do not comprehend why the area 'all around them erupted with screams' (*ibid.*: 116) until Mr Weasley explains the Mark's significance:

> 'You-Know-Who and his followers sent the Dark Mark into the air whenever they killed,' said Mr Weasley. 'The terror it inspired … you have no idea, you're too young. Just picture coming home, and finding the Dark Mark hovering over your house, and knowing what you're about to find inside …' Mr Weasley winced. 'Everyone's worst fear … the very worst …'. (*ibid.*: 127)

On the body of a Death Eater, the Mark is utilised as a reminder of the possibility of this 'worst fear' being realised, particularly after Voldemort has returned to a position of power once more. The threat comes not just from the individual Death Eater and the violence that they can perpetrate, but from the criminal gang to which they belong and the extremist ideologies that they champion.

To show the Dark Mark, then, is not only to assert superiority over those who are not members of Voldemort's exclusive gang and to force them to bend to the will of the Death Eaters, but also to establish membership of a group that will crush anyone who stands in their way. Harry is convinced that he has witnessed Draco Malfoy doing just this on a visit to Borgin and Burkes's Dark Arts shop: "'[h]e showed Borgin something we couldn't see," Harry pressed on stubbornly. "Something that seriously scared Borgin. It was the Mark, I know it – he was showing Borgin who he was dealing with, you saw how seriously Borgin took him!"' (Rowling 2005: 125). While Ron is sceptical, protesting that, 'He's sixteen, Harry! You think You-Know-Who would let *Malfoy* join?' (*ibid.*), it later transpires that Draco *has* become a Death Eater – although his Dark Mark, which features in the film version of *The half-blood prince* (Yates 2009), never appears directly in the books.

For Draco, becoming a Death Eater at sixteen signals his premature coming of age – in the wizarding world, seventeen is the legal age at which a witch or wizard becomes an adult (*ibid.*: 56). Being branded with the Dark Mark is a rite of passage, a process of initiation into adulthood. Makiko Kuwahara identifies the 'notion of "before/after"' inherent in tattooing for initiation, where '[t]he person was a boy and became a man "after" being tattooed' (Kuwahara 2005: 17). This certainly appears to be the case with Draco, who ascends to a position of adult authority after showing Borgin his Dark Mark, as Borgin responds by calling him 'sir' and making 'a bow as deep as the one Harry had once seen him give Lucius Malfoy' (Rowling 2005: 122). As Harry has predicted, Draco has 'replaced his father as a Death Eater' (*ibid.*: 125) and now occupies the position of power that Lucius Malfoy held before he failed Voldemort and was subsequently imprisoned in Azkaban. At Hogwarts, too, Draco takes advantage of his newly acquired Dark Mark to get others to do his bidding against their will:

> 'He's got Crabbe and Goyle transforming into girls?' guffawed Ron. 'Blimey … no wonder they don't look too happy these days … I'm surprised they don't tell him to stuff it …'
>
> 'Well, they wouldn't, would they, if he's shown them his Dark Mark,' said Harry. (*ibid.*: 426)

The Dark Mark, it seems, is not just an indicator of criminality and immorality but is also the ultimate symbol of power. Those who possess it use it as a means to intimidate, threaten and control those who do not. On the surface, at least, he who bears the Mark wields the power. In its resemblance to a gang tattoo, the Dark Mark constructs a crime narrative in which the criminals are easily identifiable but, ultimately, uncontainable, spreading terror through the pervasiveness and visibility of their threat.

MARKS OF POSSESSION, PAIN AND PUNISHMENT: MARKING THE VICTIM

Through its function as a gang tattoo, the Dark Mark appears to imbue its bearer with a power that they did not previously possess. Draco Malfoy clearly undergoes a transformation after being branded with the Dark Mark. Before his Death Eater days, Draco is represented as a comic villain, the butt of jokes as he is turned into 'Draco Malfoy, the amazing bouncing ferret' (Rowling 2000: 183) by the impostor Mad-Eye Moody in *The goblet of fire* and transformed into a giant slug by members of Dumbledore's Army at the end of *The order of the phoenix* (Rowling, 2003: 761). In *The half-blood prince* (2005), however, Draco is taken more seriously. Ostensibly, the Dark Mark promotes him to a position of greater power: from school bully to Death Eater; from rule-breaker to criminal. Yet the true power of the Dark Mark does not lie with its bearer. Draco's most significant transformation is not from comic figure to powerful gang member, but from villain to victim. In Draco's case, both his physical and psychological state is drastically altered in *The half-blood prince*, as Harry observes: '[w]as it his imagination, or did Malfoy, like Tonks, look thinner? Certainly he looked paler [...] there was no air of smugness, or excitement, or superiority' (Rowling 2005: 443–44). Moaning Myrtle's description of Draco in the same book further illustrates his psychological transformation after he has been branded with the Dark Mark: 'he's sensitive, people bully him, too, and he feels lonely and hasn't got anybody to talk to, and he's not afraid to show his feelings and cry!' (*ibid.*: 433). Draco is firmly redefined as a victim and, despite the apparent power that the Dark Mark affords him over those who are unmarked, his true powerlessness becomes abundantly clear when he finally confronts Dumbledore at the end of *The half-blood prince*, apparently ready to kill him. When Dumbledore attempts to reason with him, Draco reveals that 'I haven't got any options. [...] I've got to do it! He'll kill me! He'll kill my whole family!' (*ibid.*: 552). Draco, it seems, is not in control of his own body or destiny. Branded with the Dark Mark he, like the rest of his family, belongs to Voldemort.

Here, the Dark Mark does not function as a gang tattoo – a symbol of membership of a powerful group – but is reminiscent instead of the involuntary process of branding and tattooing used 'in a dehumanizing way to mark slaves, prisoners, captives and sometimes soldiers as property', a practice which continued into the nineteenth century and which has reappeared in more recent times in forms such as the Holocaust tattoo (DeMello 2014: xxxi). As Clare Anderson observes, slave tattoos and brands were 'indelible marks' which 'designated ownership and, like naming practices designed to strip slaves of extra-European identity, were powerful symbols of unfreedom' (2004: 18). In a similar manner, the Death Eaters become Voldemort's slaves as he takes possession of their bodies through the Dark Mark with which he has branded them, and this Mark denies them an identity outside the service of Voldemort. Notably, like the institutions and authority figures who branded or tattooed slaves, prisoners and other subjugated groups with marks of ownership and submission, the Dark Lord himself remains unmarked. Voldemort prides himself on being unique – on first learning that he is a wizard he tells Dumbledore: 'I knew I was different [...] I knew I was special' (Rowling 2005: 254) – and by keeping his own skin free of the Dark Mark, he clearly distinguishes himself from those who bear his Mark. He is the ruler rather than a member of his Death Eater gang. His pale, unblemished skin is symbolic both of his desire to purify the wizarding race and of his position at the head of the system – unscathed by the conflict into which he sends his marked slaves. The absence of the Dark Mark on Voldemort's body suggests his difference from and superiority to his Death Eaters, his apparent invincibility (and perhaps his inhumanity) and his lack of suffering. The Dark Mark may connect the Death Eaters as a community, but for Voldemort, branding his followers is about imposing his own ideologies upon a subservient group. Consequently, the Dark Mark is transformed from a powerful symbol of gang membership to a debilitating mark of enslavement.

Just as the real-life branding and tattooing of slaves and prisoners was often used for punitive purposes (Anderson 2000: 106), so Voldemort uses the Dark Mark to punish those who fail him. Kuwahara observes that '[t]he body is possessed, territorialized, conquered, handed over and cultivated through tattooing' (2005: 21). In Draco's case, this transference of ownership is an unwilling one. Draco is branded with the Dark Mark, not as the 'great honour' that his Aunt Bellatrix judges it to be, but rather, 'as vengeance for Lucius's mistake' (Rowling 2005: 38) of failing to obtain the prophecy about Voldemort and Harry in *The order of the phoenix*. While many of Voldemort's original followers voluntarily took the Mark and, therefore, willingly offered up their bodies to him, on Voldemort's return to power they too do his bidding out of fear rather than loyalty. Older and, perhaps, wiser after the first Wizarding war, many of Voldemort's followers have renounced their connection with the Dark Lord, in many cases to avoid prison but also, perhaps, suggesting that their own views on blood status are not as extreme as those of their master. The free choice that they made in their youth is not afforded to them after Voldemort's restoration to his body.

Suman Gupta argues that Voldemort's servant, Wormtail, is 'kept subservient by his fear of Voldemort's power' and that 'fear too is what all the other followers of Voldemort, the Death Eaters, feel for him – and it is fear too that makes them all serve him' (2003: 114). The reappearance of the Dark Mark on the Death Eaters' bodies reminds them of Voldemort's possession of them. The Dark Mark had 'been getting clearer and clearer for months' (Rowling 2000:

370) as Voldemort started to regain his strength in *The goblet of fire* and finally 'turned jet black' (*ibid.*: 560), burning the skin, as Voldemort was restored to his body and summoned his Death Eaters by pressing 'his long white fingers to the brand on Wormtail's arm' (*ibid.*). Those who are 'brave enough to return when they feel it', such as Lucius Malfoy, become his unwilling slaves, while those who are 'foolish enough to stay away' (*ibid.*), attempting to deny Voldemort's assertion of power over their bodies, such as Igor Karkaroff, are exterminated. Karkaroff's body is later discovered 'in a shack up north. The Dark Mark had been set over it' (Rowling 2005: 103); a reminder that, ultimately, Voldemort's followers cannot escape the Mark with which they have been branded. Thus, the presence of the Dark Mark upon the bodies of the Death Eaters – as both a symbol of the power which Voldemort exerts over them and as a means by which he does so – redefines Voldemort's criminal followers, who are obviously villainous in many respects, as victims.

The Death Eaters are not the only victims whose bodies are branded by Voldemort with a mark of ownership. Harry's lightning-bolt scar also becomes a mark of Voldemort's possession in the second half of the series. While the mark inflicted upon Harry by Voldemort is described clearly as a scar throughout the series, the magical act of cursing and the burning pain associated with it comes closer to the act of branding than any other form of scarification. In the earlier books, Harry's scar just burns as a sign of Voldemort's presence. For example, when Harry encounters Voldemort in the Forbidden Forest in *The philosopher's stone*, 'a pain pierced his head like he'd never felt before, it was as though his scar was on fire' (Rowling 1997: 187). Like the Dark Mark which burns again on the return of Voldemort (a process of re-branding), the lightning-bolt scar recalls the initial wounding, a wound the infant Harry Potter is too young to recall but one he is repeatedly forced to face. On Voldemort's restoration to his body in *The goblet of fire*, however, Dumbledore reveals to Harry his belief that 'your scar hurts both when Lord Voldemort is near you, and when he is feeling a particularly strong surge of hatred [...] Because you and he are connected by the curse that failed' (Rowling 2000: 521–22). The burning of Harry's scar, like the burning of the Death Eaters' Dark Marks when summoned by Voldemort, can be linked to the punitive and possessive act of branding. What is notable about these magical marks, however, is that the burning pain is not confined to the initial act of branding itself, but extends to the moments where Voldemort makes contact with and takes possession of the body which he has marked. In *The deathly hallows*, the extent of Voldemort's connection with Harry becomes clear, as Dumbledore reveals to Snape that: '[p]art of Lord Voldemort lives inside Harry, and it is that which gives him the power of speech with snakes, and a connection with Lord Voldemort's mind that he has never understood' (Rowling 2007: 551). Just as the Dark Mark is a symbol of Voldemort's ownership of his Death Eaters' bodies, so Harry's curse scar is a sign of Voldemort's more literal and extreme possession of *his* body, a possession which makes Harry feel 'dirty, contaminated, as though he were carrying some deadly germ, unworthy to sit [...] with innocent, clean people whose minds and bodies were free of the taint of Voldemort' (Rowling 2003: 435). Initially, Harry's scar burns like the Death Eaters' Dark Marks but, as Voldemort regains power, Harry begins to detect his opponent's emotions and, later, full visions of Voldemort's actions. While these visions help him to determine and thwart Voldemort's plans at times,[3] by the end of *The order of the phoenix*, Voldemort has discovered the extent of his connection with Harry and sends him a false vision of Sirius in danger in order to lure Harry into the Department of Mysteries to obtain the crucial prophecy for him. Just as he uses the Dark Mark to summon his Death Eaters, so Voldemort uses the mark of possession with which he has branded Harry as a means of forcing Harry to do his bidding. Harry's scar may mark him out as 'the Chosen One' who must thwart Voldemort, but it is also Voldemort who has chosen Harry as his adversary and who continues to pull the strings for as long as he possesses Harry. Like Draco and the other Death Eaters, Harry becomes the marked victim of the unmarked master criminal.

The curse scar, however, is not the only mark of possession upon Harry's body. In *The order of the phoenix*, Harry gains a new scar, a type of textual tattoo, this time not from Voldemort, but from a source which turns out to be equally villainous. Dolores Umbridge, Ministry official and newly appointed headmistress of Hogwarts, is representative of a flawed and corrupt wizarding government who refuse to mobilise against Voldemort. Sent to Hogwarts to discredit the news that Voldemort has returned, Umbridge takes drastic measures to silence Harry and his supporters. In the detention that Harry must serve with Umbridge for refuting her statement that news of Voldemort's return is a lie, she instructs him to write 'I must not tell lies' with her own 'special' quill 'with an unusually sharp point' for 'as long as it takes for the message to *sink in*' (Rowling 2003: 240):

> Harry placed the point of the quill on the paper and wrote: *I must not tell lies*. He let out a gasp of pain. The words had appeared on the parchment in what appeared to be shining red ink. At the same time, the words had appeared on the back of Harry's right hand, cut into his skin as though traced there by a scalpel – yet even as he stared at the shining cut, the skin healed over again, leaving the place where it had been slighter redder than before but quite smooth. (*ibid*.)

This inscription on Harry's hand is reminiscent of the punitive *godna* marks – penal tattoos – applied by the authorities in Bengal and Madras in the eighteenth and nineteenth centuries to convicts to inscribe their crimes upon the body for all to see. Just as perjurers were marked on the forehead with the word '*duroghgo* (liar)' as a form of 'public shaming' (Anderson 2004: 18), so Harry's status as a 'liar' is marked upon his 'public skin'.[4] Harry's 'crime' is not only marked *on* his hand but *by* his hand. Like the systems of punishment discussed by Michel Foucault in *Discipline and punish*, which involve bodily torture and public spectacle, Harry's punishment by Umbridge makes 'the guilty man herald his own condemnation [...] thus attesting the truth of what he had been charged with' (1977: 43). Despite his innocence – it is Umbridge who lies about Voldemort's return, not Harry – Harry is forced to endure a ritual of torture which serves to 'mark the victim: it is intended, either by the scar it leaves on the body, or by the spectacle that accompanies it, to brand the victim with infamy' (*ibid.*: 34). By inflicting a permanent and visible scar upon Harry, Umbridge aims both to discredit Harry and to warn his peers about the dangers of dissention. Umbridge, like Voldemort, stamps her own mark – the Ministry's mark – upon Harry and attempts to control him through it, hoping that it will 'serve as a reminder' (Rowling 2003: 244) of what happens when the individual rebels against the dominant system of control. Like Voldemort, Umbridge is also an unmarked authority figure who imposes bodily marks upon her victims as a sign of possession and punishment. These punishments inscribe the ideologies of the system that she represents upon the bodies of those who resist Ministry control.

Similarly to Voldemort, Umbridge and the Ministry are oppressive forces who, at this point in the series at least, are unscathed by the conflict which is escalating around them. Umbridge is not a member of Voldemort's faction but, as Sirius warns Harry, 'the world isn't split into good people and Death Eaters' (*ibid.*: 271). Umbridge, and all that she stands for, is no better than Voldemort and his philosophy. She may not be a murderer, but Umbridge reveals the extent of her own corruption and criminality as she attempts to use the illegal Cruciatus Curse on Harry and reveals that she 'ordered Dementors to go after Potter last summer', maintaining that '[s]omebody had to act' to discredit Harry's claim that Voldemort had returned (*ibid.*: 658; author's emphasis). Notably, in *The deathly hallows*, Umbridge becomes 'Head of the Muggle-born Registration Commission' (Rowling 2007: 206), suggesting her commitment to Voldemort's eugenics policies. This adds further significance to her unmarked status. Like Voldemort, Umbridge's lack of bodily markings is symbolic of her desire to purify the wizarding race and, consequently, the marks which she inscribes upon Harry and other dissenters in *The order of the phoenix* bear resemblance to the dehumanising tattoos applied by the Nazis at Auschwitz to Jews, homosexuals, communists and other groups who did not conform to Nazi ideologies and genetic ideals (Apel 2001: 302; Schiffmacher and Riemschreider 2014: 17). Harry, like the Holocaust victims, is marked out as different, deviant and dissident – a figure who must be subjugated and, eventually, eliminated. In the *Harry Potter* series, to be marked is to be a victim of a tyrannical and unjust system of control. Thus, while brands and scars initially appear to define their bearers as heroes or villains, those whose bodies are marked – be they Harry the hero or Draco the Death Eater – are soon redefined as victims, struggling to resist the marks of power by which the unmarked inscribers of these marks – the true villains – have taken possession of their bodies. The world is no longer 'split into good people and Death Eaters', but into unmarked criminals and marked victims. This inversion of the stereotype by which criminals bear the bodily marks which assert their deviancy and guilt emphasises the maturation and growing complexity of the series' crime narrative.

MARKS OF RESISTANCE: MARKING THE HERO

Not all of the brands and scars featured in the *Harry Potter* series permanently mark their bearers as victims and possessions of those who have marked them, however. Beeler argues that 'tattoos are linked to various forms of resistance. Historically, and even mythically, the tattoo has been associated with subversion, and it continues to serve this function in contemporary culture' (2006: 6). While the bodily marks acquired by Rowling's characters are often imposed against their will, they are, in some cases, the result of an act of resistance to an oppressive and corrupt system of control. These marks of resistance are symbols of heroism rather than victimhood. Harry's friend Neville Longbottom becomes a bearer of such marks in *The deathly hallows*. Harry is taken aback by Neville's physical transformation when he first encounters him on returning to Hogwarts: '[t]he longer Harry looked at Neville, the worse he appeared: one of his eyes was swollen, yellow and purple, there were gouge marks on his face, and his general air of unkemptness suggested that he had been living rough' (Rowling 2007: 460). However, while he initially appears to be a victim of the Death Eaters' violent rule at Hogwarts, Neville proudly displays his scars, explaining their significance:

> 'That's how I got this one,' he pointed at a particularly deep gash in his cheek, 'I refused to do it' [...] 'Alecto, Amycus's sister, teaches Muggle Studies, which is compulsory for everyone. We've all got to listen to her explain how Muggles are like animals, stupid and dirty, and how they drove wizards into hiding by being vicious towards them, and how the natural order is being re-established. I got this one,' he indicated another slash to his face, 'for asking her how much Muggle blood she and her brother have got.'
>
> 'Blimey, Neville,' said Ron, 'there's a time and a place for getting a smart mouth.'
>
> 'You didn't hear her,' said Neville. 'You wouldn't have stood it either. The thing is, it helps when people stand up to them, it gives everyone hope. I used to notice that when you did it, Harry.' (*ibid.*: 462)

By drawing attention to his scars and providing a narrative for them, Neville becomes reminiscent of the tattooed subject of the nineteenth-century freak show who, as Margo DeMello observes, 'would tell the crowd about how he had acquired his tattoos. These stories centred around his capture and forcible tattooing by savage natives [...] the pain involved in the tattooing, and his heroic escape from captivity' (DeMello 2000: 56). Yet, where these freak-show tales were often fabricated for sensational effect and financial gain, Neville's account of his violent altercations with the Carrows is much more authentic and less gratuitous and, hence, its impact more powerful. It is within Neville's scarification narrative that the connection between bodily marks and eugenics is most strongly asserted. The scars that Neville receives at the hands of Alecto and Amycus Carrow directly mark his resistance to Voldemort's pureblood ideology. Neville is not a victim of the Carrows – rather he invites their violence and, consequently, marks himself as an enemy of Voldemort's eugenic purging of those with Muggle blood. Thus, Neville uses the Carrows' own intolerance against them, playing on their insecurities about their own blood status to goad them into violence. He then constructs a new identity for himself through the scars which they inflict upon him; as Susan Benson claims, 'tattooing, piercing or branding can also act as [...] a way of "reclaiming" the body for the self' (2000: 249). Neville is not a victim of the Carrows but a hero, continuing Harry's work at Hogwarts in the name of Dumbledore's Army, and resisting the corrupt agencies which attempt to impose control upon the Hogwarts' students.

The mark with which Harry is branded by Umbridge as punishment also functions as a mark of resistance in the later books. While this scar initially appears to mark him out as a victim and possession of Umbridge and the Ministry, the fact that Harry gains it during an act of resistance against the Ministry enables him to reclaim it for his own purpose. As Harry predicts, the words 'etched into the back of his hand' by Umbridge's quill do not 'ever fade entirely' (Rowling 2003: 295), and while Harry initially conceals the mark as he does not want to give Umbridge 'the satisfaction of knowing she's got to me' (*ibid.*: 246); as the Ministry's corruption grows, he begins to display his mark openly as a sign of resistance to the Ministry's control. When the new Minister for Magic, Rufus Scrimgeour, approaches Harry in *The half-blood prince* with a proposition to 'stand alongside the Ministry, and give everyone a boost' – a task that would involve 'popping in and out of the Ministry from time to time' to 'give the right impression' (Rowling 2005: 323–24), Harry refuses outright to become the Ministry's poster boy and, hence, their possession:

'I don't want to be used,' said Harry. [...] You don't care whether I live or die, but you do care that I help convince everyone you're winning the war against Voldemort. I haven't forgotten, Minister ...'

He raised his right fist. There, shining white on the back of his cold hand were the scars which Dolores Umbridge had forced him to carve into his own flesh: *I must not tell lies.* (*ibid.*: 325; author's emphasis)

Harry thus uses the Ministry's own edict against them. In the defiant act of raising his fist, he refuses to give the wizarding world the impression that he is supporting the Ministry. In fact, he openly opposes their policies, such as their imprisonment of the harmless Stan Shunpike as a Death Eater. Harry refuses to 'tell lies' for the Ministry and by drawing attention to his Ministry-inflicted scars, he emphasises the Ministry's hypocrisy. Through their initial denial of Voldemort's return and their subsequent desire to pretend that Harry is working for them, the Ministry show that they are perfectly willing to tell lies to suit their own ends. In his confrontation with Scrimgeour, Harry takes possession of these scars and, in doing so, takes ownership of his body – refusing to acquiesce to those who have inflicted the marks upon it. In *The deathly hallows*, Harry again exposes the marks to Scrimgeour as a sign of his resistance to the power of the corrupt Ministry when the Minister seeks his allegiance once more:

> 'We ought to be working together.'
> 'I don't like your methods, Minister,' said Harry. 'Remember?'
> For the second time, he raised his right fist, and displayed to Scrimgeour the scars that still showed white on the back of it, spelling *I must not tell lies*. (Rowling 2007: 110–11)

The scars inflicted upon Harry by the Ministry, therefore, become 'the marks of self-possession, not defeat' (Benson 2000: 249), as he, like Neville, uses them to define himself as an active opponent, rather than a passive victim, of those who have marked him.

Taking ownership of bodily marks, however, becomes more difficult when the bearer has been passive during the process of their inscription. Harry's curse scar, for example, is not a mark of resistance gained through his rebellion against a system of control. He is a passive recipient of this mark – an innocent victim rather than a hero standing up for what he believes in. Rather than using the scar to construct an identity for himself, Harry, as a baby, has an identity imposed upon him by his scar. While, through the mark of resistance imposed upon him by Umbridge on behalf of the Ministry, Harry defines himself as leader of Dumbledore's Army, the organisation established by Harry and his friends in defiance of the Ministry and their rules, his curse scar defines him first passively as Voldemort's victim; initially, as 'the boy who lived' and then later as Voldemort's nemesis 'the Chosen One'. Critically, Harry is always defined in relation to Voldemort through his scar and it remains a symbol of Voldemort's possession of him throughout the series. For Harry, the curse scar is a mark of shame, a constant reminder of Voldemort's control over him and, consequently, he often wishes to conceal it. After witnessing Tonks's ability to change her appearance at will, Harry reveals his desire to rid himself of his scar:

> 'Can you learn how to be a Metamorphmagus?' Harry asked her, straightening up, completely forgetting about packing.
>   Tonks chuckled.
>   'Bet you wouldn't mind hiding that scar sometimes, eh?'
>   Her eyes found the lightning-shaped scar on Harry's forehead.
>   'No, I wouldn't mind,' Harry mumbled, turning away. He did not like people staring at his scar. (Rowling 2003: 52)

Although Harry attempts to resist the power of the scar, and tries to permanently conceal or erase his scar, it is Voldemort who initially severs the connection between himself and Harry established through the scar.

As Dumbledore reveals to Harry in *The half-blood prince*: 'Lord Voldemort has finally realised the dangerous access to his thoughts and feelings you have been enjoying. It appears that he is now employing Occlumency against you' (Rowling 2005: 61). When the connection is re-established in *The deathly hallows* and Harry begins to have visions again, Hermione begs him to resist Voldemort's possession once more: '[y]ou mustn't let that connection open up again – Dumbledore wanted you to close your mind! [...] Harry, he's taking over the Ministry and the newspapers and half the wizarding world! Don't let him inside your head too!' (Rowling 2007: 75). Failing to heed Hermione's advice, Harry begins to seek the connection with Voldemort's mind when he is overcome with a desire to possess the Elder Wand, an all-powerful wand which enables its owner to become a master of death: 'Harry wished his scar would burn and show him Voldemort's thoughts, because for the first time ever, he and Voldemort were united in wanting the very same thing ...' (*ibid.*: 352). But accessing Voldemort's thoughts is a double-edged sword and while Harry gains valuable information about Voldemort's movements, he does not want Voldemort to learn of the actions or whereabouts of him and his friends. It is only after the trauma of Dobby's death that Harry is able to shut down his dangerous connection with Voldemort: '[h]is scar burned, but he was master of the pain; he felt it, yet was apart from it. He had learned to control at last, learned to shut his mind to Voldemort [...] Grief, it seemed, drove Voldemort out' (*ibid.*: 387). Yet since Harry's grief is an involuntary reaction, prompted by the actions of Voldemort and his Death Eaters, Harry is not fully in control and his resistance of the mark's power over him is only temporary. In the end, it is Voldemort himself who performs the act which destroys the magical properties of Harry's scar. After defining Harry as '[t]he boy who lived' (*ibid.*: 564) once more, Voldemort reasserts Harry's status as his passive victim rather than his active opponent and withdraws from Harry's body by performing the Killing Curse upon him for a second time. Despite Harry's attempts to gain a measure of control over his connection with Voldemort, his curse scar never truly becomes a mark of resistance, but instead continues to mark Harry as Voldemort's property until Voldemort himself relinquishes ownership of Harry's body.

Former Death Eater Severus Snape is more successful than Harry in his attempt to resist the identity imposed upon him by another symbol of Voldemort's ownership: the Dark Mark. Just as Harry desires or attempts to conceal his curse scar, so the Death Eaters hide the Mark beneath their robes, only exposing it in order to do Voldemort's bidding: to summon him, to respond to his summons, or to intimidate people in his name. By contrast, when Snape uncovers his Dark Mark in *The goblet of fire*, it proves his loyalty to Dumbledore and his defiance of Voldemort as he shows it to the Minister for Magic as evidence of Voldemort's return:

> Snape strode forwards, past Dumbledore, pulling up the left sleeve of his robes as he went. He stuck out his forearm, and showed it to Fudge, who recoiled.
>
> 'There,' said Snape harshly. 'There. The Dark Mark. It is not as clear as it was, an hour or so ago, when it burnt black, but you can still see it. [...] This Mark has been growing clearer all year. Karkaroff's too. Why do you think Karkaroff fled tonight? We both felt the Mark burn. We both knew he had returned.' (Rowling 2000: 616)

Snape cannot remove his Dark Mark or his past as a Death Eater – as Barty Crouch Junior states 'there are spots that don't come off [...] Spots that never come off' (*ibid.*: 410), but he is able to resist the identity imposed upon him by Voldemort through the Dark Mark. Unlike his fellow Death Eaters, Snape is able to use the Dark Mark to construct a new identity for himself outside the service of Voldemort: that of spy and, ultimately, that of hero.

In the wake of *The deathly hallows*, critics are beginning to acknowledge Snape's heroic status. Christina Flotmann argues that in the chapter of *The deathly hallows* entitled 'The Prince's tale', in which Snape's true colours are revealed, the word 'Prince':

> does not now refer to Snape's mother's maiden name, his arrogance in youth or his seeming double-dealings, but is used as the title 'Prince' and emphasises Snape's true nature and nobility. It is noteworthy that Snape alone, among all the characters in the stories who assume a title, is truly worthy of it. (Flotmann 2013: 181–82)

Maria Nikolajeva identifies the 'crosswriting' involved in the construction of Snape as a hero:

> Heroic deeds on battlefields and direct confrontations are more tangible and easy to understand. Hero worship is mainly based on outward features and actions. For a sophisticated reader, however, Snape presents a considerably higher-standing hero. In fact, viewing the novels as a whole, they can be read on a certain level as Snape's rather than Harry's story. (Nikolajeva 2011: 204)

Snape is certainly the foremost detective figure at the centre of the series' crime narrative and it is his detective role that most clearly defines him as a hero. While Harry views Snape's constant skulking around as a sign of his villainy, it is really an indication of his commitment to his detective role and his loyalty to Dumbledore. In *The philosopher's stone*, it is Snape who is suspicious of Quirrell and keeps a close watch on him, protecting Harry in the process. Again, in *The prisoner of Azkaban*, Snape is on hand to catch Sirius Black, whom he thinks is a Death Eater and a mass murderer who poses a threat to Harry. More crucially, after Voldemort's resurrection, Snape works undercover to gain information for the Order that will lead to the defeat of the master criminal, Voldemort. From this point onwards, the actions that ostensibly mark him out as a villain – becoming Voldemort's right-hand man, swearing the Unbreakable Vow to protect Draco, offering to help Draco to kill Dumbledore and, finally, killing Dumbledore himself – are performed in the service of the right side as a 'spy and double agent' (Flotmann 2013: 180) and, consequently, as a protector and hero.

Snape is no longer a Death Eater, nor is his body enslaved by Voldemort. He is not controlled by the Mark and does not respond to Voldemort's summons in one of the two ways anticipated by Voldemort. When Snape feels his Dark Mark burn, he neither returns to serve Voldemort nor flees from him. Instead, he reacts to Voldemort's summons by returning as an enemy in the guise of a friend, ready to betray Voldemort for his own personal reasons, which are revealed to Harry after Snape's death. Snape's self-possession of his own body and his identity, which he has successfully reclaimed from Voldemort, is underlined in his final act as he lies dying from a 'bloody wound at his neck' inflicted upon him by Nagini: 'A terrible rasping gurgling noise issued from Snape's throat. "Take … it … Take it …" Something more than blood was leaking from Snape. Silvery blue, neither gas nor liquid, it gushed from his mouth and his ears and his eyes' (Rowling 2007: 528). This silvery blue liquid contains Snape's most crucial memories and this final bodily emission reveals the full extent of Snape's heroic status. He is the series' true seeker of justice, resisting Voldemort's ownership of his body in order to avenge the death of the woman he loved and to protect her son. Snape's heroic status is confirmed in the epilogue of *The deathly hallows*, set nineteen years after Voldemort's final defeat, where Harry tells his son, Albus Severus, that Snape 'was probably the bravest man I ever knew' (*ibid.*: 607). On Snape's body, the Dark Mark is no longer a symbol of Voldemort's control, but of Snape's courage in defying his power. Through his resistance and subversion of the Dark Mark's original significance and function and his subsequent redefinition of the Mark upon his own body, Snape becomes the true hero of the series.

CONCLUSION

While the brands and scars present in the *Harry Potter* series are permanent (spots that never come off) their symbolic status and functions are more fluid. Just as 'Snape's choice to "join the side of the angels" after a long association with the Death Eaters is a distinct one that defies a black and white moral scheme' (Klaus 2012: 31), so the marks on the bodies of Rowling's characters are not simply shorthand for distinguishing good from evil. As this chapter has demonstrated, the Dark Mark is not just a symbol of criminality or evil, just as Harry's curse scar is not solely a mark of heroism. The representation of brands and scars supports the series' moral complexity. Those who are defined by their bodily marks become victims of the people or systems that have imposed the marks upon them, while those who define themselves through their marks become heroes, resisting the control of those who have marked them and setting themselves up as opponents of corrupt systems of control. It is not the bodily marks themselves, therefore, but the relationships between the marks, the markers and the marked that positions the bearers of the marks upon the moral spectrum and defines their roles as criminal, victim or hero – and sometimes as all three. The fluidity of these relationships contributes to the complexity of the series' overarching crime narrative. The stigma commonly attached to brands and scars is challenged in the second half of the *Harry Potter* series as the stereotype of the deviant and/or criminal marked body is interrogated and inverted. Those who are marked are drawn in 'shades of grey' and only those who inflict marks fit into 'a black and white moral scheme': the unmarked heads of oppressive systems of power – Voldemort and Umbridge – are marked as the series' only permanent and irredeemable criminals. By leaving the real criminals unmarked, the *Harry Potter* series subverts expectations and shows itself as a mature and sophisticated crime narrative which acknowledges that the indisputable villains are those who implement systems of control which impose bodily marks and who are themselves left unscathed by conflict. Here, the absence of marks of pain and suffering, oppression and possession, becomes the true indicator of guilt.

NOTES

1 Voldemort and his Death Eaters are initially thwarted in chapter one of *The philosopher's stone*. The Dark Mark has not been seen within the wizarding community since the events of this chapter and is not mentioned at all in the first three books in the series.
2 There is also an interesting link here between the Dark Mark and American naval tattoos of the mid-twentieth century where, Margo DeMello observes, a popular tattoo choice included the words 'death before dishonour, usually found on a snake-encircled dagger or skull' (DeMello 2000: 64). Again, this connection reinforces the significance of the Dark Mark as a symbol of membership of, and loyalty to, a specific group and the adoption of a particular ideology.
3 An example of this is Harry's vision of the attack on Mr Weasley by Voldemort's snake, Nagini, which enables the Order to rescue Mr Weasley before Nagini's poison takes full effect (Rowling 2003: 408–16).

4 Clinton R. Sanders and D. Angus Vail define 'public skin' as 'above the neck and below the wrist' – an area upon which '[m]ost tattooists routinely refuse to place tattoos' (Sanders and Vail 2008: 78).

BIBLIOGRAPHY

Anderson, Clare (2000), '*Godna*: Inscribing Indian convicts in the nineteenth century', in J. Caplan (ed.), pp. 102–17.

— (2004), *Legible bodies: Race, criminality and colonialism in South Asia* (Oxford and New York: Berg).

Apel, Dora (2001), 'The tattooed Jew', in B. Zelizer (ed.), *Visual culture and the Holocaust* (London: The Athlone Press), pp. 300–20.

Beeler, Karin (2006), *Tattoos, desire and violence: Marks of resistance in literature, film and television* (Jefferson and London: McFarland).

Benson, Susan (2000), 'Inscriptions of the self: Reflections on tattooing and piercing in contemporary Euro-America', in J. Caplan (ed.) (2000), pp. 234–54.

Caplan, Jane (ed.) (2000), *Written on the body: The tattoo in European and American history* (London: Reaktion).

DeMello, Margo (2000), *Bodies of inscription: A cultural history of the modern tattoo community* (Durham, NC and London: Duke University Press).

— (2014) *Inked: Tattoos and body art from around the world* (California: ABC-CLIO, LLC).

Elster, Charles (2003), 'The seeker of secrets: Images of learning, knowing, and schooling', in E. E. Heilman (ed.), *Critical perspectives on Harry Potter* (New York and London: Routledge), pp. 203–20.

Falconer, Rachel (2009), *The crossover novel: Contemporary children's fiction and its adult readership* (New York and Abingdon: Routledge).

Flotmann, Christina (2013), *Ambiguity in Star wars and Harry Potter: A (post)structuralist reading of two popular myths* (Bielefeld: Transcript).

Foucault, Michel (1977), *Discipline and punish: The birth of the prison* [English edition]; [*Surveiller et punir: Naissance de la prison*: French edition (1975)], trans. A. Sheridan (London: Penguin Books).

Gupta, Suman (2003), *Re-reading Harry Potter* (Basingstoke: Palgrave Macmillan).

Klaus, Anne (2012), 'A fairy-tale crew? J. K. Rowling's characters under scrutiny', in C. J. Hallet, and P. J. Huey (eds), *J. K. Rowling: Harry Potter* (Basingstoke: Palgrave Macmillan), pp. 22–35.

Kuwahara, Makiko (2005), *Tattoo: An anthropology* (Oxford and New York: Berg).

Nikolajeva, Maria (2011), 'Adult role models and heroism in the Harry Potter novels', in K. Berndt and L. Steveker (eds), *Heroism in the Harry Potter series* (Farnham and Burlington: Ashgate), pp. 193–206.

Routledge, Christopher (2001), 'Harry Potter and the mystery of ordinary life', in A. E. Gavin and C. Routledge (eds), *Mystery in children's literature: From the rational to the supernatural* (Basingstoke: Palgrave Macmillan), pp. 202–09.

Rowling, J. K. (1997), *Harry Potter and the philosopher's stone* (London: Bloomsbury).

— (1998), *Harry Potter and the chamber of secrets* (London: Bloomsbury).

— (1999), *Harry Potter and the prisoner of Azkaban* (London: Bloomsbury).

— (2000), *Harry Potter and the goblet of fire* (London: Bloomsbury).

— (2003), *Harry Potter and the order of the phoenix* (London: Bloomsbury).
— (2005), *Harry Potter and the half-blood prince* (London: Bloomsbury).
— (2007), *Harry Potter and the deathly hallows* (London: Bloomsbury).
Sanders, Clinton R. and D. Angus Vail (2008), *Customizing the body: The art and culture of tattooing* [revised and expanded edition] (Philadelphia: Temple University Press).
Schiffmacher, Henk and Burkhard Riemschneider (2014), *1000 tattoos* (Köln: Taschen).
Yates, David (dir.) (2009), *Harry Potter and the half-blood prince* (USA: Warner Bros)
Zipes, Jack (2002), *Sticks and stones: The troublesome success of children's literature from Slovenly Peter to Harry Potter* (New York and London: Routledge).

10

'Since the schism': Reading the tattoo in Lemony Snicket's *A series of unfortunate events*

Caroline Jones and Katharine Cox

INTRODUCTION

An eye tattoo, formed of the letters VFD, is crucial to the detective and interpretative functions of Daniel Handler's *A series of unfortunate events* (1999–2006).[1] Written under the pseudonym of Lemony Snicket, the series features a significant tattoo on the left ankle of members of a secretive organisation, the Volunteer Fire Department. The series is narrated by Snicket and explores the fate of the orphaned Baudelaire children (Violet, Klaus and Sunny). We meet the children after the death of their parents in a fire, which also destroys their home. These events are characterised as the first in a series of unfortunate events. However, as the story develops, the children's unusual skills (essentially the foundations of training in the ways of the VFD) reveal that their circumstances are manipulated by members of the VFD from both sides of the schism that split the organisation. As orphans, they are put under the custodianship of their family's banker, Mr Poe (one of Handler's many textual nods to the genres of gothic and crime fiction), who places them with a series of unsuitable guardians. These guardians range from manipulative and despicable (such as Count Olaf and Esme Squalor), to well-meaning but ineffectual (such as Uncle Monty and Jerome Squalor). The series documents a rapid development for the children through a series of offered or forced communities (a theatre troupe, circus, lumberyard, island commune and so on), until they establish a wider self-sufficient family unit (incorporating the Quigley triplets and the latest Snicket child). During this process of personal growth and establishment of community by the children, the meanings of the VFD, and the tattoo that appears to represent it, are a focal point for their detective activities.

Crucially, the tattoo, the insignia of the organisation, has been inked on members prior to a schism which splits the organisation and so transforms the meaning of the tattoo. The reading of the tattoo is irrevocably altered by the schism. The children's initial reading of the tattoo is to equate its appearance with the shattering of their world: the death of their parents, their subsequent passage into 'care', and with Count Olaf's evil schemes. The eye tattoo symbolises the protagonists' place under the gaze of the villain, initially presented as a parental gaze. However, *The vile village* (the seventh book) sees a shift in the detective function of the series. The children progress beyond their use of detection to unmask Olaf and instead use their VFD skills to interpret textual and moral ambiguities, resulting in a more complex reading of the tattoo.[2]

The Baudelaire children initially encounter the tattoo on the ankle of their first guardian and nemesis Count Olaf, a distant relative, who intends to steal their vast fortune. By the end of the first book, the children have escaped Olaf's clutches, but their reprieve is temporary. Each subsequent book sees them forced to escape another of his plans (though the schema of the stories alters after the seventh book) until his death in *The end* (2006). While the early part of the series charts their attempts to uncover the tattoo literally, after the seventh book, the series moves into its detective phase with the children's consideration of the tattoo and the organisation that it represents. After being thwarted by Olaf, disguised as Detective Dupin, the children adopt the role of detectives themselves. The hunted become the hunters.

AUTHORSHIP, NARRATIVE FRAGMENTS AND EMPTY LIBRARIES

The children's readings of the tattoo emphasise the importance of knowledge and research and that interpretation can and will vary over time. Their approach to reading the tattoo is constructed as a type of detection. There are various acts of detection that occur in the series, including some that are encouraged as processes for the reader. One of the most important concerns the reader and Lemony Snicket himself. The books purport to be the Baudelaires' true history as researched and written by the narrator. He too is a detective, following the children's journey and its relation to his lost love, Beatrice (ultimately revealed as the Baudelaires' mother). It is Snicket's name that appears on the cover as the author, rather than Handler.[3] At the end of each book, sections entitled 'about the author and illustrator' continue the fictionalisation of Snicket and his supposed correspondence with his publishers. In addition, the series illustrator is set alongside the fictional character of Snicket, and so continues this blend of fiction and reality.

The simple structure of the orphans' story is disrupted by acts of metafiction and literary asides and jokes. The youngest child Sunny's language development, for example, includes her timely utterance of neologisms, homophones, literary references and cooking recipes. In addition, Snicket interrupts the story of the Baudelaires to provide a contemporaneous account of his own fictional situation. There is a deliberate attempt in book twelve (2005: ch. 2) to turn the reader into a detective. Portions of the texts are reversed which requires the reader to use a mirror and actively engage with the text in order to read these portions effectively. The narrative is, therefore, revealed to 'competent' readers as multi-layered.[4]

Sara Austin identifies Snicket's style of narrating as mock-didactic, providing a 'metafictional link between the series and the didactic tradition' (2013). Snicket has an explanatory function whereby he takes care to interpret and define words which the (child) reader may be encountering for the first time. These digressions to illustrate and define terminology are also provided in a more curt fashion by Klaus. Typically, Klaus's glosses are more reliable than Snicket's interventions. This forms part of the series' interest in language, interpretation and meaning. Snicket's overlong definitions and explanatory analogies are used to provide a hesitation between the word or concept, its definition and meaning, and test the competence of the reader. This emphasises the importance of reading and the slipperiness of language and meaning, and is reflected in the changing readings of the tattoo. The tattoo is a visual manifestation of the children's understandings of the complexities of society and culture.

Elizabeth Bullen (2008) claims that Handler, writing in a 'serio-comic Victorian-gothic style' (qtd Cullinan *et al.* 2005: 655), turns the didactic narrative and the convention of children's fiction generally on its head by not providing a happy ending either to the individual books or the series as a whole. The narrator repeatedly warns the reader that this will be the case and uses prolepsis to tempt the reader to stay reading. The lack of a conventional ending is flagged up from the very beginning of the first book, where the reader is implored not to read any further – 'if you are interested in reading books with happy endings, you would be better off reading some other book' (Snicket 1999: 1) – and repeated throughout the series.[5] However, the ending is not unambiguously unhappy either. The Baudelaires finally establish their family unit and the fundamental basis of their community. The end of the series sees them experienced and self-sufficient. Their research and experience has shown them that the 'black and white' mentality of the VFD is to be avoided, that schisms are cyclical, that unfortunate events happen to all (Olaf's personal history is a testament to this), and they recognise the importance of literature and reading to develop empathy.

As the series progresses, it becomes increasingly difficult to tell which side members of the split VFD are on. The tattoo encompasses both sides of the schism and cannot be fully claimed by either side. Typically, the organisation is split into fire starters and fire extinguishers. This division is also reflected in literary taste, whereby 'good' members of the VFD revere 'good' literature

(Herman Melville, Elizabeth Bishop, Samuel Taylor Coleridge, T. S. Eliot and so on) and 'bad' members resort to 'bad' poets such as Edgar Guest (this difference is explored in *The grim grotto*). Particularly sinister characters enjoy the opportunity to burn books regardless of their literary merit. Snicket, himself a fire extinguisher, mediates this taste, though it is shared by Klaus.[6]

Towards the end of the series, the binary of the schism is repeatedly contested and is physically evident in the second set of twins to be revealed as triplets: the Denouement brothers. The Baudelaires meet with Ernest and Frank Denouement who reflect the absolutism of the split factions, both of their names reporting to truth, before meeting their other brother Dewey. Dewey offers a more nuanced understanding of VFD, emphasised by his establishment of the VFD library as the Hotel Denouement. Despite the orphans' wish to retain a strong moral compass,[7] their actions (both deliberate and inadvertent) see them become fire starters as they destroy (under Olaf's orders) an area of the hinterlands and cause Hotel Denouement, and with it the VFD library, to burn. The consequences of their actions see the children question whether they are able to choose a side in the schism and, indeed, whether there actually are only two sides. Clearly, Handler is drawing on the structure of detective stories which typically have a denouement, or final unravelling of the mystery or crime (*The penultimate peril*). The mysteries of the VFD are more impenetrable than most, though, and it takes a further book, *The end*, for the children to see their situation with clarity.

Dewey's record keeping and construction of a library is significant. With his advanced research skills, Klaus is repeatedly called upon to draw disparate narrative fragments together to cohere some meaning. While he has some limited success in solving literary puzzles (Aunt Joesphine's encrypted notes and Isadora's poetry, for example), he struggles to contextualise his knowledge. He improves on this after meeting Quigley Quagmire (the triplet brother of 'twins' Isadora and Duncan) who recommends the use of a VFD commonplace book. Klaus uses the commonplace book to establish a continuity of thought about VFD and essentially create a record for consideration. His record keeping is part of a long tradition of VFD practice, but the organisation's knowledge is repeatedly threatened by the impermanence of written records caused by the burning of archives and libraries (so threatened by the fire starters of the VFD). The process of creating an archive is revealed to be both political and partial. It teaches the children to interrogate written records, consider the idea of completeness and to think about the record's context.

The children are often confronted with empty or destroyed libraries, incomplete archives and textualities. It is as though the fire that burnt their familial library has distributed literary fragments throughout their world. These fragments and loss of meaning emphasise the children's world as a postlapsarian state. In a reworking of the Garden of Eden, the Incredibly Deadly Viper saves the children by feeding them hybrid apples (cultivated by their parents) from a tree at the centre of the island 'paradise'. This tree is literally revealed as a tree of knowledge. It houses their parents' notes, diary and scientific equipment. It even appears to pre-empt Sunny's enthusiasm for cooking as there is a kitchen hidden in its hollow boughs as well. To eat of this fruit is to rip away any vestments of childhood innocence. The fruit is the literal fulfilment of their parents' involvement in VFD. It causes the children to review their sentimental, one-dimensional and biased view of their parents and to acknowledge the complexity of the world and their role within it. Olaf's revelations of the Baudelaire parents' involvement in the death of his parents completes this process. Certainly, some critics have viewed this as a negative ending since it reflects the end of the children's innocence. However, the children positively embrace this state of experience, aware of their skills and their journey ahead.

BEFORE AND AFTER THE SCHISM: SECRET ORGANISATIONS AND ALTERNATIVE COMMUNITIES

In keeping with a tradition of detective narratives, Olaf is forced to don a range of disguises to hide his distinguishing features: his one eyebrow and his tattoo. Olaf's more outrageous disguises include mimicking a disability (as a sea captain with one leg), cross dressing (as a receptionist and as Kit Snicket) and donning a religious disguise (he wears a turban as Coach Genghis). It initially appears that Olaf's disguises form part of his daily work as an actor in a troupe; however, the disguises are later revealed as outfits from the VFD's wardrobe. It is thanks to their own increasing skills and growing self-reliance, rather than the misguided help of the adults entrusted with their care, that the Baudelaire children repeatedly escape his clutches – something also very much in keeping with the traditions of children's mystery and detective fiction (Pickrell 2008).

To emphasise how unfortunate and unlucky the children are, each book has thirteen chapters and there are thirteen books in the series.[8] The children begin by being victims of Olaf's crimes and gradually take on the role of detectives and so gain their own agency. Their identification of Olaf, by seeing through his various disguises, is a detective trope that becomes routine practice for the children. The children's principle deliberations are the meaning of the eye symbol which is variously and repeatedly represented (most prominently as a tattoo), the investigation into the mysteries of the secret VFD society, their parents' role in the VFD, their own training for their present situation, the mystery of their parents' deaths and the whereabouts and importance of the VFD's missing sugar bowl (a McGuffin device). Through literary references to *Moby-Dick*, including naming the submarine after the heavily tattooed Queequeg, Handler foreshadows the fact that the series will end with the majority of its mysteries equally 'unsolved to the last' (2004b: 451).

The tattoo is originally introduced as a pictorial representation of an eye on the ankle of the books' main villain, Count Olaf. To begin with, it is associated with authority, violence, danger and surveillance more generally. This reading is complicated by the revelation of the tattoo on other characters' ankles (such as Jacques Snicket in *The vile village*, Kit Snicket in *The penultimate peril*, and Ishmael in *The end*), including those deemed to be not villainous, which affect its original connotations and reshape the tattoo as it begins to take on different meanings. This occurs in conjunction with the complicating of the children's ideas about good and evil as they are tempted to act in villainous ways 'for the greater good' (see Snicket 2004a and 2005a). Their reading of the tattoo also changes in that the image itself alters – the initials which form the eye become visible to them (2004a) but their meaning does not. The changing meaning of the tattoo from being apparently fixed to something more ambiguous reflects this confusion. The image has two main readings throughout the series: that of a sinister eye with its gaze fixed on the Baudelaires and that of an insignia denoting membership of the ambiguous VFD. However, since the change in the tattoo's meaning has its roots in the VFD schism (an event occurring before the advent of the series), pre- and post-schism landscapes read through the tattoo reflect a modern, postlapsarian state. This state of experience is exacerbated by the capitalist industrialised processes and industries that the children encounter. The link between the series and modernity is clear from the Baudelaires' name since, according to Sandra Miller (2012), among others, the poet Charles Baudelaire brought the idea of 'modernity' to the fore.

This idea of a modern society is important in reading the tattoo. In pre-literate societies, tattoos were 'permanent, collective, and largely obligatory' (Turner 2000: 39) meaning that within such societies, 'the significance of tattoo could be read unambiguously' (39). This reading of the tattoo in such pre-literate societies tallies with the tattoos in pre-schism VFD. According to Lemony Snicket's *The unauthorized autobiography* (2007), prior to the schism, children were removed from their parents and taken to be trained by the VFD to work for the organisation. Part of this process involved the children being tattooed with the letters VFD in the shape of an eye on their left ankle, whether they consented or not. This custom, then, reflects the way that tattoos were important in signifying transitions in the life cycle, or rites of passage, but also marks the recipients as property and denotes their (in)voluntary membership of the organisation, meaning that it fulfils Turner's other criteria of pre-literate tattooing of being both permanent and collective but also obligatory. In the tenth book, an encounter with the villainous 'woman with hair but no beard' reveals that labour under the VFD before the schism was not egalitarian either, when she refers to having 'an infant servant once – a long time ago' (2004a: 32). Membership of VFD then seems to originally have been obligatory, meaning a large degree of free will and autonomy has been taken from members.

Turner argues that while tattoos were once 'embedded in social processes' in modern societies 'these social linkages are either broken or at least eroded', leading to tattoos becoming 'optional, playful, and ironic' (2000: 41). Post-schism, the VFD tattoo could be said to reflect this modern consideration of tattooing. The original links between members are broken, and the organisation itself has abandoned the practice of tattooing, because, 'since the schism, we have realized that it is not wise to permanently mark oneself with a symbol when the meaning of the symbol may change at any moment' (2007: 191). The character of Esme Squalor, Olaf's girlfriend, is indicative of the sense that tattoos and other symbols have become both ironic and playful. Squalor is obsessed with a binary fashion dynamic, refusing to associate with anything considered 'out' and adorning herself with the latest 'in' things, regardless of how ridiculous these may be. Rather than get a tattoo, she marks her entry into Olaf's villainous troupe and her status as Olaf's girlfriend by her outlandish outfits, often adorned by the VFD eye. For the Baudelaire children it seems as though the eye is watching them explicitly and unrelentingly.

The tattoo on Olaf's ankle, while suggesting danger and a villainous identity for the children, also reflects Olaf's forcible and traumatic entry into VFD. While Olaf is still presented as a villain throughout the series, questions are raised as to why this is. Reference is made to the death of his own parents with an accusation that this may have been at the hands of the Baudelaire parents (2005a: 9, 308). This presents the option of reading part of the narrative as Olaf seeking retribution for his own loss. The children make the assumption that it was Olaf who burned down their house, killing their parents in the process, but this is something Olaf strongly denies when the children finally confront him about it during his drawn out death (2006: 314). Of course, as a spectacularly nasty villain, he may well be lying, but there is also scope for a reading in which Olaf is actually innocent of the crime, leaving the question of what really happened to the Baudelaire parents open.

THE TATTOOED GAZE

There are many representations of eyes in the series: it features in interior design, as an image on a necklace, as the circle on the running pitch, clothing design, on door carvings and as patterns on china as well as in the shape of the reoccurring tattoo. For the first five books, there is only one tattoo: the tattoo of an eye on Olaf's left ankle. The idea of the Evil Eye[9] is one of the oldest superstitions in the world (Bohigan 1997), is a part of many religions and an active superstition in many places (Dundes 1992). Significantly, Count Olaf's tattoo can be read *as* the Evil Eye. It is one of the first things that the children notice about their new guardian when they are delivered to his house: 'Count Olaf had an image of an eye tattooed on his ankle, matching the eye on his front door'

(2001a: 25). The tattoo is proprietorial and makes a connection of ownership between the house's architecture, the décor and Olaf.

The tattoo also serves as a significant function in unmasking and revealing Olaf, as he cannot disguise the tattoo for long. Eyes continue to haunt the Baudelaires. In *The carnivorous carnival* (2002d), the children find themselves surrounded by representations of the eye: '[t]he eye matched the one painted on her caravan, and the one tattooed on Count Olaf's ankle. It was an eye that seemed to follow the Baudelaires wherever they went, drawing them deeper and deeper into the troubling mystery of their lives' (*ibid.*: 49–50). Here, they finally realise that the eye tattoo is made up of the letters 'V.F.D.' (*ibid.*: 121) and is the insignia for the organisation.

The shape of the tattoo leads the Baudelaire children to feel that they are constantly under the gaze of this inked eye. Long before the children recognise the tattoo as insignia, they see it as an eye and so read it in terms of someone watching them. From their first encounter with Olaf, the idea is foreshadowed: 'they wondered [...] whether, for the rest of their lives, they would always feel as though Count Olaf were watching them even when he wasn't nearby' (2001a: 25). The tattoo of an eye, then, is both all-seeing, terrifying and engaged in watching over the Baudelaire children in place of their parents. This is a sinister parental gaze in the place of a protective one.

Later on, as the children become more aware of the full extent of Olaf's villainy following his kidnap of Sunny, the idea of the eye as all-seeing recurs:

> Violet looked over in the direction of Count Olaf, but could not meet his eyes. The eyes on his face, that is. She was staring at his feet, and could see the tattooed eye that had been watching the Baudelaire orphans since their troubles had begun. (*ibid.*: 104)

This theme continues in *The reptile room* (2001b), where the tattoo is positioned as the most terrifying (and permanent) thing about Olaf's appearance. The idea of the eye tattoo watching over the Baudelaires, in *loco parentis* following their parents' death, is returned to in *The slippery slope* (2004a) when Sunny wakes up after spending the night in Count Olaf's custody in a casserole dish:

> Tattooed on Olaf's ankle was the image of an eye, and it seemed to Sunny that this eye had been watching the Baudelaires throughout all of their troubles, from the day on Briny Beach when they learned of the terrible fire that destroyed their home. [...] It was almost as if this eye had replaced the eyes of their parents, but instead of keeping watch over the children and making sure that they were safe from harm, this eye merely gave them a blank stare. (*ibid.*: 104–05)

In this instance, the meaning of the eye is acknowledged as being unknown, blank and potentially benign rather than obviously benevolent or malevolent; however, when considered as a replacement for the caring gaze of a parent, it becomes sinister. This gaze has replaced the loving protection of their parents and is brought to the fore throughout the series. Olaf's uncanny ability to find the children reinforces this idea of being under surveillance.

However, while Olaf is always able to eventually locate the children, he does not know where they are at all times, which suggests that the sense of being constantly under surveillance is more figurative than literal. Olaf relies on a fortune teller, Madame Lulu, to predict the children's whereabouts. The Baudelaires, believing in an empirical world, reveal Madame Lulu to be a VFD researcher whose archive of sources about the Baudelaires, coupled with some news reports, enable her to keep track of their whereabouts. This research element to her character suggests that she might be on the side of the fire extinguishers prior to the schism, though her attraction to Olaf proves her downfall.

From its first appearance, the tattoo is synonymous with fear and mystery, and as *The bad beginning* progresses, it becomes linked to both real and implied violence. At one point, Olaf assaults Klaus, who: 'fell to the floor, his face inches from the eye tattooed on Olaf's ankle' (2001a: 53). Like the eye, the reader is a witness to the assault but powerless to intercede. Unlike the reader, the tattoo is bound up with the assault. It is the first thing Klaus sees after it, and makes the connection between the eye and the violence explicit for the reader. During *The wide window*, Klaus reveals that he still has nightmares about 'the terrible tattoo' (2001c: 41) which continues to terrify him due to its violent associations, in addition to ideas of surveillance. Karin Beeler has connected tattoos, violence and desire; as she notes, 'because tattoos are so intimately linked with the body, it requires very little effort to see the connection between tattoos and the concept of desire' (2006: 6). Handler clearly links Olaf's tattoo with violence, and, like Beeler, also makes a link with desire. Desire is present when the children first meet Olaf's entourage and a bald-headed member of the group puts his hands on Violet's face and comments on her prettiness (2001a: 49). Prior to this, Olaf has behaved neglectfully towards the children and has verbally abused them, but it is here that the idea of potential sexual abuse begins.

In chapter six, Olaf's plan to marry Violet in order to get hold of the Baudelaire fortune begins to unfold. This desire is positioned as a threat of incest. While encouraging the children to see him as a father, he tries to seduce Violet to take the role of his bride in a play, stroking her 'on the chin, looking deep into her eyes' (*ibid.*: 78). His desire for her surfaces repeatedly throughout the series and is often linked with violence, both literal and symbolic. During the proposal, 'Violet swallowed, and looked down at Count Olaf's tattoo' (*ibid.*: 109). It is here that the link between the tattoo and desire comes to the fore. She is unable to take her eyes off the inked image as Olaf continues his attempt at seduction: 'you're such a lovely girl, after the marriage I wouldn't dispose of you like your brother and sister' (*ibid.*). While she can avoid meeting Olaf's gaze directly, Violet is unable to avoid the unwavering gaze of the tattooed eye, thus connecting the eye tattoo to Olaf's unwanted desire for her. As John

Berger states: 'women watch themselves being looked at' (1972: 47), and Violet cannot avoid being the subject of the male gaze. Olaf's desire for Violet is never realised and is most explicit in the first book; it is, however, hinted at in other books in the series. In *The reptile room*, Olaf spends an entire meal rubbing a knife against Violet's knee under the table, something that Danel Olson sees as making 'the dark Gothic promise of a hundred novels before this one: Stephano/Olaf can rape and kill her at any time if she violates any wish, so she must obey' (2001b: 515).

MARKED AS 'GOOD' AND 'EVIL': COMPLICATING A DICHOTOMY

While various commentators have written about Handler's blurring of the good and evil dichotomy (Austin 2013; Bullen 2008; Langbauer 2007; Nguyen 2012), the connection between this blurring and the tattoo motif has not been explicitly addressed, yet it is apparent throughout the series. The first six books follow a very similar structural pattern.[10] The orphans are placed in a new situation by Mr Poe where the safety of their new home is threatened by the arrival of Olaf in disguise (after the first book). The orphans are unable to convince any of their guardians that this interloper is actually Olaf until eventually Olaf is unmasked, usually through the revelation of his tattoo and single eyebrow. Finally, as the orphans are saved, Olaf makes good his escape. The tattoo, therefore, is not just an object of fear but also a means – sometimes the only means – available to the Baudelaires of unmasking Olaf and escaping his clutches. While at this point in the series the main characters are still presented as on one side or the other of a simple dichotomy of good and evil, the symbolism of the tattoo itself is already more complex. While the Baudelaires are frightened of seeing it since it means that they are in the presence of Olaf and so in danger, they are also relieved when it is publicly revealed since this means that the adults positioned as their protectors must now acknowledge the danger and address it. This gives the tattoo an early double meaning of both danger and reprieve.

In *The reptile room*, Olaf has simply masked the tattoo with make-up, and is revealed by Mr Poe, which results in the children 'for the first time in their lives' (2001b: 174) being happy to see the tattoo. By book three, Olaf has gone a step further and hidden the tattoo under a fake leg, leading the children to wonder just how far he is willing to go to perfect his disguises: '"[d]o you think he actually let leeches chew off his leg," Klaus wondered, shuddering, "just to hide his tattoo?"' (2001c: 62).[11] The unveiling of the tattoo is the pinnacle of each book: the point at which it looks as if Olaf will be not only unmasked but captured; however, each time he manages to escape.[12]

The basic pattern begins to change during *The vile village* (2002c). In this book, Mr Poe takes the maxim that 'it takes a village to raise a child' to heart and sends the children to live in the Village of Fowl Devotees. During their stay, the villagers inform them that Olaf has been captured based on the children's description of the tattooed eye. However, the prisoner turns out to be Jacques Snicket (brother of the narrator, Lemony). Like Olaf, Jacques possesses a single eyebrow and, perhaps most damningly, a tattoo of an eye on his left ankle. He proclaims his innocence – '"but lots of people have only one eyebrow", Jacques cried, "and I have this tattoo as part of my job"' (*ibid.*: 115) – but to no avail. This is the first time that the tattoo appears on someone other than Olaf, and its appearance causes confusion for the Baudelaire children. Jacques is murdered before the children are able to really speak to him, but from the little that they do see of him, they believe him to be on the same side as themselves. However, his tattoo means that they cannot be certain of this. Jacques's remark about the tattoo's connection to his job creates further confusion, since it is the first time that the idea of the tattoo serving a function other than just that of the merely decorative is raised.

It is no coincidence that this change in the symbolism of the tattoo from something automatically to be feared into something more complex is paired with a deviation from the former pattern of endings. This is the point at which the children, and to a certain extent the reader, become aware of additional narratives. Olaf's pursuit of them – and their parents' deaths – become part of something bigger, a story that began before theirs and will continue after them (this is made explicit in *The end*).

The Baudelaires move from potential victims trying to escape a villain to active participants in their fate, who seek their own answers and attempt to solve the mysteries surrounding their parent's deaths and the VFD organisation. This begins as they outwit Olaf, disguised as detective Dupin. Although the children do manage to escape Olaf, they are also accused of his murder and make the decision to run away rather than risk being burnt at the stake by the village elders. They are unwilling to trust in a justice system run by adults who, since their parents' death, have continuously let them down. This change in the ending means that the Baudelaires are now for the first time on the wrong side of the law. They are now, like Olaf, fugitives (although Olaf has the advantage of being presumed dead). This means that they can no longer rely on the assistance of Mr Poe and that they must, like Olaf, rely on a range of disguises in order to avoid arrest.

As the tattoo becomes more complex than a marking to enable a villain to be unmasked, so the Baudelaires' situation changes to one in which they must rely entirely on themselves, and their idea of themselves is challenged. *The daily punctilio* prints articles falsely claiming that the children have murdered Olaf (2002c: 248), which means that they are forced to deny who they are and don disguises to retain their freedom, since many of the people that they encounter share the belief that 'if the newspaper says somebody is a murderer, then they are a murderer and that's the end of it' (2003: 11). This literal reading of text subtly informs the ways in which the children read the tattoo. The children's experiences lead them to move from a structuralist reading of meaning. Their journey is toward an acceptance that there is no single truth and this becomes central to the narrative of the rest of the series, embodied by the idea that there are multiple readings of the tattoo.

The hostile hospital is the first to feature the Baudelaires in disguise and also the first in which Olaf is not unmasked. The books no longer follow the simple pattern detailed earlier. From here, the children are placed in a similar position to Olaf in that they are also on the run from the law, and the book ends not with Olaf's unmasking, but with the children's. Disguised as medical professionals, Sunny and Klaus have their surgical masks ripped from them by Esme Squalor, revealing them to an audience who believe them to be murderers (*ibid.*: 208). This book is the beginning of the series concentrating on the Baudelaires' attempts to uncover the truth behind their parents' deaths and find out what the secret society of VFD is, as well as to avoid being arrested. It is the start of more involved, multi-stranded and less repetitive story arcs. It is also in this book that the narrator Lemony Snicket reveals that he has a tattoo in the same place as Count Olaf and Jacques Snicket, stating, while reminiscing: 'now the only trace I have of those happy days is the tattoo on my left ankle' (*ibid.*: 214). The children are obviously unaware of this since Snicket is narrating their tale, but since the reader has presumably located Lemony Snicket on the 'good' side of a dichotomy of 'good and bad', this complicates not just the idea of who has a tattoo and what this might signify, but also who is 'good' and who is 'bad', which began with Jacques Snicket in the previous book. This is something that the protagonists begin to contend with themselves from *The hostile hospital* onwards. As Kim Hong Nguyan points out, 'Olaf's acts of villainy do not outstrip the Baudelaires' abilities to sympathise with him' (2012: 273), as the children begin to recognise when they justify their own 'villainous' actions as necessary to save their lives (2003: 241–42). Similarly, the change in the narrative structure repositions the children so that they share in Olaf's experience, and so causes them to empathise further with him. This idea that their actions, despite being done for the best intentions, may mean that the children are now villainous is explored throughout the remainder of the series, in addition to the process of humanising Olaf.

In *The carnivorous carnival* (2002d), the children are once more in disguise, this time as circus freaks, although none of them take the role of the traditional circus tattooed man or woman. Madame Lulu informs them of the schism in VFD and explains that since then, 'it's been hard for me to know what to do. I never thought I'd be the sort of person who helps villains, but now I do' (*ibid.*: 158–59). This leads the Baudelaires to address their own behaviour, which they defend because they 'always had a good reason' (*ibid.*: 159), but, as Lulu points out, 'everybody thinks they have a good reason' (*ibid.*). As good and evil become complicated, and motivation is analysed by the children, so the tattoo shifts from a talisman of violence to a sign of membership of a society, albeit one which has split into two warring factions.

At this point, the Baudelaires still see this split as one of 'good' versus 'bad', but this simple analysis is complicated as the series unfolds. For example, in *The slippery slope*, the children meet a new ally, Quigley Quagmire, who reveals that he associates the eye tattoo with noble people. Unlike the Baudelaires, therefore, he considered the building shaped like an eye which appears in *The miserable mill* as a potential place of safety (2004a: 172). This further complicates the Baudelaires' previous reading of the tattoo as carrying mainly negative connotations, since Quigley clearly reads only positive traits in the tattoo (*ibid.*). Their association of the eye with danger results in their viewing the building with fear, which is justified since Olaf is working in it disguised as Shirley, a female receptionist. Quigley, by comparison, arrives after Olaf has left, so is not harmed or threatened by those in the building.

CONCLUSION

The eye tattoo can be a seen as a simple symbol of fear, of surveillance, of parental violence mingled with desire. It denotes membership of a mysterious secret society; yet, following the society's split, it is impossible to tell whether this means the bearer of the tattoo is good or bad. The fact that the tattoo is in the shape of an eye leads to the idea of it as all-seeing, watching everything that unfolds; yet, whether this gaze is protective, neutral, dangerous or a mixture of the three is, like so much of the series, never fully explained. As the series grows more complex, bringing in subplots and unfolding more mysteries, so the meaning of the tattoo becomes complicated. Initially, it is simply a symbol of fear, violence and desire (complicated already by being a sign of hope that Olaf will be unmasked and apprehended), but from book seven onwards it begins to be read differently, revealed as a sign of membership. This reading of the tattoo appears to fit with a history of tattoos as signs of group membership from pre-literate traditional societies (Turner 2000) to more recent biker groups (DeMello 2000), where in many cases the meaning of the tattoo is known only to those initiated within the group. However, the VFD is a split organisation and so neither side are able to reclaim what was originally meant by the tattoo or simplify its contemporary meanings. Like the textual fragments the children locate that are researched and revealed to have layers of meaning, the readings of the tattoo complicate its apparent straightforward meaning as an eye or the VFD organisation it represents. The complexity and evolving meaning of the tattoo mirrors the children's increasingly sensitive readings of literature and character. The tattoo is central to Handler's representation of the slipperiness of meaning, of the promotion of research alongside reading, demonstrated through the children's growth in understanding that the world is complex.

NOTES

1 This chapter gives the original date of publication when discussing the novels. Quotations are given from the edition used by the authors. See Bibliography for further details (eds).

2 Throughout the series, the tattoo and its design are linked to architecture (where it forms the signage for an opticians, a lumber mill and a carnival sign, as well forming the arch in Olaf's house, and a spyhole cut into a door). This plays on the idea of a space where the central child protagonists will be safe, and emphasises the tattoo's ambivalent representations of safety and danger.

3 This takes the conceit of metafiction further than other children's authors such as J. K. Rowling (who used her initials to suggest gender neutrality, creating a kind of pseudonym), as Sara Austin points out (2013).

4 As is usual with children's literature which is both suitable for being read by adults to children and read by children for themselves, the narrative works on a number of levels including a more erudite literary level. We use the term 'competent' to identify the reader (child or adult) who recognises the literariness and self-reflexiveness of this text.

5 The notion of the books as forbidden is undoubtedly part of their appeal, and the technique has proved very lucrative with over fifty-one million copies having been sold worldwide (Langbauer 2007: 506).

6 This literary taste is complicated, for the reader, by Isadora's dull poetry.

7 It is Sunny, the character without VFD training, who is the sibling that often refers to the children's moral compass and identifies the ambiguity and confusion of their actions.

8 Handler has launched a prequel series entitled 'All the wrong questions' (2012–14), a companion novel *File Under: 13 Suspicious Incidents* (2015; which it could be argued is #2.5 of the *All the wrong answers* series), and there is a final chapter fourteen to conclude *The end*. It seems inevitable that the stories set in the Baudelaire world will grow. See http://www.lemonysnicketlibrary.com/ for more details.

9 Conversely, the representation of eyes can be read positively. In ancient Egypt, the eye of Horus represented protection and good health (Bohigan 1997), and the symbol of the all-seeing eye of god (or the Eye of Providence) is used by freemasons and is depicted on the reverse of the Great Seal of the United States to indicate god watching over those on Earth (Case 1935). In some cultures, tattoos have been used to ward off the Evil Eye (Hildburgh 1955).

10 This simple structuring has been criticised by Bruce Butt (2003), and yet conversely is identified as part of the series' attraction by other critics (Austin 2013; Olson 2011).

11 The idea of tattoo removal is never addressed in the books, so engrained is it with ideas of identity, community and belonging.

12 In *The reptile room*, Sunny bites off Olaf's wooden leg, revealing the tattooed ankle underneath (2001b). In *The miserable mill* (2005b), Olaf himself, disguised

as Shirley, hitches up his skirt to reveal the eye tattoo. In *The austere academy* (2002a), Sunny once again reveals the tattoo when she removes Olaf's shoes, but none of these revelations are enough to ensure Olaf's capture since these revelations generally occur at the same time as (or just before) he runs off.

BIBLIOGRAPHY

Austin, Sara (2013), 'Performative metafiction: Lemony Snicket, Daniel Handler and the end of *A series of unfortunate events*', *The looking glass: New perspectives on children's literature*, 17:1, n.p. Available: https://www.lib.latrobe.edu.au/ojs/index.php/tlg/article/view/387/381 [accessed 5 December 2018].

Beeler, Karin (2006), *Tattoos, desire and violence: Marks of resistance in literature, film and television* (North Carolina: McFarland).

Berger, John (1972), *Ways of seeing* (London: Penguin).

Bohigian, G. H. (1997), 'The history of the Evil Eye and its influence on ophthalmology, medicine and social customs', *Documentaophthalmologica*, 94:1–2, 91–100.

Bullen, Elizabeth (2008), 'Power of darkness: Narrative and biographical reflexivity in *A series of unfortunate events*', *International research in children's literature*, 1:2, 200–12.

Butt, Bruce (2003), '"He's behind you!": Reflections on repetition and predictability in Lemony Snicket's *A series of unfortunate events*', *Children's literature in education*, 34:4, 277–86.

Caplan, Jane (ed.) (2000), *Written on the body: The tattoo in European and American history* (London: Reaktion Books).

Case, P. F. (1935), *The great seal of the United States* (Los Angeles: Builders of Adytum).

Cullinan, Bernice E., Bonnie L. Kunzel and Deborah A. Wooten (eds) (2005), *The Continuum encyclopedia of young adult literature* (London: Continuum).

DeMello, Margo (2000), *Bodies of inscription: A cultural history of the modern tattoo community* (Durham, NC: Duke University Press).

Dundes, A. (1992), *The Evil Eye: A casebook: Volume 2* (Wisconsin: Wisconsin University Press).

Hildburgh, W. L. (1955), 'Images of the human hand as amulets in Spain', *Journal of the Warburg and Courtauld Institutes*, 15:1–2, 67–89.

Langbauer, Laurie (2007), 'The ethics and practice of Lemony Snicket: Adolescence and generation X', *PMLA* 122:2, 502–21.

Miller, Sandra (2012), 'Seigfried Kracauer: Critical observations of the discreet charm of the metropolis', in D. Berry (ed.), *Revisiting the Frankfurt school: Essays on culture, media and theory* (Surrey: Ashgate), pp. 7–26.

Nguyen, Kim Hong (2012), 'Mourning *A series of unfortunate events*', *Children's literature Association quarterly*, 37:3, 266–84.

Olson, Danel (2011), 'The longest gothic goodbye in the world: Lemony Snicket's *A series of unfortunate events*', in D. Olson (ed.), *21st century gothic: Great gothic novels since 2000* (Plymouth: Scarecrow Press), pp. 506–27.

Pickrell, H. Alan (2008), 'Juvenile and young-adult mystery fiction', in C. E. Rollyson (ed.), *Critical survey of mystery and detective fiction: Volume 4* (Pasadena: Salem Press).

Snicket, Lemony (2001a), *Book the first: The bad beginning* [1999] (London: Egmont).

— (2001b), *Book the second: The reptile room* [1999] (London: Egmont).
— (2001c), *Book the third: The wide window* [2000] (London: Egmont).
— (2002a), *Book the fifth: The austere academy* [2000] (London: Egmont).
— (2002b), *Book the sixth: the ersatz elevator* [2001] (London: Egmont).
— (2002c), *Book the seventh: The vile village* [2001] (London: Egmont).
— (2002d), *Book the ninth: The carnivorous carnival* (New York: HarperCollins).
— (2003), *Book the eighth: The hostile hospital* [2001] (London: Egmont).
— (2004a), *Book the tenth: The slippery slope* [2003] (London: Egmont).
— (2004b), *Book the eleventh: the grim grotto* (London: Egmont).
— (2005a), *Book the twelfth: The penultimate peril* (London: Egmont).
— (2005b), *Book the fourth: The miserable mill* [2000] (London: Egmont).
— (2006), *Book the thirteenth: The end* (London: Egmont).
— (2007), *The unauthorized autobiography: The unfortunate life of Lemony Snicket* (London: Egmont).
Turner, Bryan (2000), 'The possibility of primitiveness: Towards a sociology of body marks in cool societies', in M. Featherstone (ed.), *Body modification* (London: Sage), pp. 39–50.

PART 5

Film: Adaptation, memory and constructions of self

11

The ink of the real: Memory and identity in Christopher Nolan's *Memento*

Peter Figler

INTRODUCTION

Near the close of Christopher Nolan's 1999 neo-noir film *Memento*, Leonard Shelby (Guy Pearce) intentionally mistranscribes the license plate number of his partner, Teddy (Joe Pantoliano), initiating a series of events culminating in Teddy's murder by Leonard's hand. However, Nolan's disjunctive chronology begins at the end,[1] opening the film with Leonard killing his partner and presenting the question of why he has done so as the primary conflict. Throughout, black and white episodes depicting the past are intercut with colour scenes taking place in the present. The time streams synchronise close to the end of the film; though, to complicate matters, a sequence of flashbacks intercuts the black and white scenes. The film's structure parallels the psychological mindset of Leonard, who suffers from a condition called *anterograde amnesia*. Thus, it is only at the end of the film, but the chronological beginning of the story, that we discover that Leonard criminally manipulates his own disorder after Teddy reveals details of his past. Up to this point, he epitomises an average,[2] everyday individual lured to crime by circumstances out of his control. The revelation that Leonard is the opposite is jarring for audiences, paralleling Leonard's own condition and triggering our own reframing retrospection.

MEMENTO'S DOUBLES: THE AVERAGE JOE, PSYCHOLOGICAL TRUTH AND THE NEO-NOIR

The motif of the 'regular Joe' turned criminal is common in noir cinema, and in this section I foreground its use from classic to neo-noir texts with an eye toward situating *Memento* within the larger scheme. Leonard's almost enthusiastic transformation to murderer to protect his lie closely follows fellow insurance investigator Walter Neff (Fred MacMurray) in Billy Wilder's classic,

Double indemnity (1944). Like Leonard (*Memento*), Wilder's Neff is not a stereotypical criminal and is even quite likable. A host of double-crosses occur after Neff agrees to help Phyllis (Barbara Stanwyck) murder her husband, framing it as an accident to collect a doubled insurance payout. Neff soon discovers Phyllis is having an affair behind his back. Rightly guessing her double bluff, he informs her of his plan to kill her and pin it on her (second) boyfriend. In the climactic scene the would-be lovers shoot each other, both die,[3] and we are left wondering if there was a 'good guy' in the film at all.[4] Despite the role of the femme fatale to lure Neff into violence for her sake, it does not take Phyllis long to convince Neff to commit murder. Perhaps Neff's only regret is that he was unable to get away with the crime, not that he is now a murderer.

Though *Memento* does gesture toward *Double indemnity*'s noir conventions, Leonard's persona mirrors Neff's in more insidious ways. When first approached by Phyllis, Neff balks at the idea of murdering her husband.[5] Though she does sway him with the promise of sex and money, her claims that she 'can't breathe' and is 'scared' of her husband immediately precede his complicity; in the same way Natalie (Carrie-Anne Moss) convinces Leonard that she fears for her life while Dodd (Callum Keith Rennie) still lives. Neff may be motivated by the drive to protect, however his turn to violence inspired by jealousy, as well as the ruthless way he kills Phyllis – as she embraces him, pleading, he remarks 'goodbye, baby' and fires into her point-blank – troubles notions that he is either a white knight or merely a dupe lured by a payday. While Leonard is motivated by money and the signs of wealth,[6] he is also disturbingly comfortable with sudden violence. Ironically, it is a defence of his wife, herself allegedly brutalised by male violence, that drives Leonard to hit Natalie. He sets up Teddy for death not because his partner has wronged him, but rather because Teddy has seen through him. Films from *The third man* (1949) to *The killers*[7] (1964) to *Fargo* (1996) and beyond depict everyday individuals willingly plunging into the criminal world to protect their own self-interest.

If, as Sharon Cobb points out, the shift from 'classical' noir to the 'real revival' of neo-noir cinema is demarcated by Roman Polanski's *Chinatown* (1974), the genres still have more in common than not.[8] Joan Copjec notes that 'film noir discourse' (1993) is marked by highly recognisable conventions that 'anyone familiar with the study … can recite: a femme fatale, a morally compromised detective, an urban setting, voice-over narration, convoluted plot structure, chiaroscuro lighting, skewed framing, and so on' (qtd in Fluck 2001: 380). But though they are common, it is in the subversion of these traditional elements that neo-noir distinguishes itself. Cobb writes that both periods emphasise 'primarily antiheroes [whose] motives are usually dishonourable … many *Noir* characters are liars, at times even deceiving themselves' (*ibid.*: 207); as I will explore, the boundary dividing Leonard's lies is opaque, and complicated, which is consistent with *Memento*'s genre. If initially obscure, the underlying motivations of classical noir characters are generally less complex than their neo-noir counterparts. Sam Spade (Humphrey Bogart), hero PI of John Huston's *The Maltese falcon* (1941), is violent, but it is understood to be an occupational hazard, not grounded in latent psychological trauma. Contrast Spade with Bud White (Russell Crowe) in Curtis Hanson's *L.A. Confidential* (1997). Both men eagerly break the rules in pursuit of justice, muddying moral lines, but Bud's rage derives from the childhood trauma of his father murdering his mother, potentially deferring his own violence.[9] Unlike Bud, however, Leonard cannot rely on the law as a plausible cover for his violence.

Neo-noir's increased focus on psychological characterisations allows for a greater flexibility in character development and plot complexity, often intermingling violence and self-deception. Winfried Fluck calls noir criminality 'a metaphor for "dark" dimensions of the self that remain incomprehensible' (2001: 379). Verbal Kint's (Kevin Spacey) deception of Agent Kujan (Chazz Palminteri) in Bryan Singer's *The usual suspects* (1995) is impressive because he fabricates a narrative (presented as flashback) based solely on objects inhabiting the office space where he is interrogated. *The usual suspects*, like *Memento*, is a 'puzzle film', aimed at injecting higher levels of complexity than are generally found in more classical plots.[10] Like Leonard, Verbal constructs a psychological self in place of a cover story, and his ability to not just perform the role of a sad-sack criminal, but convincingly sell the corresponding psychology, truly defines his character. Mid-story, Verbal relates the legend of Keyser Söze's brutal sacrifice of his own wife and children, a sacrifice that transforms him from low-level to overlord in criminal culture; whether or not the story is true is inconsequential, as it is primarily useful to both supplement Söze's mythology and set him in binary distinction to Verbal. The authorities never suspect that the sniveling, psychologically weak Verbal could double as the dreaded Söze. We are left to wonder if Söze-*qua*-Verbal has ever even committed a crime, or if legend alone drives violence committed by others on his behalf. In any case, Verbal's story underpins the neo-noir conflation of violence as a mediator of identity. All of this stands in distinction to Leonard, whose own construction of identity plunges much deeper into permanence.

MEMENTO'S DECEPTION BY PERMANENCE:
LEONARD'S TATTOOS

Brian Snee, writing about Joel and Ethan Coen's fulsome body of neo-noir cinema, notes the importance of perspective, especially from the point of view of unreliable characters. In this way, we must not only mistrust what characters like Leonard Shelby tell us, but we must question their perspectives as represented on-screen. Snee identifies the commonplace of characters in noir where just 'looking at something changes it' (2009: 212). Nolan literalises this convention in Leonard's (mis)transcription of Teddy's licence plate.[11] He realises he will soon forget the self-deception and instead track down the holder of the plate in the belief that this will fulfil the quest to avenge his wife's rape and murder. Leonard quickly has Teddy's license number tattooed on his thigh, rendering it permanent and another addition to the collection of 'facts' scrawled on his body. In total, Leonard has twenty-six tattoos,[12] some professionally applied and others self-made.[13]

Anterograde amnesia affects short-term recall, preventing victims from forming new memories after an initial trauma, while retaining those memories developed prior to the injury. To compensate for his disability, Leonard's tattoos pair with handwritten notes and annotated Polaroid photographs to create a reality which must be reassembled every hour or so. *Memento*, as opposed to most other cinematic treatments of amnesic disorders, has been lauded as quite faithful in its depiction of the condition (Baxendale 2004: 1483). In Leonard's recounting of his injury, his head is driven into a bathroom mirror, striking the left-front of his head and knocking him unconscious; his assailant (whom he identifies as John G.) proceeds to violate and murder his wife. In general, anterograde amnesia affects the temporal cortex and the hippocampus contained therein,[14] which is consistent with his story. However, though the assault may have damaged his short-term memory, Leonard's 'self' should have remained intact. As Sallie Baxendale points out, post-trauma 'personality and identity are unaffected' (2004: 1480). Leonard is able to instil behaviours and trigger new memories through conditioning, however. This is perhaps most prominent in the first tattoo we encounter, 'Remember Sammy Jankis', which is placed conspicuously on the outside of his left hand.

The flashback sequence details Leonard's encounter with Sammy, who is also afflicted with anterograde amnesia. Leonard was an insurance investigator in his past, and Sammy's case was his first investigation. Through interviews and testing, he concludes that Sammy's condition is psychological, not physical. Mental illness is not covered by Sammy's policy and so triggers the claim's rejection. Sammy's diabetic wife, unsure of what to believe, 'tests' him herself, leading to her inadvertent murder at his hands through an overdose of insulin. It is important that Sammy's story in its entirety is Leonard's recollection, adding to the ample evidence suggesting Leonard has either partially or wholly subsumed Sammy's identity – or invented him outright. In the colour present, we *see* Leonard falsify evidence to put himself on the trail of Teddy and *hear* him justify manipulating his own disorder to 'be happy', if only for a brief moment. In this way, the whole of the film – now contained in the memory of the audience – must itself be reconfigured, notably aspects told exclusively through his perspective. Until the end, Leonard is portrayed as operating in the criminal milieu only by necessity and circumstance. However, his willingness to falsely implicate and murder to preserve a lie marks him squarely as a criminal, and one can only speculate how many others have been set up beyond the 'real' John G., if such a person even existed.

Leonard's agency in Teddy's murder makes him particularly cold and abhorrent, though I suggest his rationalisation of self-deception to provide even temporary existential satisfaction is not abnormal, but quite the opposite. Psychologically speaking, it is not uncommon for people to condition identitarian self-perceptions to appear as they desire to be, often removed from actuality. Slavoj Žižek roots this process in culture and terms it *ideological fantasy*, which 'consists in overlooking the illusion which is structuring our real, effective relationship to reality', allowing individuals to rationalise beliefs and behaviours through intentional self-deception (1989: 30); this deception, however, is unstable and the past leaks out in unpredictable ways. Carlos Gallego reads the formal structure of *Memento* as analogous to notions of postmodernity and Leonard to the postmodern subject (2010: 33–35). His analysis recalls Fredric Jameson's notion of the postmodern subject (whom Jameson reads through Jacques Lacan's schizophrenic) as existing in a state of constant present, initiating a temporal breakdown and destabilisation of identity. The parallel with Leonard Shelby is compelling. Like others, however, Gallego implicitly takes the position that Leonard's 'tragic story' and 'desperate search for revenge' is rooted in accurate recollection of his injury (*ibid.*: 39) and suggests, again implicitly, that the Sammy Jankis sequence is a reliable, albeit 'dead' memory (*ibid.*: 41). Conversely, I find compelling evidence intimating that he has not only fabricated nearly every facet of the Leonard we encounter in the film, but also will stop at nothing to promulgate a new self, including the extreme body modification of nearly thirty tattoos.

In this chapter, I argue that Leonard's tattoos function well beyond tools of remembrance and instead help him manipulate his condition to form structures of truth in order to (re)define his identity, ultimately rationalising his crimes. Moreover, culturally as well as individually, the permanence of tattoos lends credence to their identitarian embodiment, functioning as signifiers of the self even more so than projections to others.[15] Tattoos quite literally inscribe and reinscribe psychological truths onto an individual, reflexively recreating the self in a fantasy image and projecting it to others. Tattoos have long been culturally viewed as markers of resistance and delinquency,[16] perhaps unconsciously allowing Leonard more access to the criminal underground in his search; or, conversely, they are conceivably mere cover for his inherently violent and unstable self. Arguably, Leonard's numerous tattoos are an unconscious extension of criminal persona; that is, criminals are frequently socially marked by their tattoos, reciprocally reinforcing cultural stereotypes. In Robert Futrell and Pete Simi's examination of tattoos and identity in white power activists, they find them to be 'physical symbols of intensifying identification' and represent 'increasing separation from the mainstream' (2004: 30). Recent cultural trends signal transference of the tattoo from subculture to the mainstream, though for many delinquency and tattooing are intertwined. Even in contemporary crime narratives, the tattoo still holds a special place to highlight criminal identitarian markers.[17] Importantly, however, as *Memento* demonstrates, wilful self-deception frequently comes at a cost, often rationalising aberrant behaviour or even violence; to that end, complex interactions involving desired and actualised self-identity are exacerbated and artificially altered by methods such as tattooing, which may trigger an unstable sense of self couched in fantasy.

LEONARD SHELBY, REAL AND FEIGNED

During a voiceover, a hallmark of film noir, Leonard asserts that he suffers from anterograde amnesia, which triggers an inability to form new memories in victims of brain trauma, though events occurring before the trauma remain intact. However, symptoms of anterograde amnesia often present with those of *retrograde amnesia* in the same patient. Functionally, the primary difference details which memories are retained post-trauma. I have already described anterograde as loss of memories following amnesic inception; in retrograde amnesia, memories prior to injury are lost. In defining these disorders, there is a clear-cut difference, though the inherent unreliability of memory makes accurate and truthful diagnoses difficult to assert. Proper diagnosis of either disorder hinges not only on honest presentation of symptoms, but perhaps most importantly on the subject being able to parse out actual memories from desires and projections (which may present through repetition or hallucination coded as actual memory). In Leonard's case, there is significant question as to which disorder, or what combination of both, he suffers – and ultimately, given his potential complicity in several deaths, if the distinction even matters. I contend that his attempts to condition his memory to an adulterated version of actuality, though largely successful, do not fully internalise, leading to the psychological 'leakage' of his past onto a state of constant present; when notes and Polaroids do not function as planned, he relies on the extreme alteration of tattoos, permanently reinscribing a narrative onto his body, which becomes a locus of truth.

It is vital to imagine Leonard as potentially an actual person, and not simply because of the ways he is allegorical of the postmodern, performative subject whose self is constantly written and rewritten in reaction to (or against) cultural or historical narratives. Todd McGowan observes in his chapter on the film that the 'subject of knowledge' is not interested in 'neutral truth' but instead 'accesses truth through distortion or deception' (2013: 41). Leonard is, of course, a fictional construct, but one that Nolan renders analogous to this subject of knowledge; as such, how he adapts his psychological/physiological condition/disability to make more self-fulfilling versions of himself is as important as how he uses tattooing for the same purpose – both strategies are commonly understood by viewers, bringing them more fully into the world of the film. McGowan writes that, as opposed to typical films, Leonard appears to act 'for the same reasons that the spectators watching him imagine themselves to act' (*ibid.*: 51).

To understand Leonard's identitarian issues, it is helpful to attempt to parse out the claims most likely to be the truth. Much has changed since William Lennox published 'Amnesia, real and feigned' in 1943,[18] though one constant remains: the difficulty in determining objectively which memories amnesiacs have retained and which are coloured by unreliable, post-trauma subjectivity; and this is to say nothing of ulterior motives in hiding symptoms or fabricating portions of recollected experience. There is ample evidence that Leonard does indeed suffer from a short-term memory disorder. Running from Dodd and later waiting in Dodd's motel room, the condition manifests in ways that seem illogical to feign, not to mention the initiation of Teddy's murder itself. Though this condition appears present, other facets of his recounting are less reliable, including the genesis of the injury itself.

Over the history of amnesia studies, consolidation theory has dominated clinical thinking. It states that though memories are processed (or consolidated) after initial experience, if 'this process is somehow disrupted, for example, by a concussive head injury, the memory fails to be stored' (Riccio *et al.* 2003: 42). In the early 2000s, however, consolidation theory was called into question through a series of experiments indicating 'a window of time following the amnestic insult (minutes to hours) during which the critical information remains available for recall; forgetting does not occur until sometime later' (*ibid.*: 42). If Leonard's recounting of his assault is truthful, this would help contextualise several brief flashes of memory depicting his wife surviving the assault; if, however, he has fabricated this event, the cut scenes still likely represent valid memories, though in this possibility he remembers his wife about to die by his own actions. It is important that *all* of the information regarding his condition is provided by Leonard himself; flashback scenes, often utilised in film to present objective versions of the past, are in *Memento* merely depictions of Leonard's well-rehearsed version, rendering them questionable. The mere notion that he is aware – without notes or tattoos – that his condition exists by name highlights either the strength of his conditioning or outright duplicity.[19]

One rather important aspect of Leonard Shelby is that, like Walter Neff, he is unequivocally not a good guy, and there is reason to believe he never was. Because of his condition and the pathos contained in his story, however, it is easy to position Leonard as a good man gone bad. For example, Tracey K. Parker argues that Jimmy's (Larry Holden) murder, as a direct result of

Teddy's duplicity, 'foreshadows [Leonard's] moral decline as he transitions from avenger to a murderer who premeditates his crime' (2008: 3). If this is true, however, it happens with remarkable alacrity, given that in the span of about five minutes, Leonard would need to suffer a complete reversal of personality and immediate 'moral decline'. It is more likely that Teddy's abuse of his partner's condition *coupled* with Leonard's own violent nature motivates him to add Teddy to his forgettable list of crimes. Beyond his agency in Teddy's murder, Leonard hits Natalie when she verbally berates him and generally demonstrates a propensity (and aptitude) for violence in ways average citizens typically do not; he is remarkably unaffected after discovering that he has murdered Jimmy under false pretenses and summarily steals his clothes and Jaguar car. Parker's belief that Leonard so quickly shifts a foundational ethical-personality dimension and thus experiences a 'complete shift in values and behavior [*sic*]' feels more like the 'unrealistic' manner in which amnesia is popularly depicted in film (Baxendale 2004: 1481).

REMEMBERING TO FORGET: AUTOBIOGRAPHICAL AND EPISODIC MEMORY

I would like to extend some 'what ifs' at this point, with respect to Leonard's story, which help illuminate the absolute necessity of his overabundance of tattoos as viewed through his potentially violent character. If his amnesia is anterograde, evidence suggests that while he must rigorously condition himself to retain information after the injury, he has full prior recollection, with retrograde presenting an opposing frame. However, as I mentioned earlier, the likelihood of both states either existing simultaneously or in a process of oscillation is probable. This state, known as global amnesia, would serve to explain Leonard's confusing mélange of imagistic recall as well as the strong suggestion that Sammy is an aspect of an amnesia-induced dissociative disorder.[20]

His recollection may then necessarily include both aspects of Sammy's identity and the events just before his injury, which he presents as an ill-conceived robbery. According to his story, Leonard kills one of the assailants assaulting his wife but is then knocked out from behind by another, initiating his amnesic condition. Leonard's version of the story stands in opposition to the police report (parts of which Teddy maintains have been blacked out by Leonard to prevent him facing this different account) which found no evidence of a second robber and, crucially, that his wife was not killed; moreover, close inspection of the pages Leonard peruses shows the conspicuous title of 'psychiatric report'. Nolan's cross-cuts suggest that buried under conditioning, Leonard does remember his wife's survival. The tight point of view shot depicting her blinking on the bathroom floor follows Teddy's revelation that she survived. Afflicted with anterograde amnesia, Leonard would recall a prominent yet fragmented version of these events, their importance highlighted as his freshest memories. Problematically, however, the cross-cutting depicts repressed post-trauma memories, agreeing with symptoms of retrograde, not anterograde, amnesia. It follows that, given the actuality of his condition, Leonard indeed suffers from global amnesia, most likely triggered by extreme stress and re-exposure to trauma. Studies have drawn conclusive links between fantasy-alteration of memory after witnessing particularly violent crimes.[21] Leonard himself tells Teddy that '[m]emory's not perfect. It's not even that good. Ask the police, eyewitness testimony is unreliable.' His statement, while most certainly underscoring major themes of the story, may be an unconscious 'slip', grounded in his own experience.

Though Leonard tries hard to suppress his past, it nonetheless seeps into his present. He passes time waiting in Natalie's apartment by watching television. His posture, expression and steady channel-changing rhythm parallel those shown of Sammy in the flashback sequence. As he turns the remote over in his hand, Leonard absently studies the 'Remember Sammy Jankis' tattoo. Very briefly, the scene cuts to a closeup of a hand flicking a needle, which corresponds with Teddy's later (earlier) revelation that it was Leonard's wife who was diabetic and that Sammy did not even have a wife. Had Leonard projected his own experience onto Sammy, it follows that her inadvertent death by insulin overdose correlates directly with his condition. These memories reinforce Teddy's claim that Leonard's wife survived the assault but oppose a diagnosis of anterograde amnesia, instead supporting a condition of retrograde amnesia. The remote, like a tattoo, functions here as an object of memory that triggers involuntary recall. Of course, while the remote accesses a memory he would like to suppress, it is a disposable object, unlike a tattoo.

These objects prompt Leonard to engage with his *reflexive identity*, which is a psychological mechanism that uses 'material objects in private to define [himself] prior to and independent of [his] social roles as perceived by others. The act of daily identity creation and affirmation through goods ... indicates the extent to which human cognition and psychological sense of self are inextricably linked to the handling of material culture' (Smith 2007: 412). Though M. L. Smith asserts that memory-objects like tattoos are intimate and intended to introject private self-identity, Leonard also utilises them to project a public identity, as I would argue that most people do; however, by necessity he often makes them more public to support the narrative.

It may be simplistic to suggest that Leonard opportunistically takes advantage of different states of amnesia. Rather, I would like to complicate his story by mediating all understanding of Leonard Shelby through his clear ethical flaws and ready willingness to engage in violence. It is the fantasy-narrative of heroic husband questing to avenge the brutalisation of his wife in the face of a debilitating disorder that Leonard desires; however, both his guilt and his condition stand in the way of fully inscribing this narrative solely through conditioning. As I mentioned earlier, it is not uncommon to revisit and alter memory to project an ideal self. To that end, Leonard's desire to reconfigure his own memory is not abnormal; yet, when those memories implicate him in a series of deaths, each seemingly more cold-blooded than the next, now there is considerable ethical slippage. Thus, the specific type of amnesia is less important than the agency with which he manipulates this condition, irrespective of when and how it was initiated or to what extent he has accurate recall. Arguably, it may be more important that Leonard asserts one type of amnesia as part of his self-manipulation than what form it takes.

With respect to his situation, two types of memory are important though: episodic and autobiographical. Experimental psychologist Martin Conway defines them:

> Episodic memory is reconceived as a memory system that retains highly detailed sensory perceptual knowledge of recent experience over retention intervals measured in minutes and hours ... Autobiographical memory, in contrast, retains knowledge over retention intervals measured in weeks, months, years, decades and across the life span. (2001: 1375)

Because Leonard is most likely to suffer from complex global amnesia, he is able to utilise both types of memory to varying degrees. It is here that conditioning is most important, as it allows different structures of knowledge contained within memory formations to best shape his ideal self. Leonard insists that, as opposed to Sammy, he can function because of his 'habit and conditioning', though he immediately states that it is due to 'acting on instinct'. On the surface these statements appear contradictory, but I will read them through permeable knowledge-creating structures of memory. Conway asserts that rather than working as discrete modes of retention, 'autobiographical memory provides the instantiating context for sensory-perceptual episodic memory' (2001: 1375).

Conway's research focuses most closely on autobiographical memory, though it functions by linking to episodic memory. Notably, the two work together to create objects of knowledge. Their differences involve episodic memory's 'experiencing self (or the "I")' and the autobiographical 'experienced self (or the "me")' (*ibid.*). Though it is overly simplistic, it is useful to consider the difference as those of subject and object. I will draw a parallel between these types of knowledge and Lacan's theoretical framework of the *je* and *moi*, or the subjects of the *enunciation* and the *enunciated*, respectively. Conway's notion of the experienced self follows Lacan's *moi* in that it functions as autobiographical knowledge, based in largely stable memories of activity – that is, this knowledge has a relatively static sense of permanence because it functions as 'recollective experience', or experience that a person has drawn from participation. These memories function as objects of knowledge accessible through direct recall. Leonard's autobiographical memory (now) includes his vain attempt to save his wife, only to be struck down by her eventual killer, creating an object of revenge; in the linguistic schema of Lacan, the enunciated statement of his *moi* might sound like, 'I am a faithful husband and will stop at nothing to gain justice for my wife'. In order for Leonard to believe in lies of his own design, he must interpolate non-lived experience into permanent autobiographical objects of knowledge. Conway cautions that while autobiographical knowledge 'functions to ground the self in memories of actual experiences and remembered reality', it 'does not always, even though it may usually correspond to actual reality' (*ibid.*: 1377). Most people cannot arbitrarily reassign meaning to autobiographical knowledge because their involuntary recall *knows* the truth of their circumstance. Leonard's condition provides a ready-made workaround.

Conway's research shows that autobiographical experience is supplemented by episodic experiencing – while these moments are ephemeral, lasting no more than minutes, they provide the necessary context for retrieving and interpreting autobiographical knowledge, including fantasies and wish-promise projections. Everyday objects, including sensations and emotions, trigger autobiographical memory in short bursts, or episodes. These bouts of episodic information work consciously and unconsciously with autobiographical to continuously reinforce identity. Among the most important functions of episodic knowledge is to 'keep track of progress on active goals as plans are executed' (*ibid.*: 1381). So, while the *moi* says, 'I am', the *je* says, 'I desire to be', or perhaps more importantly, 'I will be'. This attention to syntactic elements is critical to Leonard's manipulation, as it concretises the goals and plans which comprise the bulk of his existence.

There is good reason to believe that in moments of clarity, like Teddy's revelations at the end of *Memento*, Leonard proactively takes steps to make his condition work for him, to allow him to perpetually pursue the quest that defines his self; all the while fortifying the reinscribed narrative that deflects guilt away from his wife's death and alters his autobiographical memory. It is my belief that Leonard cannily games his own disability by morphing episodic into autobiographical knowledge. As he encounters episodic information useful to the overarching narrative, he transcribes the information on notes and pictures which he checks and rechecks 'religiously'. Once the amnesia activates, his episodic buffer is lost but the inscriptions remain, waiting to be assimilated into permanent memory. Conway points out that episodic memories will rapidly degenerate unless they are 'integrated at the time or consolidated later'; or, in other words, by using habit and routine – of which Leonard exists in a perpetual state – to internalise one structure of truth over another (2001: 1376). Short-term memory loss coupled with rigorous psychological conditioning provides ready-made relearning after each episode. Of course, as we see, this plan is not without its faults, and the cross-cuts intimating that Leonard and Sammy are one and the same self suggest that despite a clever inversion of his disability, he must take more extreme steps. Notes and photos may be lost and destroyed, and thus he must literally inscribe new knowledge into memory by way of the tattoo.

SCRIPTED CRIMINALITY: CONDITIONING THE CONDITION

Lacan is vital here because of the strict correlation between Leonard's conflation of the signifying function of tattoos and his self-manipulation. I want to stress the linguistic dimension of what has come before in this chapter. Lacan's analysis hinges on the 'speaking[22] subject' as one whose identity is engendered by signification, by language. Desire is mediated through language at the close of the 'mirror stage', and an infant begins the journey to human subject through socialising dimensions of language. Stemming from Hegelian principles, Lacan posits that the identitarian self is formed through recognition and dialectical encounters with others, but emphasises the form and function of language in these encounters as indispensable. Thus, the splitting of the self (*je*/*moi*) couples with performative dimensions of enunciation. Performativity and signification contextualise the relationship between Leonard's former existence and his new fantasy-projected identity; they help mould his *je* subjectivity into his *moi* permanence.

The usability of performative utterances has been widely adapted since J. L. Austin first coined the term in his work on speech-act theory: *How to do things with words* (1962). Austin differentiates between utterances which contain truth or falsehood based on experience and actuality ('I did …'), calling them *constatives*, and those which project a self's desire ('I will do … I promise to do …'), calling them *performatives*. In Conway's structure, constatives align with autobiographical knowledge, while performatives follow closely with episodic; in Lacan's terms they parallel *moi* and *je*, respectively. In Leonard's case, his drive to instil a permanent present by way of a new past means he must change both types of knowledge. To accomplish this, he transforms notes and Polaroids into a series of performatives inscribed directly onto his body; thus, once the condition manifests, the performative aspect permeates the constative dimension.

I claim that Leonard is unable to block latent images of his wife's death at his own hands and so instead improves his conditioning. However, it follows that, as Nolan shows us, basic behaviourist-repetition training did not take. Leonard extols his own system over Sammy's, saying '[c]onditioning didn't work for Sammy, so he became helpless. But it works for me. I live the way Sammy couldn't. Habit and conditioning. Acting on instinct … Sammy had no drive. No reason to make it work. Me? I got a reason.' He says this during the phone conversation that frames the Sammy flashback sequence. Note the strong presence of constative utterances in the passage: '... it works for *me* ... *I* live ... *I* got a reason ...'. Leonard's *moi* discourse internalises these scripted statements as truth based on repeated and, as we see in the passage, self-referential conditioning.

Leonard is aware, in a moment of stress near the end of the film, that to destroy the pictures he takes 'you have to burn them'. While it is not impossible to presume this information might already be contained within his autobiographical lexicon, it is much more likely that he has internalised this knowledge from a series of episodic encounters. While the visual history shows that he supplements tattoos (a homemade 'or James' is appended to the professionally applied 'Fact 3: First Name John'), he cannot destroy them, making them an invaluable source of autobiographical knowledge. Thus, as the opening lines of his restructured narrative, Leonard tattoos 'John G raped and murdered my wife' on his chest and 'remember Sammy Jankis' on his hand, motivating the signifying function of the tattoo within his *moi* to *je* discourse.

CONCLUSION

This chapter's exploration of terminology is necessary not only to highlight parallels among psychological and linguistic lines, but also to support the absolute necessity of Leonard's tattoos within the revenge narrative. As I contend, his experience helps to bridge the psycholinguistic linkage between tattoos and identity, notably in the form of ideological fantasy; though Leonard's condition marks him as an outlier, well removed from the average person, his desire to assuage the ghosts of his past does not. While there is a case for argument-by-degree, it is common in psychoanalysis to encounter patients with a range of identity-dissociative issues, with some grounded in latent violence or crime.

Drawn into Leonard's psychological perspective, we want to believe his story of overcoming his condition. Unlike Harry Powell or Max Cady, Leonard's tattoos are narratively framed as memorials to his wife, which is likely why it is such a dramatic reversal at the end of the film when he is revealed to be a selfish and murderous criminal rather than an average Joe drawn inexorably into crime. Leonard constructs an identity through the visually signifying dimension of tattooing, though ultimately even this construction is unable to hide his true self. Because of the chronological structure of *Memento*, the audience only discovers the falsification of his story and propensity for violence at the film's end, triggering a retroactive review of all that has come before. Leonard utilises the tattoo as a projection of identity aimed at convincing an audience, but crucially Leonard must also convince himself. Apart from Teddy, who appears to know Leonard's background best of all, others in *Memento* take his story at face value not only because he believes it, but because the tattoos function as (painful and dedicated) vehicles of sincerity.

NOTES

1 The film is often erroneously said to run 'backwards'. To be clear, which is quite necessary in discussions of this work, only the opening scene actually runs backwards.

2 Of course, terms like average are problematic, given that their use presupposes a societal normal/abnormal binary that signifies based on factors like sexuality, belief or appearance. Much of Michel Foucault's later work deals with socially constructed stigmatisations of abnormality. My overarching point is that while Leonard's use of tattoos to (re)construct identity is extreme, it is not uncommon.

3 Neff's ultimate fate is ambiguous. After entering his full recounting into the Dictaphone, he tells Keyes he is fleeing for the border but makes it only as far as the doors outside the office before collapsing. If Neff does live to be arrested, however, the strong implication is that his final destination is the gas chamber.

4 It could be argued that Barton Keyes (Edward G. Robinson) is closest to the conventional 'good guy' in the film. As the film ends, Keyes overhears Neff's confession and, far from being horrified that his friend has murdered several people, instead appears tired and perhaps feels sorry for him.

5 'Who'd you think I was?' he protests, after accusing her of plotting her husband's death.

6 It is foolhardy for Leonard to take the clothes and especially the Jaguar car of a local and high-level drug dealer, but he does so anyway. This level of visibility clashes with his stated revenge motive. Equally, Neff is distracted by the expensive anklet that Phyllis wears when they first meet, seduced both by her sexuality as well as her ubiquitous signs of wealth.

7 Don Siegel's 1964 film, with John Cassavetes, Lee Marvin and Angie Dickinson, is an adaptation of Ernest Hemingway's short story of the same name. An earlier (1946) version starring Burt Lancaster and Ava Gardner also translates Hemingway's work to the screen. The story has also been adapted as *Out of the past* (1947), *One false move* (1992) and *A history of violence* (2005) which demonstrates a fascination with the average Joe turned killer.

8 Cobb's brief essay in *Film noir reader 2* (1999) outlines thirteen traits common to classical noir that are both paralleled and subverted in neo-noir. Her illustrative examples are useful for situating the fine periodising differences.

9 For example, shooting a suspect and planting a gun on him, threatening an informant by putting his gun in his mouth and playing Russian roulette, and engaging in regular beatings of criminals in an abandoned motel used as a 'black site' interrogation location.

10 See Warren Buckland's collection, *Puzzle films* (2009), for a comprehensive take on the genre, including a chapter dedicated to *Memento*.

11 And quite literally at that. When Leonard takes down Teddy's plate, he mistakenly substitutes one letter; he writes down and summarily tattoos on his leg 'SG13 71U', an error that careful viewers can corroborate thanks to Nolan's tight shot of the plate actually reading 'SG13 7IU'. This should prevent him from tracing the plate to

Teddy. Later however, when Leonard and Teddy roll Dodd out of the motel room, the change becomes *real*, as we see another tight shot of the plate, now physically changed to match his original transcription. This 'error', which is actually noted in Nolan's shooting script, further emphasises the idea that Leonard has altered his reality to suit himself, and moreover that we, the viewing audience, see actuality only through his perspective.

12 Technically there are twenty-seven, though this total includes the 'I've done it' tattoo which appears only in a fantasy sequence at the end of the film.

13 All critical materials on *Memento* mention Leonard's tattoos as central to the film, though in general these mentions are ancillary to their respective analyses. Notable scholarship includes: Claire Molloy's *Memento* (Edinburgh, 2010) which details a wealth of backstory about the film's inception, including a comprehensive history of its distribution. Her third chapter presents a detailed examination of the plot and its intricacies, and reads well alongside Stefano Ghislotti's similarly-aimed chapter in *Puzzle films*; Jaqueline Furby and Stuart Joy's collection *The cinema of Christopher Nolan: Imagining the impossible* (Wallflower, 2015) includes several useful pieces on the film, including Margaret Toth's '*Memento*'s postmodern noir fantasy: Place, domesticity and gender identity' and Fran Pheasant-Kelly's 'Representing trauma: Grief, amnesia and traumatic memory in Nolan's New Millennial Films'; Todd McGowan's psychoanalytic reading of *Memento* in his book *The fictional Christopher Nolan* (2013); Tony Jackson's '"Graphism" and story-time in *Memento*' discusses technologies of writing and the ways in which they relate to identity, with key passages focusing on the tattoos.

14 Though this is only in general. Andrew Mayes and Neil Roberts point out that '[a]mnesia is caused by brain lesions in any number of regions: the medial temporal lobes, the midline diencephalon, the basal forebrain, and possibly the ventromedial frontal cortex' (2001: 1398–99).

15 See Rosemary Joyce on tattoos and other body ornaments as societal metaphors, as 'marking already-given aspects of social status of the individual person, or as media for the communication of given social identities' (2005: 142).

16 There are numerous texts exploring this aspect, including the recent publications: *Bodies of inscription* by Margo DeMello (2000); *Tattooed: The sociogenesis of body art* by Michael Atkinson (2003); and *Bodies of subversion* by Margot Mifflin (2013); though perhaps the most comprehensive is Steve Gilbert's *Tattoo history: A source book* (2000). In addition, see 'Tattoos and ratings of personal characteristics' by Douglas Degelman and Nicole Deann Price (2002); 'Why do people get tattoos?' by Miliann Kang and Katherine Jones (2007); and 'Marked difference: Tattooing and its association with deviance in the United States' by Josh Adams (2009).

17 For example, reformed neo-Nazi Derek Vinyard covers the swastika tattoo over his heart with his hand near the end of *American history X* (1998), signaling both its proximity to his (former) identity and his desire to repress it. Flashbacks detail Derek's immersion in the neo-Nazi movement paralleling his membership with the marking of his body. Robert De Niro's portrayal of the sadistic ex-convict Max Cady in Scorsese's 1991 remake *Cape Fear* is augmented by his numerous prison tattoos, the most prominent a large cross spread across his back, its arms suspending the words 'truth' and 'justice' like a scale. He is terrifying at times, and it is difficult to ignore the presence of the tattoos that complement this terror. Cady's

tattoos recall one of the first and most memorable appearances of tattoos in film. Charles Laughton's *The night of the hunter* (1955) is itself a testament to the power of fantasy and projected identity. Though lacking the population of tattoos on Leonard Shelby's body, Harry Powell's (Robert Mitchum) tattoos are conspicuous and symbolically laden. Bearing two seemingly homemade tattoos of 'LOVE' and 'HATE' on the knuckles of each hand, Powell, a self-identified Reverend, claims he is the vehicle for cleansing lustful and vile women of sin. 'Cleansing' is thinly veiled code for murder, and Powell is an archetypal villain. His tattoos mark him as a wolf in sheep's clothing for even the most unlettered viewer.

18 Lennox identifies the three most important causes of amnesia as 'alcohol, epilepsy, and hysteria' (1943: 298). To these he suggests 'pathological, psychological, and feigned' (*ibid.*: 299). From a viewpoint of the early twenty-first century, Lennox's analysis is rudimentary. His analysis forms part of an important trajectory in understanding the disorder, including grounding terminology later adapted and assimilated into neurological and psychological science.

19 If, for example, Leonard has entirely fabricated Sammy, it is plausible he has read the term in his 'police reports' (most are actually psychiatric reports). Ultimately, Sammy is the most unreliable character in the film, as he is presented only in Leonard's recollection. This makes his existence or degrees thereof impossible to prove. It is my belief that Sammy is (was) a real person, though Leonard has displaced/transferred elements of his own past onto Sammy.

20 See Edmund Howe (1984, especially 257–63).

21 See C. J. Stanny and T. C. Johnson (2000).

22 Speaking here need not strictly refer to verbal communication, but may include writing and gestures.

BIBLIOGRAPHY

Adams, Josh (2009), 'Marked difference: Tattooing and its association with deviance in the United States', *Deviant behavior*, 30:3, 266–92.

Atkinson, Michael (2003), *Tattooed: The sociogenesis of body art* (Toronto: University of Toronto Press).

Austin, J. L. (1962), *How to do things with words* (Harvard: Harvard University Press).

Baxendale, Sallie (2004), 'Memories aren't made of this: Amnesia at the movies', *BMJ: British medical journal*, 329:7480, 1480–83.

Buckland, Warren (ed.) (2009), *Puzzle films* (New York: Wiley).

Cobb, Sharon (1999), 'Writing the new *noir* film', in A. Silver and J. Ursini (eds), *Film noir reader 2* (New York: Limelight Editions), pp. 207–13.

Conway, Martin (2001), 'Sensory-perceptual episodic memory and its context: Autobiographical memory', *Philosophical transactions: Biological sciences*, 356:1413 ('Episodic Memory'), 1375–84.

Copjec, Joan (1993), *Shades of noir: A reader* (London: Verso).

Degelman, Douglas and Nicole Deann Price (2002), 'Tattoos and ratings of personal characteristics', *Psychological reports*, 90:2, 507–14. Available: https://doi.org/10.2466/pro.2002.90.2.507 [accessed 5 December 2018].

DeMello, Margo (2000), *Bodies of inscription: A cultural history of the modern tattoo community* (Durham, NC and London: Duke University Press).

Fluck, W. (2001), 'Crime, guilt, and subjectivity in "Film noir"', *Amerikastudien/ American studies*, 46:3, 379–408.

Furby, Jaqueline and Stuart Joy (eds) (2015), *The cinema of Christopher Nolan: Imagining the impossible* (n.p.: Wallflower).

Futrell, Robert and Pete Simi (2004), 'Free spaces, collective identity, and the persistence of U.S. White Power activism', *Social problems*, 51:1, 16–42.

Gallego, Carlos (2010), 'Coordinating contemporaneity: (Post) modernity, 9/11, and the dialectical imagery of *Memento*', *Cultural critique*, 75 (Spring), 31–64.

Gilbert, Steve (2000), *Tattoo history: A source book* (n.p.: Juno).

Howe, Edmund G. (1984), 'Psychiatric evaluation of offenders who commit crimes while experiencing dissociative states', *Law and human behavior*, 8 (3/4: Psycholegal Assessment, Diagnosis, and Testimony), 253–82.

Jackson, Tony (2013), '"Graphism" and story-time in *Memento*', *The fictional Christopher Nolan* (Austin, Texas: University of Texas Press).

Jameson, Fredric (1991), 'Culture: The cultural logic of late capitalism', in F. Jameson, *Postmodernism, or the cultural logic of late capitalism* (Durham, NC: Duke University Press), pp. 1–54.

Joyce, Rosemary A. (2005) 'Archaeology of the body', *Annual review of anthropology*, 34, 139–58.

Kang, Miliann and Katherine Jones (2007), 'Why do people get tattoos?', *Contexts*, 6:1, 42–47. Available: https://doi.org/10.1525/ctx.2007.6.1.42 [accessed 5 December 2018].

Lacan, Jacques (2006), *Écrits: English edition*, trans. B. Fink (New York and London: W. W. Norton).

Lennox, William G. (1943), 'Amnesia, real and feigned', *The University of Chicago law review*, 10:3, 298–312.

Mayes, Andrew R. and Neil Roberts (2001), 'Theories of episodic memory', *Philosophical transactions: Biological sciences*, 356:1413, 1395–408.

McGowan, Todd (2013), *The fictional Christopher Nolan* (Austin: University of Texas Press).

Mifflin, Margot (2013), *Bodies of subversion: A secret history of women and tattoo* (New York: Powerhouse Books).

Molloy, Claire (2010), *Memento* (Edinburgh: Edinburgh University Press).

Nolan, Christopher (dir.) (2000), *Memento* (Newmarket: Los Angeles).

Parker, T. K. (2008), '"Do I lie to myself to be happy?": Self-help culture and fragmentation in postmodern film', *Interdisciplinary literary studies*, 10:1, 1–15.

Riccio, David C., Paula M. Millin and Pasacle Gisquet-Verrier (2003), 'Retrograde amnesia: Forgetting back', *Current directions in psychological science*, 12:2, 41–44.

Smith, M. L. (2007), 'Inconspicuous consumption: Non-display goods and identity formation', *Journal of archaeological method and theory*, 14:4, 412–38.

Snee, Brian (2009), 'Soft-boiled cinema: Joel and Ethan Coens' neo-classical neo-noirs', *Literature/film quarterly*, 37:3, 212–23.

Stanny, C. J. and T. C. Johnson (2000), 'Effects of stress induced by a simulated shooting on recall by police and citizen witnesses', *The American journal of psychology*, 113:3, 359–86.

Wilder, Billy (dir.) (1944), *Double indemnity* (Paramount Pictures: Los Angeles).

Žižek, Slavoj (1989), *The sublime object of ideology* (London: Verso).

12

The *Bounty* mutiny and its adaptations: Tattooing, primitivism, class and criminality

Matt Oches

INTRODUCTION

The date of the infamous mutiny is well known. Fletcher Christian led a bloodless mutiny against William Bligh's command of HMAV *Bounty* on the morning of 28 April 1789. It occurred only a few weeks after leaving Tahiti, where the crew had collected 1015 breadfruit plants for transportation to the West Indies as a cheap source of food for plantation slaves. Bligh and eighteen men loyal to him were cast adrift in the ship's launch. The event has been variously recorded in historical record, claim and counter claim, and has been consolidated as part of the public consciousness through fictional, non-fictional and filmic representations. This chapter firstly explores the historic practice of tattooing and its representation in this group of seamen on the *Bounty*, through Bligh's sole authored list of mutineers and the collectively recalled second list. These form some of the earliest records of this type of cross and intercultural exchange between European and Tahitian societies but, significantly, Bligh's reconstruction of these is in the criminological context of the mutiny. Here, Bligh's account also connects the ideas of primitivist idealisation, degeneration and criminology. Opposing narratives, primarily from Fletcher Christian's brother, consider a more noble form of primitivism whereby Christian's tattoos reveal a class-kinship with the social hierarchy in Tahiti. I expose the role of the tattoos in this process of criminological blame and consider the construction of primitivist idealisation in Bligh and Christian's narratives. Their opposing viewpoints are represented in the variety of adaptations of the event in literature and film. Because every adaptation of the *Bounty* story revolves around and attempts to explain the mutiny, these narratives can be understood as examples of crime fiction. I trace the visual and narrative uses of tattooing in Charles Nordhoff and James Norman Hall's novelisation *Mutiny on the Bounty* (1932) and the three American films (1935,

1962, 1984).[1] Through an understanding of adaptation as intertextual dialogue,[2] I consider how the presence of tattooing is used to promote a cause of primitivist idealisation for the mutiny.

Although numerous theories in fiction and nonfiction have been advanced about the *true* cause of the mutiny,[3] this event cannot be reduced to one element of the voyage. A confluence of circumstances – such as Bligh's abusive language, the five months spent at Tahiti, the small size of the ship, the delay in the Admiralty sending Bligh his sailing orders and the lack of marines – not only precipitated the mutiny, but also allowed it to be executed. Almost all of the mutineers were tattooed while at Tahiti and yet, despite the significance given to the representations of these tattoos in Bligh's two lists of the mutineers, these body modifications tend to be minimised or obfuscated in representations of the mutiny. The two lists of the mutineers Bligh wrote in 1789 include whether, to what extent, and in some cases, where and with what designs each man was tattooed. These lists produce a strong correspondence between tattooing, criminality and rejection of Western civilisation.

Coming only twenty years after the initial Pacific–European cultural exchange of tattooing at Tahiti in 1769, during James Cook's first voyage, the mutineers' tattoos helped facilitate primitivist and criminological discourses about tattooing in the West. In the most prominent fictional representations of the mutiny from the twentieth century, tattooing is represented with different degrees of historical accuracy. The varying role of tattooing in these adaptations of the *Bounty* – ranging from erasure to representing the tattooing operation itself – indicates whether more importance is granted to the supposed cruelty of Bligh or to a primitivist idealisation of the Pacific Islands as the impetus for the criminal act of mutiny.

ENCOUNTERING TAHITI

During Captain James Cook's first Pacific voyage (1768–71) on the *Endeavour*, he spent three months in 1769 at Tahiti to record the transit of Venus across the sun. In 1767, the *Dolphin*, commanded by Samuel Wallis, had made first European contact with Tahiti; in 1768, the French captain Louis-Antoine de Bougainville of the *Boudeuse* also stopped at Tahiti in the course of his circumnavigation. The *Endeavour* stayed at Tahiti far longer than either of the ships captained by Wallis or Bougainville, who 'were both preoccupied by the need to obtain fresh supplies and ensure the security of ships and crews ... Wallis used extreme force to suppress Tahitian assaults on the ship' (Douglas, 2005: 36). Since the Tahitians' first contact with Europeans was characterised by violent interaction, the local reaction to the *Endeavour* can be viewed as a different strategy of dealing with the European intruders. As Nicholas Thomas explains, 'those visitors who came after Wallis met with what they considered friendliness and benevolence; the hospitality and generosity were real, but were also certainly *interested*. For the first time during any Pacific encounter, Cook and his crew were invited to enter into Tahitian sociality' (Thomas 2005: 18; author's emphasis). This integration included *taio* friendships, name exchange and tattooing. In addition to being the source of the etymological derivation of the term tattoo (*tatau*), this cultural exchange represents the reintroduction and reinvigoration of a historically discontinuous practice of European body modification.[4]

Lieutenant William Bligh was master of the *Resolution* during Cook's third and final voyage and was present at Kealakekua Bay when Cook died. Instead of spending three months at Tahiti for astronomical observation, on his return Bligh was there for five months to collect breadfruit. The *Bounty*'s mission, proposed by Sir Joseph Banks – who was himself tattooed at Tahiti during the *Endeavour*'s voyage – was to transport breadfruit from Tahiti to the West Indies to provide a cheap source of food in the diet of plantation slaves. Bligh himself understood this mission as the first practical application of the 'knowledge' procured by previous voyages of 'discovery' to the Pacific (see Bligh 1792: 5). The mission of the *Bounty* attempted to bolster the institution of slavery through an explicitly capitalist, imperial utilisation of the 'knowledge' produced by the voyages of Cook and others.

TATTOOS AND THE MUTINY:
WILLIAM BLIGH'S FIRST AND SECOND LISTS

The men who mutinied against Bligh's command of the *Bounty* were not average sailors who returned to Europe and America with tattoos obtained in the Pacific. Only ten of the twenty-five who stayed on the *Bounty* ever returned to England; two of these ten were not tattooed.[5] Some of the tattoos received at Tahiti were European names, dates or motifs (such as hearts, darts and stars), which became common designs of the nineteenth-century mariner tradition of tattooing. Others were Tahitian designs, which were the types of tattoos received by Euro-Americans in the Pacific to help facilitate their integration into a specific community. Coming only twenty years after the initial cultural exchange of tattooing, both types of designs could be read as signs of an attempted, at least partial, integration into Pacific Islander life. Because the 'savage' practice of tattooing was indelibly inscribed within 'civilised' skin, these tattoos destabilise the civilised/savage binary. Combined with the notoriety of the *Bounty* mutiny and the numerous adaptations and (re)presentations that followed it, the mutineers' tattoos helped facilitate both the primitivist and criminological discourses about tattooing.

Rather than a specular, corporeal phenomenon, the *Bounty* mutineers' tattoos were produced textually for the British public in two very similar documents written by Bligh himself. These are the two lists and physical descriptions of the mutineers. There is no indication as to whether any of the eighteen men who joined Bligh in the launch were tattooed during this visit to Tahiti, and Bligh himself was not tattooed. Because the mutiny was a spontaneous, chaotic affair in which loyalties were unclear and shifting, the lists reinforce the artificial split between the ship and the launch. As Greg Dening states, '[b]eing on the ship and not the launch did not necessarily make one group guilty and the other not' (1992: 43). Bligh's lists, however, produce staying on the ship and having tattoos as signs of criminality.

The first list was written on the *Bounty*'s launch and comprises part of Bligh's log of the voyage to Timor. The second was drawn up at Batavia (modern Jakarta), and copies were sent to different colonial administrators to aid in apprehending the mutineers. Bligh also included it as the fifth of the fifteen documents that he published as 'An answer to certain assertions' (1794) in which he defended himself against accusations in Edward Christian's 'Appendix' (1794).[6] This second list especially relates to the primitivist and criminological discourses about tattooing, because it was the only primary document published at the time that catalogued the tattooing of the *Bounty* crew.

The silence and obfuscation surrounding these tattoos outside Bligh's lists of the mutineers, which are essentially descriptions of wanted men for identification and apprehension, signals that submitting to the tattooing operation at Tahiti became a sign of criminality in the wake of the mutiny. Bligh does not mention tattooing at all in *A narrative of the mutiny* (1790). The three passages in his expanded *A voyage to the South Seas* (1792) that mention tattooing are all concerned with the body modifications of Pacific Islanders.[7] Edward Christian does not discuss tattooing in the two documents he published in defence of his brother. James Morrison, the boatswain's mate who was found guilty by the court martial but was subsequently pardoned, provides a rather detailed ethnographic account of Tahitian tattooing in the only other extant first-hand account of the mutiny besides Bligh's; however, he is silent about the tattooing of the *Bounty* crew, including his own tattoos.[8] Since Morrison likely began writing this document while waiting trial,[9] this obfuscation indicates that Pacific tattoos could be signs of potential criminality.

In his two lists, Bligh implicitly associates a high level of tattooing with guilt in the mutiny. There are subtle differences between the two documents with respect to tattooing, which are partially attributable to the circumstances in which they were composed. The list from the log of the launch's voyage seems to have been compiled solely from Bligh's personal memory, while the second version written at Batavia was a more collective effort that incorporated information from the loyal men. At the end of the list in 'An answer to certain assertions', Bligh includes the following note: '[t]his description was made out from the recollection of the persons with me, who were best acquainted with their private marks' (Bligh and Christian 2001: 165). This note indicates that, despite the close quarters of the ship and Bligh's concern for the physical health of the men, there was distance between the commander and crew of the *Bounty*. The first document was composed in a schematic list form, while the second was written in more standard prose. Both documents detail height, complexion and hair colour; the private marks include scars, deformities and the placement and design of tattoos. Bligh's descriptions of the mutineers' tattoos indicate the growing prevalence of body modification among mariners: 'Bligh unknowingly pre-empted a trend that emerged in the navy over the coming decades and became formalized practice by the 1830s' (White 2005: 75). Bligh can also be considered a forerunner of the criminological interpretation of tattooing, which views tattoos as specular signs of a criminal disposition.

In Bligh's first list of the mutineers, tattooing is not mentioned in the descriptions of six men: John Mills, Henry Hilbrant, John Williams, Michael Byrne, Thomas McIntosh and Charles Norman. Furthermore, Bligh claimed that four of the men 'are deserving of mercy being detained against their inclination', and he identifies these as Byrne, McIntosh, Norman and Joseph Coleman (Bligh and Bach 1987: 218). All four were acquitted by the court martial. Bligh describes at least one specific tattoo design on the bodies of eight of the men: Fletcher Christian, George Stewart, Peter Heywood, Edward Young, James Morrison, John Millward, Thomas Ellison and Joseph Coleman. Of the remaining eleven men that were tattooed, Bligh sometimes details the extent and placement of the body modifications.[10] For these men, less detailed descriptions, such as 'very much tatowed' and 'tatowed in several places', appear multiple times (Bligh and Bach 1987: 214–17). Of the three found guilty by the court martial and hanged – Millward, Burkitt and Ellison – all were tattooed.

With respect to tattooing, the differences between the first and second lists of the mutineers are indicative of the correspondence between body modification, guilt in the mutiny and idealisation of the Pacific Islands that Bligh implicitly traces in finding the cause of the mutiny. The entries about tattooing in the second document are different for six of the twenty-five men who did not join Bligh in the launch. For example, the descriptions of tattooing for William McCoy and William Muspratt were expanded.[11] Three of the men for whom tattooing was not mentioned in the first list – Henry Hilbrant, John Williams and Thomas McIntosh – are now marked as having been tattooed at Tahiti. Both Williams and McIntosh are described as 'tatowed', and Hilbrant is 'tatowed in several places' (Bligh and Christian 2001: 164). It is notable that McIntosh, acquitted by the court martial, was one of the four Bligh identified as deserving of mercy.

However, the description of the tattoo on Joseph Coleman, another of the men Bligh believed to be innocent, is actually shorter in the second list. While the original description states he has 'A Heart Tatowed on One of his Arms and

5777', the second list omits the numerals (Bligh and Bach 1987: 217). Coleman was the armorer of the *Bounty* and had been an able seaman during Cook's third voyage to the Pacific. As Caroline Alexander notes, 'the date beneath, "5–7–77," suggests that this was a souvenir from his first Pacific voyage, when he – and William Bligh – had been at Tongatapu en route to Tahiti' (2003: 250). By omitting this date in the published version, Bligh implicitly represents Coleman as having been tattooed in 1788–89, though it appears that he did not receive another tattoo during the *Bounty*'s stay at Tahiti. Even the tattoos of men whom Bligh knew to be loyal to him – Coleman was detained by the mutineers because of his skills as an armourer – become signs of a potentially criminal disposition, or perhaps signs of passive complicity in the criminal act of mutiny.

Some men received tattoos that appear to be souvenirs, commemorating their visit to Tahiti, such as Coleman's marking of a prior trip. For example, Edward Young had on his right arm 'a Heart & Dart through it with E.Y. underneath and the date of the year 1788 or 1789', and Thomas Ellison '[h]as got his Name tatowed on his Right Arm and dated October 25th 1788', which was the day the *Bounty* sighted Tahiti (Bligh and Bach 1987: 213, 217). Others requested specifically British designs from the Tahitian tattooists.[12] Bligh describes one explicitly Tahitian design, on the body of John Millward, who was hanged: 'is marked the Pit of the Stomach with a Taoomy [*taumi*] or Breastplate of Otaheite' (Bligh and Bach 1987: 214). Christian, George Stewart and Matthew Quintal are all described as 'tatowed on the backside' (Bligh and Bach 1987: 213, 215). This indicates that they had undergone traditional male tattooing in Tahiti, which included a black area covering the buttocks with arches curving over the lower back. These tattoos signal more strenuous attempts to integrate into Tahitian sociality than European motifs. Other men who are described by Bligh as extensively tattooed may also have received Tahitian designs.

Although he does not explicitly connect them, Bligh describes one common tattoo design and placement on the bodies of four men: Christian, Stewart, Morrison and Isaac Martin all had a star tattooed on the left chest. They may have followed a group of messmates from Cook's second Pacific voyage who also all had a star on the left chest. These tattoos were inspired by the *arioi*, 'a society of orators, priests, navigators, travelling performers, and famed lovers. These men and women were dedicated to "Oro [god of fertility and war], each grade having its distinctive tattoos and special garments"' (Salmond 2009: 28).[13] These tattoos of both Cook's men and the four *Bounty* mutineers combine British and Tahitian significations. As Anne Salmond explains, these star tattoos could represent 'the star of St George, one of the insignia of the Order of the Garter, the highest honour in Britain, but at the same time, evoking the large spot or bar tattooed on the left chests of senior *arioi*' (Salmond 2011: 178). The tattoos of the *Bounty* mutineers signal partial knowledge and integration into Tahitian social structures, as well as an appropriation of Tahitian tattooing as a means to express identification with the Pacific Islands through syncretic bodily presentation.

INTEGRATION AND PRIMITIVIST IDEALISATION

Whether the mutiny is viewed as an act of piracy, a bit of enlightenment heroism or an early example of primitivist idealisation, Bligh's physical descriptions, combined with his explanation of the mutiny, situate tattooing as the specular marker of a rejection of Western culture and of an idealised, primitivist appropriation of Tahitian sociality. His representation of the mutiny in both *A narrative of the mutiny* and *A voyage to the South Seas* are nearly identical in tone, with a few changes in diction.[14] In the first published account, *A narrative*, Bligh identifies primitivist idealisation as the cause of the mutiny:

> It will very naturally be asked, what could be the reason for such a revolt? in [*sic*] answer to which, I can only conjecture that the mutineers had assured themselves of a more happy life among the Otaheiteans, than they could possibly have in England; which, joined to some female connections, have most probably been the principal cause of the whole transaction … they imagined it in their power to fix themselves in the midst of plenty, on the finest island in the world, where they need not labour, and where the allurements of dissipation are beyond anything that can be conceived. (Bligh 1790: 9–10)

This explanation is very similar to two letters Bligh wrote at Batavia in October 1789 to Duncan Campbell, his uncle by marriage and former employer in the West Indian merchant service, and Sir Joseph Banks, who was responsible for Bligh's appointment on the *Bounty*.[15] The discourses about the Pacific that Bligh believes to have inspired a level of primitivist idealisation sufficient to induce a mutiny are superabundance, lack of work and sexual availability. Bligh also claims that, '[t]he chiefs were so much attached to our people, that they rather encouraged their stay among them than otherwise, and even made them promises of large possessions' (Bligh 1790: 9). The reported cheer of the mutineers – 'Huzza for Otaheite' (Bligh 1790: 7) – reinforces the importance of primitivist idealisation for Bligh. In the letter to his patron Banks, Bligh answers his own question about the cause of the mutiny in a different manner: '[i]n Answer to which I have only to give a description of Otaheite, which has every allurement both to luxury and ease, and is the Paradise of the World' (Bligh and Brunton 1989: 35).[16] This statement indicates that both the crew and the commander of the *Bounty* perceived Tahiti through the lens of laudatory primitivism.

While Bligh's identification of primitivist idealisation certainly contributes to his attempts to divert blame from himself, it should not be discarded as an important factor leading up to the mutiny. The congruence between published documents and private correspondences – many phrases and sentences reappear verbatim – supports this. At the same time, Bligh excludes the aspect of the *Bounty*'s voyage that opened the space for the crew to consider whether they could have happier lives in Tahiti: the five months spent on shore. These five months were unprecedented: '[i]t was the most extended period of authorized cross-cultural contact yet experienced between Europeans and Pacific islanders' (Lamb *et al.* 2000: 120). These five months were also unplanned. Because of the Admiralty's delay in sending Bligh his sailing orders, the *Bounty* arrived at Tahiti at the end of October 1788, 'near the outset of the western monsoon season, which ran from November to April [… and] Bligh knew he had to await the eastern monsoon, which would begin at the end of April or early May' (Alexander 2003: 107). Without this delay, the *Bounty* would have only been at Tahiti a few weeks: '[b]y the last days of November [1788], Bligh already had a full cargo of breadfruit plants' (Salmond 2011: 161). These five months allowed the crewmembers to form friendships and sexual relations, integrate partially into Tahitian sociality and receive tattoos, some quite extensively.

The acquisition of tattoos and the strategic decision to gain acceptance and integration seem to have been intimately connected for the *Bounty* crew, which is indicated in a document written by Peter Heywood. In a letter to his mother from 15 August 1792 that he composed while imprisoned on the *Hector* at Portsmouth, Heywood explains his tattoos as a means of facilitating social interactions at Tahiti: 'I was tattooed, not to gratify my own desire, but their's [Tahitians, *sic*], for it was my constant Endeavour to acquiesce in any little Custom which I thought would be agreeable to them, though painful in the Process, provided I gained by it their Friendship and Esteem' (Heywood and Heywood 2013: 88). He positions the absence of tattoos as a specular sign of non-integration within Tahitian sociality: 'The more a Man or Woman there is tattooed, the more they are respected, and a Person who has none of those Marks is looked upon as bearing a most indignant Badge of Disgrace, and considered as a mere Outcast of Society' (Heywood 2013: 88). Under the aegis of primitivist idealisation, Heywood's account represents the tattoo as the indelible sign of a volitional attempt to integrate into the social structures of Tahiti.

CLASS TATTOOING

The different tattoo designs and motifs received by members of the *Bounty* indicate that the identification with, and integration into, Tahitian customs and social structures operated along two mains lines of projected similarity, both related to class positions. If Bligh is correct about the promise of large possessions, this could have been a powerful inducement for the lower-class able seamen. Bligh mostly spent his time with the Pomare family, specifically Tu, the paramount chief of the island and Bligh's *taio* (bond friend), and his wife 'Itia. At the same time, 'the *Bounty*'s petty officers also took *taio* among the chiefs and were given "wives" from their families, the status of these women mirroring their own ranks on board the ship' (Salmond 2009: 456). It is likely that the wives and *taio* of the able seamen shared roughly analogous class positions. Bligh did not report the tattoos of Fletcher Christian in great detail, describing them as a '[s]tar tatowed on the left breast and tatowed on the backside' (Bligh and Bach 1987: 213). We do know, however, that Christian had 'adopted a full Tahitian tattoo, rather than a composite of British and local cultural symbols', though the star as previously discussed sits somewhere between England and Tahiti (Smith 2010: 256). Almost all of the able seamen stayed on the ship as did some of the officers, including Christian, who was master's mate and promoted to acting lieutenant by Bligh during the outward voyage, and Peter Heywood, Edward Young and George Stewart, who were midshipmen. Bligh describes both Christian and Heywood as 'of a respectable family in the north of England', and Stewart as 'a young man of creditable parents' (Bligh 1790: 8). While Heywood had a British design on his leg, he is also described by Bligh as 'very much tattowed', which likely included Tahitian motifs (Bligh and Bach 1987: 213). When Heywood and Stewart swam out to the *Pandora* and surrendered themselves, 'they were so tanned and heavily tattooed that at first the crew mistook them for Tahitians' (Salmond 2011: 397). It is important to note that none of the *Bounty*'s crew could have been tattooed without the consent of Tahitian tattoo artists, if not the community at large.

The tattoos of the *Bounty* mutineers can be understood as mediating class divisions, particularly between Christian and the lower-class mutineers. Christian's full Tahitian tattoo signifies a different type of engagement with and integration into Tahitian sociality than tattoos of names or dates, as well as bodies that bore both European and Tahitian designs. In his 'Appendix', Edward Christian, who was attempting to exonerate his brother, identifies a naturalised aristocratic standing as that which drew the Tahitians and Fletcher to each other:

> There is no country in the world, where the notions of aristocracy and family pride are carried higher than at Otaheite; and it is a remarkable circumstance, that the Chiefs are naturally distinguished by taller persons, and more open and intelligent countenances, than the people of inferior condition; hence these are the principal qualities by which the natives estimate the gentility of strangers; and Christian was so great a favourite with them, that according to the words of one person, 'They adored the very ground he trod upon'. (Bligh and Christian 2001: 143)

Despite Bligh's pejorative depiction of Christian's physical characteristics, 'bow legged' and 'subject to violent perspiration & particularly in His hands so that he soils anything he handles' (see Bligh and Bach 1987: 213), this passage structures the relationship between Christian and his Tahitian hosts through a naturalised aristocracy in which physical characteristics signify social standing. As Vanessa Smith states, Edward Christian 'sees a natural aristocracy as uniting Christian with the Tahitian noble savage' (2010: 260). This naturalised connection becomes specular and indelible through the cultural practice of tattooing. An implicit acceptance of class divisions partially structured the form of primitivism that led many members of the *Bounty* to be tattooed, as well as the different designs they received.

Two types of primitivist identification based on social class can be discerned in the tattooing of the *Bounty* mutineers: identification with the 'noble savage' and with the racial Other. Fletcher Christian's full Tahitian tattoo indicates a primitivist identification with the figure of the 'noble savage', which is accomplished through the naturalisation and expansion of the British class system. The inclusion of both European and Tahitian tattoo designs on the bodies of common sailors represents an identification with the racial Other on the part of the class Other. The tattooing of European names, dates and motifs by Tahitian artists reinforces the crewmembers' connection to their home culture while drawing a projected line of similarity between themselves and non-aristocratic Tahitians. These tattoos imbue lower-class status with positive connotations through the primitivist identification with 'common' Tahitian subjects. This ostensibly rejects the very class divisions that structure the form of idealisation. The adoption of indigenous designs represents a more strenuous attempt at integration because they do not produce specular references to British culture. Fletcher Christian's identification with the 'noble savage' through his full Tahitian tattoo seems to be a rejection of Western civilisation and his aristocratic standing, but this class-based identification ensures that Christian still retains the cultural authority and ascendancy of an aristocrat.

Primitivist idealisation appears to dissolve class divisions among the mutineers through the specular marker of the tattoo, but this idealisation was structured by class position, as differences in designs indicate. The disjuncture in the crewmembers seemingly only identifying with what they perceived as their Tahitian class equivalent, which would appear to preserve the divisions of the British class system, is covered over by the fetishistic cathexis of tattooing. The shared attempt to integrate into Tahitian social structures through variable, uneven appropriations of tattooing obfuscates the maintenance of class divisions. The connection between class and primitivist identification within the tattooing of the *Bounty* mutineers seems to naturalise class divisions, because an image related to a certain class position becomes indelibly fixed at a specific site on the body, which serves to essentialise a condition that has no natural or inevitable connection to the body. The mutineers' tattoos not only facilitated primitivist and criminological interpretations of tattooing, but also contributed to the production of the tattoo as a bodily sign indicative of class.

TATTOOING IN ADAPTATIONS OF THE *BOUNTY* MUTINY

The story of the *Bounty* was first adapted in 1811 with Mary Russell Mitford's narrative poem 'Christina, the maid of the South Seas', which focuses on Fletcher Christian's daughter. In 'The island, or Christian and his comrades' (1823), Lord Byron utilised Bligh's *Narrative* as one of his sources. The descendants of the mutineers on Pitcairn Island have appeared in short stories by Mark Twain, 'The great revolution in Pitcairn' (1882), and Jack London, 'The seed of McCoy' (1911). The *Bounty* has also inspired numerous works of popular fiction and children's literature. The mutiny and the tattoos of the crew continue to provide material for crime narratives into the twenty-first century. Val McDermid's crime fiction thriller, *The grave tattoo* (2006), uses the discovery of a corpse (which may be Fletcher Christian) in the Lake District with Pacific tattoos as the catalyst for a narrative that mobilises the theory that Christian escaped Pitcairn and returned to England. The conceit of *The grave tattoo* is that Christian told his version of events to William Wordsworth, who transcribed Fletcher's story and composed a poem from the material; the crime narrative revolves around the search for these documents. The novel also suggests a new potential explanation for the mutiny, that Bligh accused Christian of engaging in sexual intercourse with Peter Heywood at Tahiti.

While many *Bounty* adaptations strive for certain forms of historical accuracy, such as recreations of the ship for the films, each puts forth an interpretation of the historical record, which is itself contested and subject to revision. It is not my purpose here to catalogue all the points at which *Bounty* adaptations align with and diverge from the historical record,[17] or to engage in fidelity criticism.[18] As Robert Stam argues, dialogism and intertextuality 'help us transcend the aporias of "fidelity" and of a dyadic source/adaptation model which excludes not only all sorts of supplementary texts but also the dialogical response of the reader/spectator' (2005: 27). The *Bounty* adaptations function as hypertexts whose anterior texts are the historical documentations of the mutiny, which include Bligh's lists. Following my argument about the role of the mutineers' tattoos in primitivist and criminological discourses about tattooing, I position the varying representations of tattooing in *Bounty* adaptations as indicative of each text's explanation of the cause of the mutiny. High visibility of tattooing roughly aligns with more importance granted to primitivist idealisation, the lure of Tahiti as a 'paradise', while the obfuscation or erasure of tattooing generally indicates the production of Bligh as a violently cruel tyrant.

Nordhoff and Hall's novel of historical fiction *Mutiny on the Bounty* served as the basis for the first two major film versions of the mutiny, both titled

Mutiny on the Bounty (Lloyd 1935 and Milestone 1962). The 1935 film stars Clark Gable as Christian and Charles Laughton as Bligh, and the 1962 film stars Marlon Brando and Trevor Howard respectively. Richard Hough's *Captain Bligh and Mr. Christian* (1972), a work of nonfiction, was the main source for the third film, *The Bounty* (Donaldson 1984), with Mel Gibson as Christian and Anthony Hopkins as Bligh.[19]

The narrator of the novel *Mutiny on the Bounty* is Roger Byam, a fictional character loosely based on Peter Heywood. The narrative is thus filtered through the subjective vantage point of a young, upper-class midshipman. The discourse of the Pacific Islands as a paradise appears at different points in the novel. Byam represents Tahiti through laudatory primitivism, claiming it was 'a veritable paradise for the seaman – one of the richest islands in the world ... abounding in every variety of delicious food, and inhabited by a race of gentle and hospitable barbarians' (Nordhoff and Hall 2003: 89). In terms of sexuality, which is referred to as dissipation, it 'could only be described as a Mohammedan paradise' (*ibid.*: 89). The similarities to Bligh's description of Tahiti are evident, but the novel depicts the Pacific as possessing a certain unreality. After the *Bounty* leaves Tahiti, Byam claims that, 'the memory of our life there seemed like that of a dream' (*ibid.*: 113). Toward the end of the novel, he states that his connections to the Pacific 'all seemed to lose substance and reality, fading to the ghostliness of a beautiful, half-remembered dream' (*ibid.*: 369). The violently cruel punishments of Bligh, specifically flogging, possess substance and reality in the novel. While Bligh was certainly a verbally abusive commander, which Nordhoff and Hall depict, he was neither a physically violent man nor a 'flogging captain'. In contrast with his reputation in the twentieth century (largely produced by these fictional adaptations), Bligh 'flogged the sailors less often than almost any other British commander in the Pacific during this period – for instance, only 10 per cent of the crew on the *Bounty* were flogged, compared with 25 per cent on Captain Cook's *Resolution*' (Salmond 2011: 164). In the novel, Bligh orders far more floggings than the historical record shows, and he seems to derive a sadistic pleasure from the punishment, especially as a means of asserting his authority over the men.

Tattooing in the novel is almost entirely erased from the bodies of Tahitians and obfuscated or minimised for the *Bounty* crew. Only one Tahitian, the historical Vehiatua III, is explicitly described as tattooed. Vehiatua, who was the high chief of southern Tahiti, is represented through the trope of the 'noble savage', with beautiful and intricate tattoos 'which covered every portion of his body save his face' (Nordhoff and Hall 2003: 179). This description occurs in Tahiti after the mutiny and before the arrival of the *Pandora*; significantly, this is not during the five months of the *Bounty*'s stay. Outside a few references to crewmembers already wearing tattoos, which signals them as mariners, the tattooing of the *Bounty* crew is not mentioned until the ship has left Tahiti.

Byam states, '[i]n colour we were almost as brown as the Indians, and most of us were tattooed on various parts of our bodies with strange designs that added to our exotic appearance' (*ibid.*: 111). In contrast to Heywood's letter to his mother, Byam claims that the men submitted to tattooing 'for the sake of carrying home such evidence of their adventures in the South Sea' (*ibid.*). Rather than manifestations of integration, the tattoos become signs of a temporary visit shaded with notions of tourism. Only Edward Young's supposed tattoos are described – as coconut trees on each leg, a breadfruit tree on his back, and 'wide bands of conventionalized design' on his thighs (*ibid.*) – which relate to the mission of the *Bounty* and Tahitian culture. The narrator's own tattoos, which are said to cover his arms, are not mentioned until the crew of the *Pandora* mistakes him for a Tahitian. This obfuscation indicates the criminality associated with the tattoos, especially as Byam repeatedly professes his innocence. While not entirely excluded from the novel, tattooing is minimised and represented through exoticism and as a Pacific souvenir, rather than as a sign of identification with, and integration into, Tahitian social structures. This allows the narrative to deemphasise primitivism as a contributing factor in the mutiny, which opens the space for Bligh to become a physically violent tyrant.

The 1935 film expands upon this representation of Bligh and further obfuscates the tattooing of the *Bounty* crew. While Charles Laughton delivers an excellent performance, his portrayal of Bligh as a psychotically violent tyrant greatly influenced the misrepresentation of Bligh in the twentieth century. The film erases tattooing from the specular representation of the Tahitians and does not depict the mutineers receiving tattoos. There are, however, two references to tattooing present. The film opens with Christian leading a press gang into a pub to collect sailors for the *Bounty*'s voyage; this is an invention, as the crew consisted of volunteers. The first man to protest being pressed into service claims that he is a tailor rather than a sailor. Christian rips open his shirt to reveal a tattoo of a ship with British flags on the man's chest and quips, '[w]hat's that, your needlework?' (Lloyd 1935). As such, tattooing is depicted as already a standard mariner practice which identifies seamen. While the surgeon is tending to a man after a flogging during the outbound voyage, he attempts to comfort him: '[a] bit tattooed on the back, perhaps, but just the right style for Tahiti, eh?' (*ibid.*). This comparison between the wounds inflicted by the punitive action of flogging and the indelible designs produced by the tattooing operation seems to draw a line of similarity between Bligh's cruel actions and the 'savage' practice of tattooing. The film thus suggests that there is something 'uncivilised' about Bligh's methods of command. Because Tahitian tattooing is not visually depicted in the film and the Tahitians are mostly represented as noble savages, this reference to tattooing actually reinforces the violently cruel command of Bligh as the impetus of the mutiny. While Tahiti is represented as paradisal, the lack of tattooing indicates that the crew does not integrate into

Tahitian social structures. Primitivist idealisation becomes subordinated to resistance against tyrannical command.

In the 1962 film, which is the filmic adaptation that modifies the historical record the most, Brando adopts a lisp in his over-determined portrayal of Christian as an English gentleman. Bligh is again a violent and cruel commander; the struggle between him and Christian, a reductive depiction that many adaptations of the mutiny share, becomes a class conflict. As Greg Dening writes, the film depicts Christian 'as a gentleman fop finding true honour in standing up against Bligh's populist austerity' (1992: 346). Tattooing is absent from the bodies of the Tahitians, none of the *Bounty* members have tattoos and tattooing is not even mentioned in the film. This does not mean that the primitivist representation of Tahiti as a paradise of superabundance, lack of work and sexual availability is absent from the film. However, idealisation of the Pacific is not positioned as an important contributing factor leading up to the mutiny. Rather, the film invents a trigger for the mutiny when Bligh kicks a ladle of water out of Christian's hand when the master's mate attempts to comfort a man who drank seawater, while Tahiti mostly functions as a lush background for Brando's posturing.

The 1984 film *The Bounty* depicts tattooing on most of the Tahitian characters, shows many *Bounty* members with tattoos acquired at Tahiti, and even displays Christian receiving a tattoo: a Tahitian design on his backside. Bligh is a verbally abusive commander, but he is not depicted as violently cruel. Tahiti is again a primitivist paradise, with the discourse of sexual availability represented more explicitly; the film contains an extremely gratuitous amount of indigenous female nudity. Christian and many crewmembers are shown integrating into Tahitian social life. This film modifies the historical record the least, which is partially attributable to its putative source material being nonfiction. However, it only indirectly portrays Richard Hough's controversial conclusion about the cause of the mutiny. Hough conjectures that 'Bligh and Christian had enjoyed for a long period a homosexual relationship' (Hough 1979: 300), and that after engaging in a heterosexual relationship at Tahiti, Christian was unwilling to resume his intimate connection with Bligh on the homeward voyage, which led to Bligh's verbal abuse and public humiliation of Christian. In the film, Bligh suspiciously watches the beginnings of Christian and Mauatua's courtship, and scenes of their romance are cut with shots of Bligh lying alone in his cabin looking anxious, distressed and sweaty.

After these hints of sexualised jealousy, tattooing becomes a point of contention between Bligh and Christian while they are still on the island. After the scene in which Christian is being tattooed, he belatedly joins Bligh and other men for dinner on the ship. Bligh instructs Christian to put on his jacket; the master's mate protests that the tattoos are too painful, but Bligh insists.

The conversation turns to the breadfruit plants and when they will be ready for transportation. Bligh is anxious to leave the island because of the gradual breakdown in discipline, including not inspecting the plants every day; Christian believes the plants need more time to grow. Bligh states, 'I want to be advised of their progress every day, Mr. Christian, unless, of course, you need the time to cover the rest of your body in pretty pictures' (Donaldson 1984). Later in the film, Bligh informs Christian that three men deserted; Christian evinces no surprise, presumably because of the lure of Tahiti. Bligh claims he is not surprised because of the example being set by Christian: '[j]ust look at yourself, man. Look at the way you're dressed. Come on! You're no better than one of these natives' (*ibid.*). Bligh understands tattooing as the specular bodily sign of an idealisation of, and integration into, Tahitian social life, a sign of 'going native' that is contributing to the erosion of discipline. However, *The Bounty* also invents a trigger for the mutiny. Bligh announces that the return voyage will be made by way of Cape Horn to complete a circumnavigation. Because of the dangerous, and failed, attempt to round the Horn on the outbound voyage, this decision quickly leads to rebellion.

CONCLUSION

The tattooing of the *Bounty* mutineers occurred near the beginning of Euro-American discourses about tattooing derived from the cultural exchange of 1769. Like the mutiny itself, these tattoos were produced through multiple and overlapping circumstances: cross-cultural interaction, primitivist idealisation, class divisions, different embodied cultures and sexuality. Their contribution to primitivist discourse – which views tattooing as a 'savage' or 'primitive' practice that signals idealisation and integration on the bodies of Euro-Americans – and the criminological interpretation – which views tattoos as the sign of a criminal disposition – tends to be obfuscated or ignored. However, Bligh's lists of the mutineers indicate that these tattoos were interpreted through criminality, which was intimately connected with primitivist idealisation by the naval officer. Because of the notoriety of the mutiny and its numerous adaptations, the *Bounty* mutineers' tattoos are forerunners of the criminological interpretation of tattooing and the utilisation of the tattoo in crime and detective narratives. In the adaptations, the obfuscation of tattooing indicates a lack of narrative emphasis on both primitivism and criminality.

NOTES

1   This chapter gives the original date of publication when discussing novel: *Mutiny on the Bounty*. Quotations are given from the edition used by the author. See Bibliography for further details (eds).

2 For intertextuality and dialogism in adaptation studies, see Linda Hutcheon, *A theory of adaptation* (2006: 21) and Stam (2005: 26–31).

3 For comprehensive engagement with the *Bounty* mutiny, see: Donald A. Maxton *The mutiny on H.M.S. Bounty* (2008).

4 This understanding of tattooing at Tahiti in 1769 is advanced throughout Thomas *et al.* (2005). While not denying a discontinuous presence of tattooing practices in Europe, such as the body modifications of the Picts, Roman punitive tattooing and the Jerusalem cross, the editors emphasise the importance of the cultural exchange, its corporeal effects and the discourses it helped shape, beginning with Cook's first voyage. Thomas *et al.* respond to Jane Caplan (ed.) *Written on the body: The tattoo in European and American history* (2000). Especially in Caplan's 'Introduction', *Written on the body* argues for the importance of European body modification practices over Pacific exchange in contemporary understandings of tattooing.

5 Of the remainder, nine settled on Pitcairn and never left that island; two died at Tahiti during the eighteen months between the failed settlement at Tubuai and the arrival of the *Pandora* to bring them back to England for court martial; four died when the *Pandora* was wrecked on the Great Barrier Reef.

6 The transcription and facsimile of the list written in the launch can be found in *The Bligh notebook* (1987: 213–18 and 331–36, respectively). The second list can be found in *Awake, bold Bligh!* (Bligh and William Bruton 1989: 84–86) and in the collection *The Bounty mutiny* (2001: 162–50). Edward Christian's 'Appendix', Bligh's 'An answer to certain assertions' and Christian's 'A short reply to Captain Bligh's answer' (1795) are reprinted in *The Bounty mutiny* (2001).

7 The three passages that mention tattooing in Bligh's *A voyage to the South Seas* are on pp. 75, 144 and 148.

8 For Morrison's descriptions of Tahitian tattooing, see *Mutiny and aftermath* (2013: 245–47 and 260).

9 In their 'Introduction' to *Mutiny and aftermath*, Vanessa Smith and Nicholas Thomas write that Morrison's text 'was apparently written up in 1792, first as its author awaited trial and then as he recuperated after receiving the king's pardon' (2013: 4).

10 These men were Charles Churchill, Matthew Thompson, William McCoy, Matthew Quintal, John Sumner, Thomas Burkitt, Isaac Martin, William Muspratt, Alexander Smith (aka John Adams), Richard Skinner and William Brown.

11 In the first list, Bligh states that McCoy 'is Tatowed', and describes Muspratt as 'Tatowed' (Bligh and Bach 1987: 215–16). Respectively, these entries become 'is tatowed in different parts of his body' and 'is tatowed in several places of his body' (Bligh and Christian 2001: 163–64). Muspratt was found guilty by the court martial but won a reprieve and eventual pardon on a legal technicality.

12 Peter Heywood 'on the Right Leg is tattowed The Three legs of Man as that coin is', and James Morrison had 'a Garter round his Left leg with the Motto of Honi Soit Qui Mal y Pense', which is the motto of the Order of the Garter – 'Shame on him who evil thinks' (Bligh and Bach 1987: 213, 214). Both Morrison and Heywood received pardons.

13 For *arioi* grades and the corresponding tattoo designs and body placements, see Alfred Gell, *Wrapping in images* (1993: 146–58).

14 See *A narrative of the Mutiny* pp. 9–10 and *A voyage to the South Seas* pp. 162–63 for the similarities.
15 See *Awake, bold Bligh!* p. 26 for the letter to Campbell, pp. 31 and 35 for the letter to Banks.
16 The letter to Banks seems to be the only document in which Bligh identifies the lack of marines on the *Bounty* as a contributing factor in the mutiny: '[i]f I Had been equipped with more Officers & Marines the piracy could never had happened' (Bligh and Brunton 1989: 31).
17 As Greg Dening explains of the films, 'it was their purpose to be inaccurate. They could not say what they wanted to say without invention' (1992: 346).
18 For the limitations of fidelity criticism, see Hutcheon (2006: 6–7) and Stam (2005: 14–16).
19 Two other films about the *Bounty* have been made and they are both Australian productions. In 1916, Raymond Langford wrote, directed and produced a silent film titled *The mutiny of the Bounty*. The celluloid film deteriorated and only a handful of stills remain. In 1933, Charles Chauvel wrote, directed and produced *In the wake of the Bounty*, which starred Errol Flynn as Christian in his film debut. It is part drama and part documentary, with footage from Pitcairn Island in the 1930s (see Maxton 2008: 205–10).

BIBLIOGRAPHY

Alexander, Caroline (2003), *The Bounty: The true story of the mutiny on the Bounty* (New York: Penguin).

Bligh, William (1790), *A narrative of the mutiny on board His Majesty's ship the Bounty and the subsequent voyage of part of the crew in the ship's boat, from Tofoa, one of the friendly islands, to Timor, a Dutch settlement in the East Indies* (London: George Nicol).

— (1792), *A voyage to the South Seas … for the purpose of conveying the breadfruit tree to the West Indies in His Majesty's ship the Bounty* (London: George Nicol).

— and John Bach (1987), *The Bligh notebook: "Rough account – Lieutenant Wm Bligh's voyage in the Bounty's launch from the ship to Tofua & from thence to Timor," 28 April to 14 June 1789; With a draft list of the Bounty mutineers* [Facsim ed.] (North Sydney: Allen & Unwin in association with the National Library of Australia).

— and Paul Brunton (1989), *Awake, bold Bligh!: William Bligh's letters describing the mutiny on HMS Bounty* (North Sydney: Allen & Unwin in association with the State Library of New South Wales).

— and Edward Christian (2001), *The Bounty mutiny* (New York: Penguin).

Caplan, Jane (ed.) (2000), *Written on the body: The tattoo in European and American history* (London: Reaktion Books).

Dening, Greg (1992), *Mr. Bligh's bad language: Passion, power and theatre on the Bounty* (Cambridge: Cambridge University Press).

Donaldson, Roger (dir.) (1984), *The Bounty* (Orion Pictures Corporation: n.p.).

Douglas, Browen (2005), '"Cureous figures": European voyagers and tatau/tattoo in Polynesia, 1595–1800', in N. Thomas, A. Cole and B. Douglas (eds) (2005), pp. 33–52.

Gell, Alfred (1993), *Wrapping in images: Tattooing in Polynesia* (Oxford: Clarendon Press).

Heywood, Peter and Nessy Heywood (2013), 'Letters', in D. Maxton and R. Du Rietz (eds), *Innocent on the Bounty: the court-martial and pardon of Midshipman Peter Heywood, in letters* (Jefferson: McFarland).

Hough, Richard (1979), *Captain Bligh and Mr. Christian: The men and the mutiny* [1972] (London: Cassel).

Hutcheon, Linda (2006), *A theory of adaptation* (Routledge: New York).

Lamb, Jonathan, Vanessa Smith and Nicholas Thomas (2000), *Exploration and exchange: A South Seas anthology, 1680-1900* (Chicago: University of Chicago Press).

Lloyd, Frank (dir.) (1935), *Mutiny on the Bounty* (MGM: n.p.).

Maxton, Donald A. (2008), *The mutiny on H.M.S. Bounty: A guide to nonfiction, fiction, poetry, films, articles, and music* (Jefferson: McFarland).

McDermid, Val (2006), *The grave tattoo* (London: HarperCollins).

Morrison, James (2013), 'James Morrison's account', in V. Smith and N. Thomas (eds) with M. Nuku, *Mutiny and aftermath: James Morrison's account of the mutiny on the Bounty and the island of Tahiti* (Honolulu: University of Hawai'i Press).

Nordhoff, Charles and James Norman Hall (2003), *Mutiny on the Bounty* [1932] (New York: Back Bay Books).

Salmond, Anne (2009), *Aphrodite's island: The European discovery of Tahiti* (Berkeley: University of California Press).

— (2011) *Bligh: William Bligh in the South Seas* (Berkeley: University of California Press).

Smith, Vanessa (2010), *Intimate strangers: Friendship, exchange, and Pacific encounters* (Cambridge: Cambridge University Press).

Stam, Robert (2005), 'Introduction: The theory and practice of adaptation', in R. Stam and A. Raengo (eds), *Literature and film: A guide to the theory and practice of film adaptation* (Malden: Blackwell), pp. 1–52.

Thomas, Nicholas (2005), 'Introduction', in N. Thomas, A. Cole and B. Douglas (eds) (2005), pp. 7–29.

Thomas, Nicholas, A. Cole and B. Douglas (eds) (2005), *Tattoo: Bodies, art, and exchange in the Pacific and the West* (Durham, NC: Duke University Press).

White, Joanna (2005), 'Marks of transgression: The tattooing of Europeans in the Pacific Islands', in N. Thomas, A. Cole and B. Douglas (eds) (2005), pp. 72–89.

Television: Branding, tech-noir and fan culture

13

Hunting for the branded body in *Supernatural*: Tattoos, the Mark of Cain and fan culture

Karin Beeler

INTRODUCTION

The highly popular American fantasy detective serial *Supernatural* (filmed in British Columbia, Canada)[1] has generated a good deal of interplay between production elements, intertextual connections and fans. *Supernatural*'s positioning of characters (*mise en scène*), the show's reliance on other texts such as literary or film narratives that become part of a particular *Supernatural* episode or story arc, and the role of fans and consumer culture help create a permeable boundary between fact and fiction, actors and characters. Not only does the show depict how its protagonists, brothers Dean and Sam Winchester, solve specific cases based on their knowledge of supernatural lore, but supernatural symbols are used to reinforce the connections between storylines within this fantasy detective serial. As fans follow the episodes over the course of a season, many try to solve the crimes as they watch Dean and Sam carry out their work as detectives or hunters of supernatural phenomena. Some of these fans may also express a desire to incorporate symbols associated with these characters into their own lives. A significant illustration of the show's interconnectivity is evident in the way *Supernatural* presents the trope of the tattoo and the story arc of the Mark of Cain. The Mark of Cain has been called the 'first' tattoo (Gray 1994: 25), and it is therefore not too surprising that tattoos and the Mark of Cain in *Supernatural* serve as images which acquire the status of a 'brand'. This brand is both symbolic and literal, identified and embodied by the show's fanbase and fed back into the 'world' of the serial, an exchange which differentiates it from other shows. The tattoo is a strong thematic thread in the serial *Supernatural* that links the two protagonists and other characters to both radical and mysterious elements; the tattoo is an image that both conceals and reveals.

As hunters of supernatural phenomena, Dean and Sam regularly masquerade as FBI agents in order to access crime scenes, interact with local officials and interview victims and suspects to help them solve unusual and supernatural crimes. As federal agents, albeit phony ones, Dean and Sam display their badges and immediately become extensions of a familiar symbol, a badge of authority, that is associated with crime solving ability; thus their identities become firmly linked to the discourse of detective narratives. Their role as detectives is a layered one, both through the drive to solve these supernatural crimes and the masquerade of adopting FBI detective personae to aid this. In many ways, *Supernatural* carries on 'detective fiction's supernatural engagement' (Cook 2014: 179) that is evident in the early works of the crime and detective genre, including 'Poe, Collins or even Conan Doyle' (*ibid.*: 180). In *Supernatural*, tattoos and the Mark of Cain serve as symbols with special powers that help shape the mystery and patterns of identification that contribute to the show's detective genre components, while simultaneously reaffirming the *Supernatural* brand outside of the immediate narrative space of the show. The tattoo transcends the particularity of the individual character's experiences and operates outside the confines of the show to create a sense of community among fans. Fan culture is then also circulated back into the show via a character's tattoos, thereby illustrating how the fan experience becomes part of the cultural capital of *Supernatural*.

The tattoo has a longstanding history of serving the narratives of detection and crime, as I have explored in my study of tattoos in literature, film and television (2006: 76).[2] Tattoos facilitate the alternation between concealment and revelation that occurs in detective literature, film and television. This is also the case in detective narratives of the supernatural variety, including supernatural television drama.[3] Regarded as a form of protection by various cultures, including Samoan and North American aboriginal societies (Schiffmacher and Riemschneider 1996: 11–12), tattoos are applied to the bodies of characters in *Supernatural* to protect them from harm. During Season 3 (3.12) of *Supernatural*, anti-possession tattoos on the bodies of the hunter-detective brothers serve as a means of protection against evil powers.[4] Suzette Chan has commented on the 'aesthetically pleasing' representation of the anti-possession tattoos on Sam and Dean's bodies (2010). However, these diegetic tattoos (tattoos that are represented within the narrative world of the television show) have gone beyond the boundaries of the show's storyline; tattoos or tattoo-like images in *Supernatural* have become a recognisable 'brand' in the marketing sense of the word, and have entered the realm of fan space. As Bridget Kies notes, 'many fans have adopted the [anti-possession] tattoo design as a mark of their passion for the show' (2014: 25). The fan response to diegetic tattoos and their desire to 'brand' themselves with show-specific designs (anti-possession tattoos or the Mark of Cain) suggest that the images, characters and storylines of *Supernatural* are easily transplanted onto the bodies of fans who wear *Supernatural* merchandise or who sport tattoos from the show. In a cyclical manner, the creative team of *Supernatural* has also introduced fan culture's desire to consume these tattoos as a narrative trope for the show by introducing the tattooed fan as a character – Sam and Dean pretend to be fans of a series of *Supernatural* books and display their tattoos to 'prove' this in 'The monster at the end of this book' (4.18). This facilitates the solidification of the concept that fans are part of the *Supernatural* family. *Supernatural* therefore facilitates an interplay between character tattoos, fan tattoos, consumer culture and group membership.

In this chapter, I will be focusing on three major facets of tattooed images and narratives. I will consider how *Supernatural* uses production or televisual elements, such as *mise en scène* and character connections, to represent the mysterious power of tattoos and the 'criminal' Mark of Cain. I will also address how the show incorporates intertextuality, references or allusions to other iconic or canonical texts (literature or film) and elements of popular culture to reinforce images of tattooed bodies. These include *The girl with the dragon tattoo* (a Swedish crime novel that was published posthumously and has been adapted into film), the *Star wars* films, *The wizard of Oz* (novel and film) and the Bible (*Book of Genesis*). An examination of how these production and intertextual elements cross over into the fan experience forms part of a process of demystification as *Supernatural* engages in the process of making the unknown known or familiar. Third, this analysis will also demonstrate how fandom feeds back into the show as a construct, specifically in relation to tattooed or marked bodies.

SUPERNATURAL AND MISE EN SCÈNE: CONCEALMENT AND REVELATION

If we look at the production context for *Supernatural*, we can see how the show relies on closeup shots and *mise en scène* or careful staging and positioning for showcasing the matching tattoos on Sam and Dean Winchester (see, for example, 3.12 'Jus in bello').[5] These chest tattoos identify them as individuals who are working against forces of evil. This is similar to the fake FBI ID badges that they pull out of the inner chest pocket of their jackets. Both the anti-possession tattoo and the FBI badge are symbols of protection, and even though the badges are examples of 'false' identity (the Winchesters are not FBI agents, nor do they bear the names listed on the ID wallets), they still perpetuate the Winchester identity as protectors. In narrative terms, the tattoo is carefully intertwined with the personalities or psychological issues of characters in *Supernatural* to one another, much like the use of a tattoo in a military or gang context in order to suggest membership in a group.[6] The Winchesters just happen to be hunter-detectives and 'men of letters' (a secret order of scholars who research the supernatural) instead of gang members or soldiers.

Representations of the tattoo in *Supernatural* rely on common associations of the tattoo with protection, and this protective element is further reinforced through the strong familial connection between Sam and Dean. Both brothers acquire these tattoos, thus reinforcing their brotherly bond. In episode 3.12 ('Jus in bello') the brothers are even shown revealing their tattoos in a similar way as they pull down their shirts simultaneously and at a similar angle to reveal the anti-possession tattoo consisting of a pentagram or endless knot surrounded by a circle of flames.[7] The *mise en scène* or staging of characters suggests parallels between them. In 2008, Sera Gamble (former writer and showrunner for the serial) talked about Sam and Dean's matching tattoos in the Season 3 episode 'Jus in bello' (3.12):

> FFN: Those matching tattoos are pretty cool. How long has that been planned?
> SG: I remember talking about it with Ben Edlund last season, while Cat was writing 'Born under a bad sign.' We agreed that if we were Sam, the first thing we'd do is take that anti-possession amulet and head for the nearest tattoo parlor. He reminded me of it while we were working on 'Jus in bello', because breaking out the amulets was an important story point in that episode. So I stuck it in there, and it made for a nice moment. It's like, of course Sam and Dean have matching tats. How could it be any other way? (Cochran)

The element of protection and the familial bond associated with a tattoo are reproduced in Season 8 (8.2 'What's up, tiger mommy?') when Kevin Tran (Osric Chau) and his mother Linda Tran (Lauren Tom) acquire them to avoid demonic possession.[8] Here, mother and son are shown holding hands during their tattoo session. Kevin tries to reassure his mother, perhaps because the tattoo is often associated with a deviant context; however, Linda replies, '[w]hat, like it's my first tattoo?' thus addressing the subversive aspect often attached to a tattoo. Kevin is forced to see his mother in a different light because of this revelation; and yet Linda's tattoo is not revealed. This ensures that the narrative continues to follow a pattern of concealment even as it hints at revelation. In this way, the tattoo serves as a way of maintaining the tension between concealment and revelation that is typical of the detective genre (see Nickerson 2010).

DIEGETIC AND NON-DIEGETIC TATTOOS: FAN CULTURE AS A TELEVISION TROPE

In addition to establishing connections between its key characters, *Supernatural* has incorporated the concept of fandom into its episodes in an interactive display and play with its characters. This is a reciprocal relationship and reflects the way elements of the show (such as tattoos) have entered fan space. Brigid Cherry indicates that '*Supernatural* has always been in dialogue with its fandom. Representations of fans began early in the series' (Cherry 2011: 206). For example, *Supernatural* absorbed fan culture into its own production context in Season 4. The serial challenged the notion of a clear boundary between textual and extratextual elements by having Sam and Dean pretend to be fans of a series of books called *Supernatural* which are based on their lives as hunter-detectives (4.18 'The monster at the end of this book'). In this episode, they use their tattoos as proof of their fan-based knowledge of the characters Sam and Dean, thus taking an element of the television narrative (the anti-possession tattoo) and repurposing it so that it looks like a tattoo (or an extratextual element) acquired by a fan of the diegetic book series. As Paul Booth states, '*Supernatural* not only parodies itself within the boundaries of the show, straining the meta-nature of the genre, but also goes out of its way to depict fandom and fannish behavior [*sic*], both as a specific nod to the work of fans in keeping the show on the air and as a way to generate more fandom and to motivate the fans that exist to continue to watch' (2015: 91). The *Supernatural* episode 'The French mistake' (6.15) incorporates this self-reflexive narrative technique by highlighting the television production aspect of the show. Sam and Dean discover that they are television actors called Jared Padalecki and Jensen Ackles. When Dean sees a 'Bienvenue à/Welcome to Vancouver' sign, he says to Sam, 'Dude, we're not even in America'. This comment reinforces the episode's meta status as a show that is aware of the fact that *Supernatural* is shot in Vancouver, Canada, even though the diegetic setting is the United States of America. Through this kind of production technique, the creative team of this drama actually engages in the process of reinforcing the cult status and the subsequent demystification of *Supernatural*, a phenomenon that is also evident in how tattoos function in the serial.

In 2008, during the show's third season, Gamble anticipated the cult following of *Supernatural* when she said, '[b]y the way, I'll be convinced we're truly a cult hit when a fan gets the same tattoo' (in Cochran 2008).[9] Gamble's definition of the show's cult status has been confirmed since, as Kies notes, 'many fans have adopted the tattoo design as a mark of their passion for the show' (2014: 25). However, *Supernatural* became a cult[10] hit even before Gamble's 2008 statement, since the *Supernatural Wiki* fan tattoos website includes the statement 'little did Sera know, that fans had been getting tattoos since early on in the Show's run. This page documents the many and varied tattoos fans have had, inspired by *Supernatural* and our fandom.' Some of the tattoos featured on this fan site date back to 2006 and 2007. A 'CoolTattooArts' web page provides more evidence of the circulation of *Supernatural* into consumer culture for current fans who may also want to imprint images from the show onto their own bodies.[11] Bethan Jones has explored tattoos and fandom or 'fannish tattoos' further through an analysis of 'sacred fannish identity' (2015:

3.4). By adopting tattoos from a particular television program, fans can be viewed as a community that makes 'choices and distinctions that set [their sacred tattoo experience] aside from the mundane' (3.5). While recognising that this act of reinscription by fans can be viewed as a way of situating the sacred in fan culture, I am more inclined to argue that as fans appropriate these television symbols inscribed onto characters for themselves, they engage in the act of demystifying elements of this detective drama which uses these symbols to suggest mysterious, supernatural powers. In this sense, the anti-possession tattoos from *Supernatural* go beyond their diegetic function as symbols that protect characters from supernatural influences; they also function as a brand. One definition of a brand is a 'name, term, sign symbol or design … intended to identify the goods and services of one seller or group of sellers and to differentiate them from those of other sellers' (American Marketing Association). The anti-possession tattoo, the sigil or symbol tattooed onto the angel Castiel's skin (9.3), the sigils Castiel engraves into Sam and Dean's ribs (5.1), and the Mark of Cain (Seasons 9 and 10), all function as brands for this television serial much like the triquetra, an ancient Celtic design (Green 2003: 243) did for *Charmed* (1998–2006).[12] In *Supernatural*, the anti-possession tattoo image has entered the domain of consumer culture; the tattoo takes on the form of cultural capital when the symbol appears on pendants[13] and t-shirts[14] that can be purchased by fans. These consumer goods function as 'pseudo-diegetic merchandise' (Johnson: 2007) because they allow the fan to 'act out their involvement with the diegetic world' of *Supernatural*. As John Fiske states, '[t]he accumulation of both popular and official cultural capital is signaled materially by collections of objects, artworks, books, records, memorabilia, ephemera' (Fiske 2008: 453), thus facilitating the demystification of the tattoo for fans as the image moves from televisual space into tactile space and ultimately back again. By wearing or displaying the tattoo brands from the show *Supernatural*, fans can also express an interest in connecting to the wider *Supernatural* fan community without even having to communicate this interest verbally. Like the tattoo community at tattoo conventions, *Supernatural* fans can use their bodies or merchandise to express a 'shared identity among members' (DeMello 2000: 41) that is not dependent on the kinds of 'geographic boundaries' (*ibid.*) which define other kinds of communities. The convention space brings together people who have already established community connections through other channels (e.g. online fan sites), but the space reinforces the transplantation of the televisual experience into the fan community.

FAN EXPECTATIONS: LIFE IMITATES ART

An example of how tattoos are subject to the pressures by fans to appropriate and demystify them is evident in a fan convention discussion with

Supernatural actors Jensen Ackles and Jared Padalecki. In some ways, fans mimic the investigative process of these hunter-detective characters by asking Ackles and Padalecki to reveal any unknown components of their lives. The blurring of the lines between television fiction and the expectations that fans have of actors who portray characters with tattoos occurred during a question and answer session with Ackles and Padalecki (henceforth Q and A). In a 2013 appearance at Burcon, a fan convention in Burbank, California, Ackles and Padalecki were asked whether they actually had tattoos or would acquire tattoos, thus suggesting the fascination tattoos (even fake ones) generate for fans of this television serial ('Jensen Ackles and Jared Padalecki' 2013). In this interview, Ackles and Padalecki indicate that neither has a tattoo; they speak of the practical difficulties of makeup sessions involved in covering up a tattoo, and Padalecki talks in a tongue-in-cheek way about revealing himself when the 'time reveals itself' and that he would probably get the Texas star (both actors hail from Texas). Interestingly enough, the Texas star bears some resemblance in terms of its shape to the pentangle of Sam's anti-possession tattoo; however, one has to remember that even an actor's appearance in a Q and A session constitutes a performance, so the 'truth' factor involved in his response is relative. Padalecki may or may not have wanted to get a Texas star; he may have simply been catering to the fans' knowledge of his Texan identity. An interesting development in Padalecki's engagement with tattoos may be found in a Facebook video posted by the actor (11 April 2015). In the video he is shown sporting a Texas star tattoo on his arm. It is not clear whether it is a real tattoo (some Facebook fans wonder about this) but it generated a good deal of fan interest as fans made attempts to demystify this particular mystery. Several Facebook posts reflect an interest in determining when he acquired the tattoo. One fan claims that Padalecki said he did not have one at the Vancouver convention in 2014. Fans often assume that actors are similar to the characters they portray – hence the question about tattoos at the Burbank convention (discussed above) and the ongoing interest in tattoos as an expression of some kind of authentic experience. A comment made by another fan about the Burcon Q and A was that 'they [Ackles and Padalecki] both need to actually get the anti-possession sign tattoo!!'. This reinforces the expectation by fans that the actors imitate their character counterparts. In a similar vein, people often assume that an actor is more authentic or legitimate in their representation of an individual or situation if they have experienced something directly them-selves. Even though this kind of correspondence between a character and an actor does not have to exist, some actors build character through a Stanislavski method approach and may view tattooing as part of this process.

It is interesting that while in this particular Q and A session Ackles and Padalecki may not be connected through identical tattoos as they were in *Supernatural*, their synchronous movement of the microphone (orchestrated or not) still indicates some kind of connection. Judging by the audience laughter that follows these gestures, one could conclude that fans find this apparent synchronicity endearing. Whether or not this was a deliberate performance is immaterial; it is not unusual for fans to expect the actors to have the kind of brotherly bond they display as characters (for example, when Sam and Dean show their matching anti-possession tattoos in 4.18). As one fan points out after watching the Q and A session, 'J2 know each other waaayyy too well. They're even coordinated' ('Jensen Ackles and Jared Padalecki' 2013, YouTube video comments). This familial bond which the tattoo emphasises for Sam and Dean also appears to extend to fans and their feelings that a *Supernatural*-related tattoo makes them part of the *Supernatural* family that includes the actors and the fanbase. Samantha Leopoldi describes how a woman at a *Supernatural* fan convention in Phoenix (2015) recounted:

> meeting the boys during autographs and telling them both how they changed her life, and how she wouldn't be here if it weren't for them. How Jensen Ackles' character Dean Winchester changed her perspective on herself. [...] Proudly showing off her anti-possession tattoo (the same as the boys have in the show), she said it was 'a reminder to myself to never give up, on myself or my family, and goddamn it – that extends to every single person at that convention. We're all a family, and I wouldn't have it any other way.'

This 'transplantation' of a character's anti-possession tattoo onto a fan's body can be seen as the acquisition of cultural and social capital. The cultural phenomenon of *Supernatural* enters fan space, and even influences the social sphere of family life.

TATTOOS, INTERTEXTUAL EXCHANGES AND BRAND CHARACTER

The desire of *Supernatural*'s fans to see similarities between characters and actors is one form of demystification or a kind of investigative process into the lives of the actors who play tattooed detectives. However, the intertextual play within the narrative of the show also highlights the interconnectivity involved in the representation of tattoos. *Supernatural* continually engages with other detective stories or texts associated with the tattooed body (for example, *The girl with the dragon tattoo* phenomenon) in a way that emphasises its place in a network of tattoo and detective narratives. As Matt Hills indicates in his discussion of the science fiction and horror varieties of cult television, 'cult texts must play with their own established rules and norms' (2004: 511) and this would also seem to apply to the way the tattoo functions in a self-reflexive manner in 'The girl with the Dungeons and Dragons tattoo' (7.20) episode. For example, the female character Charlie Bradbury (Felicia Day) is introduced as a hunter-hacker character who helps the Winchesters. The intertextual references to the blockbuster book and film *The girl with the dragon tattoo*[15] demonstrate how *Supernatural* taps into popular culture and the crime genre (the Millennium trilogy books and films), while also embracing a connection to gamer culture and specifically to Dungeons and Dragons, a fantasy role playing game. *The girl with the dragon tattoo* is a transmedia phenomenon that combines crime, violence and hacker culture. A fictional creation of Swedish author Stieg Larsson, the female protagonist Lisbeth Salander is a computer hacker who sports multiple tattoos and helps a journalist, Michael Blomkvist, in his investigations. The title of the *Supernatural* episode draws on the best-selling status of the novel and the cultural status of the award-winning film adaptations; the female protagonist Lisbeth has been described as 'one of the most compelling characters in recent popular fiction' (Punter 2010: 380).

'The girl with the Dungeons and Dragons tattoo' episode features references to tattoos and popular culture while also engaging in the pattern of concealment and revelation that is part of the detective and crime genre and a component of the tattoo. For example, in this episode we discover that Charlie, a computer hacker who also happens to be a lesbian, supposedly acquired a Princess Leia *Star wars* tattoo:

> Dean: Do you have any tattoos? Give him a little sneak peek there. All tattoos are sexy.
> Charlie: Mine is Princess Leia in a slave bikini straddling a 20-sided die. I was drunk, it was Comic-Con. (7.20)

Interestingly enough, Charlie does not comply and the tattoo remains hidden (critic Josh Raymer says 'wish we could've seen that tattoo'), so we only have Charlie's word for it. The tattoo remains shrouded in mystery despite its link to this iconic character. This mysterious tattoo is also associated with the ultimate event in fan culture: Comic-Con. The concealed tattoo may also intersect with the discomfort Charlie expresses when she is forced to suppress her lesbian identity, such as when Dean tells her to flirt with a male guard in an office building so that she can gain illegal access to an office and retrieve digital information for Sam and Dean. The visual display of the Princess Leia brand on the t-shirt and on a poster suggests the visible side of Charlie; the Princess Leia tattoo, on the other hand – with the many-sided die – suggests that Charlie has hidden identities. One such hidden side becomes more obvious in the episode 'There's no place like home' (10.11), when she divides into 'good Charlie' and 'dark Charlie' after a series of adventures in the Land of Oz. Charlie's reference to the concealed tattoo teases the audience. The lack of a visual revelation of the tattoo may also disappoint some viewers but the tattoo still serves as a tribute to fans of the science fantasy franchise *Star wars* and attendees of Comic-Con, where many of *Supernatural*'s cast members have appeared as guests. Charlie's tattoo and t-shirt both sport Princess Leia images (just the kind of merchandise that may be available at Comic-Con or fan conventions) and so display an iconic 'brand character'. As K. L. Keller notes, 'brand characters represent a special type of brand symbol, one that takes on human or special-life characteristics' (cited in Rossolatos 2014: 29) and as George Rossolatos describes, they can include live action figures (*ibid.*). It is worth noting that even though the *Star wars* symbol that Charlie wears is not an obvious *Supernatural* brand, like the anti-possession tattoos or the Mark of Cain, it still solidifies her as a tattooed character who intersects with Dean's 'brand', the Mark of Cain, as we will see in a later portion of this chapter.

THE MARK OF CAIN AS TATTOO AND 'BRAND'

The ninth and tenth seasons of *Supernatural* link the concept of the tattoo with criminal behaviour and moral ambiguity through the introduction of the Mark of Cain, which also serves as a 'brand' or easily identifiable symbol for the show. In many ways, the Mark of Cain resembles the barcode in *Dark angel*, which links branded identity and criminality (see Will Slocombe's Chapter 14 in this collection). Cain's murder of his brother Abel has been called the first murder (see, for example, Schwartz 1997: 3) and results in God's 'branding' of Cain. Studies of the Judeo-Christian story of the Mark of Cain have suggested that the mark may be viewed as a physical mark or a letter: '[s]ome [exegetes] interpreted it as a letter from the Hebrew alphabet placed on either the face or the arm' (Byron 2011: 120). The Hebrew word for mark (*oth*) is the same as that for letter, which emphasises the textual ambiguity of the Mark of Cain. The shape of the image on Dean's arm (an inverted L with two drops to the left of the inverted L)[16] resembles a stylised version of the first letter of the Hebrew word '*oth*'. The tattoo connection to Dean's mark or brand is presented in the episode 'About a boy' (10.12). Near the beginning of the episode, Dean is looking through books about tattoo removal as a way of removing the mark, thus reinforcing parallels between the mark, branding (in the sense of burning a mark into the skin) and tattoos. *Supernatural* adopts this mythic parallel of two brothers but transforms the origin of the story. In the *Supernatural* 'verse', the Mark of Cain was placed on Cain by Lucifer (not God) as part of a deal Cain made to save his brother. This disrupts the identification of the biblical mark, given as visual identification and punishment for fratricide, and creates a contrast with *Supernatural*'s Mark of Cain, which reflects a selfless pact on behalf of one brother to save the other. The production element of a closeup shot emphasises the power of this mark, just like the closeups of the anti-possession tattoos highlight their hidden power. Special effects like the animated, glowing mark differentiate it from ink-based tattoos and suggest branding. Unlike tattoos, brands are much more difficult to remove. This reality is worked into the storyline of Dean's Mark of Cain as he and Sam search for a way to remove the Mark. The Mark's similarity to a brand, which involves serious burning of the skin, is enhanced through Dean's violent acts. The Mark glows whenever Dean uses Cain's knife or 'the First Blade' (the jawbone of a donkey) to kill others in an uncontrollable rage.

In the context of a supernatural detective drama, the Mark of Cain functions in several important ways. First of all, it serves as a way of uniting the criminal with the detective. As Heta Pyrhönen notes in her analysis of Agatha Christie's detective Hercule Poirot, '[t]he brand of Cain suggests that the criminal is a person like the detective: the Self (Poirot) and Other (criminal) are, if not united until the end, fundamentally similar throughout the series' (1999: 223). In the case of Dean (and in other situations, his brother Sam), the hunter-detective and the criminal are not just similar but one and the same. The questionable morality of some of Dean and Sam's actions in the serial is something that predates Dean's acquisition of the Mark of Cain; however, the Mark reinforces this in a visually arresting and mythically relevant way.

The Mark of Cain also confirms Dean's status as a perpetrator and as a protected individual. Ruth Mellinkoff states that 'the biblical Cain is thus doubly marked – as both *perpetrator* and as the *protected* charge of the Lord' (Mellinkoff 1981:1). The Mark is responsible for Dean's unbridled killing of individuals (he has the urge to kill and appears to derive pleasure from these acts), and it protects him from 'harm' or from being killed. In a sense, it also protects him from the intervention of 'good' because it is impossible for others to remove the Mark until this takes place in the finale of Season 10. Unlike Linda Tran's anti-possession tattoo, which was burned off (8.2), Dean's Mark can only be removed at great cost and involves the use of an elaborate spell and the killing of none other than Death, who appears in human form in 'Brother's keeper' (10.23). The removal of the Mark also involves the release of Darkness into the world, as we see in the Season 10 finale – an episode which offers some form of resolution while opening the door to yet another mystery, thus reinforcing the pattern of revelation and concealment that has marked this supernatural detective drama. Season 11 reintroduces the Mark of Cain, but this time the Mark is on the body of Darkness who has taken on the female form of Amara. She bears the mark on her left clavicle and has a strong bond with Dean, the former bearer of the Mark. Although Amara leaves Earth at the end of Season 11, one suspects that there is always the possibility of the future reappearance of the Mark of Cain or another kind of mysterious tattoo in future episodes.

CHARLIE AND DEAN: WOUNDED HUNTERS

Another female character who is closely linked to Dean and who has a recurring role in *Supernatural* is Charlie (Felicia Day). Several episodes in Season 10 foster parallels between the characters of Charlie (who appeared in 'The girl with the Dungeons and Dragons tattoo' (7.20)) and Dean. Fans would probably remember Charlie from this episode and might recall that she had a concealed Princess Leia *Star wars* tattoo and is capable of criminal activity – stealing digital data for Sam and Dean. These two 'brands', Charlie's Princess Leia tattoo and Dean's Mark of Cain, are linked because they evoke suffering, albeit different forms of pain. Charlie jokingly talks about acquiring the tattoo while she was drunk and at Comic-Con (7.20), but the 'slave' component of the iconic Princess Leia image aptly applies to Charlie who puts herself in a compromising position (she flirts with a man even though she is a lesbian) to retrieve information for Sam and Dean. She also suffers a broken arm, is nearly killed, killed, resurrected and finally killed again; she is repeatedly cast as a wounded character.

In the Season 10 episode 'There's no place like home' (10.11), which aired in January 2015, Charlie's good and dark side conflict as she splits into two different Charlies; fans may easily detect similarities with Dean's good and dark side. The intertwining of texts and the stories of various tattooed characters also allow different kinds of fans to enter the space of *Supernatural* (gamers, fans interested in mythology or biblical narratives, and even fans of older films like *The wizard of Oz*). In 'Book of the Damned' (10.18), another episode that features Charlie, she has found the Book of the Damned which has the secret to removing the Mark of Cain, but she is shot by a member of the Styne family who wants the book back. As a wounded hacker-turned-hunter,[17] she resembles Dean, another hunter of the supernatural, who experiences his own torment as the bearer of the Mark of Cain.

The final episode that reunites Charlie with the Winchester brothers is 'Dark dynasty' (10.21). The narrative presents tattoo-related material since Sam and Dean identify a murderer who is a member of the Styne family based on this individual's tattoo, which happens to be the Styne family crest. The crest is an image of a doubleheaded bird (perhaps an eagle) or winged creature carrying a shield with a cross in the centre. Once again, *Supernatural* introduces the idea of a tattoo in relation to family. The Winchester brothers are able to identify the murderer Eldon Styne as a member of the Styne family because of the unique design of the tattoo: only members of this group would have this tattoo. In a bizarre way, the Styne family's interest in harvesting organs and transplanting organs into their own bodies has parallels with how tattoos are introduced in *Supernatural* as a diegetic image and then 'transplanted' onto extratextual fans in the form of actual tattoos, thus signalling a fan's membership in a group of like-minded people: other fans of *Supernatural*. In the episode, the Stynes work together just as Dean, Sam and Charlie (tattooed individuals) work together to acquire the Book of the Damned. The Stynes want to get their Book of the Damned back from Charlie who has it in her possession. According to Charlie, the book holds the secret to removing Dean's Mark of Cain (10.18). Charlie manages to translate the Book of the Damned for Sam, who is keen to access it to help Dean. However, shortly thereafter, she is stabbed to death by a member of the Styne family, who is also looking for this book. Charlie's injuries and her eventual death parallel the suffering experienced by Dean (his dual image as a victim figure and as the perpetrator of violence parallels the depiction of the tattoo in the *CSI: NY* episode 'Oedipus Hex' as 'a sign of both victimhood and aggression' (Hawthorn and Miller 2018: 261)). Dean finds it increasingly difficult to resist the thirst of the Mark for violence (the Mark being the source of power for 'the First Blade', the weapon Cain used to kill his brother Abel). Even though Dean does not fulfil the seemingly inevitable curse of killing his brother, both he and Sam experience sorrow and guilt because of the indirect roles they played in Charlie's demise. In a sense, Charlie functions as the stand in for the brother that Dean does not kill, especially given the fact that earlier in the episode she claims she loves Sam and Dean because they are 'like [her] brothers'. One could also suggest that the Mark of Cain (and by extension Dean who has killed others with the First Blade) is indirectly responsible for Charlie's death since she is stabbed to death.

FAN RESPONSE TO THE MARK OF CAIN

Fan reactions to Dean's struggle with the Mark during Seasons 9 and 10 of the show suggest a high level of involvement as viewers discuss the morality of Dean's violent actions.[18] However, if viewers wish to take their fascination with the Mark of Cain even further, as fans before them have done with the anti-possession tattoos, they can purchase Mark of Cain merchandise and continue the process of demystifying these characters' tattoos or marked bodies.[19]

Clearly, like the anti-possession tattoos and sigils, the Mark of Cain has been commodified, but it reinforces the development and serial format of the show by providing fans with an updated brand. In *Brands: The logos of the global economy* (2004), Celia Lury indicates that brands can involve change. In other words, while maintaining loyalty to a brand, customers experience a changing 'relationship with a brand in time' (*ibid.*: 3). A comparable phenomenon occurs when fans of a serialised television show adapt to a change in a brand of tattoo over the span of a serialised show like *Supernatural*, which maintains familiar elements for its fans while also building on the 'tried-and-true' aspects of the show. As Catherine Johnson points out, serial dramas are one of the genres that facilitate a sustainable programme brand (2012); thus, the longevity and serial structure of *Supernatural*, a successful programme brand, engages with fans through multiple versions of the tattoo brand.

The updating of the 'tattoo' in *Supernatural* also extends to the marketplace where a variety of 'tattoos' can be purchased by fans. However, in this context the Mark of Cain image does not simply displace the anti-possession tattoo and sigils. The Mark of Cain, anti-possession tattoos and sigils still generate fan interest, even though some fans may well gravitate towards the more recent expression of that tattoo based on their consumption of later episodes of *Supernatural*. Fans who want a combination of the older anti-possession brand of tattoo, and the more recent Mark of Cain, can actually buy a t-shirt that sports the Mark of Cain *and* the anti-possession tattoos.[20] For fans who want their reality to imitate fiction, they could consider getting a tattoo or brand of the Mark, perhaps as a sign of their devotion to the show's brand or to express some of the sentiment expressed by this tattoo – such as exile, marginality or a cursed existence. As Llewellyn Negrin indicates, 'tattoos mark the body in an indelible and largely irreversible way' (2008: 98) and can offer individuals a way of anchoring their identity (*ibid.*: 99) in a world of rapid change. This identification with Dean's or Cain's image of the exile, is a feeling that a fan could paradoxically share with other fans (for example, at a comic entertainment expo), thus affirming their membership in the *Supernatural* community or family. Yet, years down the line, if they choose to have their tattoo removed, they can always do so and oddly enough still stay faithful to their imitation of Dean, since his Mark of Cain was removed after all in the finale of Season 10 (10.23 'Brother's keeper').

CONCLUSION

The consumer 'branding' of *Supernatural*'s anti-possession tattoos and the Mark of Cain reveals how tattoo-like images have travelled beyond the boundaries of this fantasy detective show and achieved cult or even sacred status. Sam and Dean's anti-possession tattoos, and Charlie Bradbury's hidden Princess Leia tattoo, have been used by the production team to strategically insert fan culture into the show's narrative (4.18). These marks on a character's body allow the television serial to play with concepts of concealment and revelation that also imitate important strategies in detective fiction, such as the concealment of identity and the revelation of a mystery or secret. Fan conventions and Facebook sites allow fans to engage in attempts to demystify characters from *Supernatural* as they question actors about real-life tattoos. The show's writers and members of the production team have also carried the trope of the tattoo through various episodes in order to facilitate parallels between characters and their experiences (Charlie and Dean). This ensures that a tattoo or the Mark of Cain can serve as a synecdochic brand for *Supernatural*, albeit a brand that can be adapted for the consumption of its fans. The contexts of fashion and fandom make the diegetic tattoos in the show available to fans of *Supernatural* in pseudo-diegetic, extra-textual and tangible ways, thus extending the 'life' of these televisual images in this fantasy detective drama. Uniquely, the scriptwriters have developed an engagement with *Supernatural*'s fandom through conventions, fan sites and fan fiction which is fed back into the serial thorough the depictions of the fan. This representation of fandom, specifically the fandom of *Supernatural*, emphasises the textual tattoos and brands associated with the serial – which in turn calls attention to the metatextual elements of *Supernatural*.

NOTES

1 *Supernatural* is primarily set in the United States of America, but filming takes place in a variety of locations in British Columbia's lower mainland and Vancouver area (including areas like Buntzen Lake and Steveston near Richmond).

2 'Classical mystery or murder narratives, such as the story of Odysseus and the story of Cain, make use of the technique of identification. (His childhood nurse sees the scar and becomes aware of his true identity.) The permanent mark which God places on Cain not only identifies him as a criminal but also serves as a visual reminder of Cain's secret or act of concealment, the murder of his brother' (Beeler 2006: 76).

3 Jason Mittell identifies the 'supernatural detective drama' (2015: 66) as a subgenre of television drama. He analyses the series *Awake* and *Medium* and mentions that these series accept certain fantastic premises, such as characters who live split lives (*Awake*) or who are able to communicate with the dead (*Medium*).

4 Where episodes are discussed in detail the title of the episode is given. When an element of an episode is quoted a shorthand of series and episode is given, as in this case (3.12) (eds).

5 'Jus in bello' refers to the latin term for (just) conduct in war.

6 Margo DeMello states that even today 'military' tattoos serve the purpose of high-lighting group identity: '[o]ften military men (and today, women) visit the tattooists in groups while on leave and get their tattoos together. In this way, the tattoos serve to create a bond between the soldiers or sailors' (2004: 414).

7 See   http://supernatural.wikia.com/wiki/Anti-Possession_Tattoo   [accessed   5 December 2018].

8 Linda's attempt to prevent possession is short lived when her tattoo is burned off by one of Crowley's assistants, thus allowing Crowley, the king of hell, to possess her.

9 Examples of the anti-possession tattoo on fans are available at http://www.super naturalwiki.com/index.php?title=Fan_Tattoos [accessed 5 December 2018].

10 Erika Engstrom and Joseph Valenzano indicate that the inclusion of *Supernatural* in an academic work such as *The essential cult TV reader* (2009), edited by David Lavery, contributes to its designation as cult television (2014: 10).

11 See cooltattooart.com/supernatural-tattoo-artworks [accessed 5 December 2018].

12 *Charmed* is a fantasy television show about three sisters who discover they are witches. In the serial, the triquetra appears in the title sequence and on the cover of the mystical *Book of shadows* that the sisters consult. The triquetra is also a symbol

that has been transported into fandom through fansites and merchandise as a brand for the show.

13 I acquired a pendant with the anti-possession tattoo design at a local comic expo/ fan convention.

14 See cafepress.ca, an online store for popular culture products featuring several difference designs.

15 The Swedish novel was published in 2005 with the English translation in 2008. The Swedish film was released in 2009 and the English language version in 2011. For a detailed discussion of *The girl with the dragon tattoo*, see Kerstin Bergman's Chapter 6 in this collection.

16 See: http://supernatural.wikia.com/wiki/Mark_of_Cain [accessed 5 December 2018].

17 https://supernaturallydevoted.wordpress.com/tag/mark-of-cain [accessed 2 February 2017. The site has since been deleted by its authors.]

18 There is much fan interest in explaining his reasons for violence or murder, see https://supernaturallydevoted.wordpress.com/tag/mark-of-cain [accessed 5 December 2018].

19 See, for example, the Mark of Cain Supernatural Custom bleached shirt www.etsy. com/ca/market/mark_of_cain [accessed 5 December 2018].

20 See www.etsy.com/listing/208359258/mark-of-cain-anti-possession-tattoo [accessed 2 February 2017].

BIBLIOGRAPHY

Ackles, Jensen and Jared Padalecki (2013), 'Talk about tattoos', *Supernatural Burcon 2013* (24 November). Available on YouTube.com at: https://www.youtube.com/watch?v=-zKmuBlVkbU [accessed 5 December 2018].

Beeler, Karin (2006), *Tattoos, desire and violence: Marks of resistance in literature, film and television* (Jefferson: McFarland).

Booth, Paul (2015), *Playing fans: Negotiating fandom and media in the digital age* (Iowa: University of Iowa Press).

Byron, John (2011), *Cain and Abel in text and tradition: Jewish and Christian interpretations of the first sibling rivalry* (Leiden: Brill).

Chan, Suzette (2010), '*Supernatural* bodies: Writing subjugation and resistance onto Sam and Dean Winchester', *Transformative works and cultures*, 4. Available: http://journal.transformativeworks.org/index.php/twc/article/view/179/160 [accessed 21 June 2017].

Cherry, Brigid (2011), 'Sympathy for the fangirl: Becky Rosen, fan identity and interactivity in *Supernatural*', in S. Abbott and D. Lavery (eds), *TV goes to Hell: An unofficial road map of Supernatural* (n.p.: ECW Press), pp. 203–18.

Cochran, C.P. (2008), 'Interview: Sera Gamble, producer and writer for *Supernatural*', *Firefox News* (1 March). Available: www.supernaturalwiki.com/index.php?title=Sera_Gamble [accessed 21 June 2017].

Cook, Michael (2014), *Detective fiction and the ghost story: The haunted text* (New York: Palgrave Macmillan).

DeMello, Margo (2000), *Bodies of inscription: A cultural history of the modern tattoo community* (Durham, NC and London: Duke University Press).

— (2014), *Inked: Tattoos and body art around the world* (Santa Barbara: ABC-CLIO).

Engstrom, Erika and Joseph M. Valenzano III. (2014), *Television, religion, and Supernatural: Hunting monsters, finding gods* (Lanham: Lexington Books).

Fiske, John (2008), 'The cultural economy of fandom', in E. Mathijs and X. Mendik (eds), *The cult film reader* (Maidenhead, England: Open University Press), pp. 445–55.

Gamble, Sera (writer) (2008), 'Jus in bello' [Season 3, Episode 12], *Supernatural* (21 February).

Gray, John (1994), *I love Mom: An irreverent history of the tattoo* (Toronto: Key Porter Books).

Green, Terisa (2003), *The tattoo encyclopedia: A guide to choosing your tattoo* (New York: Fireside/Simon & Schuster).

Hawthorn, Ruth and John Miller (2018), 'Tattoos, deviance and consumer culture in North American television: *Criminal minds, CSI: NY* and *Law and order*', in K. Watson and K. Cox (eds), *Tattoos in crime and detective narratives: Marking and remarking* (Manchester: Manchester University Press), pp. 256–70.

Hills, Matt (2004), 'Defining cult TV: Texts, inter-texts and fan audiences', in R. C. Allen and A. Hill (eds), *The television studies reader* (London and New York: Routledge), pp. 509–23.

Johnson, Catherine (2007), 'Telebranding in TV III', *New review of film and television studies*, 5:1, 5–24.

— (2012) *Branding Television* (New York: Routledge).

Jones, Bethan (2015), 'Fannish tattooing and sacred identity', L. Bennett and P. J. Booth (eds), *Performance and performativity in fandom* [special issue of *Transformative Works and Cultures* 18].

Kies, Bridget (2014), 'The monstrous male body', in L. Zubernis and K. Larsen (eds), (2014).

Larsson, Stieg (2011), *The girl with the dragon tattoo*, trans. R. Keeland (London: Maclehose Press).

Lavery, David (2009), *The essential cult TV reader* (Lexington, Kentucky: University Press of Kentucky).

Leopoldi, Samantha (n.d.), 'Proof that *Supernatural has the most dedicated fanbase*'. Available: www.sheknows.com/entertainment/articles/1078099/proof-that-superna tural-has-the-most-dedicated-fan-base [accessed 21 June 2017].

Lury, Celia (2004), *Brands: The logos of a global economy* (Abingdon and New York: Routledge).

Mellinkoff, Ruth (1981), *The Mark of Cain* (Berkeley: University of California Press).

Mittell, Jason (2015), *Complex TV: The poetics of contemporary television storytelling* (New York: New York University Press).

Negrin, Llewellyn (2008), *Appearance and identity: Fashioning the body in postmodernity* (Basingstoke: Palgrave Macmillan).

Nickerson, Catherine Ross (2010), 'Women writers before 1960', in C. R. Nickerson (ed.), *The Cambridge companion to American crime fiction* (Cambridge and New York: Cambridge University Press), pp. 29–41.

Padalecki, Jared (2015), '5:45 am and home from work!!! (11 April). Available: www.facebook.com/JaredPadalecki/videos/366501530222115 [accessed 1 March 2017].

Punter, Jennie (2010), 'Crime and punishment in a foreign land', *Queen's quarterly*, 117:3 (Fall), 380–91.

Pyrhönen, Heta (1999), *Mayhem and murder: Narrative and moral issues in the detective story* (Toronto: University of Toronto Press).

Raymer, Josh (n.d.), '*Supernatural* watch season 7: The girl with the dungeons and dragons tattoo5:45 am and home from work!!!'. Available: www.cinemablend.com/television/Supernatural-Watch-Season-7-Girl-With-Dungeons-Dragons-Tattoo-41943.html [accessed 1 March 2017].

Rossolatos, George (2014), *Brand equity planning with structuralist rhetorical semiotics* (Kassel: Kassel University Press).

Schiffmacher, Henk and Burkhard Riemschneider (1996), *1000 tattoos* (Köln: Tasche).

Schwartz, Regina M. (1997), *The curse of Cain: The violent legacy of monotheism* (Chicago: University of Chicago Press).

Supernatural Wiki: A supernatural canon and fandom resource (n.d.), 'Fan tattoos'. Available: *www.supernaturalwiki.com/index.php?title=Fan_Tattoos* [accessed 1 March 2017].

Thompson, Robbie (writer) (2012), 'The girl with the Dungeons and Dragons tattoo' [Season 7, Episode 20] (27 April).

Zubernis, Lynne and Katherine Larsen (eds) (2014), *Fan phenomena: Supernatural* (Bristol and Chicago: Intellect Books).

14

Generic branding: Tattoos, transgenics and tech-noir in *Dark angel*

Will Slocombe

INTRODUCTION

Dark angel is an American television series that ran for two seasons between 2000 and 2002. The brainchild of James Cameron and Charles H. Eglee, it was a strange generic hybrid that acted as a precursor to the current glut of fantastic(al) premises in young adult fiction. It was based upon a strong central female character trying to come to terms with life in a chaotic, technologised and criminal world. Unlike *Buffy the vampire slayer* (1997–2003), perhaps its closest programming antecedent, *Dark angel*'s characters were all ostensibly in their late teens or early twenties, trying to earn a living and work out where they fit in a post-apocalyptic Seattle in the aftermath of an Electro-Magnetic Pulse that cripples the United States of America.

One of the most interesting aspects of the series is its mix of various generic tropes, from detective and crime fiction to science fiction (hereafter referred to as 'sf'). This is perhaps not surprising: Cameron's film credits included *Terminator*, *Aliens* and *Strange days*, whereas Eglee had been involved in serials such as *Moonlighting*, *L.A. Law* and *NYPD Blue*. With the series' focus on genetic engineering, it is seemingly most obviously sf. Surveillance drones, implants and exoskeletons, alongside the military-industrial complex's control of the city, coupled with a grimy, post-apocalyptic urban landscape might position *Dark angel* within the subgenre of cyberpunk (a combination of high tech and low life in its analysis of the grittier side of technological progress) or biopunk (a facet of cyberpunk that involves biological engineering as the technological innovation). Despite this, in terms of its actual form, setting, characterisation and plotting, it is more akin to *film noir* and the 'hardboiled' crime genres, perhaps especially through the voice-over narrations that begin and end most episodes and the assumed corruption of law enforcement and city officials. Moreover, there are also 'superhero' and occasional gothic tropes and motifs present throughout in its exploration of superhuman abilities and monstrosity, respectively.

Dark angel's genre hybridity is best understood in relation to Emily E. Auger's filmic concept of tech-noir. Named after the nightclub in James Cameron's 1984 film, *Terminator*, tech-noir functions by way of a development and conflation of the gothic, detective and *film noir*, and sf genres; a response to the ways in which technologies are seen to frame experience. The series, as it develops into its second season, shifts across various genres and emphasises the corruption of systems – whether environmental, technological or socio-political. This means that the world itself is re-configured as criminal and corrupt, and this is reflected in the ways in which *Dark angel* manifests particular generic tropes. Given this generic hybridity and corruption, and referencing the work of Auger, this chapter examines the world of *Dark angel* as an instance of tech-noir and considers the role of body-marking (tattoos, brands and barcodes) as a central metaphor in this examination of the 'generic' body. 'Body-marking' in *Dark angel* not only occurs at the level of content (representations of tattoos and branding within the show), but also formally (how its own generic 'body' is 'marked'). Thus, depictions of body-marking are more than mere traces of contemporary social concern, and are etched firmly into debates about its narrative arc and generic identity.

In contrast to such generic debates, one of the most popular elements of the series was the cast, especially Jessica Alba. *Dark angel* increased Alba's public profile and led to her being cast in large-budget productions such as the *Fantastic four* (2005) and *Sin city* films (2005; 2014). The series functioned as a vehicle for Alba, with Eglee even admitting that the pilot was, 'written "kind of backwards"', 'for her cadences, rhythms, sensibilities, attitude, and slang' (qtd Bobbin 2000). As such, Alba's body – as much as her character Max's – serves as the locus for the aforementioned generic debates and is reflected in critical work on the series. Alba/Max's body is emphasised on both a narrative and visual level throughout. Kathleen McConnell, for instance, notes the mythic origins of *Dark angel*, arguing that it 'provides an iteration of the Pygmalion myth' (2002: 178) and explores the gender politics that such a reading produces; Lorna Jowett argues that '*Dark angel* situates its postfeminism [...] in (the body of) Max' (2005: np), and like McConnell makes use of the gothic genre to examine the series. Similarly, Cynthia Fuchs's brief analysis of *Dark angel* vis-à-vis *Buffy* is focused on the body of Max and her 'overt racial multiplicity' (2007: 111). More recently, Ramona Fernandez (2014) has analysed the 'somatope' or body-place of *Dark angel*, asserting the centrality of bodies to the narrative, and Clarice Butkus's examination of the soundscape of *Dark angel* reveals another aspect of the gender dynamics at work in the series (2012).

What has not been so clearly identified, however, in this focus upon bodies and gender in *Dark angel*, is the role of tattoos, brands and barcodes. Butkus, given the focus on the aural not the visual, never explicitly references them. The omission in Fernandez's article is harder to explain, given the exploration of the technological body as somatope, as is the brief mention in Jowett's work, where she states that 'the barcode on the back of [Max's] neck' is a 'key image' (2005: n.p.). Similarly, Fuchs notes briefly that a 'standard plot point' is Max's attempts to hide her barcode from her pursuers (2007). McConnell's passing description that barcode numbers emphasise characters 'as interchangeable units' (2002: 181) is disputable. Rather than the body *per se*, the *marked* body is the dominant image for understanding these various political readings of Alba/Max and, following Jowett's lead, serves as the point of intersection for the generic hybridity that the series manifests. That is, the barcode adumbrates the series in its totality, both generically and genetically, through the emphasis on bodies, and explains how *Dark angel* navigates across various genres and discourses.

BRANDED IDENTITIES AND BARCODES

Dark angel utilises several familiar tropes with regard to tattoos, through associations with criminals or gang members. In this respect, within the world of *Dark angel* tattoos tend to signify someone as deviant from mainstream society.[1] Given the problematic definition of mainstream society as it might be understood within its world, this initial observation is merely a visual encoding of contemporary (to us) social norms of tattoo imagery rather than part of the internal ideology of the world of *Dark angel*.

To give an example of how the world of *Dark angel* works, and how it might key into generic debates, Max, after the pilot episode of the show, becomes something akin to a private investigator. Logan, her paramour, has a secret identity as 'Eyes Only', a crusader against the corruption he sees everywhere in the city. Within the pilot, Max is a cat burglar, but in subsequent episodes she uses her skills to facilitate Logan's investigations. Episodes in Season 1 often involve a socially acceptable but (morally, if not legally) criminal malfeasant being identified by Logan/Eyes Only and brought to justice by Max.[2] So as much as gangs might have tattoos within *Dark angel*, most often the criminals are businesspeople, politicians and corrupt police officers, many of whom never reveal tattoos.

What complicates the role of the tattoo in *Dark angel* is a very particular kind of visual marker – the barcode. Alba's character, Max Guevara, is the product of a genetic engineering project run by the military. All subjects of this 'Project Manticore' have barcodes on the backs of their necks (Max's designation X5–332960073452 means that she is of the X5 series, and 332960073452 is her barcode number), serving to distinguish their chimeric natures from those of baseline humans, from whom the X series are otherwise visually indistinguishable. The pilot episode details an escape from Manticore by a group of children, including Max, in 2009. The narrative arc of Season 1 follows Max some ten years later as she tries to find her fellow escapees while Manticore is hunting her. In fact, Max Guevara is not her real name, but one she creates to escape from her assigned identifier, the barcode number itself. Although, her barcode identifies her as 'deviant' (from both normal humans and the military organisation that created her, despite it being 'their' mark upon her body), she in fact becomes more 'moral' than many of the normative systems that define her world.

In actuality, barcodes are only quasi-unique identifiers. Barcodes distinguish one product from different products, and so are unique to that product, but not to an individual item (which shares the barcode with other items of that type). They are Universal Product Codes, a collection of lines configured to be unique, and which are then attributed to a group of ostensibly identical items. As such, they have no inherent meaning, but only gain meaning when tracked within a database as being linked to that item (a similar mechanism to a tattoo symbolising a certain act or accomplishment within a subgroup). Their cultural resonance, however, relates to a decline of individuality and, perhaps more importantly, as a signifier of ownership and control – the barcode is a symbol of mechanisation and technologisation. This is perhaps because the barcode is perceived to be the encoding of an individual as disembodied data. Passports with the equivalent of unique identification chips, and everything from barcodes on library cards to fingerprints, retinal and biometric scans, re-create the individual as code. These measures, not visible to the individual, track and record that a datum is accurate and correctly correlated to another datum. In contrast to the significatory practices of most tattoos, which may embody or emblematise a life event, to tattoo a barcode onto a person is to concretise a piece of data and re-inscribe it on a person. This practice has become closely linked with well-established images of tattooing of prisoners for identification and the resultant dehumanisation that such an act embodies. In short, the barcode is a visual marker of data that obscures the individual, and its inclusion in *Dark angel* provides the techno-scientific backdrop so necessary for Auger's notion of the tech-noir.[3]

BARCODES AS 'BRAND' MARKS

The barcode tattoo operates in an ambivalent manner, especially in relation to how it has been conceived in recent sf productions. It is a symbol of control and dehumanisation, an encroachment of the machine or technology into the human (unlike tattoos, barcodes are deliberately designed to be machine-readable rather than by the human eye). In *Dark angel* these genetic barcodes are also unique to the individual. Thus, there is a tension at the heart of such representations of the barcode tattoo between the individual and the generic.[4] They dehumanise in the sense of being symbols of technologisation and creating the human-as-data, they also identify a 'product group' in the X series but they are not barcodes as we currently understand them, as means of distinguishing a group of identical products from another group. The barcode denotes her as a product of the secret militaristic organisation, marking her as distinct or somehow deviant from members of everyday society, yet also defines an individual, albeit socially-engineered, identity for her. The barcode denotes ownership of the subject, and their role as a function of an organisation. Likewise, the barcode functions both as a military group tattoo and a secret society tattoo.[5] *Dark angel* translates this 'secret society' body-mark into a cyber- or bio-punk context, and uses barcodes to indicate membership of a covert subgroup concerned with quasi-military actions and/or assassinations. The genetic barcode tattoos in *Dark angel* remain unique and individual.[6]

Dark angel emphasises the barcode, and its location on Alba's body, as a marketing tool or brand identifier. Much is made of the barcode in the opening credits for *Dark angel*, emphasising its importance at a thematic as well as visual level. The credits open and close with a static burst, symbolising the Pulse or the subversive transmissions from Eyes Only 'streaming freedom video bulletins'. Within this, however, the image of the barcode takes precedence. As actors' names appear on the screen, the words morph into barcodes. In Butkus's examination of the soundscape of the series, and the ways in which this contributes to the gender dynamic of the series, she notes that the credit's theme song, a collaboration between Public Enemy and MC Lyte, 'syncretises the breathy neo-soul "ahhs" with the mostly discordant elements of the post-apocalyptic industrial soundscape' (2012: 192). She then quotes from the CD liner to the track, which contrasts 'a world in chaos, a ruined landscape, society, a broken machine, corrupt, anguished, criminal' with 'the voice of an angel, delicate, erotic, at peace ... female' (*ibid.*). Evidently, the tension between technology and humanity (or, more precisely, femininity) is played out both visually and aurally during the credits, as the barcode imagery reinforces the message of the soundtrack, imbricating bodies, identities and technological tattoos together.[7]

More importantly, barcode imagery even 'brackets' the credits; a barcode resolves into the words of the title *Dark angel* after the initial static burst and, at the end of the credits, a camera pans around an image of Alba sitting on the ruins of the Seattle Space Needle. During this shot, and as the wind blows the hair from the nape of her neck, we see the barcode, which then resolves into the phrase: '[c]reated by James Cameron and Charles H. Eglee'. We might cynically transpose this sequence onto the politics of casting Alba and the subsequent development of the series and her persona as we move between Alba, the barcode and 'created by...'. This perhaps implies the extent to which Cameron and Eglee created Alba's 'brand' through *Dark angel*, and again reveals the extent to which the body and its markings serve to define the identity of the series.[8] Far from a potential triumph of femininity over technology, the prevalence of the barcode, and its location on Max's body, serves to conflate the physical with the technological in an uneasy tension.[9]

IDENTITY POLITICS I: TATTOO VERSUS BARCODE

Over the course of Season 1 of *Dark angel*, the audience is introduced to various Manticore escapees, and learns something of their lives since the escape. The arc, from the Manticore escape in the pilot to the return to it in the final episode, marks the narrative development of the first season. We discover what happened to the separated transgenic siblings, and follow Max's journey towards social engagement from her initial attitude of non-involvement and self-interest to a sense of responsibility and moral growth. It is noticeable that throughout the series, transgenics are identified – and identify each other – through their barcodes. In episodes such as 'Pollo loco' (1.18), Max identifies and misidentifies a fellow Manticore escapee Ben through his barcode (the X series Ben has been tattooing his barcode onto baseline humans who turn up murdered) and in 'The kidz are aiight' (1.14) barcodes are used to mark the graves of transgenics.[10] Similarly, in the final episode of Season 1, '… and Jesus brought a casserole' (1.22), a fellow transgenic, Zack, says to Max, seeing her barcode on one of the receptacles in the DNA lab at Manticore, 'it's you … and me … and Brin … and Tinga' and she responds, '[n]o, Tinga's dead'. In short, these barcodes are indeed definitions of identity, and however much Max wishes to escape from the constraints of that identity, it is one to which she, and the others, return to by default.

One key example of this is in the use of clones, particularly of the adult characters. For example, Jensen Ackles, who plays Ben in 'Pollo loco', is re-introduced in Season 2 as Ben's clone, Alec. For obvious reasons, there is no visual clue as to their difference, only the assumed one of behaviour and a distinct barcode designation (Ben is X5–493 whereas Alec is X5–494). These two characters never appear on screen at the same time. However, the episode 'She ain't heavy' (2.19) makes deliberate use of this interchangability of appearance, but not of barcode, by introducing the audience to an adult clone of Max, X5–453. The arc of this episode is predicated precisely on this mistaken identity. X5–453 is targeted as the agents sent to capture her assume she is Max, at least until they check her barcode. Max swaps roles with X5–453 as a means of escaping capture. Thus, at the textual level, the only difference between the two is the barcode and the fact that for some reason X5–453's genetic code is different from Max's. That said, on a meta-textual level, the audience is given deliberate visual cues of clothing and the fact that X5–453 smokes to enable the audience to further distinguish between them. Thus, what defines the individual in this episode is their coding – internal genetics and external barcode – and therefore McConnell's sense that 'the barcode numbers of the back of their necks [emphasise] them as interchangeable units' (2002: 181) is too broad. She uses this to define how Lydecker, the antagonist of Season 1, refers to his 'kids' through their barcodes; rather, Lydecker knows them as individuals through their barcodes, and it is merely a militaristic form of address as apposed to their self-designated names. The barcode serves the function of making their physicality, rather than their identities, as the barcodes actually 'de-face' the transgenics' bodies. Again, it is the process of dehumanisation and technologisation signified by the barcode that is foregrounded, not interchangeability.

There is an important distinction is to be drawn, however, between tattoos and barcodes within *Dark angel*. This is seen early on in Season 1, in the episode '411 on the DL' (1.6), as the audience learn more about the barcodes when Max finds Zack. She traces him after she finds out that a '[m]ale adult had a barcode removed from his neck at a tattoo parlor', and later in the episode Logan and Max discuss it:

> LOGAN: Might want to think about having your barcode removed, too.
> MAX: Tried once. Feels like someone's pouring acid on your skin after it's been sandblasted. Came back in a couple weeks. It's etched into our genetic code.
> LOGAN: The Mark of Cain. So why would this guy bother?
> MAX: Zack's the kind of guy that does whatever it takes as often as it takes.[11]

It becomes clear that the barcode is not just a tattoo, skin deep as it were, but etched into the transgenics' DNA. This collapses the internal/external dichotomy, and makes the barcodes a more persistent component of their identities than tattoos. Thus, *Dark angel* envisages that the barcode is part of the physical being of the transgenics, encoded at the genetic level and identifying them as somehow 'deviant' from normal humans (and, compounding the metaphor, as 'branded' criminals and outcasts from the itself corrupt organisation that created them). This further emphasises the technological paradigm of *Dark angel* (engineering a barcode birthmark within DNA) and serves to differentiate between externalised symbols of control and those enacted within individuals.[12] Whereas a tattoo can theoretically be removed or altered, a transgenic's recuperative qualities and adapted DNA mean that the barcode is created by their own body, re-inscribing the link between tattoos and ownership via the barcode mark.

Indeed, many of the Manticore subjects describe the barcodes as tattoos to their partners, who might be unaware of the truth, or in instances when the barcode is accidentally observed. As the truth about transgenics becomes more widely known to the public in Season 2, when Max facilitates the destruction of the Manticore site and the freedom of its former residents, this identification of the barcodes becomes both more pressing and more complicated. Many of the escaped subjects are so markedly different from the human norm (including a mermaid; Joshua, a 'canine with human DNA'; and various environmental adaptations for hot and cold climates) that they are visually apparent as transgenics. With the growing public awareness that there are transgenics who can pass as human, the barcode becomes a way of identifying them as transgenic, and of confirming the transgenic nature of the 'anomalies'.

In 'Proof of purchase' (2.3), for example, there is a co-location of consumerism and identity overtly pointed out through the symbol of the barcode. Alec, one of the recent Manticore escapees, is captured and allowed to go free if he can kill three other transgenics. Ames White, the leader of the NSA taskforce sent out to capture the transgenics, wants 'proof of purchase', and tells Alec to bring back the barcodes of those transgenics he kills, cutting them off their necks. A more complicated instance of identity politics explored in Season 2 again foregrounds the distinction between tattoo and barcode in the episode 'Love in vein' (2.14). Here, a gang of youths are mistakenly identified as transgenics – even by Max's character – as they have barcodes on the backs of their necks and seemingly superhuman strength and agility. When Max challenges one of them, however, it becomes clear that they are not transgenics at all, and it subsequently emerges that they have been receiving blood that acts like a battlefield drug from another type of transgenic. In the manner of 'fannish' tattoos, members of this gang have barcodes tattooed onto their necks, creating a criminal gang identified by and identifying with this one 'tattoo' (see fn 9). Logan, talking to one of the group, explains why this is such a problem for Max:

> They [the X5s] wanted out so much they escaped, and they've spent the last eleven years defending their freedom with their lives. That barcode on the back of their necks? That was put there to keep track of them, like a brand. So when she sees someone like you, eager to be a slave, wearing it … it kills her inside.

The rhetoric here is one of control, and the barcode demonstrates the extent to which *Dark angel* is predicated upon the ways in which barcodes subvert identity and choice, whereas tattoos are elective, simultaneously reinforcing and de-constructing normative senses of gang body-markings within its generic confines.

IDENTITY POLITICS II: BARCODES AND SELF-DEFINITION

The main thrust of Season 2 is concerned with the public exposure of the Manticore programme, and the barcode plays a central role in this aspect. Early on, for example, an old flame of Max's, Rafer, dresses up on Halloween as a 'genetically-engineered killing machine escaped from a government lab' by wearing black clothes and sticking a cut-out barcode on his neck, although at this stage it is described as a tabloid rumour ('Boo' 2.5). Later, in 'Hello, goodbye' (2.17), a transgenic worker is caught on camera; this finally reveals the existence of transgenics to the public. In the report, the media takes an interest in the barcode, zooming in on Mule's neck, '[y]ou can see it right there, the barcode. Unconfirmed reports suggest these tattoos were used to keep track of the various soldiers involved in the program'. Although the recording is clearly not of a baseline human, the writers foreground the barcode/tattoo as a means of confirming that this is a transgenic and therefore proving the existence of the Manticore program to the public. (The episode retains the slippage of the term 'tattoo' as the media would be unaware of the true nature of the barcodes.)

Within *Dark angel* at least, tattoos are elective and barcodes are not; this usage thereby implies social deviance rather than the lack of self-determination which the audience already associates with the transgenics' lives. The transgenics are perceived in this instance not as the victims lacking agency (as the barcode signifies), but as the (deviant) agents of fear (which a tattoo at least alludes to). After 'Hello, goodbye', when the barcode has been proven as a means of identifying 'human-like' transgenics, hiding the barcode becomes far more urgent, and in contrast to Max's attitude in Season 1, she too starts obscuring it. 'She ain't heavy' includes a scene where Alex checks Max's neck and says, '[y]ou need a little laser touch-up', indicating that it is now becoming a common way of identifying transgenics and that she has started to hide it. The need to do so is highlighted earlier in the episode when one of the other couriers at Max's work gets stamped with a fake barcode as a joke, leading to the owner of the business pulling a gun on the courier.

This need to obscure the barcode is also repeated in 'Freak nation' (2.21), the final episode of the show, where a transgenic asks, '[d]o I need a touch up?' in reference to her barcode. Although 'Freak nation' brings various instances of the symbolism of the barcode together, it shows that the barcode still occupies an ambiguous place in self-identification for the transgenics. Before the 'touch-up' scene, the audience is shown a flag Joshua has painted. This tricolour per fess flag, with a prominent white dove, is created to symbolise the transgenics, and within the black band at the base of the flag, a red barcode stands out. Joshua goes on to explain the symbolism to Max:

JOSHUA: This is you, me, even them. It's all of us.
  Joshua points to the black band at the base
  This is where we came from – where they tried to keep us.
MAX: In the dark.
JOSHUA: Secret.
  Joshua points to the red band in the centre
  This is where we are now, because our blood is being spilled.
  Joshua points to the white band at the top
  This is where we want to go.
MAX: Into the light.

Thus, the barcode signifies all transgenic identity, whether the human-looking X series, Joshua (the first transgenic, who has no barcode) or the clearly transhuman transgenics. But adopting the barcode as a symbol is not a positive appropriation of a negative image; after all, it is located at the base of the flag, where they 'came from,' not the (pure) white band of 'where [they] want to go'. This becomes clearer at the end of the episode, when a new baby (the product of two X5s) is born. One of the first things the mother checks for is a barcode, saying, '[n]o barcode. She doesn't have one', to which Max replies '[s]he's free then'. The barcode is still, at the close of the series, something that defines the transgenics but which they nevertheless seek to escape. In a shot reminiscent of Joe Rosenthal's iconic Iwo Jima image, the flag is raised at the end of the episode over Terminal City (an area that the transgenics claim as their own), but it appears that they seek a form of purity away from the barcode as much as take pride in their difference from Ordinaries (that is, baseline humans) that the barcode symbolises. That is, the barcode exists in almost colonial terms: the transgenics' bodies have been colonised by the Manticore program, and their search for a new identity, independent of Manticore, is problematised by the fact that they have no past before such colonisation and because the symbol of the barcode is the only feature uniting their disparate bodies and experiences together.

FROM TRANSGENICS TO EUGENICS

Given the politics of the barcode that *Dark angel* explores, especially in relation to tattoos, it is perhaps no surprise that it also attempts to examine the issue of branding. In Season 2, a breeding cult called the Conclave is introduced. The Conclave is also a genetic breeding programme, but rather than genetic manipulation through science, their programme is through selective breeding and eugenics. The brand is used most explicitly in the episode 'Exposure' (2.16), when Max uncovers more information about the activities of the Conclave and their initiation ritual. This ritual involves branding an individual with the pommel of a ceremonial knife that has been dipped in the blood of a snake which carries a lethal 'pathogen or viral agent'; the initiation test is to be able to survive this infection. As Logan outlines in the episode 'Hello, goodbye', those who survive the ordeal gain a brand in the shape of 'a modified version of a caduceus' to prove that they have survived the ritual and are worthy of being considered a member of that group, rather than having a mark – such as the barcode – written into their very DNA.

The contrast between these two groups, the transgenics of Manticore and the eugenics of the Conclave, is thus signified through their respective 'brands'. The barcode is encoded into the DNA as part of the individual transgenic. The caduceus brand, however, is a sign of membership in an elite group, a badge of genetic superiority. The barcode is imposed, the caduceus elected; the barcode technological, the brand ritualistic. In each case, the mark denotes membership of a group and the ways in which they are distinct from 'Ordinaries' (see note 15). Whereas all transgenics are genetic chimeras, ostensibly composed of the DNA of different animals, familiars – as members of the Conclave are known – are bred specifically to enhance certain superior physical or mental attributes. The transgenics seemingly never have tattoos: both because of their evident recuperative powers and their predisposition against marking themselves, having been so marked by Manticore. In contrast, the Conclave make use of tattoos as well as brands. The most obvious instance is in 'Freak nation', where the elite warrior breeding line of the Conclave known as the Phalanx are introduced. In a normative view of such subgroupings that emphasise physical prowess and militaristic attitudes, both male and female members appear to have tattoos in the style of tribal warriors. The distinctions between barcode, brand and tattoo, then, are an externalisation of the conceptual, biological and ideological differences between transgenics and eugenics. The debate here shifts between the 'natural' and 'pure' bodies of the eugenics, who can optionally modify their own bodies with tattoos and brands as a mark of pride, and the 'chimeric' and 'technological' bodies of the transgenics, who bear the barcode as a mark of shame.

Attempting to bridge between the two seasons, and develop more of a back-story to the Conclave, it emerges that the government's Manticore programme was a spin-off operation by a defector from the Conclave, Sandeman. While the Conclave seek to survive a lethal disease that is prophesised to occur at some point in the future, Sandeman intended to save humanity, not just members of the cult. Spurred by the realisation that one of his sons would not survive the initiation process after testing his genetic make-up (something notably forbidden by the Conclave), Sandeman engineered the immunity into the transgenics. Thus, the Conclave hunt the transgenics not only because the transgenics are not eugenically 'pure' but also because they too will survive the coming apocalypse. Moreover, Max has the ability to pass on this immunity to Ordinaries, facilitating the survival of the human race as a whole, threatening the Conclave's goal. This is discovered in the penultimate episode of the show, 'Love among the runes' (2.20), when a series of strange characters start appearing on Max's body. Like her barcode, it appears that Sandeman encoded the information in Max's genes, as both the cure and the message for understanding the Conclave's goals. In another instance of encoding information, like the barcode, Sandeman literally writes Max's destiny into her body, as she is special enough to have no junk DNA ('Bag 'em' 2.2) and can transmit the immunity to humanity.

Given the differences between the two seasons, we might further understand the politics of branding, barcodes and tattoos as demarcating the generic shifts that *Dark angel* undergoes, and its relationship to the hypothesised genre of tech-noir. Auger's definition of the tech-noir genre, as a genre of film, is predicated upon a series of key ideas regarding the interrelationship of elements of *film noir* and detective fiction, sf and gothic genres. It is fundamentally structuralist in conception, predicated upon a linear (and perhaps overly simplified) model of genre, and too schematic in application in many respects. There are problems with the ways in which it creates definitions of genres to demonstrate the characteristics of tech-noir. That said, it serves as a useful means of analysing the ways in which popular genres encode different facets of social expectations and mores, and does suggest ways in which the above genres interact within contemporary films.

THE GENRE OF TECH-NOIR

Auger asserts that '[t]ech-noir is to sf what detective fiction is to gothic'; 'there is a certain affinity between tech-noir and film noir' (2011: 36) precisely because it is a visual representation/encoding of a shift towards a questioning of the scientific paradigm and a query of the model of progress she argues that sf texts embody.[13] She continues later:

> Tech-noir film may be regarded in relation to numerous pre-existing genres: it is not only an accumulation of elements common to literary gothic, detective, and science fiction, it also shows an accumulation of motives and elements from film genres and subgenres. For example, it is, in some respects, a kind of social problem film, simply because it treats technology as a social problem; but, since tech-noir commonly treats the social problem as being so well fuelled by technology that it will soon, or indeed, has already, resulted in complete or near complete disaster, it also has a marked affinity with the disaster film. Furthermore, tech-noir is rarely far from horror in its representation of confrontation with the ultimate evil, and many tech-noir exemplars have stylistic affinities with film noir, insofar as they deliberately incorporate fashionable markers from that genre, such as the hardboiled detective, certain types of gangsters, femme fatales, shots of dark alleys on rainy nights, and so forth. (*ibid.*: 53)

Auger discusses many specific characteristics of this genre, which share at least superficially many characteristics of cyberpunk, and recreates tech-noir as a type of filmic version of that literary genre (*ibid.*: 111–64). She usefully articulates many common elements and tropes across many such films, including the conflation of biological and technological in transhuman and robotic bodies, the natural being supplanted by technological means, the role of surveillance versus secrecy, and a querying of what it means to be human in such settings and environments.

Given this brief description, it is evident that there are some issues regarding the conceptualisation and premises of tech-noir as a genre, but one can see that

Dark angel utilises such tropes as well as a number of established *noir* tropes that it sets against the problems of scientific progress.[14] As mentioned previously, the most obvious *noir* tropes are set up within Season 1: Logan, Max's love interest, is a cyber-hacker and journalist who seeks to expose corruption in the police state that Seattle has become. Max becomes his 'go-to' girl in terms of breaking into police headquarters and infiltrating gangster's houses and hideouts to gain information and/or rescue people. Max tries to evade capture from the military, epitomised by Lydecker, who wants to capture the X5 escapees, while enlisting the aid of a private eye, Vogelsang, to track down her brothers and sisters herself (interestingly, Vogelsang is murdered by a transgenic when it appears that he will lead Manticore to Max and the others).[15] The setting is often at night, and is predominantly urban and ruined (albeit including the obligatory neon, recalling the Tech Noir nightclub). Emphasising the limited roles of woman offered by *film noir*, Max's outfits shift between black figure-hugging costumes (at night; when robbing buildings) often revealing her midriff in low-cut jeans with youth-wear cap (when a courier), 'hooker' outfits (leather, hotpants, etc.) and dresses (for occasions when, as Fuchs note, she is 'undercover' (2007: 112) as an Ordinary, or when fitting into high society). These, when combined, certainly give a *noir* aesthetic and feel to the first season of *Dark angel*.

But the second season explodes this *noir*-esque setting by expanding its vision to examine the politics of the transgenic experience: rather than focus on a nexus of crime and crime fighting, *Dark angel* morphs into a paradigm of cloning rights and an exploration of anthropic principles and broader definitions of 'crime' (for example, the Conclave are 'criminal' in their aim to sacrifice humanity for their own eugenic purposes). Max's clothing does not change markedly, but there is less variation to it and less overt symbolism attached to her attire as she becomes distanced from committing and solving crimes, and more concerned with protecting her fellow transgenics. Night-time urban and underground settings are still common, but they are more often interspersed with daylight shots to juxtapose the distinction between being 'out in the open' and 'safe and hidden' for transgenics. The criminals disappear here, at least in the traditional sense of the term, as it is the breeding cult, the Conclave, who become the covert enemy (attempting to profit from the destruction of the Ordinaries), and the Ordinaries and the media who become an overt enemy (attempting to hurt or destroy the transgenics).

CONCLUSION

The shift from *noir* to tech-noir is central to the narrative development of what might be called the tech-noir genre of *Dark angel*, and what symbolises this movement is the barcode. From secret government labs that create genetic hybrids to dark conspiracies and secret societies who engage in mystical practices, from the seedy urban setting to the post-apocalyptic urban setting, and from natural to unnatural and monstrous bodies, the scientific premises of *Dark angel* collide sharply with its use of tropes from teen and crime dramas. Played out on the very bodies of the characters, particularly evident in Alba's role as Max and the distinctions between the Conclave and Manticore, the barcode is a brand of the ways in which it utilises older tropes of tattoos, criminality and contemporary experience, and manifests them within a sf setting. Despite its exploration of various kinds of body-marking, the 'tattoo' itself remains encoded within *Dark angel* as a marker of deviance from the norm, being depicted primarily on criminals and the military. Yet it is precisely through the correlations and discontinuities between such 'tribal' tattoos, 'ritualistic' brands and 'techno-scientific' barcodes that its body-politics – and the politics of its own generic body – emerges. Thus, encoded throughout its generic DNA, *Dark angel* is a chimeric mix of pre-existing tropes marshalled together to query the role of the human in a technological and perhaps already transhuman world, 'branded' by such marks at various textual and meta-textual levels.

NOTES

1   One character, Kendra, even refers to being addicted to tattoos at one point, in the episode 'Flushed' (1.4). For more on the relationship between body-marking and criminality, see Kate Watson's 'Mapping the mark' (2016: 52–54). Watson's piece also usefully demonstrates the links between gender and tattoos in nineteenth-century fiction, and the ways in which this proves salacious/erotic, as well as a badge of shame, for female characters.

2   This plays into debates about female power, agency, moral growth and socialisation (Max is 'controlled' by Logan despite her superhuman abilities) – McConnell's 'recombinant Pygmalion' – alongside generic markers from superhero comics (for example, wheelchair-using Professor X guidance of genetically enhanced humans).

3   In 2012, sf author Elizabeth Moon caused a public outcry by seemingly espousing on *The forum* that barcodes should be imprinted on individuals soon after birth. The resultant uproar clearly demonstrated concerns about loss of privacy and identity that are figured in the image of the barcode tattoo (www.facebook.com/BBCFuture/posts/232149166900826), while apparently eliding the fact that such issues are eroded in more subtle ways already, from RFID tracking of children (for protective purposes) to GPS in mobile telephones.

4   This tension between the individual and the generic is also played out in debates about the role of tattoos in contemporary society. Negrin, *contra* Susan Benson, argues how the 'individualistic' tattoo facilitates the commodification of a brand because it 'standardized items under the guise of them being individual statements' (2008: 98). Moreover, Benson's view that tattoos indicate 'ownership over the flesh' (qtd Negrin 2008: 101), is shifted from self-determination to corporate control by many texts that deal with barcode tattoos.

5   One of the most recent examples of the criminal 'secret society' tattoo is in the television series, *The mentalist*, especially in the final season, from the episode 'Fire and brimstone' [6.6.], in which members of the Blake Association (corrupt law enforcement officers and politicians) are all revealed to have three dots on their left shoulder).

6   Within the young adult market of sf books, subsequent iterations of this link between identity, branding and barcodes include texts such as Max Berry's (corporate) dystopian satire, *Jennifer government* (2004), and Suzanne Weyn's *Bar code trilogy* (2004–12). Both authors explore how barcodes serve to undermine the ways in which individuals can assert their own identities, and express concerns about the level of state, government and/or corporate control over individuals. Barcodes are overt symbols of a mechanised, capitalist society, with the loss of individual identity that such 'branding' entails. Conceptually, Christopher Sebela's Agent 47 is a close affiliate of Max Guevara's X5–452 and worthy of comparison (2017).

7   The description of the series identified by Butkus similarly emphasises the 'broken', 'criminal' elements of the world within *Dark angel*, albeit without tying it into generic debates.

8   Alba references her first tattoo following a significant break-up (probably Michael Weatherly, her co-star on the series, and ex-fiancé). In August 2016, she reflected that she would tell her younger self to 'think twice before getting a tattoo'. However, it might equally be asserted that the 'tattooed' image interferes with Alba's own 'brand', Honest Company (founded in 2011), and her public image of chic elegance. There is also an interesting set of observations to be made about the 'brand' of the series itself, through the 'transmedia storytelling' (see Evans 2011) of the three spin-off novels from the series, by Max Allen Collins: *Before the dawn* (2002), *Skin game* (2003) and *After the dark* (2003).

9   The series left its own 'mark' upon Alba because of its focus upon her body. Alba reported in 2012 that the series made her feel objectified (Lennon 2015). Moreover, in a blog post that engages with the interview, one respondent noted that they 'even have a barcode tattooed on the back of my neck' (daniel c, in McKnight 2012). This barcode 'branding' functions outside of *Dark angel*, and may be contrary to the overall message of the series in terms of valorising the 'barcode' image through the act of 'brand' identification. This branding between series and fan is explored at length by Karin Beeler Chapter 13 in this collection, and also in Bethan Jones' work on fan tattoos (2015).

10 Where episodes are discussed in detail the title of the episode is given (as in this case 'The kidz are aiight'). When an element of an episode is quoted a shorthand of series episode is given, as in this case (1.14) (eds).

11 The resonances of 'Mark of Cain' are interesting, trying to equate a 'genetically engineered killing machine' (that is, Max) with Cain, although this seems a little skewed if it is meant to be both a punishment and a measure of protection. For more on the 'Mark of Cain', see Karin Beeler's chapter in this collection (Chapter 13).

12 The relationship between body-as-technology and the control/surveillance paradigm is also identified by Shoshana Magnet, who argues that barcodes in *Dark angel* illustrate three 'technofantastic elements of biometric representation' (2011: 132).

13 Essentialising Auger's mapping of the genres somewhat, it is akin to a 'darkening of vision' via what she calls 'realms of experience'; the gothic genre emphasised

marriage and then the detective genre emerged, which envisages a cast of characters who uphold or seek to topple the products of that institution (and *film noir* arguably does the same to the detective genre). Similarly, sf asserted the primacy of science, which tech-noir then interrogates. However, Auger's model problematically assumes that sf and gothic texts never questioned the premises of our social contexts of science and marriage, respectively, arguing that 'both gothic and science fiction are all about getting there, and not so much about the consequences that follow' (2011: 36).

14 Auger's description of the relationship between DNA and computing (2011: 128–29) and the brief discussion of tattoos and graffiti as 'the art forms of the poor or signs of territoriality' (*ibid.*: 132) are also pertinent here.

15 It is for this reason that Fuchs identifies Max's attempts to cover the barcode as a 'standard plot point' (2007: 108) of *Dark angel*. The barcode, like tattoos more broadly, is seen within the world it creates as something to define an attitude or group of people, and in this case transgenics. This makes the barcode of visual signifier of difference from baselines humans, or 'Ordinaries', as they come to be known.

BIBLIOGRAPHY

Auger, Emily E. (2011), *Tech-noir film: A theory of the development of popular genres* (Portland: Intellect).

Barry, Max (2004), *Jennifer Government* (London: Abacus).

Bobbin, Jay (2000), 'James Cameron's *Dark angel* fights the future in new Fox series', *Boca Raton News* (29 September). Available: https://news.google.com/newspapers?id=dP9TAAAAIBAJ&sjid=Bo4DAAAAIBAJ&pg=4288%2C3054832 [accessed 12 February 2016].

Butkus, Clarice M. (2012), 'Sound warrior: Voice, music and power in *Dark angel*', *Film and television*, 5:2, 179–99.

Cameron, James and Charles Eglee (creators) (2000-2002), *Dark Angel* (Twentieth Century Fox Television).

Collins, Max Allen (2002), *Before the dawn* (n.p.: Del Rey Books).

— (2003) *Skin game* (n.p.: Del Rey Books).

— (2003) *After the dark* (n.p.: Del Rey Books).

Evans, Elizabeth (2011), *Transmedia television: Audiences, new media, and daily life* (Abingdon: Routledge).

Fernandez, Ramona (2014), 'The somatope: From Bakhtin's chronotope to Haraway's cyborg via James Cameron's *Dark angel* and *Avatar*', *Journal of popular culture*, 47:6, 1122–38.

Fuchs, Cynthia (2007), 'Did anyone ever explain to you what "secret identity" means? Race and displacement in *Buffy* and *Dark angel*', in E. Levine and L. Parks (eds), *Undead TV: Essays on 'Buffy the vampire slayer'* (Durham, NC and London: Duke University Press), pp. 96–115. Reprinted in D. Lavery and R. V. Wilcox (eds) (2007), *Slayage* 6:4 [24] (Summer).

Jones, Bethan (2015), 'Fannish tattooing and sacred identity', *Transformative works and culture* 18.

Jowett, Lorna (2005), 'To the Max: Embodying intersections in *Dark angel*',

Reconstruction: Studies in contemporary culture, 5:4 (Fall). Available: http://recon struction.eserver.org/Issues/054/jowett.shtml [accessed 12 February 2016].

Lennon, Christine (2015), 'Jessica Alba: View from the top', *Marie Claire* (15 May). Available: http://www.marieclaire.com/celebrity/a7122/jessica-alba-interview/ [accessed 28 June 2017].

Magnet, Shoshana Amielle (2011), *When biometrics fail: Gender, race, and the technology of identity* (Durham, NC and London: Duke University Press).

McConnell, Kathleen (2002), '*Dark angel*: A recombinant Pygmalion for the twenty-first century', *Gothic studies*, 4:2, 178–90.

McKnight, Brent (2012), '*Dark angel*'s sexuality made Jessica Alba uncomfortable', *Giant freakin robot* [blog] (16 May) Available: www.giantfreakinrobot.com/scifi/ dark-angels-sexuality-jessica-alba-uncomfortable.html [accessed 28 June 2017].

Negrin, Llewelyn (2008), *Appearance and identity: Fashioning the body in postmodernity* (New York: Palgrave Macmillan).

Watson, Kate (2016), 'Mapping the mark: Tattoos, crime fiction, and gendered cartographies', in C. Cothran and M. Cannon (eds), *New perspectives on detective fiction: Mystery magnified* (New York: Routledge), pp. 52–72.

Weyn, Suzanne (2004, 2006 and 2012), *The bar code tattoo trilogy* (New York: Scholastic).

15

Tattoos, deviance and consumer culture in North American television: *Criminal minds, CSI: NY* and *Law and order*

Ruth Hawthorn and John Miller

INTRODUCTION

Writing in 2006, Mary Kosut asserts: 'America has become a tattooed nation. If you turn on your television, open a magazine or go see a movie, you will likely encounter a tattooed body' (1035). The much cited 'tattoo renaissance' – a term coined by Arnold Rubin in 1988 – has seen what was previously considered largely as a mark of psycho-sexual deviance and social marginality make steady progress into mainstream culture. Tattoos are no longer the province of the outlaw; as Mindy Fenske observes: 'even Barbie has had a tattoo' (2007: 1).[1] Ironically, it is precisely tattooing's 'alternative' status that has to a significant extent underpinned its recent rise. Its apparent embodiment of unique self-expression, allied to an aura of edginess, even danger, is proving remarkably seductive in a neo-liberal era characterised by hyper-individualism and the relentless commercial production of novelty and excitement. Tattoos, like other 'subcultural signs' (Hebdige 2003), appear to have been thoroughly conscripted by the very ideologies (steady job, family values, cultural conformity, high-street fashion) that historically they were held to contest. As the prominent visibility of tattoos in numerous mass advertising campaigns testifies (from the hip world of Jean-Paul Gaultier to the conservative domain of banking),[2] the marked body now has notable purchase in an economically-driven popular culture.

Consequently, contemporary tattoo culture finds itself caught in a paradox. Although tattooing is more lucrative than ever before, its seeming ubiquity tarnishes the allure of an outsider art for many practitioners. Dick Hebdige's study of subculture, although predating the phenomenal upsurge in tattooing, remains pertinent: '[i]t is [...] difficult', he contends, 'to maintain any absolute distinction between commercial exploitation on the one hand and creativity/ originality on the other, even though these categories are emphatically opposed in the value systems of most subcultures' (2003: 95). The line between conformity and deviance or between capital and subversion becomes increasingly difficult to locate (which is one reason why subcultural studies has been supplemented or even supplanted by a 'post-subcultural studies' that finds the distinction between mainstream and alternative very difficult to locate or maintain).

Before assuming that tattoos have been entirely absorbed into the post-modern marketplace, however, a note of caution needs to be sounded. As Josh Adams and others argue, the 'focus on the "new tattoo generation" of tattooed middle-class professionals' sidelines the continuing role of tattooing within contexts outside the mainstream of consumer capitalism, for instance – at the risk of reviving some of tattoo's most notorious stereotypes – in gang and prison cultures (2009: 106). Tattoos are clearly not *just* the province of a middle-class hipsterism. Given its relative permanence, tattooing also comprises a different order of experience from other more ephemeral aspects of contemporary fashion.[3] So, as Hebdige concludes, '[t]he relationship between the spectacular subculture and the various industries which service and exploit it is notoriously ambiguous' (2003: 94). Tattooing, consumer culture and conceptions of the deviant are entwined in complex ways.

Evidently, as Kosut's remarks testify, television both reflects and contributes to body art's growing popularity. From the rise of the reality tattoo show,[4] to the unavoidable visibility of tattooed athletes, actors and other celebrities, tattooing is firmly established in televisual culture. As such, the tattoo has come to articulate Sarah Thornton's conception of 'subcultural capital' in which the media functions as a 'primary factor governing the circulation' (1995: 13) of subcultural practices. Within the 'economy of subcultural capital', Thornton argues, the media appears as a 'network crucial to the definition and distribution of cultural knowledge' (1995: 14). This line of argument, refined by Thornton in relation to the nineties rave scene, fits rather awkwardly with tattooing as an artform that significantly predates late-twentieth-century media cultures. There remains a profound tension between tattooing and its representation, concerned, in particular, with the idea that the folkloric transmission of tattoo knowledge between practitioners and from practitioners to clients might be co-opted by corporate media interests. TV represents a sizeable challenge to the idea of a tattoo tradition.

It is hardly surprising, given the longstanding connection of tattoos to criminality, that contemporary TV crime dramas, such as *Criminal minds, Law and order: Special victims unit* and *CSI* and its spin-offs, should comprise one of the most recurrent narrative uses of tattooing. These dramas reflect what Ken Dowler, Thomas Fleming and Stephen Muzzatti term 'the public's unending thirst for information on bizarre and violent crime' (2006: 838). A companion book to *Criminal minds*, for example, luridly promises a revealing look into 'the evil behind some of the most heinous murderers, sexual predators, and psychopaths in history [and] their unspeakable crimes' (Mariotte 2010: back cover). The huge ratings figures for these shows and others like them (including *Bones*, *Cold case* and *NCIS*) confirm a widespread fascination with the most vicious and grotesque aspects of society.[5] Tattooing's representation in this context places it intriguingly between its marginal roots and its apparently mainstream commercial present. Tattoos function as symptoms of a psychological and social deviance commodified in the construction of crime as entertainment, but also as signs of a self-confident and empowered youth culture closely linked to tattooing's subcultural origins. The ostensibly divergent roles of tattooing as atavistic outsider art and emergent fashion become difficult to disentangle.

This chapter offers three case studies of the depiction of tattoos in North American TV crime drama in order to interrogate these multiple ironies in the cultural politics of the tattoo renaissance. Starting with the *CSI: NY* episode 'Oedipus Hex' (3.5, 2006), we examine the eroticisation of the tattooed female body within the conservative framework of the show's format.[6] The episode's focus on *SuicideGirls*, an 'adult lifestyle brand' (*SuicideGirls* n.d.) – 'porn even feminists could love', apparently (*Feministe* 2005) – perfectly encapsulates the marketable cachet of tattooing's alternative mystique. With over six million 'likes' on Facebook, *SuicideGirls* is a globally significant cultural enterprise. As Carlen Lavigne argues, however, *CSI*'s formulaic narrative arc has an essentially punitive structure: heroic investigators are pitched against deviant criminals and all non-recurring characters are necessarily either victims or suspects. Accordingly, 'it is almost impossible to view the show as positive toward women, queer cultures, or sexual subcultures' (Lavigne 2009: 385). Any sense of the tattoo as a counter-normative form of embodiment is thoroughly eroded, most notably by the show's slick, 'sexy' conclusion.

Our second episode, '… A thousand words' (5.20, 2010), sees the *Criminal minds* team pitted against a serial killer whose body is covered with tattooed portraits of his victims. Here we find a return to the nineteenth-century Italian criminologist Cesare Lombroso's conception of tattoos as 'ideographic hieroglyphs' which '[enable] us to discern the obscurer sides of the criminal's soul' (1895: 798, 803). As the team read the tattooed corpse in order to save the final victim, the monstrous spectacle of tattooing is subjected to a kind of anthropological scrutiny or, in the show's own terms, 'behavioural analysis', in order to safeguard the public from the depredations of marked outsiders. Importantly, at the same time, there are also telling hints here of a cool but necessarily sanitised version of tattooing available to law-abiding citizens.

Finally, 'Strange beauty' (13.22, 2012) from *Law and order: Special victims unit* depicts tattoos as a portal to more extreme and dangerous body modifications, most notably amputation. While tattooing is here presented as fashionable and widely (though not universally) accepted, practitioners of body modification are shown to form a close-knit, cabalistic network, operating on the illicit fringes of society. Ultimately, however, the episode's narrative logic appears to (partially) exonerate tattooing from its association with darker elements of body modification and to leave space for the tattoo as part of a rich, alternative aesthetic. In each case, we argue, these crime dramas are involved in the tense procedure of retaining the tattoo's potency as the mark of the deviant, while simultaneously reclaiming body modification for a conservative, and, most importantly, marketable identity politics.

CSI: NY: 'OEDIPUS HEX'

One of the most noteworthy aspects of the tattoo renaissance has been a shift in the gender demographic of the tattooed. Formerly identified largely as a masculine preserve, tattooing has risen remarkably among women. According to a Harris poll, the percentage of US women with a tattoo increased from 15% in 2003 to 23% in 2012. The phenomenon of tattooed women has a long history, of course, particularly as 'titillating enticements' in circus sideshows, promising the double spectacle of 'a peep show within a freak show' (Mifflin 1997: 18). Evidently, it is the adjustment of conventions of female beauty that energises such displays and associates them in some quarters with the aberrant or even the monstrous. For Lombroso, in his much-quoted 1895 critique of tattooing, tattoos were antithetical to the ideas of 'refinement and delicacy' which he attributed to 'the most beautiful half of the human race' (1895: 793). Tattooing's increasing popularity among women has a good deal to do with the overturning of these kinds of gender stereotypes. Margot Mifflin describes how:

> Tattoos appeal to contemporary women both as emblems of empowerment in an era of feminist gains and as badges of self-determination at a time when controversies about abortion rights, date rape, and sexual harassment have many women thinking about who controls their bodies. (1997: ii)

Even more ambitiously, for Christine Braunberger '[t]attooed women … [stage] an aesthetic revolution in "feminine" beauty' (2000: 1). To Megan Jean Harlow, tattooing 'is a radical form of feminist self-identification' (2009: 1), while Beverly Yuen Thompson argues that for 'many women' tattoos 'symbolize a reclaiming of their bodies and a form of resistance to normative femininity' (2015: 6). For each of these critics, tattooing operates as a mark of feminist self-possession. Mifflin does add a welcome degree of nuance, arguing that 'it would be silly to suggest that wearing [tattoos] makes women de facto feminists' (1997: vi).[7] As we shall see, the way that pornography appears to have embraced the tattoo renaissance provides striking evidence of the limits of tattooing as a sign, or at least a stable sign, of feminist struggle.

'Oedipus Hex' presents us with precisely this tension between alternative feminist embodiment and (for the most part) masculine consumption. The episode focuses on the murder of a Suicide Girl immediately after a sexually-charged performance at a 'punk show'. Initially, suspicion falls on her fellow Suicide Girls, before the murderer is revealed as a male tattoo artist. With members of the *SuicideGirls* (*SG*) community playing themselves, 'Oedipus Hex' has a very close relationship with the *SG* enterprise to the extent that one blogger, 'Modified Girl', complains that it is 'nothing but a one hour advertisement for the website' (2006). Undoubtedly, there is a strong element of self-promotion in the representation of the Suicide Girls. As they explain themselves to the bemused Detective Messner:

> MISSY: We're a sisterhood of 1,200 punk rock, pierced, goth, glam, pin-up girls. We're not the Baywatch girls or the Playboy bunnies.
> ZOLI: Or the Pussycat Dolls.
> MISSY: We're the Bettie Pages of this generation. The Suicide Girls are about being strong, sexy and confident, and above all ... unique. (*CSI: New York* 3.5, 2010)

In language that has the ring of a marketing campaign, the *SG* aesthetic is defined in stark opposition to the mainstream, patriarchal erotic capital of *Baywatch* and *Playboy*. The origin of the provocative name *SuicideGirls* affirms the aggressive assertion of an alternative identity, sometimes referred to as 'grrrl power'. As Al Suicide suggests elsewhere, the *SG* lifestyle is sufficiently non-conformist to amount to 'social suicide' (CrashBoxKid 2007). The significant pause before the clinching adjective 'unique' emphasises the perceived distance of this 'sisterhood' from conventional forms of female beauty.

There are numerous contradictions, however, behind this assumption of alterity. Bettie Page did in fact model for *Playboy*, and the extent to which the *SG* reclamation of the pin-up tradition can be seen as empowering is questionable. Moreover, in *CSI: NY* the Suicide Girls claim to be 'women-owned and women-operated', but the business is in fact owned and co-founded by Sean Suhl – described by one former Suicide Girl as an 'active misogynist', hardly an indicator of feminist business credentials (Fulton 2005). Controversies surrounding his management emerged in 2005, the year before this episode was broadcast (*ibid.*). Cynically, 'Oedipus Hex' has the feel of a public relations exercise in the face of a wave of negative publicity that emerges from an apparent disparity between feminist idealism and corporate practices.

Despite the significant commercial edifice of *SuicideGirls*, the episode begins by fixating on the supposed danger inherent to this community. In doing this, tattooing's importance, as a signature element of the *SG* alternative aesthetic, is quickly established. The opening sequence dramatises the journey of an innocent small-town girl, Carensa Sanders, into the perilous subculture of body modification. We begin with an *SG* audition video showing her as a conservatively dressed young woman, unhappy with her appearance as a 'typical high school senior' (*CSI: New York* 3.5, 2010). The scene ends with Carensa expressing her desire to be part of a different community: '[a]ll I've ever wanted is to be around other girls like me who can accept me for who I really am' (*ibid.*). Jumping a year into the future, we find a scantily clad, notably tattooed Carensa (now 'Omen Suicide') raining down 'blood' on her fellow Suicide Girls in a burlesque take on the famous prom scene from the 1976 horror film *Carrie*. As the show's creator Anthony E. Zuiker comments, she goes 'from being little miss innocent to being blood-soaked' in the space of a few minutes (CrashBoxKid 2007). Carensa's graduation into Omen echoes *Carrie*'s disruption of the heteronormative American rite of passage of the High School prom. The opening sequence makes the point, rather bluntly, that Carensa is not, at all, the 'typical high school senior'.

There is a further, more disturbing, transformation to come, however, as the following scene cuts to the examination of her corpse by crime scene investigators. The manner of Omen's death loads the representation of tattooing with significance. A fresh tattoo of a winged love heart is the site of the fatal blow on her chest, delivered, we later discover, with the heel of a green stiletto, part of the Suicide Girls' costume for the *Carrie* skit. The subsequent investigation characteristically focuses on the murder weapon; in a perversion of the Cinderella story (and another punk twist on culturally embedded narratives of heterosexual normalcy), finding who the shoe fits will, it seems, lead them to the murderer. As the *CSI: NY* team interview their suspects, the episode becomes a tour of the women's alternative bodies, honing in on their extensive tattoos and piercings. Given the context, and with the stiletto as a clearly gendered weapon (reminiscent of Hedy's use of the stiletto as a weapon in *Single, white, female* (1992)), the *SG* aesthetic helps to locate the women firmly within the violent and libidinal tradition of the femme fatale. Interrogations are heavily sexualised; questions from male investigators are responded to with erotic overtures.

As 'Oedipus Hex' sets up the mystery in its early stages, the representation of tattooing therefore has a double function. First, the location of Omen's injury, through the ink and into the heart, imagines the tattoo as symbolic wound. In seeking to participate in a community of difference by marking her skin, she exposes herself to a culture of violence. Second, and connectedly, the spectacle of the suspects reprises Lombroso's assumption of the inherent criminality of the tattooed. The tattoo, then, functions as a sign of both victimhood and aggression.

In a formulaic plot twist, as the narrative progresses the assumption of the Suicide Girls' guilt is revealed to be false. The investigation takes the *CSI: NY* team to the studio of Omen's tattooist for a fairly routine series of questions, but when they later find him brawling with Al Suicide, Omen's girlfriend, he begins to draw suspicion. In the classic crime scenario of the love triangle, it emerges that the tattooist – also called Al – has also slept with Omen. He is then quickly identified as the murderer. The discovery of the tattooist's guilt exonerates the Suicide Girls and partially redeems their aesthetic from its violent associations. Conversely, however, the tattooist as murderer reinforces the broader connection between tattooing and criminality which inevitably reflects back onto the *SG* subculture. Importantly, the tattooist's lethal outburst affirms the tattooed female body as a location of social anxiety and intersects with a complex of issues concerning gender and power in the context of tattooing. Omen's tattoo, inscribed 'Till Death Do Us Part – Omen and Al' operates not just as a wound but also as a contract affirming her loyalty to the Suicide Girls' lifestyle and provoking the tattooist's jealous rage. A flashback to the application of Omen's tattoo shows the tattooist above his subject in a dominant, clearly sexualised position, cockily supposing he is marking his own name on the girl's chest. The tattoo machine functions here, in Nancy Kang's phrase, as a 'trans-dermal phallic substitute' (2012: 72). His role as the bad-boy lover is usurped, however, by the assertive figure of Al Suicide (who humiliatingly beats him when they fight); the murder evidently responds to a fear of emasculation in the face of the apparently subversive subculture of 'grrrlhood' from which he is inevitably excluded.

The overarching view of tattooed women appears by the end of the investigation to be the stereotypical one: the Suicide Girls are enticing, sexualised, dangerous and threatening to traditional gender power structures. Any sense that this might amount to or support a radical feminism is undone by the episode's closing scene. We return here to Carensa's initial audition in a moment that re-includes her in the conventional American family values she appeared to have abandoned. She concludes the tape poignantly: 'I just want to be happy … I just want to be loved. Mom – I love you' (*CSI: New York* 3.5, 2010). As Omen is revealed finally to be, in many ways, just a regular girl, the scene cuts to the surviving Suicide Girls from the *Carrie* performance, walking away from the still bemused Detective Messner. The last shot offers closeups that focus on a staple pornographic imagery to which body modification appears suddenly rather incidental. The stark juxtaposition between the redeemed Carensa and the promiscuous Suicide Girls (a point emphasised by Nixon Suicide's parting come-on to Messner) ultimately adds little to feminist identity politics. Above all, what we are left with is an image of the sexual availability of the tattooed body in the online economy, a conclusion that coheres with Lee's discovery that 'what a Google search of "Suicide Girls" produces are websites tailored for male consumption of female bodies' (Lee 2012: 161). By the end of 'Oedipus Hex', porn, tattooing and the American family appear to be finally, and perhaps rather bizarrely, reconciled.

CRIMINAL MINDS: '… A THOUSAND WORDS'

While *CSI: NY* draws on the traditional association between tattooing and monstrous female sexuality, in '… A thousand words' *Criminal minds* explores the tattoo as a sign of psychological pathology. The episode commences with a 911 call from a middle-aged man, Robert Burke, who shoots himself while speaking to the operator. Finding the man's corpse covered in tattoos of missing or murdered women, the local police call in the *Criminal minds* team, the FBI's Behavioural Analysis Unit (BAU). '… A thousand words' follows the team's investigation as they decode the tattoos, a process which echoes Lombroso's view of the tattoo as a clue to 'the fierce and obscene hearts' of criminals (1895: 798). Despite Lombroso's essentialist formulations, the link he makes between tattooing and psychopathology remains a prominent part of contemporary tattoo scholarship.[8] The BAU's work in this episode continues a longstanding supposition of the hermeneutic potential of tattooing in the context of criminology. Indeed, the episode's title, with its reference to the proverb 'a picture is worth a thousand words', highlights the proliferation of meaning that ultimately allows the team to solve the mystery of the dead man's skin.

Importantly, one of the frequently noted consequences of the rise of body modification has been a supposed denuding of the meaningfulness of tattoos. Whereas, in the context of tattooing's traditional subcultures, tattoos have often contained very specific meanings, they are now, as Llewelyn Negrin argues (following Jean Baudrillard) 'undercoded' (2008: 10). For Negrin, the meanings of 'body adornments' have become 'more and more ambiguous' (*ibid.*). In the case of Burke, however, as the team point out, the tattoos 'do tell a story', and it is the investigating team's interpretative challenge that constitutes the episode's narrative centre: decipher the tattoos and rescue the girl (*Criminal minds* 5.20, 2011). Crucially, this is a process that is concerned not only with the surface of the tattoos, but also one that requires a penetration of the depths of the artwork. A gap in the tattoo is revealed on investigation under ultra-violet light to contain the image of a foetus, tattooed in invisible ink. From this clue, the team deduce that Burke has a pregnant female accomplice who is holding the lost girl while waiting for the moment to murder her. Vitally, there is more to Burke's body art than mere aesthetics; these tattoos have a series of meaningful real-world referents that the BAU team diligently cross-reference with Burke's extensive diaries.

The image of tattooing that *Criminal minds* presents gestures predominantly towards a set of historical associations that precede the tattoo renaissance. Burke's 'giant flashy confession', as Agent Reid describes it, evokes a flamboyant criminality that identifies the urge to mark the body as a sign of the deviant nature beneath the ink (*ibid.*). What is written on the skin reveals the pathological structure beneath. This play between surface and depth in Burke's elaborate tattoo is central to the larger criminological discourse of tattooing. Such a conception would appear to notably distance the evocation of tattooing in '… A thousand words' from the emerging status of the tattoo as a fashion icon. There are two short scenes that, though peripheral to the main action of the episode, are crucial to the representation of tattooing in this context. These engage specifically with contemporary tattoo culture in relation to the BAU team's reading of Burke's atavistic skin.

As the agents attempt to track down Burke's tattoo artist, like the *CSI: NY* investigators, they pay a visit to a tattoo studio. Shown a photograph of the tattoos in isolation from the rest of the grisly scene, the tattooist they encounter is initially awed by Burke's art: '[m]an, this is beautiful work', he exclaims (*ibid.*). When he picks up on the circumstances his admiration quickly shifts to a prurient interest in the details of the gruesome death. Notably, all other characters have been deeply appalled by the scene – to the point of vomiting in one case – but the tattooist, by contrast, reveals a voyeuristic appetite for further information. He asks first: '[d]id he shoot himself?', adding creepily, 'because none of these pictures have a head' (*ibid.*). His obvious excitement is raised even further when he discovers the 'dude's a killer'. He even tries to negotiate a visit to the crime scene, claiming 'if I saw the body, I'd probably be able to tell you more' (*ibid.*). When the detectives show their disapproval, he mournfully concludes: 'so there's, like, no chance of seeing the dead dude, right?' (*ibid.*). Both his salacious curiosity and his exaggeratedly colloquial language tie the tattooist back into late nineteenth-century degenerationist discourse. Set against the morally upright BAU and a careful local detective who is profoundly affected by the case, the figure of the tattooist is demonised through his callousness, demonstrating, as Lombroso puts it, 'an inferior sensitiveness' to the string of murders (1895: 793). There is, of course, a significant irony here. While the viewer is encouraged to look down on the tattooist's ghoulishness, it is precisely this quality which the show relies on in its audience. There is always an instability in such shows' equation of prurience with otherness.

If the exchange in the tattoo studio reaffirms the connection between tattooing and criminality, an earlier scene back at the BAU headquarters complicates this stereotype. Garcia (the team's quirky, fashion-conscious IT geek) is, it seems, no stranger to the tattoo needle herself. Nonetheless, she is horrified by the images of Burke's monstrously tattooed body. Her initial statement of dismay draws a clear distinction between fashion and criminality: 'I'm into epiderm artistry as much as the next gen x-er, but this guy… eesh' (*Criminal minds* 5.20, 2011). The integrity of the divide between gen x-er and criminal is called into question, however, as she tries to help the team locate the tattoo artist. She explains: 'I'm not going to elaborate on how I know this [but] not everyone in the body art lifestyle goes through the official channels' (*ibid.*). Her own hinted experience of tattooing is located in a cultural underground that intersects with her background as a computer hacker and activist on the wrong side of the law. Critically, while the dead murderer's tattoos are hyperbolically visible, Garcia's supposed 'epiderm artistry' is never revealed, denying the possibility of her body's legibility. The anthropological imperative to decode the skin is reserved for those on society's margins: the heavily tattooed man with extreme psychological issues.

Garcia's reclamation by the FBI after her wayward youth illustrates the inclusion of the tattooed in social utility: the underground and the establishment brought together. The invisibility of her experience of 'epiderm artistry' adds an extra *frisson* to these secret markings, but also suggests a certain demureness: her tattoos (if there are any) are suitably withheld from view. The cultural acceptability of tattooing is here premised on a rather old-fashioned modesty that views excess and extroversion with dismay. Any valorisation of tattooing subculture is stymied by Garcia's necessary reserve. Both Burke's monstrosity and Garcia's restraint insist on a discourse of control through which tattooing is subject to the overriding consideration of conformity.

LAW AND ORDER: SPECIAL VICTIMS UNIT (SVU): 'STRANGE BEAUTY'

The *Special victims unit* episode 'Strange beauty' addresses more extreme forms of body modification. Although, ultimately, tattooing functions as something of a red herring, it forms an important part of the subculture the episode is concerned with. The series has previously engaged with tattooing as an entry point to deviant lifestyles, as 'the gateway to the sexual dark side' (*Law and order: Special victims unit* 13.22, 2005), and 'Strange beauty' continues in that vein. The episode begins with Detective Rollins witnessing the kidnapping of a young woman, Nina, who later is discovered dead with one leg amputated. An interview with Nina's mother reveals her daughter had been 'out of control' for some time, a 'phase' characterised, inevitably, by an interest in body modification (*ibid.*). Nina's missing limb, dredged out of a canal, is identified by an octopus tattoo and the team follow a series of leads which take them from a tattoo studio, to dubious practitioners of more unusual body modifications and, consequently, to an exclusive 'freak night' on Coney Island. The mystery's solution lies in a disturbed psychiatrist whose sexual fetish for amputating women's legs is unconnected to the tattoo community (*ibid.*). Nonetheless, 'Strange beauty' provides some telling insights into the interplay of fashion and deviance in the cultural politics of tattooing.

The episode's most illuminating discussion of tattooing takes place in the loaded setting of a morgue. Dr Warner, the pathologist, shares her insights into body modification with detectives Benson and Rollins as they scrutinise the victim's corpse, which serves as 'a record of her journey into body modification' (*ibid.*). Not only has Nina acquired more than one tattoo, but she has also undergone the more unusual procedure of 'ear pointing' (in which the ear cartilage is shaped to a point). The scene's clinical context evidently locates tattooing in the realm of the pathological, while re-emphasising the atmosphere of menace routinely associated with body modification. Like Carensa in 'Oedipus Hex', Nina's journey to victimhood ostensibly begins with a tattooist's needle. Warner's professional observations deal directly with the popularisation of tattoos as an incitement to riskier and more unusual procedures: 'tattoos used to be subversive, now kindergarten teachers have them, which means the fringe has to go even further' (*ibid.*). Tattooing, though commonplace, remains a source of social anxiety as the portal to the deviant 'fringe' embodied in the victim's 'elf ears'. The distraught mother's account of Nina's descent into rebellion confirms the anti-social edge of body modification: '[Nina] was just too wild', she laments, bemoaning how she had become 'covered' with tattoos (*ibid.*). In similar vein to the depiction of the grieving parent in 'Oedipus Hex', the mother figure of 'Strange beauty' serves to mark out a generational schism between the conservative baby-boomer and her defiantly tattooed offspring.

Following a structural pattern shared by all three episodes, 'Strange beauty' shifts from the identification of the tattoo as clue to an interview with a tattooist. Here, in stark contrast to the prurient tattooist of *Criminal minds*, the investigators find themselves in a high-end studio with a 'celebrity clientele', and an artist who pointedly distinguishes his work from that of lower status practitioners (*ibid.*). His insistence that he does not undertake 'job-stoppers' (facial tattoos, ear pointing or other extreme body modification practices) adds a certain respectability that is confirmed by his own absence of any visible tattoos (*ibid.*). As he notices Rollins' understated, 'classy', white tattoo, he establishes a hierarchy of tattooing which is also implicit in '. . . A thousand words': the tattooed professional in contrast to the tattooed deviant. The idea of job-stopping procedures he introduces is a significant phrase; any sense of tattoos as socially or economically disruptive is here immediately forestalled. The distinction between socially acceptable and culturally marginal tattooing is reinforced by the abrupt cut to a much more lugubrious establishment, operated by the artist's ex-employee, fired for encouraging clients towards more extreme practices. While the first studio is notable for its plush upholstery, the dismissed tattooist appears to work out of a ramshackle garage, complete with gas masks crudely attached to large canisters. Body modification appears bifurcated into the acceptable and hygienic and the unauthorised and perilous.

If 'Strange beauty' appears initially to resolve tattooing into a dualistic hierarchy, Fin and Rollins' subsequent visit to 'freak night' at the Mermaid Hotel in search of the darker side of body modification, depicts a world that merges the deviant and the fashionable. Coney Island has long been a place in which alternative cultures have found a commercial outlet, with a tradition of freak shows stretching back to the nineteenth century and a reputation as one of New York City's 'tattoo meccas' that endured 'well into the twentieth century' ('inkflesh' 2011).[9] Having acquired the secret password to gain admittance, the detectives arrive at the hotel. The ostentatious ritual that surrounds their entry subtly evokes the idea of the gateway, the movement from one domain to another that tattooing comprises in *Special victims unit*. Set apart from the mainstream in this way, 'Strange beauty' fetishises rather than demonises alterity. Soft red lighting and ambient music create an otherworldly atmosphere. Contortionists and acrobats interact with an extensively modified audience and the heavily tattooed form a prominent part of this carnivalesque cast of oddities. Importantly, the undercover detectives discover no air of menace, but rather a welcoming and inclusive community. This is no violent, atavistic culture, but a lush aesthetic vision of a flourishing subculture.

Finn and Rollins' visit to the freak night leads them to the one-legged Jess, a body modification practitioner who constructed Nina's elf ears. More than anything, however, Jess embodies idealism. Having lost a leg to bone cancer as a teenager, she helps people 'achieve their own perception of beauty [...] a vision of their true selves' (*Law and order: Special victims unit* 13.22, 2012). Jess' view recapitulates Carensa's quest in *CSI: NY* to become who she 'really' is and endorses a widespread conception in the tattoo renaissance of body art as the expression of a unique individuality. Body modification for Jess represents both lack and desire, compensating for her own missing leg while articulating a determination to control and shape the self. The ideal of self-construction apparent here is absolutely central to the developing appeal of tattooing. Moreover, the idea of a 'true self' expressed through the body and immaculately outside ideology might be read as one of the signature elements of late capitalism. Selfhood appears as a repertoire of limitless possibilities to be individually shaped and reshaped. While the *Criminal minds* team see through the surface of the tattoo to the depths of the tattooee's nature, the idea of the 'true self' Jess and Carensa espouse implies that the surface *is* the depth.

Such optimism, however, is ultimately founded on some sense of loss. As Alessandra Lemma writes in her psychoanalytic study of tattooing, 'the more compulsive and extreme forms of body modification reflect a difficulty in integrating the most basic fact of life: we cannot give birth to ourselves' (2010: 2). Lemma's study offers an important corrective to the naïve, essentialist individualism that Jess and the Suicide Girls propound. The desire for the 'true self' through body modification promises wholeness, freedom and the overcoming of adversity, the function, as Lemma puts it, of 'rescuing the self' (2010: 5). Yet such glib aspirations appear as a covering or obfuscation of the material conditions of being. '[I]dentity and appearance', as Negrin importantly reminds us, 'though interrelated, are not synonymous' (2008: 3).

CONCLUSION

Each of the three episodes considered here institutes a dialogue between 'traditional' and contemporary discourses of the tattoo. *CSI: NY* reconfigures the sideshow spectacle of the tattooed woman, *Criminal minds* investigates the degenerate body of the tattooed deviant, *Law and order: Special victims unit* takes us back into circus subculture. Given the location of these texts within the global commercial edifice of primetime crime drama, any sense of the subversive edge of tattooing is inevitably blunted by the genre's formulaic requirements. Nonetheless, the process of transition apparent here from tattoos as 'subcultural signs' to 'mass-produced objects' (to return to Hebdige's terms) is revealing and, despite the generic overlap between each series, not necessarily consistent (2003: 94). The apparent necessity in *Criminal minds* that the tattoo be either demonised or concealed may perhaps allow for the possibility for tattooing to retain a good measure of its subversive energy, especially in the case of the kind of large-scale tattoo project depicted on Burke. *CSI: NY* and *Law and order: Special victims unit* are notable, however, for their endeavour to incorporate the tattoo (even extensive tattooing and other more 'extreme' forms of body modification) into the dominant identity myths of the neo-liberal era, specifically the identification of consumption with self-formation.

While this analysis might seem to lead towards a pessimistic conclusion (there is no longer any outside of mainstream consumer culture), such a defeatist attitude does a disservice to the protean, continually evolving creative processes of contemporary tattoo culture and the variety of motivation and lived experience of the tattooed: the 'multiple dimensions of culture and history at play in the North American tattoo community' as Margo DeMello phrases it in her landmark study *Bodies of inscription* (2000: 2). Tattooing – for all its appropriation by consumer culture – remains, as the prominent British tattoo artist Alex Binnie commented, 'a private contract … like a folk art' (Rack 2014). The global image industry may thus be understood in exchange with, but also at a distance from, the local and multiple materialities of tattooed bodies.

NOTES

1 Barbie's first tattoo appears to date to 2008 following a collaboration between the makers Mattel and Harley Davidson. The subsequent release of a 'funky fashionista' Barbie in 2011, complete with chest and neck tattoos, resulted in its widespread condemnation as 'over-sexualised and inappropriate'. See Jon Swaine (2011).

2 Gaultier has utilised tattooing on a number of projects, most controversially with the inclusion (to some, the appropriation) of Maori *moko* for the marketing of his 2011 Le Male summer fragrances (see Ellen Carter's Chapter 5 in this collection). Tattoos appeared in a 1990s advertisement for TSB student banking in the UK, and more recently in the US, in a campaign by East River Bank in Philadelphia that

uses tattooing to emphasise its credentials as 'Philly's most advanced neighborhood bank'.

3 See Llewelyn Negrin (2008: 7).

4 The first of these were *Miami ink* (2006) and its follow-up *LA ink* (2007), and the franchise has spread with equivalents in Britain and Australia.

5 See, for example, Nielsen Ratings, www.nielsen.com/us/en/top10s.htm>.

6 Where episodes are discussed in detail the title of the episode is given (as in this case 'Oedipus Hex'). When an element of an episode is quoted a shorthand of series and episode is given, as in this case (3.5) (eds).

7 For further discussions of tattooing and feminism, see Thorsten Botz-Bornstein's 'Female tattoos and graffiti' (2012: 53–64) and Nancy Kang (2012: 65–80) both in Robert Arp (ed.) (2012).

8 For an overview of the field, see George B. Polermo's 'Tattooing and tattooed criminals' (2004: 1–25). See also Alessandra Lemma (2010).

9 Sarah Hall's novel *The electric Michelangelo* (2004) explores the practice of tattooing on New York's Coney Island and is analysed by Hywel Dix in Chapter 4 in this collection.

BIBLIOGRAPHY

Adams, Josh (2009), 'Bodies of change: A comparative analysis of media representations of body modification practices', *Sociological perspectives*, 52:1, 103–29.

Arp, Robert (ed.) (2012), *Tattoos – philosophy for everyone: I ink, therefore I am* (Chichester: John Wiley).

Bailey, Rob and Hemingway Anthony (dirs) (2010), 'Oedipus Hex', *CSI: New York: The complete season 3* [Season 3, Episode 5] (Momentum Pictures: USA).

Braunberger, Christine (2000), 'Revolting bodies: The monster beauty of tattooed women', *NWSA journal*, 12:2, 1–23.

Chapple, Alex (dir.) (2012), 'Strange beauty', *Law and order: Special victims unit: season 13* [Season 13, Episode 22] (Universal Studios: USA).

CrashBoxKid (2007), *Suicide Girls do CSI: NY*. Available: www.youtube.com/watch?v=gGprrD4VoUk [accessed 10 September 2014].

DeMello, Margot (2000), *Bodies of inscription: A cultural history of the modern tattoo community* (Durham, NC and London: Duke University Press).

Dowler, Ken, Thomas Fleming and Stephen L. Muzzatti (2006), 'Constructing crime: Media, crime, and popular culture', *Canadian journal of criminology and criminal justice*, 48:6, 837–50.

Fenske, Mindy (2007), *Tattoos in American visual culture* (New York: Palgrave Macmillan).

Fulton, D. (2005), 'SuicideGirls revolt', *The Boston phoenix*. Available: www.bostonphoenix.com/boston/news_features/other_stories/documents/05016155.asp [accessed 10 September 2014].

Harlow, Megan Jean (2009), 'Suicide Girls: Tattooing as radical feminist agency', *Advances in communication theory and research*, 2. Available: www.k-state.edu/actr/2009/12/20/suicide-girls-tattooing-as-radical-feminist-agency-megan-jean-harlow/default.htm [accessed 10 September 2014].

Hebdige, Dick (2003), *Subculture: The meaning of style* (London: Routledge).

'inkflesh' (2011), 'The death and life of New York City tattoo', *Inkflesh* [blog] (11 May). Available: https://inkflesh.wordpress.com/tag/coney-island/ [accessed 10 September 2014].

Kang, Nancy (2012), 'Painted fetters: Tattooing as feminist liberation', in R. Arp (ed.) (2012), pp. 65–80.

Kosut, Mary (2006), 'An ironic fad: The commodification and consumption of tattoos', *The journal of popular culture*, 39:6, 1035–48.

Lavigne, Carlen (2009), 'Death wore black chiffon: Sex and gender in *CSI*', *Canadian review of American studies*, 39:4, 383–98.

Lee, Wendy Lynne (2012), 'Never merely "there": Tattooing as a practice of writing and a telling of stories', in R. Arp (ed.) (2012), pp. 151–64.

Lemma, Alessandra (2010), *Under the skin: A psychoanalytic study of body modification* (London: Routledge).

Lombroso, Cesare (1895), 'The savage origin of tattooing', *Popular science monthly*, 48, 793–803.

Mariotte, Jeff (2010), *Criminal minds: Sociopaths, serial killers, and other deviants* (New York: John Wiley and Sons).

Mifflin, Margot (1997), *Bodies of subversion: A secret history of women and tattoo* (New York: Juno Books).

'Modified Girl' (2006), 'Suicide Girls on *CSI*', *BME News* (22 November). Available: http://news.bme.com/wp-content/uploads/2008/09/pubring/edit/A61122/artsuici. html [accessed 10 September 2014].

Negrin, Llewellyn (2008), *Appearance and identity: Fashioning the body in postmodernity* (Basingstoke: Palgrave Macmillan).

Polermo, George B. (2004), 'Tattooing and tattooed criminals', *Journal of forensic psychology practice*, 4:1, 1–25.

Rack, Y. (2014), 'Into you: Getting inked in Clerkenwell', *St John street news* (4 April). Available: www.stjohnstreet.net/into-you-getting-inked-in-clerkenwell/ [accessed 10 September 2014].

Rodriguez, Rosemary (dir.) (2011), '… A thousand words', *Criminal minds* [Season 5, Episode 20] (Walt Disney Home Entertainment: USA).

Rubin, Arnold (1988), 'Tattoo Renaissance', in A. Rubin (ed.), *Marks of civilization: Artistic transformations of the human body* (Los Angeles: Museum of cultural history/University of California, Los Angeles), pp. 233–62.

SuicideGirls. *Suicide Girls* [website] (n.d.). Available: https://suicidegirls.com/ [accessed 10 September 2014].

Swaine, Joe (2011), 'Tattooed Barbie doll is "oversexualised and inappropriate", say parents', *The telegraph* (20 October). Available: https://www.telegraph.co.uk/news/worldnews/northamerica/usa/8839231/Tattooed-Barbie-doll-is-overly-sexualised-and-inappropriate-say-parents.html [accessed 12 September 2018].

Thompson, Beverley Yuen (2015), *Covered in ink: Tattoos, women and the politics of the body* (New York: New York University Press).

Thornton, Sarah (1995), *Club culture: Music, media and subcultural capital* (London: Polity).

Index

EU authorised representative for GPSR:
Easy Access System Europe, Mustamäe tee 50,
10621 Tallinn, Estonia
gpsr.requests@easproject.com

www.ingramcontent.com/pod-product-compliance
Ingram Content Group UK Ltd.
Pitfield, Milton Keynes, MK11 3LW, UK
UKHW020040170726
7214IPUK00036B/345